THE CULT OF ST EDMUND IN MEDIEVAL EAST ANGLIA

THE CULT OF ST EDMUND
IN MEDIEVAL EAST ANGLIA

Rebecca Pinner

THE BOYDELL PRESS

© Rebecca Pinner 2015

All Rights Reserved. Except as permitted under current legislation
no part of this work may be photocopied, stored in a retrieval system,
published, performed in public, adapted, broadcast,
transmitted, recorded or reproduced in any form or by any means,
without the prior permission of the copyright owner

The right of Rebecca Pinner to be identified as
the author of this work has been asserted in accordance with
sections 77 and 78 of the Copyright, Designs and Patents Act 1988

First published 2015
The Boydell Press, Woodbridge
Paperback edition 2019

ISBN 978 1 78327 035 4 hardback
ISBN 978 1 78327 401 7 paperback

The Boydell Press is an imprint of Boydell & Brewer Ltd
PO Box 9, Woodbridge, Suffolk IP12 3DF, UK
and of Boydell & Brewer Inc.
668 Mt Hope Avenue, Rochester, NY 14620–2731, USA
website: www.boydellandbrewer.com

The publisher has no responsibility for the continued existence or accuracy
of URLs for external or third-party internet websites referred to in this book,
and does not guarantee that any content on such websites is,
or will remain, accurate or appropriate

A CIP catalogue record for this book is available
from the British Library

Contents

List of illustrations vii
Acknowledgements viii
Abbreviations x

Introduction 1

Part I   Texts and contexts: the legend of St Edmund

    Chapter 1   The emergence of the hagiographic tradition: Abbo of Fleury, *Passio Sancti Eadmundi* 33

    Chapter 2   *De Miraculis Sancti Eadmundi*: Herman, Osbert and Samson 48

    Chapter 3   *Vita et miracula* 63

    Chapter 4   The elaboration of the hagiographic tradition 75

    Chapter 5   The final flourish of the textual cult: John Lydgate, *The Lives of Sts Edmund and Fremund* 89

Part II   Relics, shrines and pilgrimage: encountering St Edmund at Bury

    Chapter 6   Sacred immanence, the incorrupted body and the shrine of St Edmund 115

    Chapter 7   The devotional and iconographical context of the shrine 138

Part III   Beyond Bury: dissemination and appropriation

    Chapter 8   Writing St Edmund into the East Anglian landscape 169

    Chapter 9   Miracles beyond Bury 181

    Chapter 10   Images of St Edmund 193

    Chapter 11   Texts beyond Bury: legendary collections 227

Conclusion: 'Martir, mayde and kynge', and more 239
Appendix 1   Synoptic account of the legend of St Edmund 246

Appendix 2 Chronology of significant events and texts associated
            with the cult of St Edmund   248

Bibliography   251
Index   274

Illustrations

Unless stated otherwise all images are copyright of the author.

Map
    Significant locations associated with the legend of St Edmund, church dedications and visual imagery   xi

Plates after p. 68
I   Danes attacking a town, MS M.736, fol. 10, © The Pierpont Morgan Library (New York, Pierpont Morgan MS M.736)
II   Edmund's apotheosis, MS M.736, fol. 22v, © The Pierpont Morgan Library (New York, Pierpont Morgan MS M.736)
III   Death of King Sweyn, MS Harley 2278, fol. 103v, © The British Library Board (London, British Library, MS Harley 2278)
IV   Edmund enthroned, MS Harley 2278, fol. 34, © The British Library Board (London, British Library, MS Harley 2278)

Figures
1   Carved stone spandrel of the martyrdom from St Lawrence (Norwich)   208
2   Carved wooden misericord of the martyrdom from Norton (Suffolk)   209
3   Stained glass roundel of St Edmund with arrows from Saxlingham Nethergate (Norfolk)   209
4   St Edmund and Henry VI on the chancel screen at Ludham (Norfolk)   212
5   Wolf and head benchend from Walpole St Peter (Norfolk)   221
6   Wolf and head benchend from Hadleigh (Suffolk)   221
7   Sutton Hoo purse lid, © The Trustees of the British Museum   224
8   Æthelwold seal, © The Trustees of the British Museum   225

Tables
1   Topographical references   174
2   Images of St Edmund by medium   195
3   Images of St Edmund by iconography   195

Acknowledgements

Numerous people and institutions have been of great help during the course of my research. Notable amongst these are Caroline Palmer and the team at Boydell and Brewer. Particular thanks also go to Mr Robert Yorke, Librarian at the College of Arms, for facilitating access to the Arundel 30 manuscript, and to Rear-Admiral Michael Harris of the Monumental Brass Society for his help with the Frenze brass. I was lucky enough to visit two St Edmund-related conservation projects and my thanks go to Andrea Kirkham for allowing me access to Troston during her conservation of the paintings, and to Matthew Champion for inviting me to Lakenheath to see a similar conservation project and for generously providing me with photographs, a copy of the report and frequent updates of possible new Edmund sightings. The production of this volume was supported with funds made available by The Centre of East Anglian Studies, University of East Anglia. The British Library Board, the Trustees of the British Museum and the Pierpont Morgan Library, New York have kindly granted their permission for images from their collections to be reproduced.

Family, friends and colleagues have been a great source of encouragement. The following deserve special mention: Chris Bonfield, Tom Licence, Matt Mesley, Sam Newton, Tom Rutledge, Gesine Oppitz-Trotman and George Oppitz-Trotman, and the honorary medievalist Karen Schaller. Sara Claxton was the most understanding boss and the most wonderful friend, and has kept me smiling throughout. Katherine Lewis and Margit Thøfner were supportive and helpful examiners and have continued to offer invaluable advice.

Special thanks are due to Sarah Salih, with whom I began the project on which this book is based and who first inspired me to study medieval literature. She must also take the credit (or blame) for introducing me to John Lydgate's *Lives of Saints Edmund and Fremund*, which is where this all began. Thanks also to Karen Smyth, who joined my supervisory team four years into the project and whose input and enthusiasm in the latter stages were welcome. And to Sandy Heslop, whose knowledge and intellectual generosity have inspired me throughout.

There are a few people without whom it would not have been possible for me to complete this project. Leon Doughty has been a constant comfort and support, whose unwavering belief in me and this book has sustained me throughout. He has taken some wonderful photographs on our many Edmund outings and also made the map in this volume, and for this and so much more I will always be grateful.

Above all, thanks go to my parents, for patiently enduring so many detours to obscure corners of Norfolk and Suffolk in search of St Edmund, and for so many other things that it's not possible to put into words. This book is dedicated to them, and to those people who I wish were still here to see it.

Abbreviations

BAA: Bury	*Bury St Edmunds: Art, Architecture, Archaeology and Economy*, ed. Antonia Gransden, British Archaeological Association Conference Transactions, xx (Leeds: British Archaeological Association, 1998)
es	extra series
GiL	*Gilte Legende*
GoL	*Golden Legend*
ns	new series
os	old series
SS	*Speculum Sacerdotale*
SEL	*The South English Legendary*

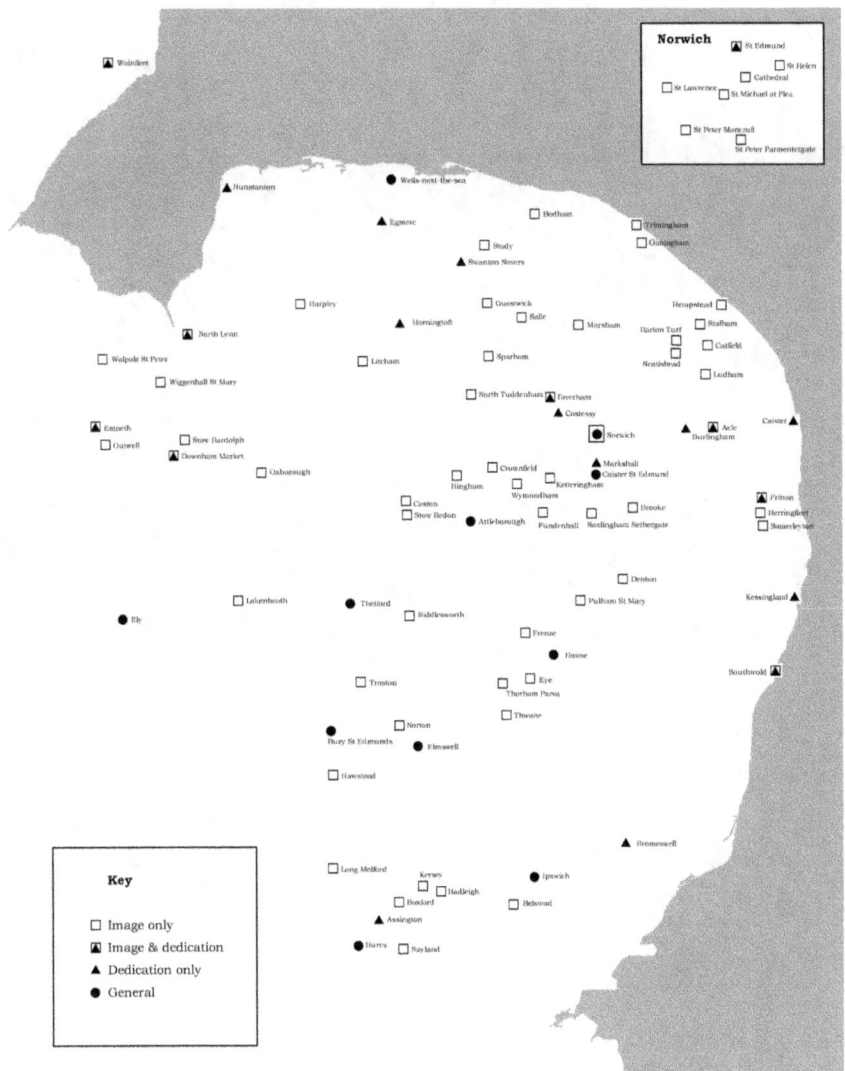

Significant locations associated with the legend of St Edmund, church dedications and visual imagery

Introduction

'To us too had the last day, the inevitable moment, come: we were monks, the glory and honour of Eastern England were, but the fierce fire is seizing it all, and mastering the holy temple.'[1]

IN November 1535 Thomas Cromwell's Commissioners arrived at the abbey of Bury St Edmunds to report on the condition of the monastery and the extent of its wealth. Three years later they returned to confiscate the abbey's possessions for the Crown, writing to Cromwell of their successes:

> Pleasith it your lordship to be advertised that wee have ben at saynt Edmondes Bury, where we found a riche shryne which was very comberous to deface. We have takyn in the seyd monastery in golde and sylver MMMMM markes, and above, over and besides a well and riche crosse with emereddes, as also dyvers and sundry stones of great value ... and we assure your lordship that the abbott and convent be very well contented with every thing that we have done there.[2]

In September 1539 the abbey was dissolved. The 'riche shryne' belonged to St Edmund, erstwhile king of Norfolk and Suffolk, who met his death at the hands of the Great Viking Army on 20 November 869. The value of the goods seized by the Commissioners attests to the wealth and prestige accrued by the abbey, 'the

---

[1] Anon., *Incendium Ecclesiae*, in *Memorials of St Edmund's Abbey*, 3 vols, ed. Thomas Arnold, *Rerum Britannicarum Medii Aevi Scriptores* (Rolls Series), 96 (London: Printed for Her Majesty's Stationery Office by Eyre and Spottiswoode, 1890-93), III, pp. 283-7; p. 285. This description of the fire which devastated the church of the abbey of Bury St Edmunds in 1465 owes much at this point to Panthus' lament on the Fall of Troy in Virgil's *Aeneid*: 'The last day comes, Troy's inescapable hour./ Troy is past, Ilium is past, and the great glory of the Trojans:/ Jupiter carries all to Argos: the Greeks are lords of the burning city./ The horse, standing high on the ramparts, pours out warriors,/ and Sinon the conqueror exultantly stirs the flames.' Virgil, *Aeneid*, trans. Sarah Ruden (New Haven: Yale University Press, 2008), II, ll. 324-9, p. 33.

[2] *Three Chapters of Letters Relating to the Suppression of the Monasteries*, ed. Thomas Wright, Camden Society, London, vol. 26 (London: Printed for the Camden Society by John Bowyer Nichols and Son, 1843), p. 144.

glory and honour of Eastern England' referred to above by the monastic chronicler, due largely to the reputation and popularity of their saintly patron. More than sixty medieval churches throughout the country bore his dedication, many of which were also adorned with his image.[3] Between the tenth and sixteenth centuries more than thirty separate accounts of his legend were written in Latin, Old English, Anglo-Norman, Old French or Middle English.[4] For much of the Middle Ages Bury was one of the most popular pilgrimage destinations in England and Edmund's cult also enjoyed some popularity abroad, particularly in Scandinavia and Iceland, at Saint-Denis near Paris, at Lucca in Italy (from the tenth to the twelfth century) and at Toulouse in the south of France (from the thirteenth century).[5]

Edmund was an enduring favourite with the English monarchy. In 945, King Edmund I (922–46) granted the abbey possession of a defined area around the monastery, later known as the Liberty of the town or *banleuca*, within which it had absolute jurisdiction to the extent that no royal official was allowed to enter.[6] In 1020 King Cnut (1016–35) replaced the community of secular clerks who tended Edmund's remains at Beodricesworth (later Bury St Edmunds) with Benedictine monks, granting them a charter of privileges the following year.[7] Arguably the

---

[3] Frances Arnold-Foster, *Studies in Church Dedications or England's Patron Saints*, 3 vols (London: Skeffington and Son, 1899), III, pp. 354 and 359.

[4] For a summary of the development of the legend see Grant Loomis, 'The Growth of the Saint Edmund Legend', *Harvard Studies and Notes in Philology and Literature*, xiv (1932), 83–113.

[5] For the cult in Scandinavia see Alison Finlay, 'Chronology, Genealogy and Conversion: The Afterlife of St Edmund in the North', in *St Edmund, King and Martyr: Changing Images of a Medieval Saint*, ed. Anthony Bale (York: York Medieval Press, 2009), pp. 27–44; for Saint-Denis see Pamela Z. Blum, 'The Saint Edmund Cycle in the Crypt at Saint-Denis', in *Bury St Edmunds: Art, Architecture, Archaeology and Economy*, ed. Antonia Gransden, British Archaeological Association Conference Transactions, xx (Leeds: British Archaeological Association, 1998) (hereafter *BAA: Bury*), pp. 57–68; for Lucca see Antonia Gransden, 'Abbo of Fleury's *Passio Sancti Eadmundi*', *Revue Bénédictine* 105 (1995), 20–78, esp. 75–8. The Toulouse cult concerned a set of rival relics, claimed to have been stolen from Bury in 1216, most of which are now under the guardianship of the Duke of Norfolk in Arundel Castle. See Richard Gem, 'A Scientific Examination of the Relics of St Edmund at Arundel Castle', in *Bury St Edmunds: Art, Architecture, Archaeology and Economy*, ed. Antonia Gransden, British Archaeological Association Conference Transactions, xx (Leeds: British Archaeological Association, 1998), pp. 45–56.

[6] See Antonia Gransden, *A History of the Abbey of Bury St Edmunds, 1182–1256* (Woodbridge: The Boydell Press, 2007), pp. 236–244 and Robin J. Eaglen, *The Abbey and Mint of Bury St Edmunds to 1279* (London: Spink, 2006), p. 6.

[7] The earliest authority for Cnut's foundation is a marginal note to the Easter Tables in the Bury Psalter, now Vatican MS Reg. Lat. 12, fol. 16v. See Antonia Gransden, 'The

most significant royal intervention came in 1043 when Edward the Confessor granted the abbey jurisdiction over the eight and a half hundreds of West Suffolk, elevating Bury to one of the foremost Benedictine houses in the country.[8] This territory came to be known as the Liberty of St Edmund and the abbots of Bury exercised the powers of a sheriff.

Edmund was a favourite of successive English monarchs, as exemplified by his appearance on the glorious late fourteenth-century Wilton Diptych where, along with Edward the Confessor and John the Baptist, he presents Richard II (1377–99) to the Virgin and Christ Child.[9] The personal relationship many monarchs enjoyed with St Edmund is also evident in Henry III's (1216–72) account of the birth of his second son, sent to the abbot of Bury, Henry of Rushbrooke (1235–48):

> Know that on Monday after the feast of St Hilary [16 January 1245], when our beloved consort Eleanor, our Queen, was labouring in the pains of childbirth, we had the antiphon of St Edmund chanted for her, and when the aforesaid prayer was not yet finished, the bearer of this present letter, our valet [Stephen de Salines, told us that she had] … borne us a son. So that you may have the greater joy from this news we have arranged for it to be told to you by Stephen himself. And know that, as you requested us if you remember, we are having our son named Edmund.[10]

The cult of St Edmund was vibrant and dynamic, widespread both throughout society and throughout the Middle Ages.

'King' Edmund

Yet, in stark contrast to the popular 'saint' Edmund, virtually nothing is known of the historical 'king' Edmund. Glimpses of numismatic evidence indicate that

---

Legends and Traditions concerning the Origins of the Abbey of Bury St Edmunds', *English Historical Review* 100, no. 394 (January 1985), 1–24; 10–12.

[8] See Gransden, 'Legends and Traditions', 12.

[9] See Shelagh Mitchell, 'Kingship and the Cult of Saints', in *The Regal Image of Richard II and the Wilton Diptych*, ed. Dillian Gordon, Lisa Monnas and Caroline Elam (London: Harvey Miller, 1997), pp. 115–24.

[10] M.J. Howell, 'The Children of Henry III and Eleanor of Provence', in *Thirteenth Century England 4*, ed. P.R. Coss and S.G. Lloyd (Woodbridge, 1992), pp. 57–72; p. 63. For a discussion of this incident in the broader context of the cult see Rebecca Pinner, 'St Edmund, "Martir, Mayde and Kynge", and Midwife? New Approaches to Medieval and Early Modern Miracles', in *Contextualising Miracles: New Historical Approaches*, ed. Matthew Mesley and Louise Wilson, *Medium Ævum* Monograph, XXXII (Oxford: The Society for the Study of Medieval Languages and Literature, 2014).

Edmund succeeded Æthelweard to the throne of East Anglia c.855. Coins were issued during his reign in sufficient numbers to suggest that he ruled for several years.[11] The earliest written mention of Edmund is in the Parker manuscript of the *Anglo-Saxon Chronicle*, complied around 890. The compiler notes the arrival of the 'great heathen army' in 865 which 'took up winter-quarters in East Anglia; and there were supplied with horses, and the East Anglians made peace with them'.[12] Leaving East Anglia, the army travelled north, capturing York, where it settled for several years before returning to East Anglia in the autumn of 869:[13]

> In this year the raiding army rode over Mercia into East Anglia, and took winter-quarters at Thetford; and in that winter King Edmund fought against them, and the Danes gained the victory, and slew the king, and subdued all that land and destroyed all the monasteries which they came to.[14]

Edmund's death is thus recorded in scant detail and the exact manner of his demise is ambiguous.[15] However, in his *Vita Ælfredi regis Angul Saxonum*, begun in 893 and based primarily upon the *Anglo-Saxon Chronicle* up to the year 887, Asser interprets the annal as claiming that Edmund died in battle:

> In the same year, Edmund, king of the East Angles, fought fiercely against that army. But alas, he was killed there with a large number of his men, and the Vikings rejoiced triumphantly; the enemy were masters of the battlefield, and they subjugated that entire province to their authority.[16]

---

[11] C.E. Blunt, 'The St Edmund Memorial Coinage', *Proceedings of the Suffolk Institute of Archaeology* xxxi (1969), 234–53; 234.

[12] *The Anglo-Saxon Chronicle*, ed. Dorothy Whitelock with David C. Douglas and Susie Tucker (London: Eyre and Spottiswoode, 1961), p. 45.

[13] The compiler for the Alfredian period began his year on 24 September; thus Edmund's death appears in s.a. 870 but actually occurred in November 869. See M.R.L. Beaven, 'The Beginnings of the Year in the Alfreidan Chronicle, 866–87', *English Historical Review* 33 (1918), 328–42, 336 and n. 36.

[14] *The Anglo-Saxon Chronicle*, ed. Whitelock, p. 46.

[15] Loomis, however, notes that two manuscripts of the *Anglo-Saxon Chronicle* (MS E: Oxford, Bodleian Library, MS Laud 636 and MS F: London, British Library, MS Cotton Domitian A.viii) refer to 'Sce Eadmund' and cites this as evidence of early cultic veneration. However, MS E appears to be written in a single hand as late as c.1121, and MS F is most likely to have been produced in the late eleventh or early twelfth century. The references to 'Sce Eadmund' may therefore be later additions in response to Edmund's growing reputation. Loomis, 'Growth', 83–4.

[16] *Asser's Life of King Alfred*, ed. W.H. Stevenson (Oxford: Clarendon Press, 1904), pp. 25–6.

No reference is made to Edmund's death as an act of martyrdom. Asser was not the only author to draw upon the *Anglo-Saxon Chronicle* for inspiration and material, and its brief description of Edmund's death is repeated virtually unchanged in subsequent chronicles produced throughout the Middle Ages.[17] Susan Ridyard concludes that the *Anglo-Saxon Chronicle*, and therefore to some extent the tradition which derives from it, records Edmund's story before it was 'subjected to the accretion of legend':

> In these nearly contemporary sources there is no reference to his patronage or childhood, to the date or means of his rise to power or even to the nature of his rule. Nor is there any indication that his death was regarded as a martyrdom: the *rex sanctissimus* of later hagiographical tradition appears here simply as one among the many leaders and rulers of the Anglo-Saxons who lost both their kingdoms and their lives in the years preceding the 'Alfredian revival' of the late ninth century.[18]

What may be called the St Edmund chronicle tradition therefore constitutes the earliest narrative account of Edmund's life and demise. The contrast between these sparse details and the vast, elaborate cult which developed by the end of the Middle Ages is remarkable. It is the filling of this narrative void which this book explores by considering how, why and when the cult of St Edmund developed.

'Saint' Edmund

Similar ambiguity pertains in the earliest days of the cult. A series of silver pennies bearing on the obverse side the legend *sce eadmund rex* (O St Edmund the King!) circulated in the Danelaw, the Danish-controlled areas of England including East Anglia, from the mid-890s. Around two thousand examples are extant, most recovered from buried hoards, indicating that the so-called St Edmund memorial coinage was issued in some quantity before production ceased c.910. It is unclear who initiated the issue, since the coins bear no identifying features other than the name of the moneyer (+VVIDBVLD MOIIE) surrounding a central cross on the reverse, although the central A on the obverse is found on other East Anglian coins from this period, suggesting their production in the region. Scholarly opinion regarding the origin of these coins is divided. Ridyard proposes that the Danes who settled in East Anglia had them minted to ease relations with

---

[17] Loomis, 'Growth', 83–105.
[18] Susan Ridyard, *The Royal Saints of Anglo-Saxon England. A Study of West Saxon and East Anglian Cults* (Cambridge: Cambridge University Press, 1988), p. 62.

the indigenous inhabitants of their new kingdom who already celebrated the sanctity of their fallen king:

> Their adoption of St Edmund may have been a move shrewdly calculated to enhance their political position within Edmund's kingdom. That position was from the outset open to challenge, and the cult of St Edmund, created by the East Angles, is most readily understood as a potent symbol of that challenge. Perhaps the Danish rulers, in acknowledging Edmund's status as 'saint', sought to perform an act of expiation and political reconciliation ... perhaps even they sought to draw the sting from a cult of rebels.[19]

In contrast, Chapman suggests that the West Saxon dynasty during the reign of Alfred (871–99) minted the coins in order to promote the cult of St Edmund as a means of enhancing their claim to the throne of the Eastern kingdom. Wessex influence over Danish East Anglia was established following the defeat of the Danish army at the Battle of Ethandun (Edington) in May 878. Alfred persuaded Guthrum and his men to convert to Christianity and they were baptised with Alfred as Guthrum's sponsor. This afforded Alfred a degree of moral sway over the warriors of the Danelaw and implied some level of cultural and political superiority. Chapman proposes that Alfred had the coins minted as an additional means of undermining Danish control over East Anglia:

> In the legend 'O St Edmund the King!', emblazoned by West Saxon moneyers across thousands of Viking pennies, Alfred and his successors managed to gloss over the last two decades of Viking rule in East Anglia. Instead of acknowledging whoever succeeded Guthrum to the kingship, they chose to honour Edmund as the only king; undermining Viking claims to legitimacy by removing them from the list of East Anglian rulers altogether.[20]

Thus numismatic evidence alone suggests that the cult of St Edmund may have originated as an expression of indigenous East Anglian resistance to their Danish overlords, an attempt by the Danes to appease the natives, or an act of West Saxon political subversion. The lack of certainty regarding Edmund as a historical figure and the subsequent origins of the cult has frustrated generations of historians. Yet it is my assertion that this ambiguity is precisely what led to Edmund's popularity.

---

[19] Ridyard, *Royal Saints*, p. 216.
[20] Anna Chapman, 'King Alfred and the Cult of St Edmund', *History Today* 53.7 (July 2003), 37–43; 43.

Scholarly context

Due to his existence as a documented historical figure, previous scholarship has typically been concerned with establishing the circumstances and facts of Edmund's life and reign. This is exemplified by two seminal works: Whitelock's 'Fact and Fiction in the Legend of St. Edmund' and Gransden's 'Legends and Traditions concerning the Origins of the Abbey of Bury St Edmunds', the titles of which hint at the preoccupations of their respective authors in recovering the historical 'truth'.[21] Each author attempts to negotiate the distance perceived to exist between history and hagiography, between 'king' Edmund and 'saint' Edmund. Gransden, for example, laments that 'Abbo knew almost nothing historical about St Edmund – not even the date of his death, which was recorded in the *Anglo-Saxon Chronicle*.'[22] Lord Francis Hervey's *Corolla Sancti Eadmundi*, in which he compiled all the versions of the medieval legend known to him, evinces similar concerns. He explains that his purpose is to 'dissect from the mass of traditions the genuine history of S. Edmund' and goes on to present 'An Essay Towards Reconstruction' in which he produces an alternative account of Edmund's life.[23] Although Hervey's endeavours seem to have been prompted by interest in Edmund as a devotional figure, his principal concern was with the historicity of the legendary tradition. In 'The Growth of the Saint Edmund Legend' Grant Loomis is similarly interested in establishing the 'definitive' account. He discusses each version in chronological order, assessing how the texts relate to their predecessors and noting any additions they make to the overall legend. His aims are less purely historicist than Hervey's; when discussing Geoffrey of Wells' innovative account of the birth and boyhood of Edmund, for example, he states that 'it is not my purpose to test the historical value of this addition' and acknowledges that details such as these were often very likely added to appease the desire for further information regarding the saint's life which grew apace with his popularity.[24] However, his focus upon innovation in the legend means that he dismisses briefly *The Liber Monasterii de Hyda*, Bartholomew Cotton's *Historia Anglicana*, the *Eulogium* and Walter of Coventry's *Memoriale* with the comment that whilst they 'all have short notices or accounts of St Edmund' they

---

[21] Dorothy Whitelock, 'Fact and Fiction in the Legend of St Edmund', *Proceedings of the Suffolk Institute of Archaeology* 31 (1969), 217–33; Gransden, 'Origins'.

[22] Antonia Gransden, *Historical Writing in England*, 2 vols (London: The Hambledon Press, 1997), I, p. 84.

[23] *Corolla Sancti Edmundi: The Garland of St Edmund, King and Martyr*, ed. Francis Hervey (London: John Murray, 1907), Preface, liv.

[24] Loomis, 'Growth', 91. See also Loomis, 'St Edmund and the Lodbrok Legend', *Harvard Studies and Notes in Philology and Literature* xv (1933), 1–23.

'add nothing to the sum of our knowledge'.²⁵ He therefore fails to consider the implications of similarities and continuities across the tradition. The preoccupation exhibited by these authors in establishing chronologies, regnal lists and the like in relation to 'king' Edmund is understandable, considering that the period in which Edmund reigned is one for which historical certainty often remains elusive. In terms of understanding the cult of 'saint' Edmund the deductions of these authors form a useful basis, illuminating the historical circumstances leading up to and surrounding Edmund's martyrdom. The tendency to prioritise the historical over the cultic in relation to historical saints remains a persistent trend. In Edmund's case this is particularly true in relation to ongoing debates surrounding the location of his martyrdom.²⁶

Despite this, scholarly emphasis has to some extent shifted towards considering the social, cultural and political dimensions of saints' cults. In his influential work on canonisation and hagiography Pierre Delooz describes saints as constructed social entities which are able to teach us about the communities which venerated them:

> All saints are more or less *constructed* in that, being necessarily saints *for other people*, they are remodelled in the collective representation which is made of them. It often happens, even, that they are so remodelled that nothing of the real original is left, and, ultimately, some saints are solely *constructed* because nothing is known about them historically: everything, including their existence, is a product of collective representation.²⁷

Similarly, the work of Donald Weinstein and Rudolph M. Bell drew attention to the ways in which 'the pursuit as well as the perception of holiness mirrored social values and concerns' in the medieval West.²⁸ In the case of Edmund, a saint about whose historical existence so little seems to have been known even at the inception of his cult, it is entirely appropriate to describe his saintly identity as constructed.

---

[25] Loomis, 'Growth', 97

[26] The most frequently suggested and vociferously advocated locations are Hoxne (Suffolk), Hellesdon, near Norwich (Norfolk), and Bradfield St Clare, near Bury St Edmunds (Suffolk). This book does not enter into this debate, except where it illuminates the development of Edmund's saintly identity. For further details and summaries of the debate see Gransden, 'Origins', pp. 7–8 and Eaglen, *The Abbey and Mint*, pp. 2–3.

[27] Pierre Delooz, 'Towards a Sociological Study of Canonized Sainthood in the Catholic Church', trans. Jane Hodgkin, in *Saints and their Cults: Studies in Religious Sociology, Folklore and History*, ed. Stephen Wilson (Cambridge: Cambridge University Press, 1983), pp. 189–216; p. 195.

[28] Donald Weinstein and Rudolph M. Bell, *Saints and Society: The Two Worlds of Latin Christendom, 1000–1700* (Chicago: University of Chicago Press, 1982), p. 6.

Furthermore, it seems likely that the ambiguity which so frustrated generations of modern scholars was actually one of the greatest strengths of Edmund's cult, as, in the absence of fact, Edmund was a blank canvas onto which could be written the ideologies and aspirations of generations of devotees.

The nature of those responsible for cultic promotion is the subject of ongoing debate. In his thought-provoking study *The Cult of Saints*, Peter Brown suggests that cults were fundamentally an expression of the dominance of institutional elites.[29] Similarly, André Vauchez's *Sainthood in the Later Middle Ages* emphasises the role of ecclesiastical authorities in controlling the cult of saints, one of the results of which was a frequent revision of the requirements for papal canonisation.[30] Although Edmund was never officially canonised, Vauchez's exposition of the ways in which saintly identities were revised in response to particular circumstances is especially relevant for a saint whose cult, I would suggest, was based upon his factual indeterminacy and resulting ability to signify in various ways.

The more popular elements of the cult of saints have been emphasised by a number of scholars. Aron Gurevich avers that medieval parishioners considered the saints to be 'their own property'.[31] Similarly, in his study of English religious culture on the eve of the Reformation, Eamon Duffy stresses the personal relationships enjoyed by many later medieval people with the saints in their roles as intercessors, the so-called 'debt of interchanging neighbourhood' referred to by Caxton in his translation of the *Legenda Aurea*.[32] Interest in the exploration of 'bottom up' influences on sanctity and devotional practices continues to grow.[33]

It is within this vibrant scholarly tradition that this study is located. The ongoing lively debates concerning the nature of medieval sanctity both indicate the vitality of research in this area and remind us that much remains to be considered. Based upon Delooz's assertions regarding the social construction of sanctity, this book explores the ways in which the cult of St Edmund developed throughout the Middle Ages, with particular emphasis upon the groups and individuals

---

[29] Peter Brown, *The Cult of Saints: Its Rise and Function in Latin Christianity* (Chicago: University of Chicago Press, 1981), esp. pp. 62–4.

[30] André Vauchez, *Sainthood in the Later Middle Ages*, trans. Jean Birrell (Cambridge: Cambridge University Press, 1997).

[31] Aron Gurevich, *Medieval Popular Culture: Problems of Belief and Perception*, trans. János M. Bak and Paul A. Hollingsworth (Cambridge: Cambridge University Press, 1990), p. 41.

[32] *The Golden Legend or Lives of the Saints as Englished by William Caxton*, 7 vols, ed. F.S. Ellis (London: Temple Classics, 1900), VI, p. 97, cited in Eamon Duffy, *The Stripping of the Altars: Traditional Religion in England, 1400–1580* (New Haven and London: Yale University Press, 1992), p. 160.

[33] See for instance, *Contextualising Miracles*, ed. Matthew Mesley and Louise Wilson (2014).

responsible for its perpetuation and dissemination. Plurality is important: Delooz stresses that texts and artefacts must be considered in their original contexts, noting 'a picture commissioned by a bishop of the Counter-Reformation period as a model destined to edify his flock should not be interpreted in the same way as a rough wooden statue born of rustic piety'.[34] Thus the human factors discernible in the development of Edmund's cult will be considered in their social, cultural and political contexts.

Several studies have informed the methodologies employed in this study. These will be discussed below in relation to their particular influences, but Virginia Blanton's monograph on the cult of St Æthelthryth of Ely deserves special mention here, due to the numerous ways in which it converges with this current project.[35] It is the only other longitudinal study of an Anglo-Saxon saint published to date and considers the development of the cult between 695 and 1615, a similar chronological range to the flourishing of Edmund's cult. Blanton likewise adopts an interdisciplinary approach, evaluating a range of textual, liturgical, documentary and visual sources. Comparisons may also be drawn between the two saints in question, Edmund and Æthelthryth: both are royal, Anglo-Saxon and renowned for their virginity and incorrupt corporeal remains. These similarities also draw attention to the ways in which this current project is original and distinctive, both in findings and approach. For example, whereas Blanton approaches the cult chronologically, discussing sources in date order, I have opted for a more thematic approach, organising material in terms of production and reception, with particular emphasis on the influence of Bury as the cult centre and the extent to which proximity to the abbey (both literal and by association) determined the construction and reception of Edmund's saintly identity. Blanton acknowledges the need to move beyond traditional periodic distinctions that separate Anglo-Saxon studies from medieval scholarship, and this is integral to my approach.[36] Despite their similarities, there are also significant differences between the two Saxon saints, most notably in relation to their respective genders, along with their contrasting lay and ecclesiastical statuses (Edmund is a king, whereas Æthelthryth flees her royal husband and takes the veil). A key question will therefore be the way in which these differences figure in the cultural and ideological signification ascribed to each saint.

---

[34] Delooz, 'Towards a Sociological Study', p. 197.
[35] Virginia Blanton, *Signs of Devotion: The Cult of St Æthelthryth in Medieval England, 695–1615* (University Park, PA: The Pennsylvania State University Press, 2007). For Blanton's methodology see in particular her 'Introduction', pp. 1–16.
[36] For Blanton's defence of her chronological approach see p. 13.

Although Blanton's study is to some extent interdisciplinary, her decision to base it around a series of textual moments means that other material can at times feel rather supplementary. Discussion of the development of the textual cult of St Edmund forms a significant aspect of this present book, but its insistently interdisciplinary focus means that each source is assigned equal merit and allowed to signify in its own right. A concomitant consequence of the realignment of scholarly attention towards saints' cults as social entities has been a shift away from hagiography as the principal method of cultic dissemination and recognition of saints' cults as multi-media phenomena. Interdisciplinary studies of single saints employ sources from various disciplines to great effect. In relation to St Edmund, the collection of useful and informative essays edited by Anthony Bale is multi-disciplinary and considers the cult of St Edmund as manifested in various social and cultural contexts and in differing media.[37] However, due to its multi-authorship it is inevitably partial in its coverage, meaning that much ground is left to be covered.

In her explicitly interdisciplinary study of the cult of St Katherine in later medieval England Katherine Lewis moves beyond the textual to consider the lives of St Katherine in their manuscript context, as well as utilising a wide range of visual and material artefacts along with documentary sources such as wills in order to locate St Katherine firmly in her historical context and demonstrate the variety of ways in which she signified for medieval men and women.[38] Samantha Riches similarly insists upon the multivalency of St George, demonstrating through his presence in various media the development of a devotional identity which remains culturally prevalent in modern England but whose origins are little understood.[39] This present study likewise employs an interdisciplinary approach. The chapters are based upon various interpretive strategies which transcend traditional disciplinary distinctions, with each exploring an aspect of the cult from a variety of perspectives in order to investigate the range of cultural roles performed by St Edmund.

A further influential and important study is Ashley and Sheingorn's collection of essays on the cult of St Anne in late medieval society.[40] Of particular relevance is the attention they devote to exploring areas of the cult where traditional

---

[37] *St Edmund, King and Martyr: Changing Images of a Medieval Saint*, ed. Anthony Bale (York: York Medieval Press, 2009).

[38] Katherine Lewis, *The Cult of St Katherine of Alexandria in Late Medieval England* (Woodbridge: The Boydell Press, 2000).

[39] Samantha Riches, *St George: Hero, Martyr and Myth*, rev. edn (Stroud: The History Press Ltd, 2005).

[40] Kathleen Ashley and Pamela Sheingorn, eds, *Interpreting Cultural Symbols: Saint Anne in Late Medieval Society* (Athens and London: The University of Georgia Press, 1990).

disciplinary boundaries overlap or 'intersect', as this allows consideration of phenomena typically marginalised by traditional disciplinary distinctions. Ashley and Sheingorn locate their study in relation to three principal intersections: popular culture, popular piety and women's studies.[41] Although seemingly a very different saint to Anne, the principal of determining the key arenas in which Edmund's cult was manifested will similarly underpin this consideration.

Central to several studies of saints' cults is the notion of how individual saints functioned as cultural symbols. Ashley and Sheingorn attest to the importance of attending to the meanings created by saints' cults in the context of the cultures in which they originated:

> In analyzing these miracle narratives [of St Foy] as semiotic entities we must simultaneously attend to three aspects of the text; we must see them as rhetorical structures (a set of internally related signs), as historically contingent constellations of signs, and as sign systems designed to have historical agency.[42]

Although primarily concerned with the *miraclua* of St Foy, I would contend that this three-fold practice of examining a text both in detail and in context is applicable to all cultic artefacts. The notion of a 'constellation of signs' is particularly relevant in an interdisciplinary context, as the systems to which cultic artefacts are related are not just textual but visual, oral, cultural, social and political. Also implied are the semioticians themselves, those responsible for making meaning through the creation of cultic artefacts, and their respective outlooks and motivations.

Karen A. Winstead locates her study of virgin martyrs in relation to Ashley and Sheingorn's investigation of St Anne, noting that she is also concerned with the 'cultural work' performed by these saints.[43] Her study is of particular relevance, as she considers how the lives of these saints developed throughout later medieval England. She concludes that the 'remarkable transformations' in the legends of individual martyrs 'signal a struggle over the meaning of these powerful cultural symbols'.[44]

In addition to the cultic artefacts themselves and those responsible for their creation, the way in which aspects of a saint's cult were received and understood is also crucial. Although an object, text or image may have been created with

---

[41] Ashley and Sheingorn, *St Anne*, p. 1. For discussion of their methodology in general see pp. 1–6 and 48–53.

[42] Kathleen Ashley and Pamela Sheingorn, *Writing Faith: Text, Sign, and History in the Miracles of Sainte Foy* (Chicago: University of Chicago Press, 1999), p. 20.

[43] Karen A. Winstead, *Virgin Martyrs: Legends of Sainthood in Late Medieval England* (Ithaca and London: Cornell University Press, 1997), p. 4.

[44] Winstead, *Virgin Martyrs*, p. 4.

a particular reader or viewer in mind, secondary recipients may also have had access to them and their participation in interpreting a cult must also be borne in mind. The title of Miri Rubin's study of the cult of the Virgin Mary indicates a similar investment in determining the reception of this all-pervasive medieval devotional figure, which she achieves by citing a wide range of sources and artefacts from across medieval and Early Modern Europe.[45] Accounting for the popularity of a saint in varying contexts is similarly a concern of the essays in Jenkins and Lewis's study of St Katherine of Alexandria, which likewise employs an interdisciplinary approach.[46]

'Blyssyd Edmund, kyng, martir and vyrgyne/ Hadde in thre vertues by grace a souereyn prys'[47]

In his lengthy mid-fifteenth century life of St Edmund, the Bury monk John Lydgate repeatedly deploys a tripartite epithet in his descriptions of the martyr, referring to Edmund as 'martir, mayde and kynge'. The longevity and variety of Edmund's cult makes it unlikely that these were the only terms in which he was understood, or at least that many meanings could be read into each aspect of his identity. Blanton demonstrates a similar multivalence in relation to St Æthelthryth. Although the saintly identity of the patroness of Ely could be reduced in similar terms to 'princess, abbess and virgin' Blanton demonstrates that St Æthelthryth's story in fact contains a far more nuanced set of cultural signs: royal asceticism, political marriage, conjugal chastity, monastic patronage, bodily incorruption, maternal nourishment.[48] This implies that Edmund's cultural signifiers will be equally complex. However, as will be discussed in detail below, Lydgate draws extensively on the pre-existing St Edmund tradition, meaning that his tripartite epithet, if somewhat reductive, is nevertheless broadly indicative of Edmund's

---

[45] Miri Rubin, *Emotion and Devotion: The Meaning of Mary in Medieval Religious Cultures*, Natalie Zemon Davies Annual Lecture Series (Budapest and New York: Central European University Press, 2009), esp. Chapter 3, 'Emotions and Selves', which explores encounters with the figure of the Virgin Mary in word, image and sound.

[46] *St Katherine of Alexandria: Texts and Contexts in Western Medieval Europe*, ed. Jacqueline Jenkins and Katherine J. Lewis (Turnhout: Brepols, 2003).

[47] John Lydgate's *Lives of Saints Edmund and Fremund* is printed in *Altenglische Legenden. Neue Folge*, ed. Carl Horstmann (Heilbronn: Henniger, 1881), pp. 376–445, I.192. The most recent edition is John Lydgate's *Lives of Sts Edmund and Fremund and the Extra Miracles of St Edmund: Edited from BL MS Harley 2278 and Bodleian Library M*, ed. Anthony Bale and A.S.G. Edwards (Heidelberg: Universitätsverlag, 2009). Prologue, 1–3.

[48] Blanton, *Signs of Devotion*, p. 4. For a similar discussion of cultural symbols see also Sarah Beckwith, *Christ's Body: Identity, Culture and Society in Late Medieval Writings* (New York: Routledge, 2003).

reception by the mid-fifteenth century. It therefore provides a useful starting point for considering the constituent aspects of Edmund's saintly identity.

Edmund the 'kyng'

The phenomenon of royal sanctity has attracted considerable scholarly attention, with particularly notable works by Susan Ridyard, David Rollason and Alan Thacker exploring the cults of sainted Anglo-Saxon monarchs.[49] A number of these studies assert that the cults of many Anglo-Saxon royal saints were promoted by royal patrons for political reasons. Alternatively, there are those who equate the popularity of royal martyr cults in Northern Europe with Germanic, pre-Christian attitudes to the charisma of royal blood and sacral qualities of kingship. The first comprehensive survey of sacral kingship was offered by Sir James Frazer in *The Golden Bough*, in which he drew upon comparative analysis of a vast array of cultures in order to examine the sacral power of the god-king, which he identified as primarily residing in his ability to influence the workings of nature.[50] Two highly influential monographs on the supernatural underpinnings of medieval kingship were inspired by Frazer: Fritz Kern's *Kingship and Law* and Marc Bloch's *The Royal Touch*.[51] Of particular relevance to this study are Kern's interest in the relationship between the supernatural and the political or social aspects of royal cults and Bloch's longitudinal approach to the charisma of royal sanctity and the ability of kings to enact healing. William Chaney's work continued the quest for pagan–Christian continuity.[52] Gábor Klaniczay has investigated similar issues in the cults of Central European saints.[53] In her discussion of Anglo-Saxon royal saints, Catherine Cubitt refines the pagan–Christian dichotomy and

---

[49] Ridyard, *Royal Saints*; David Rollason, 'The Cults of Murdered Royal Saints in Anglo-Saxon England', *Anglo-Saxon England* 11 (1983), 1–22; Alan Thacker, 'Kings, Saints and Monasteries in Pre-Viking Mercia', *Midland History* 10 (1985), 1–25.

[50] Sir James George Frazer, *The Golden Bough: A Study in Magic and Religion*, 12 vols (London: Macmillan, 1906–15), esp. vols 1–2, 'The Magic Art and the Evolution of Kings. Parts I and II'.

[51] Fritz Kern, *Kingship and the Law in the Middle Ages*, trans. S.B. Chrimes (New York: Harper and Row, 1970) and Marc Bloch, *The Royal Touch*, trans. J.E. Anderson (New York: Dorset Press, 1961).

[52] William A. Chaney, *The Cult of Kingship in Anglo-Saxon England: The Transition from Paganism to Christianity* (Manchester: Manchester University Press, 1970).

[53] Gábor Klaniczay, 'From Sacral Kingship to Self-Representation: Hungarian and European Royal Saints', in his *The Uses of Supernatural Power. The Transformations of Popular Religion in Medieval and Early Modern Europe* (Cambridge: The Polity Press 1990), pp. 79–94. See also Janet Nelson, 'Royal Saints and Early Medieval Kingship', Studies in Church History, 20 (1983), 15–30.

argues instead for the origins of royal cults in spontaneous, lay devotion, suggesting that they should be regarded as manifestations of popular religion.⁵⁴ The questions raised by these studies indicate a possible tension in the cult of royal saints between the scholarly and the supernatural, and are perhaps evident in the appearance of the wolf in St Edmund's legend.

A seminal work amongst studies of individual sainted kings is Jacques Le Goff's monograph on St Louis.⁵⁵ The structure reveals methodological objectives comparable to this book: the first part deals with the biography of the living St Louis, the second focuses on the producers and mediators of the cult and the third upon the varying ideologies and concepts that Louis was thought to represent. In methodological terms, Gábor Klaniczay's *Holy Rulers and Blessed Princesses* is similarly relevant. Rather than privileging one approach he considers a range of factors relating to sainted monarchs, including: pagan heritage, sacral kingship, martyrdom, the *rex iustus*, chastity and the *athleta patriae*, earthly versus heavenly authority and royal saints as propaganda.⁵⁶ Like Ridyard, Klaniczay traces the evolution of the notion of royal sanctity across several centuries. He notes that previous studies which focus too closely on one historical period preclude the opportunity of considering historical development within these cults, in response to which he offers 'a new synthesis, one different – and complementary – in approach and methodology from what has already been written on the subject'.⁵⁷ His principal objective is to attend closely to 'how distinctly the putatively timeless stereotypes … bore the stamp of the cultural milieu in which any concrete cult in fact found expression'.⁵⁸ This study employs a similar longitudinal approach and likewise seeks to locate responses to Edmund's royalty in a historical framework.

Edmund the 'martir'

Edmund's martyrdom guaranteed his status as a saint and was therefore an intrinsic part of his saintly identity. All saints were believed to possess intercessory ability,

---

⁵⁴ Catherine Cubitt, 'Sites and Sanctity: Revisiting the Cult of Murdered and Martyred Anglo-Saxon Royal Saints', *Early Medieval Europe* 9 (2001), 53–83. See also her 'Universal and Local Saints in Anglo-Saxon England', in *Local Saints and Local Churches in the Early Medieval West*, ed. Alan Thacker and Richard Sharpe (Oxford: Oxford University Press, 2002), pp. 423–54, esp. pp. 424–32.
⁵⁵ Jacques Le Goff, *Saint Louis* (Paris: Gallimard, 1996).
⁵⁶ Gábor Klaniczay, *Holy Rulers and Blessed Princesses: Dynastic Cults in Medieval and Central Europe*, trans. Éva Pálmai (Cambridge: Cambridge University Press, 2002).
⁵⁷ Klaniczay, *Holy Rulers*, 'Introduction', p. 16.
⁵⁸ Klaniczay, *Holy Rulers*, 'Introduction', p. 12.

but some were perceived to be particularly potent, often by virtue of the place they occupied in Christian history. Martyrs were afforded a special place amongst the ranks of saints. Weinstein and Bell describe martyrs as spiritual superheroes, 'purposeful heroes of dramatic and mortal struggles for the faith', who, through the exertion of their own will, attempted to further what they saw as God's work.[59]

Richard Gameson describes the martyrdom of a saint as the 'irreducible minimum' in terms of visual representation and refers to the tradition of depicting martyrs by allusion to, or at the moment of, their death.[60] This is also true of textual hagiographies, where the *passio* often comprises the central narrative. In the case of Edmund, his death at the hands of the Vikings is one of the few elements of his narrative that may be described as irreducible, as it constitutes his brief cameo in the *Anglo-Saxon Chronicle*, although it is the authors of the hagiographic tradition who construct the narrative of Edmund's death and portray him as a martyr, preferring to die rather than abjure his faith in favour of the Danes' pagan religion. Gameson describes the way in which Becket's death was 'used to redefine the spirituality of his life'.[61] This was a common hagiographic tendency whereby an individual's death was projected back upon the events of his or her life, which were subsequently redefined in relation to later actions: a glorious death implied a life equally well lived. Thus the manner in which Edmund's life was constructed based upon the events of his death must be a key consideration in the examination of the development of his cult.

In addition to the cause for which he died, the manner of Edmund's torture would have been significant to the medieval faithful. Sagittation was not a form of martyrdom unique to Edmund: St Sebastian also faced death by arrow, sometimes causing confusion as to which saint is depicted.[62] In addition, Edmund was eventually decapitated and many early Christian martyrs were similarly executed after enduring lingering and violent torture. This implies that not only is Edmund continuing a long tradition of defending the faith, but he is represented as on a spiritual par with the earliest founders of Christian sainthood. His martyrdom therefore integrates him into the continuous narrative of Christian history, establishing a link with individuals from all periods which transcends conventions of era or nationality.

---

[59] Weinstein and Bell, *Saints and Society*, p. 160.
[60] Richard Gameson, 'The Early Imagery of Thomas Becket', in *Pilgrimage: The English Experience from Becket to Bunyan*, ed. Colin Morris and Peter Roberts (Cambridge: Cambridge University Press, 2002), pp. 46–89; p. 53.
[61] Gameson, 'Early Imagery', p. 53.
[62] For example, it is unclear whether the image on the roodscreen at Stalham (Norfolk) is St Edmund or St Sebastian, although usually the crown worn by the former is diagnostic.

Considerable scholarly interest has been devoted to the representation of violence in saints' lives, particularly the torture endured by most martyrs before their eventual demise, and the ways in which this violence was intended to be read by varying audiences.[63] However, Jocelyn Wogan-Browne notes that 'torture is not a static sign': rather that it has 'no stable taxonomy from one legend to another ... its meaning is not instrumental but enacted, produced in front of us in each legend's narrative exchange'.[64] Is the martyrdom therefore 'irreducible' in the sense that it is static and unchanging, or is it adapted to suit the circumstances for which it was produced? For example, is the violence more or less extreme in some versions of Edmund's legend, and if so, what does this imply about the intended audience?

Edmund the 'vyrgyne'

The representation of torture in saints' lives marks the intersection of various strands of scholarly enquiry, for instance the relationship between Edmund's martyrdom and his attribution as a 'mayde', the third element of Lydgate's epithet. These coalesce in relation to the extent to which violence is gendered. This is particularly apposite in the case of a virgin martyr such as Edmund. The majority of scholarly attention to date has been devoted to the large numbers of female saints who fit within this category. The torture and sexual threats suffered by these women have been interpreted as voyeuristic or pornographic.[65] However, as a male virgin martyr, Edmund's relationship to these representational tropes must be considered. Winstead defines the typical female virgin martyr as an attractive young woman who refuses to participate in pagan sacrifices, debates with

---

[63] Robert Mills' *Suspended Animation: Pain, Pleasure and Punishment in Medieval Culture* (London: Reaktion Books Ltd., 2005) is an excellent introduction to the complicated issue of violence and its representation in medieval culture, as well as modern responses and assumptions. See especially Chapter 4, 'Invincible Virgins', pp. 106–44 and Chapter 5, 'Of Martyrs and Men', pp. 145–76. See also René Girard, *Violence and the Sacred*, trans. Patrick Gregory (Baltimore and London: The Johns Hopkins Press, 1977).

[64] Jocelyn Wogan-Browne, *Saints' Lives and Women's Literary Culture, c. 1150–1300: Virginity and its Authorizations* (Oxford: Oxford University Press, 2001), p. 108.

[65] For the ways in which torture was read see Wogan-Browne, *Saints' Lives*, pp. 106–17. For contrasting discussions concerning this debate see Kathryn Gravdal, *Ravishing Maidens: Writing Rape in Medieval Literature and Law* (Philadelphia: University of Pennsylvania Press, 1991) and Katherine J. Lewis, '"Lete me suffer": Reading the Torture of St Margaret of Antioch in Later Medieval England', in Jocelyn Wogan-Browne et al., eds, *Medieval Women: Texts and Contexts in Late Medieval Britain: Essays for Felicity Riddy* (Turnhout: Brepols, 2000), pp. 69–82.

her antagonists, affirms the fundamental tenets of Christianity, destroys idols, performs miracles and endures excruciating torments and threats to her virginity before finally meeting her death.[66] It is notable how closely Winstead's definition resembles the martyrdom of St Edmund.

Numerous scholars, such as Vauchez, Kieckhefer, and Weinstein and Bell, have established that the changing social conditions of the later Middle Ages, especially the increasingly private and introspective nature of piety and increased lay agency, resulted in changing definitions of saintliness.[67] Despite this, the often generic lives of the historically remote virgin martyrs remained popular.[68] Winstead suggests that this may in part be accounted for by clerical attempts to reinforce the barrier between the increasingly well-informed and enthusiastic laity and the saintly elite, as the virginal status of these particular saints marked their distinctiveness from the majority of a lay audience.

Wogan-Browne identifies a further key trait in the representation of virgin martyrs which points to additional complications in the representation of St Edmund. She observes that female virgin martyrs are perpetually beautiful and youthful, freed from the mortal contamination of the Fall by their renunciation of marriage and sexual reproduction:

> If virgins are vessels, they are precious but fragile. If they are flawless and eternally youthful, inhabiting bodies without menstrual and menopausal phases, then they are also excluded from historical process. Leading a life of silent veiled enclosure, 'dead to all earthly desires', virgins' real existence is in heaven, enclosed beyond mortal action and change, and they have no history.[69]

However, whilst Edmund does choose heaven and the martyr's palm, he also exists in the temporal realm, as king of the Eastern Angles. The extent to which this formulation is also applicable to male virgin martyrs must therefore be tested. Winstead notes that the virgin martyr was inherently a paradoxical symbol:

> As the most vulnerable and carnal of human beings – women – the virgin martyrs testify that the flesh can indeed triumph over corporeal desires, that weakness can prevail over strength. As women who transcend their gender

---

[66] Winstead, *Virgin Martyrs*, pp. 5–6.
[67] Vauchez, *Sainthood in the Later Middle Ages*; Weinstein and Bell, *Saints and Society*; Richard Kieckhefer, *Unquiet Souls: Fourteenth-Century Saints and Their Religious Milieu* (Chicago: University of Chicago Press, 1984).
[68] See Winstead, *Virgin Martyrs*, pp. 10–18.
[69] Wogan-Browne, *Saints' Lives*, pp. 19–21; p. 21.

to become manly, the virgin martyrs evoke the mystery of a God made man.[70]

However, this formulation is problematic when applied to male virgin martyrs such as Edmund. It implies that for a woman to triumph over weak and feeble flesh is to become 'manly'; then Edmund's virginity is a natural male state, which is clearly not the case, especially for a ruling monarch expected to perpetuate the royal line.

To some extent these questions arise due to the theoretical investigations upon which they are based being biased towards the study of female experience and sexuality. The study of medieval masculinity has experienced a relatively recent burgeoning of interest.[71] The most successful of these studies have focused on the plurality of male identities in the Middle Ages and the ways in which these were constructed and negotiated. Just as scholarship of women's roles in the Middle Ages has revealed their great variety and fluidity, medieval masculinities have proven equally diverse. Andrea Cornwall and Nancy Lindisfarne note that in many cultures the 'different images and behaviours contained in the notion of masculinity are not always coherent: they may be competing, contradictory and mutually undermining'. [72] This is reflected in a collection of essays edited by Jacqueline Murray.[73] In her introduction to the volume Murray identifies what are commonly regarded as the characteristic components of medieval masculine identity: the physical prowess and bravery of the warrior elite, honour, power, authority and responsibility, and sexual veracity and reproductive capabilities.[74] As a king, Edmund belongs to the warrior elite and might be expected to conform to these behavioural norms. Yet as a martyr he shuns violence and chooses self-sacrifice, and as a virgin he renounces the temptations of the flesh. The ways in which different manifestations of cultic devotion reconciled, or indeed elided, these apparent contradictions are a key question of this book. A number of studies provide a useful lead, in particular *Holiness and Masculinity in the Middle Ages*, edited by

---

[70] Winstead, *Virgin Martyrs*, p. 12.
[71] Ground-breaking studies in this area include *The Making of Masculinities: The New Men's Studies*, ed. Harry Brod (Boston: Allen and Unwin, 1987), *Medieval Masculinities: Regarding Men in the Middle Ages*, ed. Clare A. Lees (Minneapolis: University of Minnesota Press, 1994) and *Becoming Male in the Middle Ages*, ed. Jeffrey Jerome Cohen and Bonnie Wheeler (New York: Garland, 1997).
[72] Andrea Cornwall and Nancy Lindisfarne, 'Dislocating Masculinity: Gender, Power and Anthropology', in *Dislocating Masculinity: Comparative Ethnographies*, ed. Cornwall and Lindisfarne (London: Routledge, 1994), pp. 11–46; p. 12.
[73] *Conflicted Identities and Multiple Masculinities: Men in the Medieval West*, ed. Jacqueline Murray (New York and London: Garland Publishing Inc., 1999).
[74] Murray, 'Introduction', *Conflicted Identities*, pp. ix–xx.

P.H. Cullum and Katherine J. Lewis, and *Gender and Holiness: Men, Women and Saints in Medieval Europe*, edited by Samantha Riches and Sarah Salih.[75]

In an essay in the former volume, Jacqueline Murray explores the means by which men who entered the religious life and took vows of celibacy sought to redefine their masculinity. She concludes that by acknowledging carnal desire the clergy were able to present themselves as conquerors of the flesh, superior to men in secular life who submitted to desire. This involved the development of a vocabulary which deployed masculine militaristic imagery to describe the 'battle for chastity'.[76] Chastity could provide a useful means by which the reigns of childless kings such as Edward the Confessor or Richard II could be redefined as spiritually exalted, thus effectively diverting attention away from the dynastic difficulties brought about when no direct heir was forthcoming.[77] In their discussion of the backgrounds and origins of medieval saints, Weinstein and Bell suggest that this *topos* may largely account for the disproportionately large numbers of royal saints:

> The spectacle of reversal, of sacrifice, of inversion of worldly status was crucial to the perception of sanctity. Inherited poverty was commonplace; voluntary poverty was sanctifying ... For a farm labourer to take a vow of poverty or of humility was little more than to affirm an existing condition. But the whole point of holiness was rejection of the world and its values, overturning one way of life in favour of its opposite, shedding the 'old man' and putting on the new. The very material circumstances of the upper classes gave them the means to demonstrate to the world the fervour of their conversions.[78]

Pragmatically, virginity was not a desirable state for a monarch, but medieval writers of advice literature for kings and princes stressed the importance of self-restraint and chastity outside the sacramentally ordained bounds of marriage, arguing that a king must present the best possible role model to his people, and

---

[75] *Holiness and Masculinity in the Middle Ages*, ed. P.H. Cullum and Katherine J. Lewis (Toronto: University of Toronto Press, 2005) and *Gender and Holiness: Men, Women and Saints in Medieval Europe*, ed. Samantha Riches and Sarah Salih (London: Routledge, 2002).

[76] Jacqueline Murray, 'Masculinizing Religious Life: Sexual Prowess, the Battle for Chastity and Monastic Identity', in *Holiness and Masculinity*, ed. Cullum and Lewis, pp. 24–42. On the vocabulary of chastity see also Michel Foucault, 'The Battle for Chastity', in *Western Sexuality: Practice and Precept in Past and Present Times*, ed. Philippe Ariès and André Béjin, trans. Anthony Forster (Oxford: Basil Blackwell, 1985), pp. 14–25.

[77] See Lewis, 'Edmund of East Anglia, Henry VI and Ideals of Kingly Masculinity' and her 'Becoming a Virgin King: Richard II and Edward the Confessor', in *Gender and Holiness*, ed. Riches and Salih, pp. 86–100.

[78] Weinstein and Bell, *Saints and Society*, p. 199.

that he had no right, and little chance of success, in ordering his subjects to behave in a manner of which he was not himself capable.[79] Thus precedents existed for virginal royal saints, along with numerous strategies for accommodating this aspect of their saintly identity. The extent to which those responsible for the construction of Edmund's cult deployed these strategies, or whether they developed alternatives, will therefore be explored. St Æthelthryth is a similarly chaste saint, and the comparison between the ways in which a virginal (female) nun and a virginal (male) king are represented prove illuminating.[80]

The cult of St Edmund in medieval East Anglia

The extent of the cult of St Edmund in medieval England was such that discussing it in its entirety would be unfeasible in one book. I will therefore focus upon the cult as it developed in East Anglia (primarily the modern counties of Norfolk and Suffolk) from its inception in the ninth century to the dissolution of the abbey of Bury St Edmunds in 1539. In terms of the written legend this presents no disadvantage, as the majority of texts and manuscripts were originally authored or compiled at Bury. Norfolk and Suffolk also benefit from some of the highest concentrations in the country of surviving medieval church art, which makes the region an eminently suitable focal point for exploring the iconography of St Edmund. East Anglia was Edmund's own kingdom and the region which housed his cult centre at Bury. Aspects of the early cult in particular show the influence of popular devotion. Therefore considering Edmund in this context allows the exploration of the relationship between indigenous responses to the cult and its official, ecclesiastical perpetuation via the monastic community at Bury.

Part I: Texts and contexts: the legend of St Edmund[81]

In his assessment of the growth of the legend of St Edmund, Loomis wryly observes that 'about a mere scrap of history, a vast amount of material has gathered to form

---

[79] See Lewis, 'Edmund of East Anglia', pp. 166–9.
[80] Blanton, *Signs of Devotion*, especially pp. 81–8, 99–105, 122–9.
[81] A note on terminology: various terms are used to describe the written account of a saint's actions and the manner of his or her death. 'Life' or 'lives' is the most common and is used in this study. As a genre, a saint's life is a specific discourse governed by certain literary as well as religious conventions and tropes and refers to more than simply the period in which the saint was alive. The Latin term *vita* (lit. 'life') is used when this is the title of a text. *Passio* refers specifically to an account of a saint's death, or 'passion'. Miracle narratives were often included in saints' lives but were also collected together as independent texts and as such can be considered as a further sub-genre.

in its collected bulk a veritable saga'.[82] The 'veritable saga' which Loomis imagined the medieval legendary tradition to have become is exemplified in the Bury monk John Lydgate's mid-fifteenth-century *Lives of Sts Edmund and Fremund*, which in more than 3,500 lines of verse, accompanied by 150 full-colour miniatures, documents the life and death of his abbey's patron and his saintly cousin.[83] This is arguably the zenith of the medieval tradition: the *Lives* is the longest and most detailed version and Lydgate both unites and elaborates upon other texts from the established tradition and introduces his own original details. It was also produced in fascinating historical circumstances, being commissioned by Lydgate's abbot, William Curteys, to present to the young king Henry VI as a souvenir of his extended sojourn at the abbey between Christmas 1433 and Easter 1434. Lydgate's poem and the several illuminated manuscripts in which it is preserved are a far cry from the brief record of Edmund's death in the *Anglo-Saxon Chronicle*. The fundamental issue which Part I addresses is therefore how, why and when the legend flourished from such humble beginnings to encompass more than thirty extant versions.

Loomis's characterisation of the growth of the legend during the Middle Ages is highly informative but also somewhat misleading. In particular, 'gathering' implies a process whereby the legend is drawn together in one location and suggests an almost teleological progression and development. However, the texts vary considerably in length, detail, form and authorship and, far from offering a coherent and unified version of the life and death of St Edmund, anachronisms and contradictions are present throughout. My assessment of the development of the legend proceeds from the assertion that it is more often than not these moments of narrative instability, which generations of historians have sought to resolve, that are most revealing regarding the textual construction of Edmund's saintly identity. Particular consideration will be afforded to how factors such as authorship, patronage and circumstance influenced each retelling of the tale.

An important distinction should be noted at the outset between references to Edmund in chronicles and the contrast they present to the hagiographic sources. In most instances it is important not to overstate generic dissonance, as this has

---

[82] Loomis, 'Growth', 83.

[83] John Lydgate's *Lives of Saints Edmund and Fremund*, ed. Anthony Bale and A.S.G. Edwards, *John Lydgate's Lives of Saints Edmund and Fremund and the Extra Miracles of St Edmund: Edited from British Library MS Harley 2278 and Bodleian Library M* (Heidelberg: Universitätsverlag, 2009). All further references will be given parenthetically. For a facsimile of British Library MS Harley 2278, the manuscript presented to Henry VI, see *The Life of St Edmund, King and Martyr: A Facsimile of British Library MS Harley 2278*, with an introduction by A.S.G. Edwards (London: British Library, 2004).

led to the traditional tendency to privilege 'historical' chronicles over 'literary' hagiographies. Whilst avoiding value judgements of any kind it is certainly the case that the Edmund legend bifurcates along generic lines: whereas the hagiographic tradition was constantly evolving, with each author seeking to add new material and provide additional insights, the majority of the chroniclers replicate virtually unchanged the account of Edmund's death found in the *Anglo-Saxon Chronicle*. As noted above, this led Loomis to readily dismiss them as of little interest or value. The difference cannot be accounted for simply in terms of authorship; many chronicles were written by monks, just as the majority of the hagiographies originated in the monastic community at Bury. Both the function and form of chronicles is likely to have affected their presentation of material. The chronological scope is often broad, with the result that whilst Edmund is present, he is not the protagonist. Whilst some historical works in which Edmund appears were written at Bury and are therefore more concerned with the abbey and its interests, including its patron, many were written elsewhere. Some, such as Ranulf Higden's *Polychronicon*, are universal histories covering large periods of time.[84] As such, the amount of detail in which subjects from earlier periods in particular are discussed is necessarily limited. The physical format may have a similar effect, as the space for each annal was sometimes allocated many years in advance.[85] Whilst this does not preclude the author from writing in more depth, for example by encroaching upon the space for the next entry, such constraints make it more likely that details will be limited. The nature of what might be called the St Edmund chronicle tradition is therefore interesting for a number of reasons. Firstly, it indicates that the irreducible minimum of Edmund's narrative remained constant throughout the Middle Ages. Secondly, this sheds valuable light upon the development of the hagiographic tradition, as it provides a base line against which the innovations of subsequent authors can be assessed.

Miracles attributed to St Edmund will also be considered alongside the legends. There has been a scholarly tendency to divorce miracle accounts both from the physical contexts in which they occurred and also from the legendary contexts in which they originate. Simon Yarrow's consideration of the miracles of St Edmund reflects this trend.[86] Whilst offering insightful suggestions as to the meaning and significance of Edmund's miracles, Yarrow fails to locate his discussion within the

[84] *Polychronicon Ranulphi Higden monachi Cestrensis, together with the English translations of John Trevisa and of an unknown writer of the fifteenth century*, 9 vols, ed. Joseph Rawson Lumby, *Rerum Britannicarum Medii Aevi Scriptores*, 41 (London: Longman, Green, Longman, Roberts and Green, 1865–86).
[85] Gransden, *Historical Writing*, I, p. 29.
[86] Simon Yarrow, *Saints and their Communities: Miracle Stories in Twelfth Century England*, Oxford Historical Monographs (Oxford: Clarendon Press, 2006), pp. 24–62.

broader development of Edmund's legend and so the overall significance is lost. Subsequent studies of medieval miracles have started to address the bias hitherto evinced.[87] This study likewise treats miracles as an integral part of the formation of Edmund's saintly identity in a broader textual context.

Finally, it has been a common phenomenon in hagiographic scholarship to consider textual sources in isolation from their manuscript contexts. Cynthia Hahn goes some way to explaining this by suggesting that 'it is often assumed that pictures merely illustrate their texts' and are entirely dependent on the words they accompany, rendering them secondary and subordinate to the verbal narrative.[88] However, such logocentrism robs a text of its original performative context. In her discussion of manuscripts containing late-medieval English hagiographies, Mary Beth Long maintains that 'to ignore the physical context in which hagiographical texts are found – pictures, page material and thickness, and ink colour, as well as the content of accompanying texts and marginalia – is to miss a vital piece of the interpretative experience medieval readers would have of the individual lives'.[89] Each iteration of Edmund's life and miracles collections is therefore considered in its codicological setting and in relation to its historical, social and cultural origins.

Part II: Relics, shrines and pilgrimage: encountering St Edmund at Bury

As the custodian of Edmund's remains, the abbey at Bury was the centre of his cult and, as Part I demonstrates, the primary location from which information about his life and legend was disseminated. Although mutually dependent in terms of cultic perpetuation, the textual cult and the physical remains of Edmund functioned in distinctly different ways in terms of audience and reception. Although pilgrimage was by no means a universal experience it was more readily accessible for the vast majority in the medieval West than were the rare and precious manuscripts containing Edmund's life and posthumous deeds. By far the most public aspect of the cult at Bury were the sights and sounds encountered by the pilgrims who visited the shrine. Relatively little attention, however, has been paid to the ways in which the convent sought to determine Edmund's reception

---

[87] For example, *Contextualising Miracles*, ed. Mesley and Wilson (2014).
[88] Cynthia Hahn, *Portrayed on the Heart: Narrative Effect in Pictorial Lives of the Saints from the Tenth through the Thirteenth Century* (Berkeley and London: University of California Press, 2001), p. 45.
[89] Mary Beth Long, 'Corpora and Manuscripts, Authors and Audiences', in *A Companion to Middle English Hagiography*, ed. Sarah Salih (Cambridge: D.S. Brewer, 2006), pp. 47–69, p. 49.

by the faithful through the visual and physical orchestration of the pilgrimage experience, although consideration of this aspect of the cult of other saints has yielded valuable results.[90] Part II therefore redresses this significant gap in scholarly understanding by reconstructing the experience of a pilgrim to the shrine of St Edmund at key historical moments.

The primary reason for this scholarly diffidence is scarcity of source material, especially the physical condition of the abbey ruins. Once the third-largest Romanesque building in northern Europe, all that survive today of the site of St Edmund's shrine in the eastern arm of the abbey church are the remains of the crypt excavated in the late 1950s.[91] In his *Historical and Descriptive Account of St Edmund's Bury*, published in 1804, Edmund Gillingwater describes a model he had seen of the abbey church of Bury:

> It was ten feet long, five feet wide, and of a proportionate height, containing some 300 nitches and 280 windows, adorned with images and other Gothic figures … A model of the Abbey was likewise to be seen at Newmarket about fifty years ago, but whether this be the same as that above mentioned, we are not able to say.[92]

The interior of the church was evidently also visible, as Gillingwater remarks that the model of St Edmund's shrine was 'ornamented with images and crowns, gilt, as in its original state'.[93] At some point during the course of the nineteenth century this model disappeared from public view, as M.R. James, writing ninety years later, plaintively cites the description in the 'faint hope that the model … might yet be in existence in some lumber-room'.[94] Despite the absence of detailed models such as that described by Gillingwater, or a significant quantity of physical evidence, other sources do exist which enable a reconstruction of the interior of the abbey church.

Probably the best-known source relating to the abbey of Bury St Edmunds is the chronicle written by Jocelin of Brakelond, in which he describes life in the

---

[90] *Art and Architecture of Late Medieval Pilgrimage in Northern Europe and the British Isles*, 2 vols, ed. Sarah Blick and Rita Tekippe, Studies in Medieval and Reformation Traditions, 104 (Leiden and Boston: Brill, 2005).
[91] H.J.M. Maltby, 'Excavation of the Abbey ruins, Bury St Edmunds', *Proceedings of the Suffolk Institute of Archaeology* xxiv (1949), 256–57.
[92] Edmund Gillingwater, *Historical and Descriptive Account of St Edmund's Bury* (Saint Edmund's Bury: Printed by and for J. Rackham, Angel Hill, 1804), p. 65.
[93] Gillingwater, *Historical and Descriptive Account*, p. 65.
[94] M.R. James, *On the Abbey of S. Edmund at Bury*, Cambridge Antiquarian Society publications, Octavo series 28 (Cambridge: Deighton Bell, 1895), p. 177.

monastery between 1173 and 1202 in vivid and immediate detail.[95] In particular, his account of the fire of 1198, in which the shrine was badly damaged, suggests tantalising clues as to the appearance and arrangement of the church interior. Similarly, an anonymous account of the far more devastating fire of 1465 provides an indication of alterations made during the intervening years.[96] The *Gesta Sacristarum* (the deeds of the sacrists) lists the monastic officials responsible for various building works from the time of Abbot Baldwin (1065–97) until the end of the thirteenth century and from this may be inferred some details of the interior arrangement of the abbey church.[97] In addition, numerous chronicles are extant, along with various lists of benefactors, details in wills, inventories and registers, and a fascinating fragment of an account of the annual ritual activities of the abbey.[98]

Many of these sources were cited by M.R. James in his volume *On the Abbey of S. Edmund at Bury*, published in 1895, in which he describes his intention to collate all available materials which will be 'illustrative of the internal decorations and arrangements of the Abbey Church'.[99] Some of these texts had been published elsewhere, most notably by Thomas Arnold in his three-volume *Memorials of St Edmund's Abbey*, but James also claims to 'bring to light some new material'.[100] One of the most significant 'new' sources relating to the interior of the abbey which James claims to 'bring to light' is a manuscript in the College of Arms, London, now known as MS Arundel 30. The manuscript comprises 216 leaves and measures 9 × 5½ inches. The manuscript was owned after the Dissolution by Nicholas Bacon (1509–79), the Lord Keeper and a Suffolk landowner whose father acquired by royal grant various lands previously belonging to the abbey of Bury St Edmunds. It subsequently passed to the antiquary John Bale (1495–1563), then to Matthew Parker, archbishop of Canterbury (1559–75) and then to Lord William Howard of Naworth (1563–1640). It was acquired, along with other books from Naworth, by Thomas Howard, the second earl of Arundel (1586–1646), until William Dugdale persuaded Henry, duke of Norfolk to donate this and other volumes to the College of Arms in 1678.[101] It appears to have been written for Bury St Edmunds abbey, and contains a copy of the *Bury Chronicle* from the Fall until

---

[95] Jocelin of Brakelond, *Chronicle of the Abbey of Bury St Edmunds*, trans. Diana Greenway and Jane Sayers (Oxford: Oxford University Press, 1989).

[96] *Incendium Ecclesiae*, ed. Arnold, *Memorials*, III, pp. 283–7.

[97] *Gesta Sacristarum*, ed. Arnold, *Memorials*, II, pp. 289–96.

[98] For a summary of the sources see James, *On the Abbey Church*, pp. 115–50.

[99] James, *On the Abbey Church*, p. 117.

[100] Arnold, *Memorials*; James, *On the Abbey Church*, p. 117.

[101] See *The Chronicle of Bury St Edmunds, 1212–1301*, ed. Antonia Gransden (London: Nelson, 1964), xxxviii–xlii.

1301, with additional annals for numerous years up to 1335, along with a fifteenth-century copy of Nennius's *Historia Britonum* and other miscellaneous historical and ecclesiastical pieces.[102] The fly-leaves of the book are made up partly of palimpsest leaves of a large quarto copy of the *Aeneid*, written in an eleventh-century English hand, on which are recorded a large collection of verses inscribed on wall paintings, altar pieces, painted windows, tapestries, sculptures and a range of other artefacts in churches in Peterborough, St Mary's abbey at York, Flixton and Framlingham in Suffolk, Lincoln, Spalding, Westminster and Bury St Edmunds, with the majority pertaining to the latter location. The manuscript may be loosely dated by internal evidence: it refers to images which appear to adorn the Lady Chapel at Bury, which was begun in 1275, and also to a number of items, for example the great candlestick, which were destroyed in the fire of 1465, suggesting a date between these two events. The handwriting of the verses, however, is from the earlier portion of this period. Although James indicates that he believes a single author to have been responsible for copying down these inscriptions, at least four hands appear to be discernible, ranging from the late thirteenth to the mid-fourteenth century. It therefore appears that at various times a number of individuals visited churches, primarily in East Anglia, but also as far afield as York and Westminster, and compiled a record of the inscriptions they found on images in various media. Considering the probable monastic provenance of the manuscript, successive sacrists of the abbey at Bury would be likely candidates for showing such detailed interest in the decorative schemes of other churches, possibly gathering ideas to implement in their own abbey church. Relatively little scholarly attention has been paid to this aspect of Arundel 30, and many questions concerning its provenance remain to be answered which lie beyond the scope of this book. Despite this, the inscriptions pertaining to Bury offer a unique insight into the decoration of the abbey church and the iconographic setting of the cult of St Edmund.

Part Three: Beyond Bury: dissemination and appropriation

The final section turns away from Bury to consider manifestations of devotion in alternative locations. The difficulties in distinguishing between 'official', Bury-authorised devotional practices and those which evolved spontaneously elsewhere are considerable. It is therefore unhelpful to think in terms of direct oppositions such as 'official' and 'unofficial', clerical and lay, learned and unlearned. Instead I

---

[102] See W.H. Black, *Catalogue of Arundel Manuscripts in the Library of the College of Arms* (London: printed by S. and R. Bentley, 1829), pp. 44–57.

would suggest that the distinction should be between 'home' and 'away' and will therefore explore how Edmund's saintly identity was perceived and presented at a remove from the cult centre and how this equated to the official version of his sanctity propagated at Bury in both word and image. Chapter 8 therefore explores the way in which Edmund was written into the landscape of East Anglia and the locations which came to be associated with his legend, such as the site of his initial coming ashore near Hunstanton in north-west Norfolk.

The fundamental difference between the cult at Bury and elsewhere was proximity to Edmund's relics and their miracle-working *virtus*: the powerful aura of miracle-working potency whose strength was concomitant with proximity to the saintly remains. The miracles discussed in the first two parts of this book are primarily those associated with Edmund's relics, both before and after their enshrinement in the abbey church. The intact preservation of Edmund's corpse and Bury's vigorous promotion of its continued presence in the abbey means that any relics of the saint found elsewhere are likely to be secondary, such as the fragment of coffin which Blomefield reports was in Thetford Priory, or the portion of shirt preserved in crystal (*una pars camisie Sancti Edmundi in uno cristall*) in St Edmund's church, Norwich.[103] In Chapter 9 I will therefore consider miracles which occurred in the absence of primary relics in order to determine the impact upon the nature of the miracles and thus the presentation of Edmund's saintly identity. In the absence of relics another means by which the presence of a saint could be invoked was through the use of visual imagery. Representations of Edmund are extant in more than eighty locations in Norfolk and Suffolk and these will be used in Chapter 10 to determine the nature of his iconographic representation. Finally, in Chapter 11 we cross the regional borders to examine what happens to Edmund when he is anthologised alongside other saints in legendary collections. Although strictly outside the remit of this project, this material includes the latest medieval version of the St Edmund's legend, and also serves as a striking contrast to the many East Anglian Edmunds, thus furthering our consideration of the dialectic of 'home' and 'away'.

Implicit in all these discussions is the question of who was responsible for disseminating Edmund's cult. The complex networks of patronage, both ecclesiastical and lay, mean that even the most remote East Anglian community may have been connected to the abbey at Bury through the involvement and activities

---

[103] The Thetford relic is cited by Francis Blomefield, *An Essay Towards a Topographical History of the County of Norfolk*, 2nd edn, 11 vols (London: Miller, 1805–10) II. 118. The relic of Edmund's shirt is listed in *Inventory of Church Goods during the Reign of Edward III in the Archdeaconry of Norwich*, 2 vols, ed. Aelred Watkin, Norfolk Record Society, 19 (Norwich: Norfolk Record Society, 1947–8), I, p. 7.

of certain individuals, connections which today may be lost or, at best, difficult to recover. Nevertheless, attempting to determine the role of individuals or communities in disseminating the cult is fundamental as it provides additional insight into the social, political and cultural context in which Edmund was deployed. If saints' cults are social constructions, then saints are of the people, but which people?

PART I

Texts and contexts
The legend of St Edmund

CHAPTER 1

The emergence of the hagiographic tradition Abbo of Fleury, *Passio Sancti Eadmundi*

'On such occasions each would contribute to the others such information as he himself had obtained; and thereupon one would afterwards confer with another. I, too, used to furnish a few particulars which I had gained by word of mouth from others, or learned from reading aloud.'[1]

The hagiographic tradition

IN contrast to the largely static chronicle tradition, the hagiographic representation of Edmund was constantly evolving, with each author seeking to add to the repository of knowledge concerning Edmund's life, death and posthumous deeds. Many hagiographers make frequent intertextual references, and whilst referring to previous versions of the legends bolsters their own authorial credibility, it also indicates that they are aware of contributing to a continuous, evolving narrative. The hagiographic tradition appears to develop independently of its annular counterpart, as from the outset it offers a different version of events: whereas in the brief chronicle entries Edmund meets his death in battle, the hagiographers develop the narrative of martyrdom, where Edmund is captured by the Danes and dies in defence of his faith. The prototype for the chronicle tradition is an authoritative 'historical' work, the *Anglo-Saxon Chronicle*, but the hagiographers appear to lack a similar documentary precedent, which supports the assertion that Edmund's cult is almost entirely constructed. It also raises the question of how the alternative hagiographic versions originate and how they are authorised in ways which allow them to deviate from a source as respected and established as the *Anglo-Saxon Chronicle*.

A useful corollary is to be found in Winstead's discussion of the lives of female virgin martyrs. The early lives emphasise sensation and confrontation, whereas by the thirteenth century a more explicitly didactic mode of representation was dominant, including lavish prayers and passages of exposition.[2] Writers of the

---

[1] Geoffrey of Wells, *De Infantia Sancti Edmundi*, ed. Arnold, *Memorials*, I, pp. 93–103; p. 93.
[2] Winstead, *Virgin Martyrs*, Chapter 1, pp. 19–63.

late fourteenth century distanced the saints from the increasingly prominent laity by emphasising their miraculous abilities and their contempt for institutions such as family and state.[3] In contrast, most likely in response to fear of Lollardy and misdirected lay learning, the female virgin martyrs of the fifteenth century were significantly less radical and confrontational and more conservative. It is particularly noteworthy that Winstead identifies Lydgate's *Lives* of the female virgin martyrs Sts Margaret and Petronilla as conforming to these later medieval developments, as this allows direct comparison with his presentation of Edmund.[4] These broad trends provide a useful model with which the St Edmund hagiographic tradition may be compared. As a virgin martyr he may be expected to conform to these developments, but if this is not the case then this suggests that other areas of his saintly identity are, at least in some instances, predominant.

Abbo of Fleury, Passio Sancti Eadmundi

The first hagiographic version of Edmund's legend is the *Passio Sancti Eadmundi* by Abbo of Fleury (c.945–1004).[5] A monk of the celebrated Benedictine house of Fleury-sur-Loire, Abbo was a renowned scholar, teacher and proponent of reformed monasticism.[6] He came to England in 985 at the request of Dunstan, archbishop of Canterbury (959–88), and spent two years at Ramsey Abbey near Peterborough, teaching, and administering the community's school. It was likely during this period or shortly after his return to Fleury in 987 that he composed the *Passio*.[7] Abbo dedicates his text to Archbishop Dunstan, suggesting that it was composed before Dunstan's death in 988. Ælfric's early eleventh-century English translation of Abbo corroborates this, as he claims that Abbo arrived three years before Dunstan's death (i.e. in 985) and that he returned to Fleury

---

[3] Winstead, *Virgin Martyrs*, Chapter 2, pp. 64–111.

[4] Winstead, *Virgin Martyrs*, Chapter 3, pp. 112–146.

[5] The most recent edition of the *Passio* is in *Three Lives of English Saints*, ed. Michael Winterbottom, Toronto Medieval Latin Texts, 1 (Toronto: Centre for Medieval Studies, 1972) pp. 67–87, from London, BL, MS Cotton Tiberius B. ii (fols 2–19v), of the eleventh century. The only complete translation of the *Passio* is by Hervey in his *Corolla*, pp. 6–59. Unless stated otherwise all translations of Abbo will be drawn from this edition.

[6] The fullest treatment of Abbo's career and achievements is Marco Mostert, *The Political Theology of Abbo of Fleury. A Study of the Ideas about Society and Law of the Tenth-Century Monastic Reform Movement* (Hilversum: Verloren, 1987), pp. 17–18, 40–64.

[7] Gransden believes that Abbo wrote the *Passio* whilst at Ramsey; Gransden, 'Abbo Fleury's *Passio*', 23, 47–56. For an alternative view, that he wrote after his return to France see Mostert, *Political Theology*, pp. 17, 45.

within two years; the *Passio* was therefore composed between 985 and 987.⁸ The *Passio* is divided into chapters which fall into four sections: the first is a dedicatory epistle to Archbishop Dunstan (Epistle); this is followed by a historic and geographical preface (Chapters I–II); Edmund's reign and the events precipitating the Danish invasion are introduced (Chapters III–IV) before the martyrdom itself is described (Chapters V–XI); the *Passio* concludes with details of the aftermath of Edmund's death, the early development of the cult and a number of miracles (Chapters XII–XIX).

Provenance

The provenance of the *Passio* is noteworthy, as it not only provides an insight into the origins of an individual text but also illuminates the genesis of the entire hagiographic tradition concerning St Edmund. It is apparent that Abbo utilised numerous sources in his composition. He cites liberally from scripture, classical writers including Virgil and Horace, and there are strong echoes of Bede and allusions to the lives of other saints, most notably Sts Cuthbert and Sebastian.⁹ The *Passio* abounds with intertextual borrowings to the extent that Gransden dismisses it as 'little more than a hotchpotch of hagiographical commonplaces'.¹⁰ Whilst not denying his literary indebtedness, Abbo himself provides an alternative account of the ultimate source of his tale. He claims that the story of Edmund's martyrdom was first related to King Æthelstan (924–40) by a very old man (*sene decrepito*) who claimed to be Edmund's armour-bearer (*armiger*). This tale was told in the presence of Archbishop Dunstan, who in turn told the story to the bishop of Rochester and the abbot of Malmesbury whilst Abbo was present.¹¹ Since Edmund's demise until Abbo's arrival at Ramsey, 116 years had elapsed, and whilst it is technically possible for the story to have been transmitted in the manner Abbo describes, it is likely at the very least that the passage of the years had dimmed the memory of the events and thus doubt is cast over the credibility of Abbo's story.¹² Abbo, however, takes care to authenticate his claims. He refers to Dunstan's assertion that 'the snows of [the armour-bearer's] head (*nix capitis*)

---

[8] *Ælfric's Lives of Saints*, ed. and trans. W.W. Skeat, 2 vols, Early English Text Society, os 76 and 82 (London: Oxford University Press for the Early English Text Society, 1966), II, pp. 314–35; p. 315.

[9] For a detailed discussion of the *Passio*'s intertextuality see Gransden, 'Abbo Fleury's *Passio*', 22–3, 29–40.

[10] Gransden, 'Origins', 86–7.

[11] Abbo, *Passio*, Epistle; Hervey, *Corolla*, p. 9.

[12] Elizabeth van Houts discusses the validity of Abbo's claims in *Memory and Gender in Medieval Europe, 900–1200* (Basingstoke: Macmillan, 2009), pp. 47–8.

compel belief', relying upon the conventional association of old age and wisdom.[13] His insistence on eye-witness testimony confers further credibility:

> To them you [Dunstan] averred, while the tears ran from your eyes, that you had in your youth learned the history from a broken-down veteran, who in relating it, simply and in good faith ... declared on his oath that, on the very day on which the martyr laid down his life for Christ's sake, he had been armour-bearer to the saintly hero.[14]

In her discussion of the development of Becket's hagiography, Anne Harris suggests that the immediacy of the eye-witness is compelling because it is both performative and evidentiary.[15] In Edmund's case the armour-bearer's testimony is performative because it is affective (Dunstan weeps as he recalls the tale and in turn is compelled to retell it) and evidentiary because of the impression of incontestable proof of hearing the story from someone who was actually present and witnessed the tortures inflicted upon Edmund, which so moved the armour-bearer's audience.

The role of the eye-witness, of someone who experienced at first hand the events of the martyrdom, represents an important standard in hagiographic narration.[16] Despite its recognised tropic nature, scholars have treated this element of Abbo's *Passio* with surprisingly little suspicion. Whitelock was clearly convinced by Abbo's version of events, claiming that it must 'be treated with respect':

> On this central theme [the martyrdom], Abbo could not drastically have altered what he claimed to have heard from Dunstan ... He could not have invented the armour-bearer. Nor is it likely that Dunstan should indulge in motiveless and flamboyant lying.[17]

Ridyard reiterates this sentiment with the startling claim that 'it is at least possible that Abbo's narrative is a more reliable source for Edmund's death than either

---

[13] Abbo, *Passio*, Epistle; Hervey, *Corolla*, p. 9. For the wisdom and virtue attributed to old age in the Middle Ages see John A. Burrow, *The Ages of Man: A Study of Medieval Writing and Thought* (Oxford: Clarendon Press, 1986), pp. 107–9, 150–1, 162–4.

[14] Abbo, *Passio*, Epistle; Hervey, *Corolla*, p. 9.

[15] Anne F. Harris, 'Pilgrimage, Performance and Stained Glass at Canterbury Cathedral', in *Art and Architecture*, 2 vols, ed. Blick and Tekippe, Studies in Medieval and Reformation Traditions, 104 (Leiden and Boston: Brill, 2005), I, pp. 243–84; p. 249.

[16] Jeannette M.A. Beer, *Narrative Conventions of Truth in the Middle Ages* (Genève: Libraire Droz S.A., 1981), pp. 23–34.

[17] Whitelock, 'Fact and Fiction', 221.

the *Anglo-Saxon Chronicle* or Asser', merely adding the cautionary caveat that 'it would be a mistake to … regard the *Passio* simply as a direct and straightforward reproduction of the armour-bearer's story' on the basis that time and the retelling of the tale are likely to have resulted in the addition and embellishment of certain elements.[18] Even Gransden, normally sceptical of a literary-inspired motif, is circumspect, suggesting that 'Abbo's appeal in the Epistle to Dunstan's authority is so specific and the assertion that Dunstan's informant was a layman so unusual that it is hard to disbelieve.'[19]

Despite the willingness of modern critics to accept his claims, Abbo presents knowledge of, and interest in, Edmund's story as fragile, preserved by a few individuals but not widely known. He claims that the Ramsey monks desired the legend to be recorded partly as a result of Dunstan's regard for it, which caused him to 'store up [the armour-bearer's] words in their entirety in the receptacle of [his] memory', but also due to their fear that it would fall into 'utter oblivion', as Dunstan was an old man with whom the story could very well die.[20] Abbo avers that at the time of writing, the story 'is unknown to most people, and has been committed to writing by none'.[21] His urgency may have been heightened as there appear to be some who doubted Dunstan's version of events. Abbo himself admits that 'none would give credence' to the miracles wrought by Edmund after his death were it not for the 'irrefragable authority' of Dunstan's assertions.[22] Even so, when Dustan maintained the continuing incorruption of Edmund's body, 'one of those present anxiously raised the question of whether such things were possible?'[23] Dunstan reassures his listeners by referring to the precedent offered by St Cuthbert.[24] It is possible, of course, that Abbo invented these details in order to legitimate his composition and invest it with urgency and import. Nevertheless, it implies that the hagiographic tradition originated at a moment when the legend of St Edmund was poised precariously between obscurity and renown.

It is likely that the *Passio* functioned as far more than a straightforward life. One question in particular which continues to perplex scholars is why Ramsey commissioned the life of a saint buried elsewhere. It is possible that the congregation at Beodricesworth, only forty miles from Ramsey, may have learned of Abbo's presence and commissioned him to write the life of their saintly patron,

---

[18] Ridyard, *Royal Saints*, pp. 63–4 and p. 67.
[19] Gransden, 'Abbo of Fleury's *Passio*', 57.
[20] Abbo, *Passio*, Epistle; Hervey, *Corolla*, p. 9.
[21] Abbo, *Passio*, Epistle; Hervey, *Corolla*, p. 7.
[22] Abbo, *Passio*, Epistle; Hervey, *Corolla*, p. 9.
[23] Abbo, *Passio*, Epistle; Hervey, *Corolla*, p. 9.
[24] Abbo, *Passio*, Epistle; Hervey, *Corolla*, pp. 9–11.

although there is no evidence that this was the case. However, Archbishop Dunstan is likely to have favoured the strengthening of the Church in East Anglia after decades of Viking invasions. The development of the cult of St Edmund would enable the monastery at Beodricesworth to grow and flourish, with the burgeoning influence of the community conferring stability and administrative control over the region. David Dumville goes as far as to claim that Beodricesworth was transformed from a secular to a Benedictine monastery in this period and that Abbo wrote to commemorate its refoundation.[25] It is generally agreed, however, that Beodricesworth was refounded in 1020 by Cnut.[26] Similarly, Gransden's claim that Dunstan sought to create a second East Anglian see based at Beodricesworth and encouraged Abbo to promote St Edmund as a means of legitimising the community's elevation to diocesan status is unconvincing.[27] It therefore seems most likely that the *Passio* was written for, if not at, Ramsey.

Edmund was certainly enthusiastically commemorated at Ramsey. The *Historia Regum*, the early sections of which were produced at Ramsey, mentions the year of Edmund's death and notes that 'it would be fitting to include some thoughts on the honour of his passion'.[28] There is also a couplet in his honour in the Metrical Calendar of Ramsey:

Astra poli petit Eadmundus decoratus honore;
Gaudent Angligeni laudibus almificis.

(Edmund, decorated with honour, makes for the heavens of the high; The English people rejoice with generous praises.)[29]

The *Passio* was one of the earliest hagiographic texts of the tenth-century monastic revival in England, so it is possible that Abbo sought to provide the Ramsey

---

[25] David N. Dumville, *English Caroline Script and Monastic History. Studies in Benedictinism, AD 950–1030* (Woodbridge: The Boydell Press, 1993), pp. 77–8.

[26] Gransden, 'Origins', 10–12.

[27] For Gransden's suggestions concerning the creation of a second East Anglian diocese see her 'Abbo Fleury's *Passio*', 41–5.

[28] Symeon of Durham, *Libellus de exordio atque procursu istius, hoc est Dunhelmensis, ecclesie*, ed. and trans. David Rollason (Oxford: Clarendon Press, 2000). Much of the compiled material up until 887 is thought to derive from an earlier compilation by Byrhtferth of Ramsey. See Michael Lapidge, 'Byrhtferth of Ramsey and the Early Sections of the *Historia Regum* attributed to Symeon of Durham', *Anglo-Saxon England* 10 (1982 for 1981), 97–122.

[29] Michael Lapidge, 'A Tenth-Century Metrical Calendar from Ramsey', *Revue Bénédictine* 94 (1984), 326–69.

monks with a high-quality hagiographic model to inspire the composition of the lives of other saints.[30] Gransden suggests that the *Passio* may in fact have been commissioned by Ramsey's abbot, St Oswald, also archbishop of York, who had a well-known interest in the cult of saints. Promoting Edmund's cult would simultaneously raise the profile of East Anglia as a whole; in this context the favourable comparisons drawn between Edmund and Cuthbert should be read as attempts to place Edmund, and the region from whence he originated, on a par with the holy realm of Northumberland.[31]

In contrast, Lucy Marten suggests that Ramsey's lay founder and benefactor, the ealdorman Æthelwine, may have been directly involved in the commissioning of the *Passio*.[32] It seems that during his stay at Ramsey, Abbo had some contact with Æthelwine. Abbo's biographer, Aimo, wrote that during his stay in England he received 'only words' from King Ethelred II (978–1016) but 'from the ealdorman he had gifts worthy of his sanctity and was treated with much reverence by him as long as he was in his company'.[33] Æthelwine fostered close connections with Ramsey; the *Ramsey Chronicle* refers to him as 'father', he lived close by and visited frequently and chose to spend his final days in the monastery. Marten suggests that Æthelwine's interest in the region and its reputation may have led him to commission the *Passio*.[34]

However, the way in which Edmund is depicted would not necessarily accord with the preoccupations of a tenth-century ealdorman and is more suited to a monastic audience. Exploring the ways in which Abbo constructs Edmund's sanctity is crucial in determining the origins and function of the *Passio*. As the first hagiographic account of Edmund's demise it also sets the precedent for subsequent authors. It is thus necessary to explore in detail the means by which Abbo elucidated the characteristics of his protagonist.

A royal saint

The historical introduction with which Abbo prefaces the *Passio* enables him to establish Edmund's worthy lineage. He claims that Edmund was 'sprung from

---

[30] The earlier text is Lantfred's *Translatio et miracula Sancti Swithuni*, ed. E.P. Sauvage, *Analecta Bollandiana*, iv (1885), 367–410.
[31] Gransden, 'Origins', 83–4.
[32] Lucy Marten, *The Southfolk and the Northmen: Suffolk 840–1086* (forthcoming). I am grateful to the author for sharing her work with me before its publication.
[33] Aimo, *Vita et Martyrium S. Abbonis*, ed. Jacques-Paul Migne, *Patrologia Latina*, cxxxix, cols 390–2; col. 392.
[34] Marten, *Southfolk and Northmen*.

the noble stock of the Old Saxons' and 'descended from a line of kings'.[35] In the first chapter he describes the merits of the Saxons, who, along with the Angles and the Jutes, are invited by the Britons to be their 'protectors' and who 'defend their clients and themselves with courage' and 'unconquered bravery'.[36] Eventually frustrated by the sloth of the 'wretched natives', the three tribes seize the land for themselves, dividing it into three kingdoms and casting the Britons out.[37] Thus Edmund is shown to descend from noble conquerors. Edmund is depicted as an exemplary king, but one who differs somewhat from his warrior ancestors:

> He was in truth of a comely aspect, apt for sovereignty; and his countenance continually developed fresh beauty through the tranquil devotion of his most serene speech. To all he was affable and winning in speech, and distinguished by a captivating modesty; and he dwelt among his contemporaries with admirable kindness, though he was their lord, and without any touch of haughtiness or pride.[38]

In addition, Edmund fairly administers justice and is generous to widows and orphans,[39] evincing an admirable array of praiseworthy kingly qualities.

This portrait, however, must be understood in relation to what Abbo tells us of the events of the martyrdom, which complicate the notion of Edmund as exemplary king. Despite informing us that Edmund 'was in the prime of life, and in the fullness of vigour' and 'a keen solider', he tells us that when confronted by the Danish invaders Edmund surrenders.[40] It is this decision which leads to his capture and martyrdom and the transfer of his kingdom into Danish hands. Rather than being read as a failure of his kingship, however, Edmund's decision must be understood in terms of a different model: that of Christ. The paradigmatic shift occurs during Edmund's conversation with the bishop. In his response to the prelate's recommendation that he 'seeks safety in flight' or surrender to the Danes'

---

[35] Abbo, *Passio*, III; Hervey, *Corolla*, p. 15.
[36] Abbo, *Passio*, I; Hervey, *Corolla*, pp. 11–13.
[37] Abbo, *Passio*, I; Hervey, *Corolla*, p. 13.
[38] Abbo, *Passio*, III; Hervey, *Corolla*, p. 15.
[39] Abbo, *Passio*, IV; Hervey, *Corolla*, p. 17. For contemporary views of kingship see, for example, Abbo of Fleury's *Liber Apologeticus* and *Collectio Canonum*, written for the Capetian kings Hugh and Robert the Pious, in which he outlines ideal kingship in similar terms. *Liber Apologeticus* is printed in Jacques-Paul Migne, *Patrologia Latina*, cxxxix, coll. 461–72; *Collectio Canonum* is printed in Migne, *Patrologia Latina*, cxxxix, cols 473–508. For the extent to which Abbo's depiction of Edmund accorded with contemporary theories of kingship see Gransden, 'Abbo of Fleury's *Passio*', 45–56.
[40] Abbo, *Passio*, VI; Hervey, *Corolla*, p. 21.

demands for tribute and submission, Edmund proffers an alternative course of action:[41]

> I have always avoided the calumnious accusations of the informer; never have I endured the opprobrium of fleeing from the battle-field, realising how glorious it would be to die for my country; and now I will of my own free will surrender myself, for the loss of those dear to me has made life itself hateful.[42]

The mid-sentence caesura is the turning point of the narrative, when Edmund relinquishes the world and embraces the hereafter and the martyr's fate. This is reflected in the lexical transformation which occurs almost simultaneously in the text. Edmund is no longer depicted as a temporal king but as a champion of Christ, 'a standard bearer in the camp of the eternal king'.[43] The conflict becomes ideological, as Edmund refuses to submit to Hinguar unless the Danish chief and his army convert to Christianity.[44] Enraged, Hinguar sends soldiers to seize Edmund, who drag him before the Viking chief 'like Christ before the governor Pilate'.[45] Like Christ, Edmund is 'mocked in many ways' and 'savagely beaten' before being tied to a tree (invoking the cross) and 'tortured with terrible lashes' before being shot full of arrows until he resembled 'a prickly hedgehog or a thistle fretted with spines'.[46] Twice we are told that throughout his suffering Edmund continued to call on Christ until he was finally beheaded:

> Thus in his departure from life, the king, following the footsteps of Christ his master, consummated that sacrifice of the Cross which he had endured continually in the flesh. Just as Christ, free from all taint of sin, left on the column to which he was bound, not for himself, but for us, the blood which was the mark of his scourging, so Edmund incurred a like penalty bound to the blood-stained tree, for the sake of gaining a glory that fades not away. Christ, whose life was without stain, suffered in his great benignity the bitter pain of unmerciful nails in his hands and feet in order to cleanse away the foulness of our sins; Edmund, for the love of the holy Name, with his whole body bristling with grievous arrows, and lacerated to the very marrow by the

---

[41] Abbo, *Passio*, VIII; Hervey, *Corolla*, p. 27.
[42] Abbo, *Passio*, VIII; Hervey, *Corolla*, p. 27.
[43] Abbo, *Passio*, IX; Hervey, *Corolla*, p. 33.
[44] Abbo, *Passio*, IX; Hervey, *Corolla*, p. 33.
[45] Abbo, *Passio*, X; Hervey, *Corolla*, p. 33.
[46] Abbo, *Passio*, X; Hervey, *Corolla*, p. 35.

acutest tortures, steadfastly persisted in the avowal of his faith which in the end he crowned by undergoing the doom of death.[47]

Gransden suggests that even the passages purporting to describe Edmund's temporal rule may be inflected by the prominence they afford to the sacrality of kingship. For example, she notes the emphasis placed by Abbo upon Edmund's consecration and detects echoes of the consecration of a priest and the rites for the ordination of a bishop, such as Edmund's acceptance of the 'stole of baptism' or the 'ring of faith'.[48]

A regional saint

In addition to his universal Christology, Abbo imbues Edmund with associations which resonate in a more specific, local context. Following the description of the *adventus* of the Germanic tribes and the division of the island into three kingdoms, Abbo devotes a chapter to the geographic characteristics of one of these kingdoms: East Anglia. In a narrative gesture borrowed from Bede's *Ecclesiastical History*, East Anglia is described as a richly fertile region with 'delightfully pleasant gardens and woods', with 'abundant grazing for flocks and herds' and 'noted for its excellent sport'.[49] Thus Abbo refocuses his narrative from the general to the specific, deftly locating Edmund in the context of national history whilst asserting his regional identity. This is also an effective dramatic device, establishing the Edenic idyll soon to be shattered by the Viking scourge.

Yet Abbo's East Anglia is also wild and lonely, affording to 'not a few congregations of monks desirable havens of lonely life':[50]

> The above-mentioned eastern part attracts attention for the following and other reasons: that it is washed by waters on almost every side, girdled as it is on the south and east by the ocean, and on the north by an immense tract of marsh and fen, which starting, owing to the level character of the ground, from practically the midmost point of Britain, sloped for a distance of more than a hundred miles, intersected by rivers of great size, to the sea. But on the side where the sun sets, the province is in contact with the rest of the island, and on that account accessible; but as a bar to constant invasion by an enemy,

---

[47] Abbo, *Passio*, XI; Hervey, *Corolla*, p. 37.
[48] Gransden, 'Abbo Fleury's *Passio*', 48–50.
[49] Abbo, *Passio*, II; Hervey, *Corolla*, p. 15. Cf. Bede, *The Ecclesiastical History of the English People*, ed. Judith McClure and Roger Collins (Oxford: Oxford University Press, 1964; rpt. 1999), I.1, pp. 9–12.
[50] Abbo, *Passio*, II; Hervey, *Corolla*, p. 15.

a foss is sunk in the earth by a mound equivalent to a wall of considerable height.[51]

Marten suggests that far from describing an earthly paradise, Abbo sought to emphasise the vulnerability of the region, suggesting that to a tenth-century audience facing the continued prospect of Viking raids, 'a girdle of ocean and rivers was not a defence, but an invitation'.[52] The present threat posed by the Danes is reflected in Abbo's powerful invective in which he condemns them as cruel, barbarous cannibals, followers of the Antichrist.[53] Abbo imagines the conflict between the Danes and the East Anglians in geographical terms, suggesting that the depravity of the northmen should not be wondered at, 'seeing that they came hardened with the stiff frost of their own wickedness from that roof of the world where he had fixed his abode who, in his mad ambition, sought to make himself equal to the Most High'.[54] Abbo concludes bitterly that 'from the north comes all that is evil'.[55] Just as the Danes are products of their cold, forbidding homeland, so Edmund may be equated with his kingdom, depicted by Abbo as simultaneously rich and exposed, but also a holy kingdom which offers solace to those seeking the spiritual life. These characteristics are shared by Edmund, an admirable yet vulnerable king who privileges spiritual concerns above all others. Thus Abbo established an almost symbiotic relationship between king and kingdom.

This relationship is likewise expressed through Abbo's description of Edmund's subjects. Following the martyrdom, once the Danes had departed and relative peace was restored, Edmund's followers emerged from hiding to seek the king's severed head in order that he might be given a proper Christian burial.[56] Edmund is now both 'their king and martyr' and his subjects are 'united in great numbers', suggesting a collective and unanimous response.[57] The head guides them during their search by 'exclaiming in their native tongue, "Here! Here! Here!"' until the East Anglians find the lost remnant of their king, guarded by a wolf, who has been dissuaded from his natural proclivity to eat the head by virtue of Edmund's sanctity.[58] Edmund is portrayed as a true East Anglian who calls, literally and metaphorically, to his people, the only ones capable of discovering him. The sense of local identity is enhanced by Abbo's decision to record the head's Old

---

[51] Abbo, *Passio*, II; Hervey, *Corolla*, pp. 13–15.
[52] Marten, *Southfolk and the Northmen*.
[53] Abbo, *Passio*, V; Hervey, *Corolla*, p. 19.
[54] Abbo, *Passio*, V; Hervey, *Corolla*, p. 19.
[55] Abbo, *Passio*, V; Hervey, *Corolla*, p. 19.
[56] Abbo, *Passio*, XII; Hervey, *Corolla*, pp. 39–41.
[57] Abbo, *Passio*, XII; Hervey, *Corolla*, p. 39.
[58] Abbo, *Passio*, XIII; Hervey, *Corolla*, p. 41.

English 'her, her, her' in his Latin text, which he glosses for his non-native readers by explaining '*Quod interpretatum Latinus sermo exprimit, "Hic, hic, hic"*'.[59] Edmund is constructed as an Old English, and specifically East Anglian, saint.

This is reiterated in Abbo's depiction of the translation of the body, some years later, from its humble resting place beneath the 'chapel of rude construction' to a more fitting location in Beodericesworth.[60] The translation was made possible as 'the conflagration of war and the mighty storms of persecution were over', but Abbo claims that the people were ultimately motivated by 'the occurrence of marvellous works' through which Edmund 'made manifest by frequent miraculous signs the magnitude of his merits in the sight of God'.[61] Again Abbo is explicit that these events were witnessed by people 'of that province', and that the region was united in its devotion to Edmund, as 'high and low alike' recognised his sanctity.[62] It is also interesting to note that whilst Abbo dedicates the *Passio* to Dunstan and claims him as his authority, the commission originates from the community as a whole; Abbo is adamant that it is 'the brethren' who exhort him to write.[63] Whether genuine or another authorial conceit, Abbo implies that the creation of the textual cult had its origins amongst the people of East Anglia.

A virginal saint

Furthermore, Abbo also stresses Edmund's bodily incorruption, describing the condition of his remains upon the occasion of his first translation to Beodricesworth:

> Whereas it was supposed that the precious body of the martyr would have mouldered to dust in the long interval of time which had elapsed, it was found to be so sound and whole that it would not be out of place to speak of the head having been reunited with the body, for there was absolutely no apparent trace of wound or scar. And so the king and martyr Edmund was with reverence pronounced to be a saint, and was translated whole and entire, and wearing every semblance of life, to [Beodricsworth], where to this day without change of form he awaits the covenanted felicity of a blessed resurrection.[64]

---

[59] Abbo, *Passio*, XIII; Hervey, *Corolla*, p. 41.
[60] Abbo, *Passio*, XIV; Hervey, *Corolla*, pp. 43–5.
[61] Abbo, *Passio*, XIV; Hervey, *Corolla*, p. 45.
[62] Abbo, *Passio*, XIV; Hervey, *Corolla*, p. 45.
[63] He repeats this three times in the Dedicatory Epistle; Abbo, *Passio*, Epistle; Hervey, *Corolla*, pp. 7–9.
[64] Abbo *Passio*, XV; Hervey, *Corolla*, p. 45

Abbo explains that Edmund's wholeness was a physical manifestation of his inner purity, and a certain sign that he belonged to the noble ranks of those who had spurned the temptations of the flesh in favour of a life of chastity:

> And how great was the holiness in this life of the holy martyr may be conjectured from the fact that his body even in death displays something of the glory of the resurrection without a trace of decay; for it must be borne in mind that they who are endued with this kind of distinction are extolled by the Catholic Fathers in the rolls of their religion as having attained the peculiar privilege of virginity, for they teach that such as have preserved their chastity till death, and have endured the stress of persecution even to the goal of martyrdom, by a just recompense are endued even here on earth, when death is past, with incorruption of the flesh.[65]

Abbo thus deploys a conventional argument in relation to Edmund, suggesting that despite his life of privilege he was invulnerable to temptation:

> Let us then consider what manner of man he was, who, stationed on the royal throne in the midst of worldly wealth and luxury, strove to conquer self by the incorruptibility of his flesh.[66]

Edmund's ability to resist carnal enticement is echoed by the stoicism he displays in response to the extreme physical suffering of his martyrdom; his inner spiritual strength is equalled by his physical resistance, a sure sign to his hagiographers and devotees that he was indeed a saint.

The interest of tenth- and eleventh-century monastic reformers in promoting clerical celibacy has been discussed at length elsewhere.[67] Given the monastic audience for whom the *Passio* was most likely composed it is credible to read Edmund's virginity as an attempt to present him as a role model for clerical readers. Blanton elucidates a similar strategy at work in the tenth-century manifestation of Æthelthryth's cult, whereby Æthelwold, bishop of Winchester (963–84), another leading reformer, depicted the Saxon abbess as the embodiment of chastity, the evidence of which was likewise found in her incorrupted remains.[68] However, Blanton notes that the presence of a female body in the midst

---

[65] Abbo *Passio*, XIX; Hervey, *Corolla*, pp. 55–7.
[66] Abbo *Passio*, XIX; Hervey, *Corolla*, p. 57.
[67] For example, Jacqueline Murray, 'Masculinizing Religious Life: Sexual Prowess, the Battle for Chastity and Monastic Identity', in *Holiness and Masculinity*, ed. by Katherine J. Lewis and P. Cullum (Cardiff: University of Wales Press, 2004), pp. 24–42.
[68] Blanton, *Signs of Devotion*, pp. 73–7, 96–105.

of a now-male monastic community may have been deemed problematic. She suggests that Æthelwold sought to counter this by rendering Æthelthryth's body as a textual rather than physical entity and promoting liturgical commemoration in favour of pilgrimage to her shrine at Ely.[69] As a Bedan saint well established by the time of the reforms, it was both necessary and desirable to recast Æthelthryth to suit current circumstances. In this respect, therefore, Edmund may have presented a number of attractive advantages to the reformers: as a male saint he was an ideal role model for male religious, and as a hitherto undocumented saint his legend could be shaped from the outset to suit the prevailing ecclesiastical mood.

Manuscript tradition

The dissemination of the first version of Edmund's legend provides an insight into the geographical scope of his cult in its formative stages. It also evinces the extent to which the *Passio* remained popular in subsequent decades and centuries. The earliest known version of the *Passio* is preserved in London, Lambeth Palace Library, MS 361, a mid-eleventh-century booklet containing a copy of the *Passio* marked for eight lessons, along with three hymns and a Mass in honour of St Edmund.[70] Another early booklet pertaining to St Edmund (now Copenhagen, Royal Library, MS GI. Kgl. 1558) was produced c.1100 and belonged to the abbey of St Denis, Paris.[71] The text is marked for twelve lessons and is followed by an office of St Edmund with musical notation. Gransden suggests that Baldwin, abbot of Bury between 1065–97, was responsible for disseminating the legend of St Edmund to St Denis; he had been a monk at St Denis prior to his appointment at Bury and it is likely that he had previously taken a similar booklet of the *Passio*, along with a relic of St Edmund, to Lucca (Italy) whilst on his way to Rome in 1071 to secure for Bury the privilege of exemption from Pope Alexander II.[72] Booklets containing a life of a saint and accompanying devotional material, usually prayers and a Mass, were relatively common.[73] They were easily portable and therefore an effective method for disseminating a cult, a function evinced by the distribution of booklets featuring St Edmund as far apart as St Denis and Lucca at a relatively

---

[69] Blanton, *Signs of Devotion*, pp. 122–9.

[70] See Gransden, 'Abbo Fleury's *Passio*', pp. 63–4 and Winterbottom, *Three Lives*, pp. 8–9.

[71] GI. Kgl. 1558 is described by Ellen Jørgensen, *Catalogus Codicum Latinorum Medii Aevi Bibliothecae Regiae Hafnauensis*, 2 vols (Copenhagen, 1923–6) II. 190. See also Gransden, 'Abbo Fleury's *Passio*', pp. 64–5 and Winterbottom, *Three Lives*, pp. 8–9.

[72] See Gransden, 'Abbo Fleury's *Passio*', 72–4.

[73] See Pamela R. Robinson, '"The Booklet". A Self-contained Unit in Composite Manuscripts', *Codicologica* III (1980), 46–69.

early date and by the subsequent interest shown in the saint by these institutions.[74] At St Denis, for example, a set of eight magnificent column capitals in the crypt, installed by 1144 (the documented date of the consecration of Abbot Suger's crypt and choir) depict scenes from Edmund's legend. The fact that the cycle has no known parallels or prototypes in French or English sculpture of the period, along with the dependence of the imagery upon metaphors and other narrative devices found in the *Passio*, has led Pamela Z. Blum to assert its direct reliance upon Abbo's text, firmly establishing its influence at St Denis for at least a century.[75] Thus from the outset of the tradition, Edmund was conceived as a saint of national and international importance, but whose saintly identity was ultimately predicated upon his regional origins.

---

[74] For a full list of manuscripts of the *Passio* see Winterbottom, *Three Lives*, pp. 8–10.

[75] Pamela Z. Blum, 'The Saint Edmund Cycle in the Crypt at Saint-Denis', *BAA: Bury*, pp. 57–68. For a full list of manuscripts of the *Passio* see Winterbottom, *Three Lives*, pp. 8–10.

CHAPTER 2

De Miraculis Sancti Eadmundi
Herman, Osbert and Samson

Once introduced to the devotional consciousness through the creation of a successful *passio*, a nascent cult was more often than not confirmed and consolidated by the compilation of miracles attributed to the holy individual. Miracles serve as evidentiary proofs of saintly status and a means of defining an individual in relation to established, particularly biblical and early Church, patterns of sanctity, and are thus integral to the establishment of a hagiographic tradition.[1] Thus, when Abbo claims that the discoverers of Edmund's head 'recognised in the most blessed Edmund a worthy parallel to that enviable man who, unharmed among the gaping jaws of hungry lions, laughed to scorn the threats of those who had plotted his destruction', he credits both Edmund's subjects and the readers of the *Passio* with the ability to recognise the allusion to Daniel's miraculous escape from the lions' den.[2] The fact that this is a 'worthy' comparison to an 'enviable' man demonstrates the function of miraculous cross-referencing in the creation of a saintly typology. Abbo recounts a number of posthumous miracles attributed to Edmund. Indeed, it was Edmund's miracle-working reputation which led to the recognition of his sanctity and his translation to Beodricesworth.

In addition to miracles found in saints' lives, narratives were collected together and recorded in single volumes. These were similarly intended to demonstrate the saint's power, whether for the purposes of promoting pilgrimage to their resting place or of applying for official canonisation, but could also perform a subtly different function in the creation and dissemination of a cult. Often recorded by the keepers of a shrine, books of miracles were frequently kept on or near the shrine itself. They formed a tangible link between the textual and physical cult and a means of demonstrating to pilgrims the present power of a saint. Thus the compilation of Edmund's miracles marked a significant stage in the development of his cult.

---

[1] Benedicta Ward discusses the function of miracles in saints' *Lives* in *Miracles and the Medieval Mind. Theory, Record and Event, 1000–1215* (Aldershot: Wildwood House, 1987) pp. 166–91. Fresh perspectives on medieval miracles are offered in *Contextualizing Miracles*, ed. Matthew Mesley and Louise Wilson (2014).

[2] Abbo, *Passio*, XIII; Hervey, *Corolla*, p. 43.

Herman archdiaconi, liber de miraculis sancti Eadmundi

The first collection of Edmund's miracles is *De Miraculis Sancti Eadmundi*, which records Edmund's deeds up to 1096.[3] The immediate context was Abbot Baldwin's rebuilding of the abbey church, into which St Edmund was translated in April 1095.[4] New hagiographies were produced to accompany a number of the numerous post-conquest translations.[5] These texts fulfilled a liturgical function by providing readings for the feasts of the saints, and also a way of advertising saintly efficacy in the hope of attracting pilgrims. In *De Miraculis* the accounts are arranged chronologically and are discussed against the backdrop of English national events. The author refers to the *Passio* on a number of occasions and his work is intended as a continuation of the hagiographic tradition inaugurated by Abbo, providing details of Edmund's posthumous miracles which have occurred in the intervening years since the initiation of the textual cult.[6]

Provenance, authorship and patronage

The identity of the author of *De Miraculis* continues to incite scholarly debate. The author reveals his name in a miracle concerning Herman, a monk of Binham Priory in Norfolk, who he claims reported the miracle 'to me, his namesake'.[7] The complier of the late fourteenth-century collection of Edmund's miracles collated in Oxford, Bodleian Library, MS Bodley 240 cites Herman as one of his sources and variously labels him 'archdeacon', 'Herfast's archdeacon' and

---

[3] *Herman archdiaconi liber de miraculis sancti Eadmundi,* in *Memorials of St Edmund's Abbey,* ed. Arnold, *Memorials,* I, pp. 26–92. A partial edition was also produced by Felix Liebermann, ed. *Ungedruckte Anglo-Normannische Geschichtsquellen* (Strassburg: K.J. Trübner, 1879), 231–81.

[4] Herman, *De Miraculis,* ed. Arnold, *Memorials,* I, pp. 87–91. See Eric Fernie, 'The Romanesque Church of Bury St Edmunds Abbey', *BAA: Bury,* pp. 1–15.

[5] For example, St Augustine at Canterbury. See Richard Sharpe, 'The Setting of St Augustine's Translation, 1091', in *Canterbury and the Norman Conquest: Churches, Saints and Scholars 1066–1199,* ed, Richard Eales and Richard Sharpe (London: Hambledon, 1995), pp. 1–13.

[6] References to Abbo include '*in passione sancti eadmundi*', Arnold, *Memorials,* I, pp. 28; '*in exarato ... passionis*', Arnold, *Memorials,* I, p. 84.

[7] Herman, *De Miraculis,* ed. Arnold, *Memorials,* I, p. 78. For further discussion of the debate surrounding the identity of the author see Tom Licence, 'History and Hagiography in the Late Eleventh Century: The Life and Work of Herman the Archdeacon, Monk of Bury St Edmunds', *English Historical Review* cxxiv (June 2009), 516–44; 517–18.

'Bishop Herfast's archdeacon'.[8] When Thomas Arnold published his edition of the text in 1890 he attributed it to Herman the archdeacon.[9] A hundred years later this was challenged by Antonia Gransden, who suggested that Herman had never existed and may have been accidentally created by Henry de Kirkstead, the fourteenth-century prior and archivist of Bury commonly assumed to be the annotator of Bodley 240, as a result of a misreading.[10] It is, however, now generally accepted that Herman was once an archdeacon in the service of the bishop of East Anglia who later became a monk at Bury St Edmunds, for whom he composed *De Miraculis*.[11]

Herman seeks authority for his text by claiming that for 'some particulars' he is 'indebted to the confiding testimony of living persons'.[12] He also claims to have borrowed passages which he 'found scribbled in an impenetrable and adamantine hand by some unknown writer', although it has not been possible to convincingly identify this source.[13] It is clear, however, that Herman draws extensively on biblical authorities, a number of the classics including Horace and Virgil, and the Late Latin poets, a range of texts that were standard in a well-stocked late eleventh-century library such as that at Bury.[14] He also refers extensively to the *Chronica Anglica*, a version of the *Anglo-Saxon Chronicle* which ran at least until 1066.[15]

Like Abbo, Herman alludes to the contemporary vulnerability of knowledge concerning Edmund, claiming that Abbot Baldwin and the convent entreated him to record the miracles 'in the hope that the events which had passed through sorry neglect into oblivion, may, while I live, be restored to memory through a good use of the talent with which God has provided me'.[16] Tom Licence notes that the theme of commemoration pervades the collection, to the extent that in

---

[8] Carl Horstmann, ed., *Nova Legenda Anglie*, 2 vols. (Oxford: Clarendon Press, 1901), II, pp. 592, 614, 620, 627, 631 etc.

[9] Herman, *De Miraculis*, ed. Arnold, *Memorials*, I, xxviii–xxiv.

[10] Gransden, 'The Composition and Authorship of the *De Miraculis Sancti Eadmundi* Attributed to "Herman the Archdeacon"', *Journal of Medieval Latin*, v (1995), 1–52; 29.

[11] The debates surrounding the identity of the author are summarised by Licence, 'History and Hagiography', 517–22.

[12] Herman, *De Miraculis*, ed. Arnold, *Memorials*, I, p. 27.

[13] Herman, *De Miraculis*, ed. Arnold, *Memorials*, I, p. 27. Various scholars have speculated as to the identity of this source but it has so far not been convincingly identified. For two contrasting perspectives on this debate see Gransden, 'Composition and Authorship', 27–8 and Licence, 'History and Hagiography', 531–6.

[14] For detailed discussion of Herman's textual borrowings see Licence, 'History and Hagiography', 536–8. For the composition of late-eleventh-century monastic libraries see Michael Lapidge, *The Anglo-Saxon Library* (Oxford: Oxford University Press, 2006).

[15] For further discussion of Herman's use of historical sources see Licence, 'History and Hagiography', 538–9.

[16] Herman, *De Miraculis*, ed. Arnold, *Memorials*, I, p. 27.

the prologue alone the noun *memoria* appears eleven times.¹⁷ To Herman, it was not simply a matter of propriety that Bury should record the deeds of its saintly patron. He makes it clear that there is far more at stake:

> Before now, [St Edmund] had not to any great extent been proclaimed to the world by miraculous displays in the place where by divine guidance he had chosen for himself a most worthy sepulchre, partly, I am led to think, because of the carelessness of writers who in their great folly attached little importance to the deeds, such as there were, of the exalted martyr, partly because of the unworthiness of the people at that time and because the hour had not yet come for him to show compassion on them.¹⁸

In failing to appropriately commemorate their patron, the community at Bury were failing to fulfil what Caxton refers to in his translation of *The Golden Legend* as 'the debt of interchanging neighbourhood', whereby a saint interceded with God on behalf of an individual or community in return for their devotion and remembrance.¹⁹ Herman therefore conceived of *De Miraculis* not only as continuing the hagiographic tradition begun by Abbo but also as repaying an imagined 'debt' and ensuring Edmund's continued intercession on behalf of his devotees, particularly his monastic guardians at Bury.

Healing and hurting: the nature of the miraculous intercessions

The nature of the miraculous intercessions attributed to St Edmund provides an insight into how the monastic community sought to construct the identity of their patron in the period in which Herman was writing. Statistical analysis of the miracles reveals that just over a third involve healing, with Edmund demonstrating his ability to cure a wide range of maladies and afflictions. The range of cures he enacts is typical of those performed by saints in this period.²⁰ He is democratic

---

17 Licence, 'History and Hagiography', 540. See Arnold, *Memorials*, I, pp. 26–7.
18 Herman, *De Miraculis*, ed. Arnold, *Memorials*, I, p. 27.
19 The original text on which Caxton based his translation is the *Legenda Aurea* by Jacobus de Voragine, a compilation of saints' lives composed c.1260, and one of the most widely read texts of the European Middle Ages. Caxton's version is from 1483. *The Golden Legend or Lives of the Saints as Englished by William Caxton*, 7 vols, ed. F.S. Ellis (London: Temple Classics, 1900), VI, p. 97.
20 See Ronald Finucane, *Miracles and Pilgrims. Popular Beliefs in Medieval England* (London, Melbourne and Toronto: J.M. Dent and Sons Ltd., 1977) esp. pp. 59–82 and Tables of types of miracles pp. 144–5.

in his provision of healing, interceding on behalf of old and young, rich and poor alike, extending his posthumous protection across the whole of his kingdom with the same charitable and paternal concern which Abbo claims characterised his earthly reign.[21] In his ground-breaking survey of medieval miracle culture, Ronald Finucane analysed over three thousand miracles performed by numerous saints and determined that nine out of ten involved healing.[22] This figure attests to the centrality of healing to the medieval cult of saints. Even if we exercise a degree of scepticism regarding Finucane's statistics, this nevertheless suggests that Edmund was less concerned with healing than many of his saintly counterparts and raises the question of the nature of the remaining miracles. Herman describes a variety of wonders, including a number of rescues performed by the saint (accounting for 16 per cent of the total), the marvel of Edmund's incorrupt remains (3 per cent), his power over nature as evinced in the wolf's guarding of his head (3 per cent) and a number of miracles which are unspecified, such as the 'many wonders' which occurred at the site of Edmund's first burial (6 per cent). The nature of the remaining 33 per cent is revealed by the frequent interpolations into the generally humorous and lively tone of *De Miraculis* of narratives of vindictive and violent retribution meted out by Edmund. Licence maintains that this was a deliberate authorial strategy:

> Evidently Herman thought it a trick to please his audience should the saint sometimes give his enemies a poke in the eye. Vengeance miracles are common in hagiography, but their treatment here as outlets for comedy coupled with the author's disquieting enthusiasm for sharp instruments and for targeting the eyes – 'the most fragile members of the human body' as he admits – is vicious to an extreme.[23]

This punitive element of Edmund's saintly character is best understood in the social and political context in which Herman was writing. It is notable that the largest single category of recipients in *De Miraculis* are aristocratic men, predominantly Normans, most of whom attempt to encroach upon the lands or Liberty of the abbey in some way and are punished dreadfully for their misdeeds. This contrasts with the more balanced picture offered by Abbo, in which Edmund's intercessions are more equally distributed according to status and gender. This indicates that a change had occurred in the way in which Edmund was interpreted and deployed. In the context of post-conquest tenurial upheaval Edmund

---

[21] Abbo, *Passio*, IV; Hervey, *Corolla*, p. 17.
[22] Finucane, *Miracles and Pilgrims*, p. 59.
[23] Licence, 'History and Hagiography', 526.

is depicted as a powerful and jealous defender of his lands and people. This is not a trait unique to Edmund. Blanton, for example, describes Æthelthryth similarly deterring Norman intruders in the *Liber Eliensis*, composed at Ely in the early twelfth century:

> In the Ely narrative, the monastic community utilizes the image of Æthelthryth's royal and abbatial position to define itself as a sovereign body. In repeatedly underscoring the elements of royalty, chastity, inviolability, and immutability, the chronicle's description of the enshrined body establishes a recurring symbol of power through which the monks assert their sovereignty over the Isle of Ely and their autonomy in the monastery's governance. Using this imagery, the monks challenge anyone who might take advantage of them.[24]

Herman's characterisation of Edmund was thus part of a broader strategy developing in the wake of the Norman Conquest by which monastic houses sought to defend themselves against the prospect of wholesale social and ecclesiastical change. Like Æthelthryth's, Edmund's royalty is emphasised as a means of portraying the Liberty of Bury St Edmunds as a kingdom over which Edmund still ruled. As well as reassuring the monastic community of the ability of their patron to defend them, *De Miraculis* simultaneously functions as a stark warning to any who are tempted to transgress, indicating the imagined, or at least desired, ability of the cult of saints to infiltrate the political ether.

It is unlikely to be coincidence that Herman was writing at the time that the dispute between Norwich and Bury concerning the location of the episcopal see was at its height. The conflict raged from the early 1070s until 1081 between Baldwin, abbot of Bury St Edmunds (1065–97) and Herfast, bishop of East Anglia (1070–84). Herfast wanted to relocate the see to Bury, but the abbot and monks vigorously resisted, objecting to the encroachment on their authority which they feared this would entail. Baldwin initially frustrated the bishop's plans by travelling to Rome in 1071, where he secured papal exemption from episcopal interference.[25] The dispute was eventually settled decisively in Bury's favour by William I in 1081, but not before Herfast had incurred the wrath of St Edmund. Herman recounts with gleeful relish that whilst Herfast was out riding he cursed Edmund and his abbey for thwarting his scheme, upon which he rode into a branch, 'the saint's means, I dare say, of revenge, plunging him into spasms of unexpected

---

[24] Blanton, *Signs of Devotion*, pp. 132–3. See pp. 131–41 and 166–71 for broader discussion.
[25] V.H. Galbraith, 'The East Anglian See and the Abbey of Bury St Edmunds', *English Historical Review* xl (1925), 222–8; 228.

agony as both eyes are changed into a well of cascading blood'.[26] Herman claims that he persuaded the bishop to resolve his dispute with Abbot Baldwin, physician to the Conqueror, in order that he might appeal for the abbot's help in curing this terrible injury.[27] Herman was present at Bury whilst the bishop was treated by Baldwin and Herfast duly recovered.[28] Herman's invocation of Edmund as a fierce and faithful protector of his people should therefore be read in this broader political context, and Gransden concludes that Herman wrote *De Miraculis* as 'a piece of propaganda' in which his object 'was to increase St Edmund's and the abbey's prestige in order to fortify it against its enemies, especially the bishop of East Anglia'.[29]

Edmund likewise consistently demonstrates his determination to deter secular incursions.[30] Herman continually emphasises Edmund's kingship, describing him as 'protector' and 'glory and shield' of the East Angles and claims that Edmund remained 'the patron of the East Anglian kingdom ... winning from the Almighty the reward that no king after him, save God himself, should rule in those regions'.[31] In an incident analogous to the dispute with the bishop of East Anglia, Herman records that a Norman courtier of William I's household attempted to annex a Bury manor adjacent to his own land. He was struck blind, and was only partially healed upon offering a very large candle to the shrine.[32] Another narrative features Leofstan, a local tenth-century sheriff whom Herman describes as a savage man too eager to inflict the severest of punishments allowed by the law.[33] Whilst Leofstan was holding court in the Hundred of Thringoe (Norfolk), an 'accused woman' fled to Bury and claimed sanctuary at Edmund's shrine. Leofstan denounced both the woman's right to sanctuary and Edmund's jurisdiction in the matter, offering, according to Herman, a direct challenge to the saint to prove 'who was more powerful, either the martyr in setting her free, or the judge in condemning her'.[34] Perhaps inevitably, things went ill for Leofstan: as the sheriff's servants dragged the woman from the church the monks fell to their knees and prayed for vengeance. This was duly delivered: the plaintiff was freed and Leofstan writhed in agony, possessed by a demon for the rest of his painful life.[35]

---

[26] Herman, *De Miraculis*, ed. Arnold, *Memorials*, I, p. 62.
[27] Herman, *De Miraculis*, ed. Arnold, *Memorials*, I, p. 63.
[28] Herman, *De Miraculis*, ed. Arnold, *Memorials*, I, p. 64.
[29] Gransden, 'Origins', p. 89.
[30] For discussion of further territorial miracles see Yarrow, 'The Cult of St Edmund at Bury', in his *Saints and their Communities*, pp. 43–7.
[31] Herman, *De Miraculis*, ed. Arnold, *Memorials*, I, pp. 46, 51, 28.
[32] Herman, *De Miraculis*, ed. Arnold, *Memorials*, I, pp. 58–9.
[33] Herman, *De Miraculis*, ed. Arnold, *Memorials*, I, p. 31.
[34] Herman, *De Miraculis*, ed. Arnold, *Memorials*, I, p. 31.
[35] Herman, *De Miraculis*, ed. Arnold, *Memorials*, I. 32.

The death of Sweyn Forkbeard

The most compelling example by far of Edmund's defence of his kingdom is Herman's description of the events surrounding the death of King Sweyn Forkbeard.[36] The son of King Harold of Denmark, Sweyn was an ambitious and experienced warrior. He drove his father out of Denmark shortly before 988 and campaigned extensively in England in the first decade of the eleventh century. In 1013 Sweyn led a full-scale invasion of England. Upon Sweyn's landing at Gainsborough, Herman records that King Ethelred II (the 'unready') abandoned England and fled to Normandy with his wife, leaving the country at Sweyn's mercy, as recalled in the Peterborough manuscript of the *Anglo-Saxon Chronicle*:

> King Swein came with his fleet to Sandwich, and very quickly turned round East Anglia into the mouth of the Humber, and so upwards along the Trent until he came to Gainsborough. And then Earl Uhtred and all Northumbria immediately submitted to him, and all the people in Lindsey, and afterwards the people of the Five Boroughs, and quickly after, all the raiding-army to the north of Watling Street; and he was granted hostages from every shire. Then after he recognised that all the people had submitted to him, he ordered that his raiding-army should be provisioned and horsed; then he turned southward with his whole army, and entrusted his ships and the hostages to Cnut, his son. And after he came over Watling Street, they wrought the greatest evil that any raiding-army could do, then turned to Oxford, and the inhabitants of the town immediately submitted and gave hostages – and from there to Winchester, and they did the same; then from there they turned eastwards to London ... Then when he had travelled thus far, he turned northward towards his ships, and the whole nation had him as full king.[37]

The breathless stream of conjunctions in this extract attests to the terrifying inevitability of Sweyn's progress across the country. His reign, however, was as short as his conquest was swift: the Peterborough Chronicler rather spitefully records that in February 1014 'the happy event' of Sweyn's death occurred.[38]

Whereas the received historical narrative is of virtually unopposed conquest, the hagiographic sources which feature the invasion and death of Sweyn offer an alternative perspective. According to Herman, in the face of yet another Scandinavian invasion, all the people of East Anglia (*tota plebs*) fled to Edmund's

---

[36] Herman, *De Miraculis*, ed. Arnold, *Memorials*, I, p. 32.
[37] *The Anglo-Saxon Chronicle*, ed. Whitelock, p. 92.
[38] *The Anglo-Saxon Chronicle*, ed. Whitelock, p. 93.

shrine to exhort the saint to intervene on their behalf.[39] Edmund appeared to Sweyn in a vision and issued him with a strict warning:

> 'Cease, cease to exact tribute which they have never under any king given. It was not taken or paid in the time of any of them after me, and if you do not remove this oppression from them, you shall soon see that you displease God and me on behalf of the people.'[40]

Egelwyn, a monk of Bury, also visited Sweyn and cautioned him to heed St Edmund's warning, but Sweyn refused. According to Herman, Edmund appeared to Sweyn whilst the king was in bed, spearing him with a lance: 'stationed at God's right hand, he single-handedly strikes down his enemy, slays his adversary, halts the tribute'.[41] A later continuator of *De Miraculis* is even more emphatic in his version of events:

> And calling the king by his own name [Edmund] said, 'Do you want to have a tribute, O King, from the land of St Edmund? Rise up, behold, take it.' He who was rising up sat down again in his bed, but soon began to cry out dreadfully when he saw the weapons. As soon as the soldier made the attack, he left him, pierced through with a lance, dying. Stirred up by his shout, we ran to it and found him defiled with his own blood, his soul belched forth.[42]

The invasion of Sweyn would have had particular resonance when it was first recorded by Herman in the 1090s. East Anglia continued to suffer Viking raids in the late eleventh century, including one incident in the early 1080s when pirates burnt a settlement near Bury, killing a number of the inhabitants.[43] Ultimately, though, Sweyn embodies all invaders, just as the *tota plebs* who flock to Edmund's tomb represent the entire region's dependence on its saintly overlord. M.R. James proclaims that 'the story of Sweyn's death redounded more than anything else to St Edmund's glory'.[44] This is due partly to the type of miracle this represents: Edmund is, after all, killing a king. It is also particularly fitting that the king whom

---

[39] Herman, *De Miraculis*, ed. Arnold, *Memorials*, I, p. 33.
[40] Herman, *De Miraculis*, ed. Arnold, *Memorials*, I, p. 35.
[41] Herman, *De Miraculis*, ed. Arnold, *Memorials*, I, p. 36.
[42] Herman, *De Miraculis*, ed. Arnold, *Memorials*, I, p. 118.
[43] The raid is recorded by Goscelin of Saint-Bertin, 'The Liber *confortatorius* of Goscelin of Saint-Bertin', ed. C.H. Talbot, *Analecta monastica, troisième série: Studia Anselmiana*, xxxvii (Rome, 1955), 1–117; 67–8. See Licence, 'History and Hagiography', 522, for further discussion.
[44] James, *On the Abbey Church*, p. 137.

he kills is Danish, the successor of the Vikings who caused Edmund's own demise. In a sense, then, this episode represents Edmund's saintly 'coming of age', and completes the sequence of events begun by his own martyrdom. He has regained supremacy and wrested control of his kingdom back from those who sought once again to conquer it.

Edmund's alleged dispatching of Sweyn also has broader political implications, as Herman explains that it halted the Danish king's trajectory towards the conquest of England:

> And so the saint was held in more renown for such an unexpected event. It was believed that by his [Sweyn's] removal not only were the poor of his town free, but throughout the whole of England his greedy invasion had ceased to rage, to the relief of the poor whom God had not neglected.[45]

Herman claims that this places Edmund on a par with the early Church martyr Mercurius, 'who wrought vengeance on Julian the Apostate for his wicked blasphemies against the mother of God and St Basil'.[46] In addition to protecting his regional interests, this demonstrates Edmund's ability to intervene on behalf of the whole country, making him a saint of national importance, a defender of the faith, and integrating him into the ongoing narrative of the universal Christian Church. Like Abbo, Herman frequently alludes to Edmund's virginity, but in the context of his more aggressive sanctity it acquires additional meaning: just as Edmund's body was miraculously healed of its wounds, so too his kingdom remains inviolable.

Ridyard notes that whilst the monks of Bury sought to promote the benefits of Edmund's protection, they were cautious not to over-emphasise his regional identity, because 'a regional protector was always useful, but a separatist saint might be self-defeating'.[47] She suggests that Herman attempts to balance this aspect of Edmund's sanctity by making him a kinsman of Edward the Confessor and detailing the fifteen kings who ruled between Edmund and the Norman Conquest, with no mention of the changes of ruling dynasty which had taken place.[48] This represents a subtle but significant re-formulation of Edmund's identity, and Ridyard concludes that 'Edmund's role as patron of the East Angles was paralleled, in short, by his role as patron of the English'.[49] The miracles attributed to Edmund by

---

[45] Herman, *De Miraculis*, ed. Arnold, *Memorials*, I, p. 37.
[46] Herman, *De Miraculis*, ed. Arnold, *Memorials*, I, p. 36. For further discussion of this event see Licence, 'History and Hagiography', 539–40.
[47] Ridyard, *Royal Saints*, p. 230.
[48] Ridyard, *Royal Saints*, p. 230. Cf. Arnold, *Memorials*, I. 28 ff.
[49] Ridyard, *Royal Saints*, p. 230.

Herman therefore mark a distinct stage in the development of his saintly identity. Although he still rigorously defends the Christian faith he also proactively seeks to defend his people and his kingdom in a way previously unimagined.

Manuscript context

This is reiterated by the manuscript context of *De Miraculis*. The longest version survives in London, British Library, MS Cotton Tiberius B. ii, an extremely high-quality manuscript written at Bury by a single scribe around 1100.[50] This manuscript also includes a copy of Abbo's *Passio*, suggesting that it was intended to be a comprehensive account of Edmund's life and legend, his 'official biography'.[51] Two abridged versions are also extant: Paris, Bibliothèque Nationale, MS Latin 2621 (fols 84r–92v) and Oxford, Bodleian Library, MS Digby 39 (fols 24r–39v), a compilation of mainly hagiographical texts. The Oxford manuscript dates from the early twelfth century and originates from Bury. The Paris manuscript is of a similar date and the work of an English-based, Norman-trained scribe, but cannot definitively be identified as a Bury product.[52] Licence suggests that Cotton Tiberius B. ii and the Latin 2621 manuscript shared a lost exemplar, and that Digby 39 is a copy of Latin 2621.[53] Gransden's discovery that both abridged versions of *De Miraculis* were once unbound and self-contained suggests they may have been designed as promotional tracts for the cult of St Edmund, intended for ease of distribution and copying.[54] The majority of the material absent from the abridgements relates to historical details particular to Bury, presumably less desirable or necessary in an alternative context.[55] The miracle narratives were clearly highly adaptable texts and not only represent a significant stage in the development of the cult at Bury but also provided an additional means by which the monastic community could promote St Edmund farther afield.

Continuation

The fullest version of *De Miraculis* in Cotton Tiberius B. ii concludes with a miraculous sea rescue which occurred in May 1096. This miracle is incomplete,

---

[50] For a full description see Rodney Thomson, 'Two Versions of a Saint's Life from St Edmund's Abbey: Changing Currents in Twelfth-Century Monastic Style', *Revue Bénédictine* 84 (1974), 383–408; 385.
[51] Licence, 'History and Hagiography', 533.
[52] Gransden, 'Composition and Authorship', 6.
[53] Licence, 'History and Hagiography', 534.
[54] Gransden, 'Composition and Authorship', 6.
[55] Licence, 'History and Hagiography', 534.

terminating abruptly before the story is fully developed. It is possible that Herman's death prevented the completion of his text. However, within a few years, probably between 1098 and 1118, *De Miraculis* was rewritten by another Bury monk.[56] Only one copy of this text survives, preserved in a richly illuminated manuscript made at Bury in the early twelfth century (New York, Pierpont Morgan Library, MS M. 736, fols 23r–76r).[57] The author makes some relatively minor stylistic and exegetical alterations to Herman's text, and also completes the last, unfinished miracle of *De Miraculis* before appending an expanded version of Herman's cure of a disabled woman on the Feast of John the Baptist and adding four new miracles of his own.[58] Scholarly opinion concerning the provenance of the additional miracles is divided. Gransden believes that they were in fact written by Herman, an opinion repeated by Yarrow.[59] However, the reference in one of the additional miracles to the death of a monk named Herman seems to refer to the author of *De Miraculis*. The reviser-continuator refers to the monk as preaching from Edmund's shrine and showing the saint's bloodied undergarments to the assembled crowds. These same relics are afforded prominence in *De Miraculis* and Herman describes his handling of them in a similar manner.[60] It therefore seems likely that the monk named Herman is the same as the author of *De Miraculis*, and since his death is described in one of the additional miracles this renders it highly unlikely that they were written by the same author.

Revisions: Osbert de Clare and Abbot Samson

A fully revised version of *De Miraculis* survives in one composite manuscript, London, British Library, Cotton Titus Aviii.[61] This is a quarto-sized book containing a cartulary with miscellaneous thirteenth- and fourteenth-century material from Westminster Abbey (fols 2–64), an abbreviated copy of Abbo's *Passio* (fols 65–78v) and a revised version of *De Miraculis* (fols 78v–145v). Gransden notes that *De Miraculis* is on separate gatherings from the rest of the volume and bears the abbey's class mark, S. 153, probably entered by the fourteenth-century Bury

---

[56] Thomson, 'Two Versions', 386 n. 3.
[57] For further discussion of this manuscript and its relationship to Herman's text see Licence, 'History and Hagiography', 526–31.
[58] New York, Pierpont Morgan Library, MS. M. 736, fols 66v–67r and Arnold, *Memorials*, I, 91.
[59] Gransden, 'Composition and Authorship', esp. 40–1, Yarrow, *Saints and Their Communities*, p. 49.
[60] *De Miraculis*, ed. Arnold, *Memorials*, I, pp. 53, 54.
[61] Printed as Samson, *De Miraculis* in Arnold, *Memorials*, I, pp. 107–208. For a full description of the manuscript see Thomson, 'Two Versions', 387–9.

bibliographer Henry de Kirkstead, who also wrote notes in the margins, suggesting that it originated at the abbey.[62] This copy of *De Miraculis* dates from c.1200 and was perhaps made for the abbey's library or for Abbot Samson himself. It is divided into two books: Book I contains a prologue and sixteen chapters; Book II opens with a prologue followed by a passage extolling the merits of St Edmund, then twenty-one chapters. That the version of *De Miraculis* in Titus Aviii is a compilation is apparent both from the subtle discrepancies in the depiction of Edmund and from the prose style of the two books; Gransden observes that 'Book I is all in simple, straightforward prose' whereas the majority of Book II is written in a more 'inflated' style.[63]

It is generally accepted that Abbot Samson (1182–1211) was responsible for compiling the Titus Aviii *De Miraculis*: simplifying the prose of the Pierpont Morgan 736 version which constitutes the majority of the first Book, composing a number of original passages and inserting Book II.[64] The author of the section concerning Edmund in Bodley 240 also ascribes seventeen of the miracles he cites to '*Samson*', '*Samson abbas*', '*Samson abbas sancti Edmundi*', '*Ex libros miraculis eius Samson*' and '*Ex libro primo miraculorum Samsonis abbatis*'.[65] The simplified prose style accords with Jocelin of Brakelond's description of the abbot in which he claims that when preaching Samson concentrated 'more on plain speaking than flowery language'.[66] Thus Samson's principal role was as compiler and refiner.

The majority of the 'inflated prose' of Book II of Titus Aviii is generally attributed to a single author. In marginal annotations Henry de Kirkstead attributes chapters 8–20 to Osbert de Clare, 'prior of Westminster'.[67] Osbert was a well-known hagiographer and a particularly keen supporter of the cult of St Edward the Confessor and author of the *Vita beatii Eadwardi*.[68] He was prior of Westminster Abbey at the time of the election of Herbert as abbot in 1121, an episode which provoked controversy over the issue of free election. Osbert seems to have been at the heart of the dispute, as a result of which he spent much of his subsequent life in exile. A friend of Abbot Anselm of Bury, he probably stayed at the abbey

---

[62] Gransden, *A History of the* Abbey, pp. 122–3.
[63] Gransden, *A History of the Abbey*, p. 126.
[64] See, for example, Samson, *De Miraculis*, ed. Arnold, *Memorials*, I, pp. xxxix–xli; Thomson, 'Two Versions', 389–408; Gransden, *A History of the Abbey*, pp. 126–8.
[65] Horstmann, *Nova Legenda*, II, pp. 589, 593, 596–9, 599–600, 608–9, 609–10, 611–13, 618, 627–30, 631–2, 632, 632–3, 633–4, 637–8.
[66] Jocelin, *Chronicle*, p. 37.
[67] Samson, *De Miraculis*, ed. Arnold, *Memorials*, I, p. 152–3. Chapters 1–5 are derived from the version of *De Miraculis* in Pierpont Morgan 736, and the rest appear to date from the time of the compilation of Titus Aviii. See Thomson, 'Two Versions', 388–9.
[68] Osbert de Clare, *Vita beati ac gloriosi regis Anglorum Eadwardi*, ed. Marc Bloch, *Analecta Bollandiana* 41 (1923), 5–131.

during his period of exile, c.1125–c.1134. It is likely that Osbert composed the material relating to Edmund either during or shortly after his sojourn in East Anglia, perhaps in thanks for the convent's hospitality.[69]

Osbert's contribution to the corpus of St Edmund's miracles subtly refines the way in which the saint had hitherto been presented. The letter which appears at the beginning of Book II in Titus Aviii offers a commentary on Exodus 28:17, in which the virtues of St Edmund are likened to those symbolised by the gems found on the breastplate of Aaron:

> These precious stones signify the diverse virtues in which, we believe, the virgin king and martyr was resplendent in body, and he left himself as one to imitate in the glory of his holy works.[70]

Yarrow suggests that the placing of Osbert's letter at the beginning of the second book, before the account of Edmund's translation into Abbot Baldwin's new abbey church, is a deliberate attempt to reorganise the material of Herman's *De Miraculis* in order to depict the translation as the beginning of a more positive phase of cult activity, beginning with the reaffirmation of Edmund's virtues in Osbert's letter.[71] Although Herman's punitive miracles are retold in Book I, these represent a far lower proportion of Edmund's total miraculous activity in Titus Aviii (22 per cent, as compared with 33 per cent in the original). The lengthy description of the dispute surrounding the location of the episcopal see is also notably absent. In the Titus Aviii version, healings and cures are the predominant means by which Edmund interceded on behalf of his devotees, accounting for nearly half of the total (48 per cent). The other categories remain roughly stable, and it is therefore in the number of healings and punitive miracles where the greatest shifts occur. The recipients of the miracles also betray the authors' contrasting preoccupations. Although the proportions of recipients from each 'class' or 'estate' remain roughly equal, it is notable that the miracles of the Titus Aviii version refer explicitly to 10 per cent of those who benefitted from miraculous activity as being of the lower orders, predominantly servants but also the unspecified 'poor'.[72] Furthermore, there is greater emphasis upon the local origins of a number of the recipients, such as a young woman from Clare (Suffolk) who is healed after losing the use of her limbs, a Dunwich man cured of dropsy, or the restoration of lost money to the

---

[69] *The Letters of Osbert de Clare, Prior of Westminster*, ed. Edward W. Williamson (London: Oxford University Press, 1929), nos. 5–8, 23.
[70] Samson, *De Miraculis*, ed. Arnold, *Memorials*, I, p. 154.
[71] Yarrow, *Saints and their Communities*, p. 57.
[72] Samson, *De Miraculis*, ed. Arnold, *Memorials*, I, pp. 109–10, 140–1, 164–5, 180–1, 186.

servant of a knight of Copeland.[73] Yarrow suggests that these changes constitute a deliberate attempt by the compiler to remodel Edmund's saintly identity:

> His refinements pared down the text, replacing its earlier moral and rhetorical digressions with simpler, more direct renderings of the stories. The result was a version that sharpened the focus of its monastic audience on the social significance of the miracles rather than their historical correctness.[74]

It is notable that the majority of new or revised material is in the second book of the Titus Aviii *De Miraculis* attributed to Osbert de Clare. It is likely that Osbert's status as an outsider at Bury, albeit one who remained with the community for a considerable period of time, afforded him an alternative perspective on Edmund's sanctity, particularly in relation to the saint's vigorous defence of his lands and rights, in which as a non-Bury monk he may have had less of a vested interest.

It is equally possible that the more pastorally concerned Edmund who emerges from the Titus Aviii compilation represents Abbot Samson's vision of the saint, subtly redefined as part of his efforts to inaugurate a new period of cultic activity and promotion. Overall the Titus Aviii miracles reflect the regional emphasis and less-violent nature of Osbert's compilation. The revision of Edmund's miracles accords with Samson's attempts to revive the cult by restoring the abbey church and shrine, much as Abbot Baldwin had inaugurated a new phase of cult promotion by rebuilding the abbey church and the commissioning of the original *De Miraculis* by Archdeacon Herman. Perhaps Samson sought to promote an image of Edmund which he thought would be particularly appealing to pilgrims who might travel to Bury seeking the intercession of its patron. These earliest *miraculi* thus chart a telling shift, from an emphasis on the integrity of the abbey's lands and privileges in response to conquest and incursion, to a more confident, less defensive, phase when Edmund's intercessions became more demotic and magnanimous.

---

[73] Samson, *De Miraculis*, ed. Arnold, *Memorials*, I, pp. 178–9, 189–91.
[74] Yarrow, *Saints and their Communities*, p. 53.

CHAPTER 3

Vita et miracula

THE close relationship between Edmund's life and miracles is evinced by a number of manuscripts containing both texts.

London, British Library, MS Cotton Tiberius B. II

London, British Library, MS Cotton Tiberius B. ii is a high-status manuscript written by a single scribe at Bury St Edmunds in the last decade of the eleventh century.[1] The version of the *Passio* in this manuscript is closely related to one of the abbreviated copies, now Gl. Kgl. 1558. The manuscript also includes a copy of Herman's *De Miraculis*, suggesting that it was intended to be a comprehensive yet accessible account of Edmund's life and legend: his official biography.[2] This is reiterated by an inscription in a fourteenth- or fifteenth-century hand which claims that the manuscript was kept in the close vicinity of the shrine: (*'liber feretrariorum sancti eadmundi'*).[3] The dating of the manuscript places it within the abbacy of Baldwin (1065–97), the rebuilder of the abbey church and staunch promoter of his abbey's saintly patron. In addition to attesting to the close relationship between the life and the miracle narratives, this manuscript therefore also indicates the multi-disciplinary nature of the cult of St Edmund and reiterates the necessity of considering it from a variety of perspectives.

New York, Pierpont Morgan Library, MS M. 736

This is equally true of New York, Pierpont Morgan Library, MS M.736. This manuscript marks a striking development in the elaboration of Edmund's cult at Bury. Dated c.1125–35, the manuscript may be securely attributed to Bury by the documents on the opening folios: fols 2–4 contain copies of two letters, the first from Henry I to Abbot Anselm of Bury (1121–48) forbidding him to continue a

---

[1] Cotton Tiberius B. ii was used by Winterbottom as the base text for his translation of Abbo's *Passio* and is discussed in his introduction: Winterbotton, *Three Lives*, pp. 8–9. See also Gransden, 'Abbo Fleury's *Passio*', 65–6.
[2] For further discussion of Cotton Tiberius B. ii as the definitive version of the legend at the time of its production see Licence, 'History and Hagiography', 533.
[3] Elizabeth Parker McLachlan, *The Scriptorium of Bury St Edmunds in the Twelfth Century* (New York and London: Garland Publishing Inc., 1986), p. 74.

planned journey, and the second from the prior of Bury begging Anselm to return from Normandy in order to appease the king's displeasure. Following these on fols 3–4 are lists of pittances instituted by Anselm along with the names of the manors from which the money was to be derived.[4] Furthermore, Elizabeth Parker McLachlan identifies the various hands as consistent with other manuscripts known to originate from Bury during this period.[5]

The manuscript, now in a nineteenth-century binding, comprises one hundred bound vellum leaves measuring 274 × 187 mm. It contains three main texts: an otherwise unknown recension of Herman's *De Miraculis*, rewritten with minor alterations and five new miracles[6] (fols 23–76v); Abbo's *Passio* (fols 77–86v); a set of Offices for the Vigil and Feast of St Edmund containing selections from the *Passio* and a radically revised version of Herman's *De Miraculis*, interspersed with hymns, antiphons and responses with music (fols 87–100v); additional lections for the Vigil of St Edmund's Feast are also included in the opening folios (fols 5–6), out of sequence presumably due to the later rebinding.[7] The Morgan MS contains similar texts to Cotton Tiberius B. ii, which, along with the presence of the liturgical material, suggests that it was likewise intended for use as an altar book in the abbey church, perhaps replacing the earlier manuscript as the occurrence of new miracles necessitated an updated record of Edmund's posthumous activities.

The miniatures sequence

Of particular note is the set of thirty-two luxurious, full-page miniatures which preface the texts (fols 7–22v) and the thirty-nine initials which accompany the *Passio* and *Miracula*. The miniatures are painted on double vellum pages in rich body colour with black outlines and touches of gold. Stylistically, the miniatures owe much to the style of the Alexis Master of the St Albans Psalter, although the

---

[4] A detailed description of the manuscript may be found in Parker McLachlan, *The Scriptorium of Bury St Edmunds*, pp. 74–119.

[5] Parker McLachlan, *The Scriptorium of Bury St Edmunds*, pp. 75–7.

[6] Arnold suggests that Osbert de Clare was responsible for the version of *De Miraculis* in Pierpont Morgan M.736. See Arnold, *Memorials*, I, xxxvi. This view was later echoed by Williamson in his introduction to *The Letters of Osbert de Clare*, p. 26. However, this has been convincingly refuted by Thomson, who suggests that the author was an unknown Bury monk: 'Two Versions', 391–3. For a description of the nature of the Pierpont Morgan M.736 revisions see also Thomson, 'Two Versions', 385–7.

[7] Licence convincingly attributes this revised miracle collection, uniquely preserved in the Pierpont Morgan manuscript, to Goscelin of Saint-Bertin. See *Herman the Archdeacon and Goscelin of Saint-Bertin: The Miracles of St Edmund*, ed. and trans. Tom Licence, Oxford Medieval Texts (Oxford: Clarendon Press, 2014), cix–cxxvii.

nature of their relationship has been much debated.[8] It is now generally thought that the miniatures were produced at Bury by a visiting artist who first worked at St Albans.[9]

The miniatures form an independent narrative cycle of Edmund's life, passion and posthumous miracles, beginning with the invasion of Britain by his Germanic ancestors (fols 7–8), followed by Edmund's life and martyrdom (fols 8v–18), four miraculous episodes (one from the *Passio* (fols 18v–19v) and three from the *miracula* (fols 20–22)) and concluding with Edmund's apotheosis (fol. 22v). The sequence conflates the narrative of Abbo's *Passio* with incidents from the *miracula*, resulting in a new version of the legend. Hahn notes that whilst the artist 'expanded upon and even diverged from' the text of the *Passio*, he adheres more faithfully to the *miracula*, where his illustrative scheme 'involves primarily selection and emphasis'.[10] Thus the way in which the Morgan artist interprets the two texts and his possible reasons for doing so offer further insight into how the hagiographic tradition developed across both media.

Region and nation

The overwhelming sense of regional identity with which Abbo imbued his *Passio* is largely absent from the Morgan miniatures. Instead, the artist locates the events of Edmund's life and death in a national context. This is apparent from the opening of the sequence, where three miniatures depict the coming of the Angles, Saxons and Jutes to England (fol. 7), their defeat in battle of the native Britons (fol. 7v) and their division of the kingdom between the three tribes (fol. 8). These events are briefly described by Abbo, but in the miniatures are afforded disproportionate significance.[11]

As we have seen, the threat of invasion is ever present in Edmund's legend and the conquest of England by Germanic tribes therefore performs the same

---

[8] Otto Pächt attributed the miniatures to the Alexis Master himself. Otto Pächt, Charles R. Dodwell and Francis Wormald, *The St Albans Psalter (The Albani Psalter)* (London: The Warburg Institute, 1960), p. 167. The certainty of this attribution was questioned by later scholars, such as Katherine R. Bateman, who instead attributed the Pierpont Morgan M.736 miniatures to the 'workshop' of the Alexis Master. Katherine R. Bateman, 'Pembroke 120 and Morgan 736: A Re-examination of the St Albans–Bury St Edmunds Manuscript Dilemma', *Gesta* xvii, no.1 (1978), 19–26.

[9] This view is expounded, for example, by Parker McLachlan in her assessment of the stylistic similarities between the two manuscripts. Parker McLachlan, *The Scriptorium of Bury St Edmunds*, pp. 79–87.

[10] Cynthia Hahn, '*Peregrinatio et Natio*: The Illustrated Life of Edmund, King and Martyr', *Gesta* xxx, no. 2 (1991), 119–39; 119.

[11] Abbo, *Passio*, I; Hervey, *Corolla*, pp. 11–13.

semiotic function as the encroachments by the Vikings. Indeed, the Morgan artist utilises the same visual vocabulary to depict the Germanic and Viking invasions: both arrive in ships with animal-head prows, the armies wear similar helmets and both carry shields and spears (fols 7 and 9v). Upon landing in England, both engage in battle with the native inhabitants (fols 7v and 10). However, the nature of the skirmishes is revealing: the chivalric combat of the Germanic tribes who wear chainmail and fight on horseback in ordered ranks (fol. 7v) contrasts sharply with the frenzied, disordered rapine of the bare-legged and unshod Vikings, who hack at their victims as the bodies pile up around them (fol. 10). The location in which the battles occur is similarly significant: the Germanic tribes meet the similarly mounted and well-equipped Britons on the field of battle, whereas the Vikings attack a populated settlement, which burns as the battle rages. The fallen in the first battle are clearly soldiers and all bear arms, whereas the majority of the Viking's victims are unarmed and some appear naked, reflecting Abbo's account of the event:

> Boys, and men old and young, whom he [Hinguar] encountered in the streets of the city were killed; he paid no attention to the chastity of wife or maid. Husband and wife lay dead or dying together on their thresholds; the babe snatched from its mother's breast was, in order to multiply the cries of grief, slaughtered before her eyes. An impious soldiery scoured the town in fury, thirsty for every crime by which pleasure could be given to the tyrant who from sheer love of cruelty had given orders for the massacre of the innocent.[12]

The words and images are mutually reinforcing. Hahn notes that the Morgan artist recognised Abbo's textual cue and modelled the Danish attack on a representation of the Massacre of the Innocents. She concludes that since the Innocents were counted amongst the saints, the effect of this comparison in both word and image is to enhance the prestige of the East Anglian kingdom and the king who ruled it.[13]

The Morgan artist's disproportionate focus upon the coming of the Germanic tribes may also be explained in terms of Edmund's kingship. Abbo tells us very little of Edmund's origins and ancestry except that he was 'descended from a line of kings' and 'sprung from the stock of the Old Saxons'.[14] This has been

---

[12] Abbo, *Passio*, V; Hervey, *Corolla*, p. 21.
[13] Cf. the tenth-century *Codex Egberti* made for Egbert, Archbishop of Trier. Stadtbibliothek Trier, Ms. 24, fol. 15v. See Hahn, 'Peregrinatio et Natio', 129–30 and 138 n. 89. Cf. also the Massacre of the Innocents in the St Albans Psalter, p. 30.
[14] Abbo, *Passio*, II; Hervey, *Corolla*, p. 15.

variously interpreted by subsequent authors, both medieval and modern, but the Morgan artist clearly equates the Old Saxons with one of the Germanic tribes who arrive in the opening miniatures.[15] His efforts to present them as chivalrous are therefore understandable as he seeks to furnish Edmund with worthy ancestors. It is also likely that the visual equivalences between the two invasions are intended to equate the Vikings' invasion of East Anglia with the Germanic tribes' invasion of England as a whole. Eliding the distinction between the regional and the national locates Edmund within a broader historical context and suggests that his martyrdom, and presumably also his cult, are universally significant.

Christology

The parallels which Abbo draws between Christ's passion and Edmund's martyrdom are further emphasised in the Morgan miniatures. Parker McLachlan maintains that the resemblance is heightened by the dependence of the Morgan martyrdom upon the style and iconography of the passion of Christ in the St Albans Psalter.[16] In particular she draws attention to the similarity between the Flagellation of Christ and the scourging of Edmund (fol. 13v), where the gestures and facial expressions of the aggressors are remarkably similar. The change in Edmund's sartorial appearance in the aftermath of the martyrdom may also be similarly explained. Abbo has Edmund seized by the Danes, 'pinioned and tightly bound in chains', 'mocked in many ways', then 'savagely beaten' before being tied to a tree and 'for a long while tortured with terrible lashes'.[17] In contrast to Christ, who is stripped by his tormentors (Matthew 27: 28–29), Abbo does not ascribe this indignity to Edmund. The Morgan artist, however, in seeking to multiply the connections between Edmund's martyrdom and Christ's passion, includes a scene in which the Danes drag Edmund's outer robe from his head and shoulders, the violence of their actions apparent from their contorted facial expressions and Edmund's posture, bent double with the force of their exertions (fol. 13). In order not to deviate too far from Abbo's narrative, the artist depicts Edmund clad in a robe for the next three scenes (fols 13v–14v). However, by the time Edmund's followers discover his headless corpse on fol. 15, Edmund is naked, clad only in a blue knee-length loincloth. The visibility of his shoulders when his head is reunited with his body (fol. 17) and when he is borne away on a bier for burial (fol. 17v) indicates that he is similarly naked. Parker McLachlan

---

[15] For the likelihood that Edmund was a Continental Saxon see Whitelock, 'Fact and Fiction', 218.

[16] Parker McLachlan, *The Scriptorium of Bury St Edmunds*, p. 79; pp. 86–7.

[17] Abbo, *Passio*, X; Hervey, *Corolla*, pp. 33–5.

believes that the disparity in Edmund's appearance may be accounted for by the artist's recourse to different models for these scenes. She suggests that Edmund's body when discovered by his followers is 'articulated almost line for line after the torso of the dead Christ of the St Albans Psalter Deposition'.[18] The knee-length blue loincloths are also strikingly similar, with the delicate, translucent fabric of Christ's garment perhaps testament to the superior talent of the Alexis Master, as compared with the more solid drape of Edmund's robe. It is notable that this is the only place in the St Edmund sequence where the saint is thus attired. In this instance, then, it is apparent that the artist has interpreted visually the words of Abbo's *Passio* in order to amplify the Christological nature of Edmund's martyrdom to the extent that he borrows the iconography of the Deposition of Christ from the St Albans Psalter. Although the extent to which the viewers of the Morgan miniatures would appreciate this direct connection is debatable, the change in visual tone would draw attention to the disparity. At the very least, the viewer might be expected to recognise the posture and garments of Christ from similar depictions on painted or carved roods, perhaps present in the abbey church itself. The effect of this comparison would once again serve to emphasise the elevated nature of Edmund's sanctity.

Kingship

Two miniatures illustrate Edmund's temporal reign as king of East Anglia. Facing each other across the open book, fol. 8v depicts Edmund's coronation and fol. 9 shows the king distributing alms. The coronation scene is lively and dynamic, the cleric to Edmund's left still grasps the crown which he is placing on Edmund's head, whilst the figure to the right proffers the royal sceptre. The image captures the very moment of Edmund's investiture. Seated frontally and gazing directly out at the viewer, Edmund is larger than his companions, literally the centre of attention. The iconography of the scene is derived from late-antique and medieval frontal ruler portraits and thus serves to emphasise his royalty.[19] Other figures, too, cluster around the king. Untonsured and bearing arms, they are clearly secular, most likely the subjects of Edmund's new kingdom. They gaze towards the king in avid approval and reiterate Abbo's claim that Edmund was chosen king 'by the unanimous choice of his fellow provincials'.[20] This is similarly reflected in the

---

[18] Cf. St Albans Psalter, p. 47. Parker McLachlan, *The Scriptorium of Bury St Edmunds*, p. 86.

[19] Barbara Abou-El-Haj, 'Bury St Edmunds Abbey between 1070 and 1124: A History of Property, Privilege, and Monastic Art Production', *Art History* 6 (1983), 1–29; 14 and 27 n. 101.

[20] Abbo, *Passio*, III; Hervey, *Corolla*, p. 15.

Plate I Danes attacking a town, MS M.736, fol. 10, © The Pierpoint Morgan Library (New York, Pierpoint Morgan MS M.736)

Plate II Edmund's apotheosis, MS M.736, fol. 22v, © The Pierpoint Morgan Library (New York, Pierpoint Morgan MS M.736)

Plate III Death of King Sweyn, MS Harley 2278, fol. 103v, © The British Library Board (London, British Library, MS Harley 2278)

Plate IV Edmund enthroned, MS Harley 2278, fol. 34, © The British Library Board (London, British Library, MS Harley 2278)

united efforts of Edmund's followers to search for his head after the martyrdom and the unanimous popular acclaim by which he is acknowledged to be a saint.[21]

Apart from the coronation scene, the miniature on fol. 9 is the only image in the sequence which depicts Edmund's reign prior to the events of the martyrdom. It therefore serves as the primary indicator of the version of Edmund's temporal kingship being offered in the miniatures. Abbo is generous in his praise of Edmund's rule, but gives few specific details of his royal deeds, preferring to celebrate his moral worthiness and personal graces.[22] The Morgan artist is similarly terse. Abbo does, however, claim that Edmund was 'liberal in bounty to those in want, and like a benign father to the orphan and the widow', just as Edmund in the miniature is generously distributing alms.[23] This reflects the contemporary importance placed upon acts of charity and the protection of one's subjects as a fundamental royal function.[24]

Post-mortem intervention

The Morgan miniatures reflect the tendency of Herman's *De Miraculis* to emphasise Edmund's punitive post-mortem activities. Eight miniatures (a quarter of the total) depict Edmund's vengeance against those who transgress against his shrine or relics. One of the miracles is drawn from Abbo's *Passio*, whilst the remaining two are from Herman's *De Miraculis*. It is interesting that this collection of miracles more than any other evinces a bias towards male recipients. In the context of their excessively punitive nature, this suggests a distinction between the types of miracles experienced based on gender.

The first sequence (fols 18v–19v) illustrates Abbo's narrative of the eight thieves who attempted to break into the abbey church and plunder the shrine.[25] The first miniature (fol. 18v) shows the thieves, armed with tools according to Abbo's description, attempting to gain entrance:

> One laid a ladder to the door-posts, in order to climb through a window; another was engaged with a file, or a smith's hammer, on the bars and bolts; others with shovels and mattocks endeavoured to undermine the walls.[26]

---

[21] Abbo, *Passio*, XII, XIV; Hervey, *Corolla*, pp. 39–41, 45.
[22] Abbo, *Passio*, III–IV; Hervey, *Corolla*, pp. 15–17.
[23] Abbo, *Passio*, IV; Hervey, *Corolla*, p. 17.
[24] See William A. Chaney, *The Cult of Kingship in Anglo-Saxon England: The Transition from Paganism to Christianity* (Manchester: Manchester University Press, 1970), pp. 256–7.
[25] Abbo, XVI; Hervey, *Corolla*, pp. 47–53.
[26] Abbo, XVI; Hervey, *Corolla*, p. 49.

The façade of the church is visible, with a central gabled nave flanked by two double-storied towers. The architecture identifies the church as that begun by Abbot Baldwin (1065–97), which was almost complete at the time the miniatures were painted.[27] However, the larger central gable and the door appear to be made from multi-coloured wooden planks held together by vertical rows of nails, which the thieves attempt to extract with their tools. It is possible that the artist sought to conflate the new abbey church with its wooden predecessor, which Abbo describes as a 'church of immense size, with storeys admirably constructed of wood', in which Edmund's remains were first placed upon their translation to Bury.[28] The effect of this may be to de-historicise the episode and indicate its universal and continuing relevance. Barbara Abou-El-Haj cites analogous biblical episodes, such as Psalm 73:2–3 and 5–7, where the destruction of the Temple is a metaphor for sacrilege, noting in particular the emphasis in the psalm on the depredation of the wooden parts of the building.[29] She similarly notes the equivalences between the illustration of the psalm in the Utrecht Psalter and the Morgan manuscript's depiction of the thieves' encroachment.[30] She concludes that the Morgan artist deliberately invoked this prototype in order to emphasise the sacrilegious nature of the attempted theft.[31] This in turn justifies the hanging of the thieves and explains the excessive violence and cruelty with which their execution is depicted in the next miniature (fol. 19v). Trespassing upon Edmund's shrine is thus shown to be a heinous crime, transgressing both physical and spiritual bounds, and which will be punished accordingly. Notably, however, Edmund is not the perpetrator of this punishment, as although Abbo tells us that he ensures the thieves are transfixed to prevent their escape, it is Theodred, bishop of London (909–26), who passes judgement upon them (fol. 19r).[32] Abou-El-Haj suggests that this scene is indicative of the twelfth-century reality of clerical control over civil crimes within the Bury *banleuca*, as although the bishop was prohibited from exercising justice on Bury lands, it served the purpose of the abbey to emphasise that clerical, rather than secular, justice prevailed.[33]

The theme of Edmund's aggressive retaliation is further emphasised by the inclusion of two incidents from Herman's *De Miraculis*. Two miniatures illustrate

---

[27] See *Gesta Sacristarum*, ed. Arnold, *Memorials*, II, pp. 289–96.
[28] Abbo, XIV; Hervey, *Corolla*, p. 45.
[29] 'Axes deep in the wood, hacking at the panels, they battered them down with mallet and hatchet'. Psalm 73, 6.
[30] Utrecht, Bibliotheek Der Rijksuniversiteit, MS 32, fol. 42r.
[31] Abou-El-Haj, 'Property, Privilege, and Monastic Art Production', 8–9.
[32] Abbo, XVI; Hervey, *Corolla*, pp. 49–51.
[33] Abou-El-Haj, 'Property, Privilege, and Monastic Art Production', 10.

the removal of Edmund's remains to London by his monastic guardian, Egelwyn, in order to escape the large invading Danish force led by Thurkill the Tall, who landed at Ipswich in the spring of 1010. *En route* to London Egelwyn sought shelter with an Essex priest, Eadbricht, shown on fol. 20 standing in the doorway of his house. The priest refused and was punished for his lack of hospitality: vivid scarlet flames leap from the windows towards the roof. Edmund's vulnerability is emphasised by the respective settings of the characters. Eadbricht peers around the door, holding the handle as if preparing to shut out his visitors. In contrast, Egelwyn leads the cart bearing Edmund's relics, pulled by a despondent-looking horse, across rough terrain into the ambiguous unknown space of the margin. The peril is emphasised by the organisation of the miniatures, as the viewer must turn the page to discover the fate of the entourage. In the next miniature Egelwyn and his precious cargo are still outdoors, this time negotiating a bridge which was too narrow for the cart to cross (fol. 20v).[34] The water below is turbulent and enormous fish wait expectantly. Egelwyn looks back anxiously at the wheel suspended mid-air over the edge of the bridge. As in the preceding miniature, the hand of God appears from the upper margin and casts light upon the relics, reassuring the viewer that the cart will cross the bridge in safety.

The first miniature in the sequence of three which illustrate the death of Sweyn also features Egelwyn, who warns the king to rescind his demand for tribute (fol. 21). Sweyn is seated within an elaborate architectural frame which separates him from Egelwyn, who is once again outdoors, standing on undulating ground. The force of Sweyn's refusal and the extent of Egelwyn's (literal) marginalisation is reiterated by two of Sweyn's henchmen, who burst through the architectural frame, one with a raised weapon, and thrust the monk into the right-hand margin. The balance of power is restored by Edmund in the following miniature (fol. 21v), in which he appears before Sweyn and kills him.[35] Both kings are crowned and located under semi-circular arches, but whereas Edmund stands tall, leaping towards his opponent, Sweyn is recumbent, eyes closed, mouth open and hands thrust outwards in agony as Edmund's spear pierces his chest. In this instance the frames emphasise Edmund's power as he effortlessly penetrates the boundary with his lance. The final miniature in this sequence (fol. 22) depicts the revelation of Sweyn's demise to a dying man in Essex, who proclaims the miracle from his deathbed, ensuring that Edmund's delivery of his people is known and recorded.[36] The significance of the death of Sweyn is thus once again emphasised, not least by its placing in the overall sequence. It is the

---

[34] Herman, *De Miraculis*, ed. Arnold, *Memorials* I, p. 42.
[35] Herman, *De Miraculis*, ed. Arnold, *Memorials* I, p. 36.
[36] Herman, *De Miraculis*, ed. Arnold, *Memorials* I, p. 38.

last incident recounted before the viewer is confronted by an image of Edmund in glory (fol. 22v).

In an image which recalls the coronation miniature (fol. 8v) Edmund is enthroned and likewise depicted at the moment of coronation, except in the latter miniature angels reach down from heaven and place the crown upon his head whilst he is flanked by two others who invest him with a royal sceptre and a martyr's palm. A further pair of angels in the top corners of the miniature incline towards Edmund in gestures of veneration. This is Edmund's heavenly coronation, and the ultimate recognition of his sanctity. In the first coronation miniature the action takes place under a semi-circular arch, unifying Edmund and his subjects within a single frame. In the apotheosis miniature, however, the framing simultaneously emphasises Edmund's exalted status and his intercessory abilities. In contrast to the dynamic, asymmetrical coronation miniature, at the moment of his apotheosis Edmund faces fully to the front and appears tranquil and serene. The bold vertical and horizontal lines delineate the earthly realm below the frame, from which the monks reach up to kiss Edmund's feet, and the heavenly zone above, from whence the angels descend. Edmund occupies the central ground, his head projecting into the heavenly frame and his feet dipping below the lower border, enabling the monks to reach them. Edmund's intercessory ability is likewise emphasised in the liturgical material for his feast towards the end of the manuscript, which describes the saint as 'this day ... released from earth and ushered triumphantly into heaven' and asks him to 'intercede in heaven for us on earth who send up our sighs to you'. The image is trans-historical, eliding the facts of temporal chronology in favour of universal spiritual truths. Edmund's transition from earthly ruler to saintly overlord is thus complete.

The initials

The emphasis upon authority of various kinds is reflected in the thirty-nine initials which accompany the text. Painted by a different artist to the miniatures, the majority are purely ornamental, containing foliage, interlace and animal motifs. The remaining fifteen contain scenes or characters connected with the narratives they accompany, providing an interpretive gloss to the text. Often overlooked in favour of the more striking miniatures, the initials nevertheless provide an additional insight into the interpretive context in which Edmund appears. The first initial in the manuscript, a standing haloed figure of Edmund, is now on fol. 5 and accompanies additional lections for the Vigil of Edmund's Feast. This would most likely have originally appeared at the end of the manuscript with the other liturgical material and was misplaced when the manuscript was rebound.

The first initial according to the original binding is on fol. 23 and illustrates the opening of Osbert's *De Miraculis*. In contrast to the benevolent smiling figure on fol. 5, this image depicts a more familiar Edmund engaged in the despatching of King Sweyn. Clad in chainmail and with a helmet and shield in accordance with Osbert's version of the miracle, Edmund spears the seated Sweyn while two of the king's followers look on, their hands raised to their faces in attitudes of grief, powerless to intervene despite the axes and spears they carry. This image appears out of chronological sequence and accompanies Osbert's Prologue to *De Miraculis* rather than the incident itself. This implies that the artist selected this image as the most representative depiction of Edmund's posthumous sanctity and accords with the significance afforded to this incident elsewhere.

The remaining initials offer a more balanced view of Edmund's posthumous activity, depicting the miraculous light which radiated from his original burial place (fol. 26v), his preserved corpse as it appeared when examined by Abbot Leofstan (1044–65) (fol. 43v) and the cure of a fevered soldier (fol. 50). Thus the initials represent the defining features of Edmund's sanctity: the episode which announces his miracle-working capabilities, his bodily incorruption, his ability to heal and, perhaps most importantly, his willingness to punish.

A series of kings also accompany the miracles. Their presence led Parker McLachlan to suggest that there was no clearly discernible scheme to the initials, as the kings play little active part in the text but are mentioned towards the start of each chapter of *De Miraculis* purely as date markers.[37] On the contrary, I believe the royal initials reward further consideration as these references serve the historicising function of integrating events connected with Edmund into the context of national history. The choice of kings is also significant. Precise identification is difficult, but Parker McLachlan's suggestions, based upon references in the adjacent text, are convincing: Ethelred II, 'the unready' (fol. 28), Cnut (fol. 1v), William I, the Conqueror (fol. 49), Cnut (fol. 58), and St Edmund (fol. 74). Ethelred II's flight facilitated Sweyn's conquest and therefore resonates strongly throughout Edmund's saintly biography. Cnut was instrumental in the foundation of the Benedictine community at Bury and it is therefore unsurprising that he appears twice. As Sweyn's son, he also provides an additional reminder of arguably Edmund's greatest posthumous triumph. The presence of William the Conqueror is less readily explicable but may have served to reinforce the abbey's long history: as pre-conquest rulers, Ethelred and Cnut represent the antiquity of the abbey, whereas William marks a turning point in English history, in spite of which the viewer is reminded that the abbey has survived and flourished.

---

[37] Parker McLachlan, *The Scriptorium of Bury St Edmunds*, p. 103.

Edmund's association with the sequence of kings thus reminds the viewer of his royalty and his place in the narrative of national affairs.

The portion of the manuscript containing Abbo's *Passio* is accompanied by only one historiated initial, depicting Abbo presenting a copy of his poem to St Dunstan (fol. 77). The following lections, however, are also drawn from the *Passio*, and of these the beheading of Edmund (fol. 94v), the hidden eye-witness (fol. 96) and the wolf and head (fol. 97) are illustrated. These are the key moments of the martyrdom narrative, similarly depicted in the miniatures sequence, and are unsurprising choices for illumination. The initials therefore indicate the stability of certain features of Edmund's narrative which are emphasised in other codicological contexts, both textual and visual.

As a whole, therefore, Pierpont Morgan MS M. 736 offers a distinctive version of Edmund's sanctity. The emphasis upon punitive miracles is particularly striking, considering the likely origin of the manuscript as an altar book, kept close to the shrine of St Edmund and used to commemorate him liturgically. The function of the manuscript in the context of the physical cult and its place within the abbey church will be discussed in further detail below.

CHAPTER 4

The elaboration of the hagiographic tradition

Geoffrey of Wells, De Infantia Sancti Eadmundi

THE next major development in the St Edmund legend took place in the mid-twelfth century when Geoffrey of Wells was commissioned to write *De infantia sancti Eadmundi* by Sihtric, prior of Bury St Edmunds.[1] *De Infantia* may be dated with some precision: it is dedicated to '*dominus et pater Ording*', who was abbot of Bury between January 1148 and February 1156.[2] The author also refers to Sihtric as prior at Bury, who was appointed by 1153 at the latest but probably held the post from c.1150.[3]

Geoffrey of Wells was most likely a canon of the abbey's priory at Thetford. There were three religious houses in the close vicinity of Thetford at the time of the text's composition: a Cluniac priory founded by Roger Bigod (d.1107) in about 1104; a house of the Order of the Holy Sepulchre founded by William de Warenne III (d.1148) between 1139 and 1146; and a small community of canons that cared for the parish church of St George, which by Geoffrey's time was a priory of Bury St Edmunds Abbey. Paul Hayward suggests that the dedication of the priory church may account for Geoffrey's specification of the place of Offa's death as 'at the river which travellers call St George's arm'.[4] Blomefield claims that the priory was founded by Ufi, the first abbot of Bury (1020–44), to commemorate those who had died when Edmund's army fought the Danes at the Battle of Thetford.[5] St George

---

[1] *De Infantia* is edited by R.M. Thomson, 'Geoffrey of Wells, *De Infancia sancti Edmundi* (BHL 2393)', *Analecta Bollandia* 95 (1977), 34–42 and also appears in Arnold, *Memorials*, I, pp. 93–103. Unless stated otherwise, all quotations will be from Arnold's edition.
[2] David Knowles, Christopher N.L. Brooke and Vera C.M. London, *The Heads of Religious Houses, England and Wales, Volume 1, 940–1216*, 2nd edn (Cambridge: Cambridge University Press, 2001), p. 32.
[3] *Feudal Documents from the Abbey of Bury St Edmunds*, ed. David C. Douglas (London: Oxford University Press, 1932), nos 135 and 136.
[4] Geoffrey of Wells, *De Infantia*, ed. Arnold, *Memorials*, I, p. 96. Paul Anthony Hayward, 'Geoffrey of Wells' *Liber de infantia sancti Edmundi* and the "Anarchy" of King Stephen's Reign', in *Changing Images*, ed. Bale, pp. 63–86; p. 66 n. 20.
[5] Blomefield, *Norfolk*, I, p. 430.

would certainly be an appropriately martial dedication.[6] Regardless of his exact provenance, Geoffrey's close association with Bury is apparent from his claims that he participated in discussions about Edmund with the saint's guardians. He also maintains that Sihtric travelled to Thetford to commission him to write *De Infantia*.

It is clear that Geoffrey intended his text to be a prequel to Abbo's *Passio*. *De Infantia* concludes with the Danes preparing for invasion and, for details of the martyrdom, Geoffrey refers his readers to the version 'by an eloquent man, Abbo of Fleury'.[7] Geoffrey relates his intention to record 'the story of the saint's arrival, that is, from Saxony into England' and duly presents the first account of Edmund's parentage and upbringing and his ascension to the throne of East Anglia.[8] He tells us that Offa, Edmund's predecessor in East Anglia, visited his kinsman the King of Saxony *en route* to the Holy Land, to which he had undertaken to go on pilgrimage in the hope that his prayers for an heir might be granted.[9] His devotion was indeed rewarded, as in Prince Edmund he discovered a young man possessed of such 'studied civility and gallant bearing' that he named him as his heir.[10] Following Offa's death Edmund was duly brought from Saxony to Norfolk, where he landed at Hunstanton before travelling to Attleborough, where he was educated for a year before being crowned at Bures on Christmas Day.[11] Geoffrey also elaborates upon the identity and motivations of the invading Vikings, claiming that Edmund's fame as a virtuous and benevolent king had spread as far as Denmark, where King Lodbrok taunted his sons, claiming that they were far surpassed by Edmund in royal dignity. Angered, Hinguar, Ubba and Bern invaded East Anglia in order to prove their worth.[12]

Hayward describes *De Infantia* as 'a startling contribution to Edmund's dossier', claiming that this kind of prolegomenon appears to be unique in English hagiography and in that of royal saints in general.[13] The question of why Geoffrey was commissioned to write must therefore be addressed. His averred motivation is that as Edmund grew in reputation and popularity as a powerful miracle-working saint, interest in his life and background grew commensurately and stories began to circulate regarding his origins:

---

[6] For St George as military patron see Riches, *St George*, pp. 101–39 and Jonathan Good, *The Cult of St George in Medieval England* (Woodbridge: The Boydell Press, 2009), pp. 4, 32–4, 54–5, 62, 71–2 and 82.
[7] Geoffrey of Wells, *De Infantia*, ed. Arnold, *Memorials*, I, p. 103.
[8] Geoffrey of Wells, *De Infantia*, ed. Arnold, *Memorials*, I, p. 94.
[9] Geoffrey of Wells, *De Infantia*, ed. Arnold, *Memorials*, I, pp. 94–5.
[10] Geoffrey of Wells, *De Infantia*, ed. Arnold, *Memorials*, I, pp. 95–6.
[11] Geoffrey of Wells, *De Infantia*, ed. Arnold, *Memorials*, I, pp. 97–101.
[12] Geoffrey of Wells, *De Infantia*, ed. Arnold, *Memorials*, I, pp. 102–3.
[13] Hayward, 'De Infantia', p. 67.

It has often happened that in my presence the story of the parentage and infancy of the blessed Edmund, the most holy king, and unconquered martyr of our Lord Jesus, has been told by some of the holy confraternity of monks owing you [Abbot Ording] obedience.[14]

In contrast to Abbo or Herman, who present individual memories of the saint as precious repositories of rare knowledge, Geoffrey faces a surfeit of recollections concerning Edmund's youth and parentage. He recalls that the brethren of the abbey at Bury frequently recounted different versions of this aspect of the legend and that Geoffrey himself would often 'furnish a few particulars' that he had heard by 'word of mouth from others, or learned from reading aloud'.[15] The 'others' from whom Geoffrey acquired these details are unfortunately not specified but it is plausible that in addition to the already authorised and accepted monastic versions of the legend, the monks were hearing stories in circulation outside the monastery in popular culture. What is particularly striking is Geoffrey's assertion that, after hearing the details, the monks would 'contribute to the others such information as he himself had obtained, and thereupon one would afterwards confer with another'.[16] It appears that in response to the volume of legendary material the monks met to decide the definitive version and then employed Geoffrey to record their decisions. This impression is similarly reflected in the miracles described by Geoffrey, all of which are experienced by collective audiences comprising males and females, predominantly East Anglians. In contrast, therefore, to the pre-eminence of the individual and their ability to recall the legend in Abbo's *Passio*, Geoffrey presents his text as the product of collaborative authorship. In this instance the role of the hagiographer is not as preserver of individual recollections but as a refiner and definer of cultural memory. The impression created is of a legend by now entrenched in the popular and collective consciousness of which the monks occasionally, and seemingly accidentally, became aware. This raises the question of the extent to which conflicting versions of the legend existed within different communities, what they may have been and why this might have been the case, and of course the tantalising but unknowable possibility of what material was deemed unsuitable and edited out. Most commentators accept this account of the text's origins; Thomson, for example, maintains that *De Infantia* was 'a conscientious attempt to construct a sensible, historical narrative from scanty (unfortunately unreliable) materials, to cover an

---

[14] Geoffrey of Wells, *De Infantia*, ed. Arnold, *Memorials*, I, p. 93.
[15] Geoffrey of Wells, *De Infantia*, ed. Arnold, *Memorials*, I, p. 93.
[16] Geoffrey of Wells, *De Infantia*, ed. Arnold, *Memorials*, I, p. 93.

excessively obscure period'.[17] Hayward likewise suggests that much of the content of *De Infantia* may have been generated through an unconscious process as retelling and exegesis permitted the monks of the abbey at Bury to elaborate the story in small increments.[18]

The flourishing of hagiography in the post-conquest decades is well documented and it is possible that Geoffrey was writing in order to reinforce the cult against Norman scepticism or the growth of imported cults.[19] Hayward, however, suggests that *De Infantia* must also be read in relation to the broader historical context in which it was written.[20] He interprets Geoffrey's preoccupation with the circumstances in which Edmund succeeded to the throne of East Anglia as analogous to the turmoil following the death of Henry I, having left his daughter, the Empress Matilda, as his only legitimate heir.[21] Like Henry, Offa died without an heir, but unlike the protracted and disruptive civil war which followed Henry's death, Edmund's accession to the throne is comparatively peaceful. Offa acknowledges the potential troubles of a disputed succession and is careful to inform his followers of his chosen heir:

> 'You know how much evil disagreement spawns. In its prevalence, ambition is a friend, lording over others a familiar. For that reason it is fitting that this diabolical poison should be shunned when deliberating over the kingdom, and that the rule of peace and justice ought to prevail. Therefore, that all disagreement in electing a king might be obstructed among you utterly, I designate as my successor a forceful governor for you, namely, the son of my kinsman, the king of the Saxons.'[22]

Hayward notes that in contrast to the political wrangling and sporadic outbursts of violence of the twelfth-century succession dispute, Edmund achieves the throne through patience and submission to the will of God, concluding that

---

[17] Thomson. 'Geoffrey of Wells', p. 30. For criticism of the historical accuracy of the *De Infantia* see James Campbell, 'Some Twelfth-Century Views of the Anglo-Saxon Past', *Peritia* 3 (1984), 135–50.

[18] Hayward, '*De Infantia*', p. 86.

[19] See Ridyard, *Royal Saints*, pp. 226–33; Hugh M. Thomas, *The English and the Normans: Ethnic Hostility, Assimilation and Identity 1066–c.1200* (Oxford: Oxford University Press, 2003), p. 232.

[20] Hayward, '*De Infantia*', pp. 79–84.

[21] For detailed analysis of the causes and consequence of the various disputed royal successions in this period see George Garnett, *Conquered England: Kingship, Succession and Tenure, 1066–1166* (Oxford, New York: Oxford University Press, 2007).

[22] Geoffrey of Wells, *De Infantia*, ed. Arnold, *Memorials*, I, p. 97. Translation from Hayward, '*De Infantia*', p. 82.

'acceptance of received arrangements is the principal virtue' in *De Infantia*:[23] Edmund is chosen as Offa's heir due to his merits and personal integrity; he accepts Offa's proposition only when his father grants his assent; he spends a year studying the Psalter at Attleborough in order to prepare himself for ruling; he becomes king only when acclaimed by the people of his kingdom. Hayward suggests that this concern with approaches to royal succession constitutes an attempt 'to make a constitutional point'.[24] He admits that it is unlikely that Geoffrey would be directly attempting to influence contemporary events but rather is writing in response to them, and offering a version of resolution which must have been desired by many during the Anarchy. Bury had suffered directly as a result of the conflict; in August 1153, for example, a number of the abbey's estates had been ravaged by Eustace (c.1129–53), son of King Stephen, when the abbey refused his demands for money.[25] He died shortly afterwards and the monks were careful to attribute his death to Edmund, who caused him to be poisoned by the produce he stole from abbey lands.[26] Edmund is thus offered as a model of kingly conduct and once again an arbiter in both local and national affairs.

Anglo-Norman verse lives of St Edmund

The texts discussed thus far have each sought to contribute a fresh insight into the life and posthumous deeds of St Edmund. However, this was not a hagiographical prerequisite. Following Geoffrey of Wells' *De Infantia*, the legend was not significantly augmented until John Lydgate's contribution in the mid-fifteenth century. Versions of the legend were, however, produced in the interim. In addition to the versions of the legend written primarily for the benefit of monks and clerics, a further group of texts concerning St Edmund were in circulation during the twelfth and thirteenth centuries. In particular, a considerable number of vernacular Anglo-Norman verse lives of the saints were written during this period.[27] Legge suggests that they were intended primarily for the instruction and entertainment of secular audiences, but acknowledges the possibility that they were also enjoyed by the monastic communities themselves, perhaps being read or sung on feast days.[28] Whilst therefore yielding little information concerning

[23] Hayward, 'De Infantia', p. 82.
[24] Hayward, 'De Infantia', p. 82.
[25] *Chronica Buriensis*, ed. Arnold, *Memorials*, III, p. 6.
[26] Bodley 240, ed. Horstmann, *Nova Legenda Angliae*, II, 636.
[27] See Dominica Legge, *Anglo-Norman Literature and its Background* (Oxford: Clarendon Press, 1963) pp. 243–75.
[28] Legge, *Anglo-Norman Literature*, p. 275.

the development of the content of Edmund's legend, these texts are nevertheless useful indicators of the dissemination of the established legend in a variety of literary, linguistic and social contexts.

Denis Piramus, La Vie seint Edmund le Rei

Two Anglo-Norman verse lives of St Edmund are extant. The first, *La Vie seint Edmund le Rei*, was composed at the abbey of Bury St Edmunds c.1180–1200.[29] The author identifies himself as Denis Pyramus, but nothing is known of his life and career other than what he reveals in the poem. In the opening passage he claims that he spent his youth in frivolity and sin (l. 4), frequenting the court and associating with the aristocracy (l. 5), composing for their pleasure 'satirical verses, songs, rhymes and messages between lovers' (ll. 6–8). However, now that he is approaching old age he wishes to reform his life and turn his mind 'to other things' (l. 20).[30] It is probable, therefore, that he was a court poet who later in life became a monk at Bury.[31] In the first part of the Prologue, Denis condemns writers of verse, such as he had once been, who tell fanciful or invented fables in order to please their patrons, citing contemporary examples of these in the romance style.[32] He claims instead that he will tell a true tale which will be pleasing for both the ear and the soul and 'a pastime in verses which are full

---

[29] The best edition of *La Vie seint Edmund le Rei* is by Hilding Kjellman (Göteborg, 1935), who produced an edition of the poem based on the only manuscript then known, BL Cotton Domitian XI. It is also printed in Arnold, *Memorials*, II, pp. 137–250 and Hervey, *Corolla*, pp. 224–359. Subsequently a second manuscript was discovered and this is now in the John Rylands Library, Manchester, Rylands French MS 142. The two versions differ considerably. A full collation is given by Harry Rothwell, 'The *Life* and Miracles of St Edmund: A Recently Discovered Manuscript', *Bulletin of the John Rylands University Library* lx (1977–8), 135–80. The texts in both manuscripts are incomplete; the Domitian manuscript ends incomplete, as does the John Rylands text, which also lacks 684 lines at the beginning. See Rothwell, 'The *Life* and Miracles of St Edmund', pp. 135–6. Other saints' lives were composed in Anglo-Norman verse for female patrons. Matthew Paris, for example, wrote a life of St Edward the Confessor for Eleanor of Provence, and a life of St Edmund of Abingdon and a life of St Thomas Becket for Isabel, countess of Arundel. See Richard Vaughan, *Matthew Paris* (Cambridge: Cambridge University Press, 1958), pp. 168–81; Legge, *Anglo-Norman Literature*, pp. 268–9; Dominica Legge, *Anglo-Norman in the Cloisters: The Influence of the Orders on Anglo-Norman Literature* (Edinburgh: Edinburgh University Press, 1950), pp. 30–1.

[30] Lines 1–20, trans. Legge, *Anglo-Norman Literature*, p. 81.

[31] Gransden discusses the various theories concerning the identity of the author. *A History of the Abbey*, pp. 131–2.

[32] He refers disparagingly to the anonymous author of *Partenopeus de Blois* (l. 25) and Marie de France (l. 35); Legge, *Anglo-Norman Literature*, p. 82.

of wisdom and so true that nothing can be truer'.³³ It is therefore perhaps ironic that Denis relies primarily upon hagiographic sources; Legge comments rather plaintively that 'Denis could not be expected to know [that these versions] are the wildest fiction.'³⁴ From Denis's perspective, however, these texts are true: they represented the authoritative version of Edmund's legend, produced at Bury by those closest to the saint's remains and therefore best placed to record miracles and anecdotes. They also capture what was perceived to be the essential truth of Edmund's martyrdom, which, to some extent, transcends the burden of historical factuality. As the author of another 'in house' version of the legend, it is natural that Denis should rely upon these sources.

Traces of additional sources are nevertheless also present. In the Prologue to the second part of his poem, Denis claims that he has been asked by the senior monks to translate Edmund's legend '*e le engleis e del latin*' (l. 3268). The English text, if indeed there was one, has not been identified, but he clearly draws upon Abbo's *Passio*, *De Miraculis* and *De Infantia*. He also utilises chronicles such as Gaimar's *Estoire des Engleis* along with other Anglo-Norman sources such as Wace's *Roman de Brut*.³⁵

La Vie begins with a long account of British history inspired by the *Brut* tradition, including the invasion and settlement of the Saxons, Angles and Jutes, into which Denis integrates the account of Edmund's youth and upbringing (derived from *De Infantia*), the martyrdom (from Abbo's *Passio*) and a series of posthumous miracles (from Abbo and *De Miraculis*), including the death of Sweyn, before the text in each manuscript concludes unfinished during the description of Edmund's cure of an ailing tenant. Once again we thereby see the legend integrated into the context of national history. This was most likely inspired by Abbo's prefatory narration of the coming of the Germanic tribes into England, but is amplified by Denis in his longer digression into national mythology which he borrows from the chronicle and romance traditions. The use of the vernacular and the merging of the sacred and secular traditions suggest that *La Vie* was composed for a secular patron, or at least intended for a predominantly secular audience. This is reflected in the title, where Edmund's status as '*seint*' and '*rey*' are afforded equal prominence.

It is possible that the poem was commissioned to mark the occasion of a visit to the abbey of the secular patron for whom it was written.³⁶ Despite its primary

---

³³ '*Un dedut par vers vus dirray/ Ke sunt de sen e si verray/ K'unkes rien ne pout plus veir ester*', ll. 69–71, trans. Legge, *Anglo-Norman Literature*, p. 82.
³⁴ Legge, *Anglo-Norman Literature*, p. 82.
³⁵ See Legge, *Anglo-Norman Literature*, p. 84.
³⁶ Matthew Paris's *Life of St Alban*, for example, seems to have been composed for times when members of the secular aristocracy, perhaps even royalty, joined the monks of

reliance upon hagiographic sources, Legge felt that the overall tone of *La Vie* marked it out as distinct from its predecessors, suggesting that 'in form this life has long outgrown any association with the liturgy, and appears to be more suited to the abbot's lodging than to the church building'.[37] Gransden suggests that the occasion it commemorated may have been one of the several royal visits which occurred around the time *La Vie* was composed.[38] The small number of surviving manuscripts suggests that its circulation was limited and it may have been conceived as a unique gift for a patron whose favour the abbey sought to cultivate or maintain. In this context the prominence afforded to Edmund's temporal title acquires additional significance. That the abbey thought a life of St Edmund a suitable gift to present to a king is evinced by the fifteenth-century composition by John Lydgate, discussed below. It is plausible that *La Vie* was similarly intended not just for public performance whilst the royal party sojourned at Bury, but as a gift for the king on his departure. Thus in this instance Edmund's legend was modified to appeal to a secular audience. The saint is presented as nationally significant, on a par with the famous figures and events referred to in the Prologue, by which Denis sought to raise the profile of St Edmund amongst the aristocratic audience who would, it was most likely hoped, carry his name and legend throughout the country and beyond, and perhaps be inspired to patronise his shrine and the abbey which housed it.

La Passiun de seint Edmund

The second Anglo-Norman verse life is *La Passiun de seint Edmund*.[39] The poem is anonymous but, based on the author's familiarity with East Anglia, including allusions to a defensive dyke (ll. 145, 148) and a road which crossed the county (ll. 129–32), references which are original to this version, it is probable that the author was at least acquainted with the region. In addition, the familiarity with which the author describes the history of the abbey church (ll. 1109–44), along with the exhortations to the saint and his shrine, suggests a direct connection with Bury.

St Albans to celebrate a particular occasion. See Vaughan, *Matthew Paris*, p. 181; Legge, *Anglo-Norman Literature*, p. 268.

[37] Legge, *Anglo-Norman Literature*, p. 246.

[38] Henry II went on pilgrimage to Bury in 1177 and again in 1188; Richard I visited in November 1189 following his return to England after the death of Henry II, and again in March 1194 on his release from captivity; and King John visited Bury on three occasions, in 1199, 1201 and 1203. See Gransden, *A History of the Abbey*, p. 133.

[39] *La Passiun de seint Edmund*, ed. Judith Grant (London: Anglo-Norman Text Society, 1978).

La Passiun is essentially an Anglo-Norman verse rendering of Abbo's *Passio*, with very little additional material. It was composed c.1200 although the only known version is a thirteenth-century copy in a manuscript from St Augustine's, Canterbury.[40] It draws exclusively on Abbo and makes no reference to the versions of Edmund's legend written subsequently, such as *De Miraculis* or *De Infantia*. Like Denis Pyramus, the author of *La Passiun* has modified his source material to suit the context in which he was writing. Judith Grant notes the author's tendency to simplify and curtail some of Abbo's lengthier passages, such as the description of the origin and homeland of the Danes and Edmund's extended speech in which he rejects Hinguar's demands.[41] Conversely, some sections, such as the episode of the eight thieves, are augmented and direct speech added.[42] Grant maintains that these alterations were made in order to add to the drama of the tale, in keeping with its probable oral presentation, most likely to a similar audience envisaged for *La Vie*.

Both these lives were composed during the abbacy of Samson (1182–1211) and can therefore be considered in the light of his campaign to reinvigorate the cult of St Edmund. The translation of the legend into the vernacular would also accord with what Jocelin of Brakelond tells us of Samson's linguistic preferences:

> He was a good speaker, in both French and Latin, concentrating on plain speaking rather than flowery language. He could read books written in English most elegantly, and he used to preach to the people in English, but in the Norfolk dialect, for that was where he was brought up.[43]

Although not substantial alterations to the development of Edmund's saintly identity, *La Vie* and *La Passiun* once again reiterate the subtle influences of context and the importance of individual patrons in determining the development of the legend.

An Anglo-Latin life: Henry of Avranches, Vita Sancti Eadmundi

Similar influences may be seen at work in the third translation of St Edmund's life made in the thirteenth century, this time into Anglo-Latin. The *Vita Sancti*

---

[40] Now Gonville and Caius College, Cambridge, MS 435, pp. 105–28. For a description of the manuscript see *La Passiun*, ed. Grant, pp. 11–17.

[41] *La Passiun*, ed. Grant, p. 9. Cf. Abbo, *Passio*, V; Hervey, *Corolla*, pp. 19–21 and *La Passiun*, ll, 225–40 and Abbo, *Passio*, VIII and XIX; Hervey, *Corolla*, pp. 25–33 and *La Passiun*, 469–588 and 594–704 respectively.

[42] Cf. Abbo, *Passio*, XVI; Hervey, *Corolla*, pp. 47–53 and *La Passiun*, ll, 1209–440.

[43] Jocelin, *Chronicle*, p. 37.

Eadmundi is attributed to Henry of Avranches partly on the basis of stylistic similarities with his other works.[44] It is also included in the compilation of Henry's lives made by Matthew Paris, now Cambridge, University Library, MS Dd. 11.78, the only manuscript in which the *Vita* is extant.[45] Riggs describes Henry as 'the foremost Anglo-Latin poet of the [thirteenth] century'.[46] He is one of the first poets known to have received direct payment for his poems: from 1243 to 1260 he was paid from the Exchequer of Henry III.[47] His *Vita Sancti Eadmundi* dates from early in his career when his main literary output seems to have consisted of writing saints' lives for episcopal and monastic patrons.[48] All but two of his lives concern English saints and of these all but two are Anglo-Saxon.[49]

Henry's *Vita* consists of 598 lines in elegiacs. It is primarily based upon Abbo's *Passio*, some sections of which Henry abridges and some he omits, with the addition of a few details from *De Infantia* and the inclusion of a miracle from the later recension of *De Miraculis*.[50] Henry also alludes to the tradition established by Geoffrey of Wells that Edmund came from continental Europe, claiming that 'the Saxons sent a boy to be raised by the Angles,/ that he might restore what their fathers had plundered'.[51] This refines successive authors' concern with Edmund's personal genealogy and subsequent representation of the noble ancestors from whom Edmund descends, and instead presents him as a gift from one nation to another, able to bring about reconciliation and heal centuries-old wounds. Edmund is therefore not only of regional and national, but also international, importance.

---

[44] The most recent edition is by David Townsend, 'The *Vita Sancti Eadmundi* of Henry of Avranches', *Journal of Medieval Latin*, 5 (1995), 95–118. All references will be in accordance with this edition.

[45] The *Vita* is on ff. 125v–136v. See David Townsend and A.G. Rigg, 'Medieval Latin Poetic Anthologies (V): Matthew Paris' Anthology of Henry of Avranches (Cambridge, University Library, MS Dd. 11.78)', *Medieval Studies* 49 (1987), 352–90.

[46] A.G. Rigg, *A History of Anglo-Latin Literature 1066–1422* (Cambridge: Cambridge University Press, 1992), p. 179

[47] Rigg, *Anglo-Latin Literature*, p. 179.

[48] A canon of Henry's writings was established by Josiah Cox Russell and John Paul Heironymous in *The Shorter Latin Poems of Henry of Avranches relating to England* (Cambridge, Mass: The Medieval Academy of America, 1935).

[49] The English saints are: Birin, Edmund, Fremund, Guthlac, Hugh of Lincoln, Oswald and Thomas Becket. The exceptions are Sts Crispin-Crispianus and Francis of Assisi. For a description of each of these lives see Riggs, *Anglo-Latin Literature*, pp. 179–85.

[50] For further discussion of Henry's editorial practices see Townsend, 'The *Vita Sancti Edmundi*', 99–100.

[51] *Vita Sancti Edmundi*, ed. Townsend, ll. 17–18: '*Miserunt Anglis puerum saxones alendum/ Qui restauraret quod rapuere patres*'.

Again, however, it is not its contribution to the development of the legend which is of primary interest, but rather the insight it provides into the role of individual patrons in the dissemination of the cult. Although it lacks a preface, it is plausible that the *Vita* was composed for the abbey of Bury St Edmunds.[52] The *Vita* is dated to c.1220, which would place its composition within the first few years of the abbacy of Hugh de Northwold (1215–28). It is reasonable that a new abbot would seek to make his mark upon the cult of his abbey's patron by commissioning a translation of his legend. This would be particularly appropriate in Hugh's case, given the controversy surrounding his election. Chosen by the convent following Samson's death in 1211, Hugh was not confirmed as abbot by King John until 1215. Even after his official assumption of the post, conflicts persisted between those who supported Hugh and the party who favoured the sacrist, Robert of Graveley.[53] One of the means by which Hugh sought to assert his authority in the abbey was to grant approval for significant construction projects, including the rebuilding of the chapter-house and the casting of a great bell, known as the 'Neweport' after Richard of Newport, the sacrist who oversaw these works.[54]

Hugh was also personally devoted to Edmund. Following his promotion to the bishopric of Ely in 1228 he dedicated a chapel to St Edmund adjacent to the presbytery where a wall-painting of his martyrdom from this period is still extant. Edmund's martyrdom is also carved at the foot of Hugh's tomb in Ely Cathedral and the figures of Sts Ætheltryth and Edmund decorate the sides.[55] Hugh's activities in promoting the cult of Ætheltryth are well documented.[56] It seems likely that he would go to similar efforts to promote Edmund, perhaps taking advantage of Henry of Avranches's presence in East Anglia to commission the famous poet to rewrite the life of the saint.[57] Thus partly through personal devotion and partly for political ends, the textual cult underwent further revision.

---

[52] Riggs, *Anglo-Latin Literature*, p. 182. Townsend concurs, 'The *Vita Sancti Edmundi*', 98–9.
[53] An exceptionally detailed account of the election survives in the *Cronica de electione Hugonis abbatis postea episcope Eliensis*. This has been edited and translated by Rodney Thomson, *The Chronicle of the Election of Hugh, Abbot of Bury St Edmunds and Later Bishop of Ely* (Oxford: Clarendon Press, 1974).
[54] Hugh's patronage of building works at Bury is discussed in *The Chronicle of the Election*, ed. Thomson, pp. 195–6.
[55] Marion Roberts, 'The Effigy of Bishop Hugh de Northwold in Ely Cathedral', *Burlington Magazine* 130 (1988), 77–84.
[56] For Hugh's promotion of St Ætheltryth see Virginia Blanton, 'Building a Presbytery for St Ætheltryth: Hugh de Northwold and the Politics of Cult Production in Thirteenth-century England', *Art and Architecture*, 2 vols, ed. Blick and Tekippe, pp. 539–65.
[57] That Henry of Avranches visited East Anglia is conjectured by Townsend, who suggests that he may have composed the lives of Edmund and Guthlac whilst staying in the region in the early to mid-1220s. See Towsend, 'The *Vita Sancti Edmundi*', 99.

Oxford, Bodleian Library, MS Bodley 240

The most extensive collection of materials relating to the textual cult is found in Oxford, Bodleian Library, MS Bodley 240, a huge hagiographic compendium compiled at Bury in the last quarter of the fourteenth century, possibly by Henry de Kirkstead, prior and librarian c.1360–80.[58] An entry after the index at the start of the manuscript states that it was made in 1377 and belonged to the monks of Bury St Edmunds. The first 581 pages contain a copy of John of Tynemouth's *Historia Aurea*. Following the *Historia Aurea* are a number of short lives of mostly English saints (pp. 582–624), then a *Vita et Passio cum Miraculis Sancti Edmundi* (pp. 624–77). The rubric affirms that this was compiled from various chronicles, histories and legends. Its indebtedness to Abbo, *De Miraculis* and *De Infantia* for the events of Edmund's birth and upbringing, reign, martyrdom and posthumous miracles up to 1189 are readily apparent and acknowledged by the scribe in the margins.[59] The scribe adds a few details not known from other sources, such as the names of Edmund's parents (Alkmund and Siwara) and the place of his birth (Nuremberg). He also incorporates Roger of Wendover's augmented account of the events precipitating the martyrdom, namely that the Danish king Lothbroc is swept ashore in East Anglia and murdered by one of Edmund's men, causing Lothbroc's sons to invade, seeking retribution.[60] The scribe also includes details of various confrontations between the Danes and the East Anglians before Edmund is seized. These include Edmund's tactics in tricking the Danes into ending their siege of one of his camps and the bribing of one of Edmund's masons to reveal the weak point in the defences of another fortress.[61] Far greater emphasis is placed on the military capabilities and tactics of each side than had hitherto featured in the legend. This is particularly apparent in the section describing Edmund's martyrdom entitled '*De bello inter sanctum Edmundum et Ingwarum prope thefordiam et modo martirii sancti edmundi*'.[62] This is the first occasion where a hagiographic version of Edmund's legend depicts him engaging in battle with the Danes and is arguably the most significant feature of the text. Previous hagiographers had followed Abbo's account of the martyrdom in which Edmund is peaceable to the

---

[58] Richard H. Rouse, '*Bostonus Buriensis* and the Author of the *Catalogus Scriptorum Ecclesiae*', *Speculum* 41 (1966), 471–99.

[59] The events up to the martyrdom as described in Bodley 240 are printed in Hervey, *Corolla*, pp. 377–408.

[60] Roger of Wendover, *Chronica sive Flores Historiarum*, ed. Henry O. Coxe (London: The English Historical Society: London, 1841), I, 300.

[61] Hervey, *Corolla*, pp. 390–92.

[62] Hervey, *Corolla*, pp. 397–402.

ELABORATION OF THE HAGIOGRAPHIC TRADITION 87

extent that he willingly surrenders his kingdom in order to prevent bloodshed.[63] The scribe's attribution of these events as '*ex cronicis*' indicates the extent to which he has integrated material from the chronicle tradition which largely adhered to its prototype, the *Anglo-Saxon Chronicle*, in asserting that Edmund 'fought against' the Danish army, who 'gained the victory, and slew the king'.[64] The legend hitherto bifurcated along these lines and whilst it is not readily apparent why the scribe chose to make these alterations, the transformation in Edmund's characterisation is striking.

The contrast is particularly apparent when the activities of the martial Edmund are compared to his posthumous deeds as recounted in a series of new miracles added by the Bodley 240 scribe.[65] These are dated primarily to the thirteenth and fourteenth centuries, thereby bringing the record of Edmund's interventions up to date. Forty-five new miracles are reported in Bodley 240: 57 per cent of these involve healing, 30 per cent are rescues or miracles of general assistance (with around a third of these being rescues at sea), 10 per cent are unspecified and only one miracle involves punishment. The unlucky recipient of St Edmund's wrath in this instance was William Bateman, bishop of Norwich (1344–55), who the author claims was punished for his interference in the affairs of the abbey at Bury.[66] The statistical contrast between the nature of St Edmund's interventions in Bodley 240 and his activities in earlier miracle collections is striking. Furthermore, an apparent gender bias towards male recipients is misleading. For example, in several instances male children are healed by St Edmund, who is usually invoked by both parents. Thus, whilst the recipient of the miracle in these cases is male, the devotees, and vicarious beneficiaries of the miracles, are of both genders. Similarly, the number of individuals from ordinary, lower-status backgrounds is likely to be much higher, perhaps even including the majority whose social standing is unspecified.

This change in Edmund's saintly identity accords with patterns seen elsewhere in miracle collections. Miracles attributed to earlier periods reflect the often turbulent times in which they were recorded. This is particularly true of 'Viking-age' miracles and those occurring in the aftermath of the Norman Conquest.[67] In these contexts saints are often depicted as the patrons and protectors of their lands and interests and the monastic personnel associated with them. As this need for direct protective intervention diminished over time, the number of curative miracles,

---

[63] Abbo, *Passio*, XIII–XIV; Hervey, *Corolla*, pp. 25–33.
[64] *The Anglo-Saxon Chronicle*, ed. Whitelock, p. 46.
[65] The new miracles are printed in Arnold, *Memorials*, III, pp. 318–48.
[66] Bodley 240, ed. Arnold, *Memorials*, III, pp. 320–7.
[67] These trends are discussed by Ward, *Miracles and the Medieval Mind*, pp. 33–66.

especially of pilgrims, increased and came to dominate the collections.[68] Such generalisations are evidently not applicable in every instance, but it is significant that Edmund's cult responds to broader developments in the perception and construction of sanctity. It is possible that the Bodley 240 scribe, conscious of his saintly patron's fearsome former reputation, sought to redress the balance between Edmund as peaceable healer and his ability to defend the abbey by integrating the martial characteristics present in the chronicle tradition. Whether or not this was his intention, the resulting image of a 'super saint' was seized upon by John Lydgate and utilised to full effect in the last great flourishing of the St Edmund hagiographic tradition.

[68] For the later predominance of healing miracles see Ward, *Miracles and the Medieval Mind*, pp. 67–88.

CHAPTER 5

The final flourish of the textual cult John Lydgate, *The Lives of Sts Edmund and Fremund*

John Lydgate (c. 1370–1449) was a monk in the abbey at Bury St Edmunds, which he had entered in his youth and to which he returned in the early 1430s following several periods of clerical and ecclesiastical service, including acting as the unofficial poet for the Lancastrian regime.[1] Lydgate's *Lives of Sts Edmund and Fremund* is the culmination of the medieval hagiographic tradition concerning St Edmund, yet to date it has received surprisingly little critical interest, especially within the context of the St Edmund tradition. At 3,693 lines it is one of the longest versions produced and, written largely in rhyme royal stanzas, is the first rendering of the legend into English verse.[2] Three of the manuscripts are also extensively illustrated. One of these, now British Library, Harley 2278 (also referred to hereafter as 'the presentation copy'), was prepared as a gift for Henry VI and is one of the most sumptuous English manuscripts to survive from the fifteenth century. It is lavishly illustrated with 120 high-quality miniatures which provide a unique visual parallel to the text and offer a further opportunity to examine how St Edmund was simultaneously presented in differing media.[3]

Lydgate's life is a sophisticated and elaborate rendering of the legend, interesting in its own right for the insight it offers into how the cult of one of the most popular devotional figures of the Middle Ages developed over time. Lydgate

---

[1] Derek Pearsall, *John Lydgate (1371–1449): A Bio-bibliography* (Victoria, B.C.: English Literary Studies, University of Victoria, 1997), esp. pp. 28–31.

[2] John Lydgate, *The Lives of Ss Edmund and Fremund and the Extra Miracles of St Edmund, Edited from British Library MS Harley 2278 and Bodleian MS Ashmole 46*, ed. Anthony Bale and A.S.G. Edwards (Heidelberg: Middle English Texts, Universitaetsverlag Winter, 2009), l.192. All subsequent references will be in accordance with this edition and will be given in parentheses in the text.

[3] For a facsimile of the manuscript see *The Life of St Edmund, King and Martyr: A Facsimile of British Library MS Harley 2278*, with an introduction by A.S.G. Edwards (London: British Library, 2004). For discussion of the illustrations of Harley 2278 see Kathleen Scott, *Later Gothic Manuscripts 1390–1490*, 2 vols (London: Harvey Miller, 1996), II, 225–29 and A.S.G. Edwards's Introduction to *The Life of St Edmund, King and Martyr: A Facsimile*, pp. 8–13.

describes his poem as a 'translacion', immediately locating it within the medieval hagiographic tradition concerning Edmund. Anthony Edwards suggests that Lydgate's primary source is likely to have been MS Bodley 240.[4] However, Lydgate does not specify his source. Instead he refers rather vaguely to 'the noble story' (I. 81, 190), his 'auctours' (I. 428) or most frequently simply to 'the story'. Close reading reveals that the *Lives* is far more than a simple rendering into English of one text and is in fact extremely complex in its intertextual indebtedness, with Lydgate drawing on a variety of additional sources. Some passages are also his own inventions: for example the Prologues (Prologue, 1–80; I. 81–234); his references to contemporary issues and events such as the 'lollardis' (I. 1014); and, perhaps most interestingly, details of Edmund's battle with the Danes (II. 365–95). Although seeking authority for his composition by locating the *Lives* in the broader St Edmund tradition, Lydgate is clearly producing his own unique version of the legend. It is therefore necessary to consider the effect of these inclusions upon the narrative and the extent to which these digressions from the established tradition may be accounted for by its creation for a particular reader: Henry VI.

On Christmas Eve 1433, the twelve-year-old King Henry VI arrived at the Abbey of Bury St Edmunds. He was greeted by five hundred townspeople, his confessor William Alnwick, bishop of Norwich, and William Curteys, the abbot of Bury. Henry remained the guest of the abbey until Easter the following year, dividing his time between the abbey itself and the abbot's palace at Elmswell (Suffolk).[5] The Abbey of Bury St Edmunds was one of the largest and wealthiest religious houses in fifteenth-century England and therefore a suitable choice for such an extended stay.[6] Renowned as a shrewd clerical politician, it is unsurprising that Abbot Curteys chose to mark the occasion of the royal visit by commissioning prolific author John Lydgate to produce a translation of the legend of St Edmund 'out of Latin', with the intention, as Lydgate recounts, 'to yeue it to the

---

[4] A.S.G. Edwards, 'John Lydgate's *Lives of Sts Edmund and Fremund*. Politics, Hagiography and Literature', in *Changing Images*, ed. Bale, pp. 133–45; p. 136.

[5] Abbot Curteys records the event in his Register, now British Library Add. MS 14848, fol. 128-28v. For Curteys's Register see Rodney M. Thomson, *The Archives of the Abbey of Bury St Edmunds* (Woodbridge: The Boydell Press for the Suffolk Records Society, 1980) pp. 135–8. 'De adventu Regis Henrici VI ad monasterium de Sancto Edmundo' is pp. 136–7. Curteys's account is reprinted in Craven Ord, 'Account of the Entertainment of King Henry the Sixth at the Abbey of Bury St Edmunds', *Archaeologia* 15 (1806), 65–71.

[6] See Walter F. Schirmer, *John Lydgate: A Study in the Culture of the Fifteenth Century*, trans. Ann Keep (London: Methuen, 1961) pp. 8–23 for a concise account of the Abbey. For more detailed discussions of the Abbey's history, architecture, culture and artistic role and finances see *BAA: Bury*.

kyng' as a 'remembraunce' of his stay (I. 192).[7] The resulting text was Lydgate's *Lives of Sts Edmund and Fremund*.

Henry's significance as intended recipient is emphasised by the large miniature which accompanies the text at this point on fol. 6 of the presentation copy. In a self-referentially meta-textual gesture the miniature depicts Henry enthroned, surrounded by the monks of the abbey who present him with a book, presumably the presentation manuscript itself. It is indeed notable that Henry features in the illustrations before St Edmund, being the subject of two of the six miniatures which accompany the Prologue. The second miniature depicts Henry VI kneeling before Edmund's shrine and illustrates a prayer which Lydgate urges 'alle men, present, or in absence' who are devoted to Edmund to recite. His reference to the pardon which can be obtained by praying to St Edmund being 'write and registred afforn his hooly shryne' (Prologue, 78) locates the *Lives* within the physical context of cultic devotion and seems intended to remind the king of the lived experience of his stay at the abbey. The subject of the other narrative scene which accompanies the Prologue is Lydgate himself, shown on fol. 9 praying before St Edmund's shrine. Thus the orientation of the *Lives* is emphasised from the outset in the presentation manuscript: it is intended to remind Henry of his stay at the abbey, situating him visually in relation to St Edmund's shrine whilst also reminding him of his monastic hosts and their patronage of this lavish gift.

Abbot Curteys had himself authored a Latin version of St Edmund's legend, *Vita et Passio S. Edmundi Abbreviata*, which he copied into his Register. This summarises previous versions of the legend and places particular emphasis upon the legal precedents by which Bury gained its independence.[8] A similar composite Latin life was written around this time at Bury by the kitchener, Andrew Astone, whose *Vita et Passio Sancti Edmundi breviter collecta*, ending in 1032, has similarly legalistic preoccupations.[9] Interest in promoting the abbey's rights and privileges was evidently prevalent at the time of Henry's visit and Lydgate's *Lives* should be read in this context.

Lydgate's *Lives* begins with two prologues, the first extolling Edmund's merits as protector for Henry VI, the second introducing the poem's protagonist and

---

[7] For an account of Curteys's career see Arnold, *Memorials*, III. xxix–xxxiii.

[8] See Thomson, *Archives*, p. 137.

[9] Astone's *Vita* is on fols 32–6 of the Kitchener's Customary, dated after 1425, now British Library, Cotton MS Claudius A. xii. For details see Thomson, *Archives*, pp. 146–7. The fullest discussion of both these Latin lives is by N.J. Heale, 'Religious and Intellectual Interests at St Edmunds Abbey at Bury and the Nature of English Benedictinism, c. 1350–1450: MS Bodley 240 in Context' (unpublished D.Phil. thesis, University of Oxford, 1994).

explaining the circumstances of its composition. The main body is divided into three Books: the first describes Edmund's parentage and upbringing and the manner in which he came to succeed to the throne of East Anglia; the second tells of his reign, the events which precipitate his martyrdom and his death at the hands of invading Vikings; the third is initially concerned with Edmund's cousin Fremund, the story of whose martyrdom is followed by details of miracles associated with St Edmund and concludes with the building of a new abbey church and shrine under the abbacy of Baldwin (1065–97). A closing prayer asks St Edmund to pray for Henry VI, and two envoys humbly ask the king to accept the *Lives* and protect the abbey of Bury St Edmunds. At some point after 1441 several additional miracles, possibly by Lydgate, were appended to the end of the poem.[10] The *Lives* was a popular success; twelve manuscripts of the complete text plus a number of selections or fragments survive.[11] Interest in the poem was maintained into the sixteenth century, when John Stow copied various passages and annotated some of the surviving manuscripts.[12]

The hagiographic Lives

A saint's life was an appropriate gift with which to present the young king, as at the age of twelve Henry was already demonstrating the profound religious piety that was to be one of the most distinguishing features of his reign.[13] Lydgate was likewise an obvious choice to author this work. The most prolific English poet of

---

[10] These are found in four manuscripts as an appendix to the *Lives*: The Duke of Norfolk, Arundel Castle, *sine numero*, fols 96r–99r; Oxford, Bodleian Library, MS Ashmole 46 and MS Tanner 347, fols 87r–96v; London, British Library, Yates Thompson MS 47, fols 94r–104r. A version of the additional miracles, separate from the *Lives* and containing only the second and third, is in Oxford, Bodleian Library, MS Laud misc. 683, fols 45v–52v. See Anthony Bale, 'St Edmund in Fifteenth-Century London: The Lydgatian *Miracles of St Edmund*', in *Changing Images*, ed. Bale, pp. 145–61.

[11] The complete texts are found in: the Duke of Norfolk, Arundel Castle MS, *sine numero*; Cambridge, University Library, MS Ee.2.15; London, British Library, Harley MSS 372, 2278, 4826, 7333 and Yates Thomson MS 47; Manchester, Chetham's Library, MS 6709; Oxford, Bodleian Library, MSS Ashmole 46, Rawlinson B.216 and Tanner 347; Oxford, Corpus Christi College, MS 61. The fragments or extracts include: Exeter, Devon County Record Office, Misc. Roll 59; London, British Library, Harley MSS 247; Oxford, Bodleian Library, MSS 6930, 10174 and 11568. Lydgate's *Lives* is no. 3440 in Julia Boffey and A.S.G. Edwards, *A New Index of Middle English Verse* (London: British Library, 2005).

[12] For details see A.S.G. Edwards and J.I. Miller, 'John Stow and Lydgate's *St Edmund*', *Notes and Queries* 228 (1973), 365–9 and Alexandra Gillespie, 'The Later Lives of St Edmund: John Lydgate to John Stow', in *Changing Images*, ed. Bale, pp. 163–86.

[13] For a description of Henry VI's religious proclivities see Bertram Wolffe, *Henry VI* (London: Eyre Methuen, 1981), especially pp. 3–21.

his day, he produced nearly 145,000 lines of verse and around 200 prose texts. He wrote several saints' lives in addition to Edmund's, including his most popular work, the *Life of Our Lady*, which survives in fifty manuscripts, as well as those of Sts Alban and Amphibalus, Austin, George, Giles, Margaret and Petronilla.[14] He was well versed in the traditions of late-medieval hagiography and therefore ideally placed to undertake his abbot's commission.

The *Lives* is ostensibly a characteristic, if lengthy, example of late-medieval hagiography. Alain Boureau discusses the mimetic nature of hagiography, suggesting that hagiographic books were often objects 'endowed with sacred power' which 'signalled, recalled or evoked a vow or a past or ongoing practice'.[15] It is certainly the case that the *Lives* commemorates a particular vow and example of devotional practice. During his stay at Bury Henry displayed particular devotion to the abbey's patron, praying regularly before his tomb, and Lydgate records that before the king departed he was 'meuyd in him-silf of his benignyte,/ of ther chapitle a brother forto be' (I. 154–5), prostrating himself before Edmund's shrine as he was admitted to the confraternity of the abbey, a moment commemorated in the miniature on fol. 4 of the presentation copy.[16]

Lydgate's *Lives* is firmly located within the St Edmund devotional tradition. He draws on previous lives in order to produce a text which synthesises its predecessors, uniting the accounts of Edmund's upbringing and his accession to the throne of East Anglia (*De Infantia*), his passion (Abbo, *Passio*) and his posthumous miracles (*De Miraculis*) into one narrative. The extent to which the life accords with established hagiographies is particularly well illustrated in Lydgate's description of the events surrounding Edmund's death. Lydgate adheres to the martyrdom narrative established by Abbo and repeated by subsequent authors: Edmund is beaten with 'shorte battis rounde', bound to a tree and shot with arrows until he resembled 'an yrchoun fulfillid with spynys thikke' (II. 763), a

---

[14] *A Critical Edition of John Lydgate's Life of Our Lady*, ed. Joseph A. Lauritis, Ralph A. Klinefekter and Vernon F. Gallagher (Pittsburgh: Duquesne University Press, 1961); *The Life of St Alban and Saint Amphibal*, ed. J.E. van der Westhuizen (Leiden: Brill, 1974); 'St Austin', pp. 193–206; 'St George', pp. 145–54; 'St Gyle', pp. 161–73; 'St Margaret', pp. 173–92; 'St Petronilla', pp. 154–9, *The Minor Poems of John Lydgate*, Part 1, ed. Henry Noble McCracken, Early English Texts Society, es 107 (London: Oxford University Press, 1911).

[15] Alain Boureau, 'Franciscan Piety and Voracity: Uses and Strategies in the Hagiographic Pamphlet', in *The Culture of Print: Power and the Uses of Print in Early Modern Europe*, ed. Roger Chartier, trans. Lydia G. Cochrane (Princeton: Princeton University Press, 1989), pp. 15–58, p. 19.

[16] Curteys's Register, in Ord, 'Account of the Entertainment of King Henry the Sixth', 65–71.

simile drawn directly from Abbo and rendered by Lydgate into the vernacular, and both authors liken Edmund to 'seynt Sebastyan' (II. 764).[17]

All the lives explicitly characterise Edmund's death as martyrdom; Herman's *De Miraculis* is particularly emphatic, stating that 'Edmund, the glorious king, went the way of all flesh, taking for his viaticum the palm of martyrdom'.[18] Lydgate's repeated use of the tripartite epithet 'martir, maide and kyng' indicates that his Edmund met a similar fate, giving his life in witness to the true faith of Christ. Lydgate depicts Edmund's encounter with the Danes as a conflict between two belief systems. The Danish leader Hinguar demands not only that Edmund renounce his kingdom and its treasures and submit to Danish overlordship, but insists that he '"forsake of Cristen-dam the feith,/ And, to his [Hinguar's] goddis that thow do reuerence,/ To offre onto them with franc and with encence"' (II. 494–5). Instead Edmund renounces 'al lordshepe', both Hinguar's and his own, and submits himself to Christ, maintaining that he shall '"neuer my lord forsake"' and that he is willing to '"weel suffre my blood for him to sheede"' (II. 599, 602). His willingness to forsake his temporal kingdom for the kingdom of heaven and sacrifice himself in Christ's service accords neatly with long-established hagiographic conventions and locates Lydgate's *Lives* firmly within this tradition of devotional literature.

Similarly, Lydgate's Edmund is explicitly Christological. Lydgate follows Abbo's example and refers to Edmund's 'passion'. His textual indebtedness is further apparent in his claim, taken almost verbatim from Abbo, that Edmund was brought before Hinguar 'lyk as was Cryst whilom tofor Pilat' (II. 664).[19] Lydgate designates martyrs 'Cristis championis' (II. 775) and conforms to the common hagiographic tendency to depict them as *imitatio Christi*:

> In heuen bi grace they cleyme to haue an hoom,
> Folwyng the traces of Crist that is ther hed ...
> Which feedeth his knyhtes with sacred wyn and bred,
> Set at his table in the heuenly mansioun,
> That drank the chalis heer of his passioun. (II. 778–9, 781–3)

This description of the special honours martyrs are afforded in heaven casts Christ in the role of a figurehead whom the martyrs follow and seek to emulate. It is also reminiscent of the medieval body politic, in which martyrs are fundamental to the faith in the same way that each member of the body is necessary in order for it to

---

[17] Abbo, *Passio*, X; Hervey, *Corolla*, p. 35.
[18] Herman, *De Miraculis*, ed. Arnold, *Memorials*, I, p. 27.
[19] Abbo, *Passio*, X; Hervey, *Corolla*, p. 33.

function. Lydgate's assertion that in heaven Crist will 'feedeth his knyghtes with sacryd wyn and bred' has eucharistic connotations, and in a phrase reminiscent of the Gospel of John, he goes on to suggest that at the time of his death, Edmund was 'pressid with grapis in the vyne' (II. 787).[20]

The secular Lives

To a great extent, therefore, Lydgate adheres to the established devotional tradition in his description of Edmund's demise. There is one aspect of the martyrdom narrative, however, in which he diverges from this model: Edmund goes into battle against the Danes (II. 365–95). In this Lydgate seems to have been influenced by the account in Bodley 240, but the detail in which he describes the battle and its effect upon Edmund are unprecedented. Hinguar and his army are blown off course during the crossing from Denmark and land in 'Berwyk upon Tweede', from whence they advance towards East Anglia, killing all they encounter and despoiling abbeys and churches. They reach Norfolk, sacking Thetford and 'sleyng the peeple', before pitching camp near the remains of the settlement. When news of these events reaches Edmund he immediately leaves 'Castre' (perhaps Caistor St Edmund, near Norwich) and marches on the encamped forces, where 'euerich gan other ful mortally assaile'. In his description of the ensuing battle, which rages 'from the morwe' until 'it drouh to nyht', Lydgate is unequivocal in the part played by Edmund: he proves himself a 'ful manly knyht', from whom the enemy fly 'lik sheepe', and who sheds 'ful gret plente' 'of paynym blood'. Lydgate describes the battle in painful detail:

> The soil of slauhtre I-steynyd was with blood,
> The sharp swerd of Edmond turnyd red:
> For there was noon that his strook withstood
> Nor durste abide afforn him for his hed;
> And many a paynym in the feeld lay ded,
> And many cristen in that mortal striff
> Our feith defendyng that day lost his liff. (II. 386–92)

The wholesale loss of life on both sides is emphasised by the anaphora in lines 90–1, with the repeated conjunction conveying the almost monotonous inevitability of destruction.

Further attention is drawn to the description of the battle by the accompanying miniature on fol. 50 of the presentation manuscript in which Edmund is at

---

[20] 'I am the true vine, and my father is the husbandman' (John 15:1).

the centre of the mêlée, dressed in full shining armour, blood dripping from the sword raised above his head. The dominance of Edmund's army is represented by the proportion of the miniature which they occupy: whereas the Danes cower to the far right of the frame, the East Anglians hack their way across two-thirds of the scene, urged on by three angels flying above. Lydgate's description of the Battle of Thetford is the most detailed and explicit account to be found in the legendary tradition and the extent to which he diverges from the other lives at this point is striking.

Equally notable is the psychological effect that the battle has upon Edmund. Hinguar and his troops retreat and, left alone to survey the carnage of the battle-field, Edmund 'gan to considere in his owyn siht' (II. 397) the implications of the scene. He mourns not only the Christian dead but also the many pagans who, 'thoruh ther Iniquite' (II. 402) are condemned to 'helle' where there is 'no redempcioun' (II. 404), with this democratisation of regret recalling the anaphoric gesture of lines 390–1. Lydgate's characterisation at this point is both subtle and effective and evinces an impressive level of psychological realism in his depiction of Edmund's mental state. After Edmund 'gan to considere' the carnage before him he seems unable to rid himself of the image. He frequently ponders 'withynne himself' (II. 400) the fate of the dead, 'in his memorie narwely aduertisith' (II. 410) the follies of war, and 'ofte in his mynde and his remembrance/ This pitious mater was tournyd up so doun' (II. 421–2). Lydgate paints a convincing portrait of a man troubled by the horrors of war. He stresses that although Edmund was 'bothe manly and vertuous/ And a good knyht' (II. 406–7), he is so appalled by the day's events that he resolves 'for Cristis sake shedyng of blood teschew' (II. 427). This interpolated digression thus serves the dual function of displaying both Edmund's physical might and also the scope of his humanity, features arguably lacking in previous lives. It is at this point, when Edmund chooses the path of martyrdom in favour of further conflict, that the narrative of the *Lives* rejoins that of the previous accounts. Edmund is still described in martial terms but now, rather than fighting a physical battle, he bears a 'myhti sheeld' of 'Cristes feith' and a 'gostly swerd whettid with constance' (II. 710–11). He renounces the ways of war and submits meekly and patiently to his fate.

Like the account in Bodley 240, the *Lives* is clearly in dialogue with both strands of the established tradition. Lydgate undermines his own claim that his life is a 'translation'; his intertextuality is clearly far more subtle and complex. He reveals that he has consulted more than one text when he urges the reader to consult 'cronycle' sources (Prologue, 51) in order to corroborate his depiction of Edmund's 'royal dignyte' (Prologue, 52). Whilst his recourse to chronicles is in keeping with the education prescribed for young princes (for example, when

Richard Beauchamp, earl of Warwick, was appointed in 1428 as Henry VI's guardian during the king's minority he was instructed to 'use examples culled from history books to teach the young king to "love, worship and drede God"'), in the context of the legendary tradition of St Edmund it is a notably thorough textual gesture.[21] The emphasis Lydgate places upon Edmund's temporal kingship is therefore explicable in this context. The imperative to 'use figures culled from history books' may also go some way to explaining Lydgate's determination to incorporate material from the chronicle tradition, even when this meant departing from his hagiographic predecessors.

Lydgate's recourse to these sources in order to establish a particular aspect of Edmund's identity (his royalty) is significant, as his decision to unite both strands of the tradition may best be understood in relation to its putative reader. Theresa Coletti agrees that medieval writers were capable of tailoring their portrayals of saints to the aspirations of their readers:

> [fifteenth-century] authors sought to model [the saintly subjects of their narratives] in accordance with the values and aspirations of their well-to-do patrons even as they engaged social, religious, and political issues that were relevant both to communities of lay readers and to the fortunes of church and nation.[22]

Abbot Curteys had commissioned Lydgate to compose the *Lives* as a gift for Henry VI to mark his stay at Bury, and Lydgate frequently evokes Henry as reader and offers Edmund as an 'exaumplaire' whose devotional practices Henry should seek to emulate. In addition, Lydgate's assertion that Edmund will be 'a merour cler' (I. 419) is a verbal nod towards the mirror for princes genre, in which didactic texts exemplified the character and behaviour of the ideal ruler.[23] This suggests that Lydgate was indeed tailoring his narrative to suit his intended reader with secular as well as devotional aims in mind.

---

[21] The instructions are summarised in John Watts, *Henry VI and the Politics of Kingship* (Cambridge: Cambridge University Press, 1996) p. 54; the Privy Council's instructions are printed in Sir Harris Nicolas, *Proceedings and ordinances of the Privy Council of England*, 7 vols (London: Commissioners on the Public Records of the United Kingdom, 1834–37), 3: 296, 299. See also Nicholas Orme, *From Childhood to Chivalry: The Education of English Kings and Aristocracy 1066–1530* (London & New York: Methuen, 1984).

[22] Theresa Coletti, '*Pauperatus et donum Dei*: Hagiography, Lay Religion, and the Economics of Salvation in the *Digby Mary Magdalen*', *Speculum* 76 (2001), 337–78.

[23] For the uses of mirrors for princes in royal education see Orme, *From Childhood to Chivalry*, pp. 88–103 and Watts, *Henry VI and the Politics of Kingship*, pp. 16–38 for the norms of kingship established by mirrors for princes.

In her discussion of the exemplary nature of the *Lives*, Fiona Somerset concludes that Lydgate 'urges a spiritual model of life in place of a more secular one'.[24] She suggests that Lydgate's frequent mention of other saint-kings Fremund and Edward the Confessor in conjunction with his depiction of Edmund is an attempt to 'naturalize' the problematic aspects of Henry's kingship by providing 'an alternative spiritual lineage with which to affiliate himself' and offering a model of holy kingship more appropriate to Henry's proclivities.[25] Thus, according to Somerset, Lydgate emphasises Henry's unworldly qualities and places him on a seemingly inescapable trajectory towards martyrdom and sainthood in a pre-emptive effort to ameliorate the anticipated failure of his secular reign. However, this negative reading relies heavily on the benefit of hindsight and assumes that, even had questions been publicly raised at this point in his young life concerning Henry's fitness to rule, it would be appropriate for him to be presented with what amounts to a 'get-out clause'.

In contrast, Katherine Lewis offers a far more convincing reading of the *Lives* in relation to the more traditional, secular, mirror for princes. She compares the *Lives* with the most popular example of the genre in later medieval England, the *Secreta Secretorum*, demonstrating the ways in which Lydgate's depiction of Edmund accords with the ideal king described by this and other literary mirrors.[26] This type of mirror for princes seems a far more appropriate gift for the young king than that proposed by Somerset. Henry VI became king at the age of just nine months after the death of his celebrated father, Henry V, and as such was denied the opportunity to emulate a successful reigning monarch.[27] Yet in the absence of Henry senior, Lydgate offers Edmund as a surrogate model of exemplary kingly behaviour. On several occasions Lydgate makes it clear that Edmund is a role model whom Henry should seek to imitate; within the opening lines of the poem Lydgate advises that 'Edmund shal be his [Henry's] guide' (Prologue, 45), equating the saint with the nine worthies as a figure worthy of emulation.

Lydgate was writing for the son of one of his most important former patrons. He addresses the young king directly throughout the poem and makes reference

---

[24] Fiona Somerset, '"Hard is with seyntis for to make affray": Lydgate the "Poet-Propagandist" as Hagiographer', in *John Lydgate. Poetry, Culture and Lancastrian England*, ed. Larry Scanlon and James Simpson (Notre Dame, Indiana: University of Notre Dame Press, 2006), pp. 258–78; p. 261.

[25] Somerset, '"Hard is with seyntis for to make affray"', p. 261.

[26] Katherine J. Lewis, 'Edmund of East Anglia, Henry VI and Ideals of Kingly Masculinity', *Holiness and Masculinity in the Middle Ages*, ed. P.H. Cullum and Katherine J. Lewis (Cardiff: University of Wales Press, 2004), pp. 158–73.

[27] On Henry's youth and upbringing see Ralph A. Griffiths, *The Reign of King Henry VI* (Stroud: Sutton Publishing, 1998), pp. 51–7.

to his 'fadir, most notable of memory' and his great deeds (I. 164). Derek Pearsall characterises Lydgate as the semi-official propagandist for the Lancastrian regime, and it is likely that in accepting his abbot's commission Lydgate was hoping to cultivate a relationship of patronage similar to that which he had enjoyed with the young king's father.[28] The manner in which Lydgate offers Edmund as an alternative exemplar is particularly apparent in a number of passages, seemingly anachronistic, which describe Edmund engaging with fifteenth- rather than ninth-century enemies. Thus Lydgate's account of Edmund's suppression of the Lollards, where he claims that 'to holichirche he was so strong a wal' and that he 'hated fals doctryn in especial' (I. 1015–16), should not be read as a historical anachronism or an authorial error, but rather an allusion to the contemporary monarch and the difficulties he could expect to encounter during his reign. Less than two years before Lydgate was commissioned to write the *Lives*, Humphrey, duke of Gloucester, suppressed a Lollard uprising on the king's behalf whilst Henry was in France for his coronation.[29] Pearsall describes the anxiety experienced by the clerical establishment upon the succession of Henry VI, as it was feared that he would not prove so dedicated an upholder of the Church and persecutor of heterodoxy as was his father.[30] On this occasion Lydgate was commissioned to write *A Defense of Holy Church* as a means of reassuring the establishment, and in the ballad composed for Henry VI's coronation in 1429 he urged the king 'heretykes and Lollards for to oppresse'.[31] The reference to Lollards in the *Lives* is therefore another means of suggesting to King Henry the approach he should adopt towards the defence of the Church, by means of the exemplum of the saint-king Edmund.

Lydgate is also keen to emphasise the similarities between the two rulers. On several occasions in the poem he makes reference to Edmund's youth, claiming, for example, that he was fifteen at the time of his coronation (I. 857). Yet Edmund's youth is not seen as problematic, rather it serves to emphasise his exemplary nature, as Lydgate writes that despite his youth he was a wise ruler: 'Yong of yeeris, old of discresciuon/ Flourying in age, fructuous of sanesse' (I. 396–7). The natural imagery presents the young Edmund as vital and imbued with life and potential. Henry was himself a young king, and Edmund would therefore have been a particularly appropriate role model, with such positive references to Edmund's youth at the time of his succession emphasising that good kingship was possible at any age.

---

[28] Pearsall, *John Lydgate: A Bio-bibliography*, pp. 28–31.
[29] For details of this incident see Griffiths, *The Reign of King Henry VI*, pp. 139–41.
[30] Pearsall, *John Lydgate: A Bio-bibliography*, p. 18.
[31] 'Ballad to King Henry VI on His Coronation', *Minor Poems*, II, ed. McCracken, ll. 9–10.

Other references to Henry VI throughout the poem also invite comparisons between him and the saint. The prayer in the Epilogue repeatedly describes Henry as 'thenherytour off Ingelond and France', referring to the dual monarchy he had inherited from his father (Epilogue, 1464). Lydgate prays to St Edmund to help Henry VI govern both realms, apparently anticipating the problems presented in the ruling of what had effectively become two kingdoms.[32] The position of this prayer at the end of the poem means that it will already have been seen how Edmund, a Saxon king, was able to successfully rule a foreign kingdom originally not his own, suggesting again that if Henry VI follows his example then he will be equally successful.

Lydgate's emphasis upon Edmund's kingship is apparent throughout. He frequently refers to Edmund by means of the tripartite epithet, and in the opening line of the poem Edmund's royal identity is mentioned first: 'Blyssyd Edmund, kyng, martir and vyrgyne' (Prologue, 1). Lydgate describes Edmund's war banner which he bore 'Lyk a wys kyng' in battle against the Danes (Prologue, 9) and which Lydgate avers 'shal kepen and conserue/ this lond from enmyes' (Prologue, 41–2). This banner is carried into battle against the Danes in the miniature on fol. 50. The emphasis from the outset is therefore upon Edmund as king and his martial responsibilities to defend his realm. This is reiterated in the description of Edmund's second banner:

> This other standard, feeld sable off colour ynde,
> In which off gold been notable crownys thre:
> The first tokne, in cronycle men may fynde,
> Grauntyd to hym for Royal dignyte,
> And the second for virgynyte,
> For martirdam the thrydde in his suffryng;
> To these annexyd Feyth, Hope and Charyte,
> In tokne he was martyr, mayde, and kynge. (Prologue, 49–56)

Kingship is again the first attribute to be mentioned, and in the miniature which accompanies this description (fol. 3v) each 'tokne' is represented by a crown, the symbol of royal authority.

Lydgate likewise emphasises Edmund's royal pedigree.[33] We learn in Book I that Edmund was born in 'Saxonie', the son of King Alkmond and his queen Siware. Alkmond is himself depicted as a model ruler:

---

[32] For discussion of the dual monarchy see Griffiths, *The Reign of King Henry VI*, esp. pp. 178–230.

[33] For uses of royal genealogies as Lancastrian propaganda see J.W. McKenna, 'Henry VI of England and the Dual Monarchy: Aspects of Royal Political Propaganda, 1422–1432' *Journal of the Warburg and Courtauld Institutes* 28 (1965), 145–62.

> A manli prince, vertuous of leuyng,
> And ful habounde of tresour and richesse,
> Notable in armys, ful renommed of prowesse,
> A semly persone, hardi and corageous,
> Mercuries in wisdam, lik Mars victorious,
> Eyed as Argus be vertuous prouidence,
> And circumspect as famous Scipioun;
> In kyngli honour of most excellence (I. 237–44)

Just as Abbo and the artist of the Morgan miniatures sought to glorify Edmund's ancestors, Lydgate follows Geoffrey of Wells' example and emphasises that although Edmund was not born to the throne of East Anglia, he was nevertheless of royal extraction and schooled from birth in the ways of good kingship, thus reiterating his ability to be a good ruler. Edmund's inherent regality is recognised by Offa when he makes the young prince his heir (I. 431–507) and his royal potential is realised when, following Offa's death, he assumes the throne of East Anglia.

Following Lydgate's account of Edmund's arrival in his new realm, his acceptance by the people and his coronation, is a 'chaptile' which describes 'the Roial gouernance of seynt Edmond aftir he was crownyd kyng of Estyngland' (I. 858–1088). Here we learn in detail of Edmund's rule of good government, his provision of justice and his concern with matters of state. He ensures that the Church, the law and trade are honourably run by honest men (I. 892–934), and defends the Church vigorously against heresy (I. 1015–16). Edmund is charitable: 'geyn poore folk shet was not his gate,/ His warderope open, alle needy to releue' (I. 1084–5). He governs in accordance with the four cardinal virtues and his rule is one of temperance and 'noon excesse' (I. 869). Edmund encourages his nobles to follow his example by ensuring they attend church and by joining them in suitable pastimes such as hunting and hawking and other knightly activities at which he excels (I. 1047–53). Lydgate uses the conventional image of the body politic to illustrate Edmund's maintenance of 'dew ordre' and the balance between the various social estates (I. 941). In the miniature which accompanies this passage on fol. 34 Edmund is depicted enthroned and cradling symbols of the estates: four knights bearing banners and weapons circumnavigate his head, a church (perhaps the abbey church at Bury) hovers before his abdomen, a ship floats above his lap and a plough-team labours at his feet. Edmund is seated outdoors in a landscape which echoes the shape of his throne, gesturing towards the ground in blessing or recognition, thus emphasising the bond between the king and his kingdom and his duty to protect it, another potent symbol of ideal kingship to present to the young Henry.

Codicological context

The emphasis which Lydgate places upon Edmund's kingship and the importance of acknowledging the circumstances in which the *Lives* was written is particularly apparent when the poem is considered in its codicological context, especially in the case of a poet such as Lydgate. He was a multi-media poet in every sense of the word: his poems were frequently accompanied by images, not only in manuscripts but also stitched into wall-hangings and alongside paintings (perhaps most famously accompanying a large painting of the Dance of Death on the wall of the cloisters of Old St Paul's Cathedral) or accompanying a series of decorative allegorical pastries presented at Henry VI's coronation banquet. He also wrote poems for performance, to be either acted or sung.[34]

Lydgate's *Lives* enjoyed a far wider distribution than any other separately circulating Middle English saint's life.[35] The manuscript circulation of the *Lives* indicates that its readership was not exclusively royal. In most instances it is bound into manuscripts alongside other works by Lydgate or other writers. Copies of the *Lives* in the British Library's Harleian manuscripts provide a representative illustration: in MSS 372 and 7333 the *Lives* is included alongside a wide range of other texts, varying from short devotional poems, treatises on genealogy, moral tales and, in the case of the latter, a large selection of Chaucer's *Canterbury Tales*. MS 247 is even more eclectic and contains a fragment of the *Lives* as one of sixty-five individual texts.[36] In MS 4826, however, Edmund's life (fols 4–50v) is accompanied by Lydgate's *Secrees of Old Philisoffres* (fols 52–81) and Hoccleve's *De regimine principum* (fols 84–144v). The nature of the accompanying texts suggests that in this instance Lydgate's *Lives* was treated as a mirror for princes. The general manuscript context of the *Lives* therefore reflects its popularity but is less informative concerning its reception.

In contrast, the content and patronage of the illustrated copies of the *Lives* provide a clearer indication of how the poem was disseminated. Three copies of the *Lives* are extensively illustrated: British Library MS Harley 2278, British Library MS Yates Thompson 47 and the so-called Arundel Castle Manuscript (*sine numero*). Of these, the first to be produced was the presentation copy made for Henry VI contained in Harley 2278. In this manuscript the ratio of illustrations to text is extremely high: they average more than one for each leaf and are

---

[34] Pearsall, *John Lydgate: A Bio-bibliography*, esp. pp. 25–32.
[35] For comparisons see Boffey and Edwards, *A New Index of Middle English Verse*.
[36] For the contents of the MSS see *A Catalogue of the Harleian Manuscripts in the British Museum*, 4 vols (London: British Museum Department of Manuscripts. Printed by command of H.M. King George III, 1808–12).

more or less equally distributed throughout the text. Apart from the two full-page illustrations at the front of the manuscript, the rest are usually carefully positioned in relation to the textual narrative. Edwards notes that they are embedded within the text and 'illustrate faithfully what is described', with the overall effect being 'an unusually powerful synthesis in which the verbal and visual elements of the manuscript complement one another in a carefully integrated way', noting that it is difficult to identify precedents for this degree of integration of text and image elsewhere in the presentation of fifteenth-century Middle English verse manuscripts.[37]

My reading of the *Lives* as a mirror for princes is emphasised by the unity of word and image. For example, the lengthy descriptions of Edmund's kingship in Book I are accompanied by several miniatures. First we see Edmund's coronation, depicted in a larger miniature, underlining its importance (fol. 31). The next folio contains an image of Edmund holding court (fol. 32), followed by illustrations of Edmund on his throne (fol. 34), Edmund hearing pleas (fol. 36) and Edmund engaging in kingly sports (fol. 37). By way of contrast we next see the Danish king Lothbroc and his sons worshipping idols (fol. 39): Edmund's just Christian kingship is directly contrasted with the pagan Danes. In this instance the illustrations of Harley 2278 are clearly reinforcing the *Lives*'s didactic message by placing considerable emphasis upon Edmund engaged in appropriate kingly behaviour. Except for a small number of scenes which may derive from older iconographies it is likely that most of the pictures were created for Lydgate's newly composed poem.[38] It is also probable that Lydgate had a hand in the selection of scenes. In Harley 2278 the miniatures therefore form a coherent visual parallel to the text of the poem and both the verbal and visual narratives reinforce the understanding of the *Lives* as a mirror for princes.

However, subsequent copies do not share this emphasis. The two extensively illustrated descendant manuscripts (Yates Thompson 47 and the Arundel Castle Manuscript) have around fifty miniatures each and can be dated to after 1461 by internal references to Edward IV, where this later king's name is substituted for Henry VI's in the original text.[39] They were produced by the so-called Edmund-Fremund workshop, which flourished in Bury in the 1460s.[40] The provenance of

---

[37] See Edwards's Introduction to the facsimile of Harley 2278, *The Life of St Edmund, King and Martyr*, p. 11.

[38] Kathleen Scott, *Later Gothic Manuscripts, 1390–1490*, 2 vols (London: Harvey Miller, 1996), II, p. 228.

[39] For Yates Thompson 47 see Scott, *Later Gothic Manuscripts*, II, pp. 307–10 and for the Arundel Castle MS see Kathleen Scott, 'Lydgate's *Lives of Saints Edmund and Fremund*: A Newly Located Manuscript in Arundel Castle', *Viator* 13 (1982), 335–66.

[40] Scott, 'A Newly Located Manuscript', 335–8.

the Arundel Castle manuscript is untraceable until it came into the possession of William Stow (1525?–1605). Yates Thompson 47 was also acquired by Stow, and the precise identity of its original owner is similarly unknown, although an inscription on page 213 provides some clues: 'Thys gyfen to my lady beaumoun be har lovfenge moder Margaret ffytz wauter wt all my hart'. Scott believes that the giver of the gift was probably Margaret Fitzwauter, or Fitzwalter, the second wife of Sir John Radcliffe (?1452–96) of Attleborough (Norfolk), although Lady 'beaumoun' has not been identified.[41] The production of deluxe copies at Bury suggests that the poem continued to enjoy a significant local appeal. Doubtless affluent patrons of the abbey felt it desirable and appropriate to possess a memorial of its patron saint, with its royal associations adding to its prestige.

Kathleen Scott describes the two descendant manuscripts as 'virtual twins'.[42] They were written by the same scribe and there are few differences in illustration and only minor variations in iconography and composition: the miniatures always have the same subject, always occur in the same position on the page, are always made to the same height of one or two stanzas and are usually identical in composition and frequently so in their repetition of colours for the same objects. Admittedly, Harley 2278 seems to have exerted some influence over the format of the pictures in the descendant manuscripts as they are similarly embedded within the text. However, if we inspect the manuscripts more closely its influence on their iconography appears limited: only five miniatures from the presentation manuscript appear to have been used as models in the later copies. There are also more than twice as many illustrations in Harley 2278, so there is no question of a page-by-page similarity between the three. However, the extent to which there are thematic similarities, in the sense of similar episodes being depicted in similar ways, enables the emphasis of the presentation manuscript to be further considered.

All the major episodes of the legend are illustrated in Yates Thompson 47 and Arundel Castle; the martyrdom sequence, for example, is illustrated in ten miniatures in Harley 2278 and seven in the descendant manuscripts, a remarkably similar number, given the relative total number of miniatures. Other important episodes, such as the murder of Lothbroc which precipitates the Danish invasion, are illustrated in similar detail. There are, however, some notable disparities. In particular, sequences of miniatures in Harley 2278 which endorse the *Lives* as a mirror for princes are absent from the later copies. All three manuscripts show Edmund being crowned and in each the illustrations are of the larger size (Harley 2278, fol. 31 and Yates Thompson 47 and Arundel, fol. 21v). However, in Yates

---

[41] Scott, *Later Gothic Manuscripts*, II, pp. 307–9; p. 308.
[42] Scott, *Later Gothic Manuscripts*, II, p. 308.

Thompson 47 and the Arundel Castle manuscript the next illustration occurs at the beginning of Book II, where we see Lothbroc hunting with his hounds (fol. 30). The sequence of miniatures illustrating Edmund's kingly conduct is lacking. Similarly, the emphasis upon the importance of taking counsel from lords or bishops is absent from the miniatures of the descendant manuscripts. Whereas in Harley 2278 we see Edmund's father consulting his lords, in the descendant manuscripts we see none of this decision-making process. Likewise, following the Battle of Thetford, in contrast to his Harley counterpart the descendant Edmund goes straight from victory in battle to martyrdom without consulting his bishop on how next to proceed.

These differences between the illustrative schemes may be variously accounted for. It is probable that whilst it was appropriate in the presentation copy to emphasise the role of the *Lives* as a mirror for princes, when the poem was reproduced in different circumstances this was no longer fitting or desirable and the illustrative scheme was adjusted to accommodate these new conditions. Far from merely illustrating the text they accompany, therefore, the miniatures are possessed of their own agency and are able to influence reception and understanding. Hahn suggests that the relationship between text and image is shaped by the principal of selection, as 'depending upon which parts of a written story they choose to represent, artists can shape pictorial narrative in ways radically different from texts'.[43] This is certainly the case with these three manuscripts and demonstrates the fundamental importance of the presence of Henry VI as imagined reader in determining both the visual and textual substance of the *Lives*.

St Fremund

Thus far little has been said concerning St Fremund, the other eponymous saint whose life Lydgate recounts. Described by A.G. Riggs as 'obscure and possibly fictional', virtually nothing is known of St Fremund.[44] His appearance in the *Lives* is therefore curious and has puzzled generations of scholars, the majority of whom have overlooked his much shorter section of the narrative in favour of the main body of the poem concerning Edmund. Indeed, Lydgate himself gives no indication of his intention to write about Fremund, announcing that he will 'putte in remembrance' 'the noble story ... of saynt Edmund' (I. 1–2). Fremund's 847-line interjection at the beginning of Book III therefore comes as something of a surprise. This is reflected in the transition between the two narratives, which is sudden and awkwardly executed. Having concluded his account of Edmund's

---

[43] Hahn, *Portrayed on the Heart*, p. 46.
[44] Rigg, *Anglo-Latin Literature*, p. 182.

passion and posthumous miracles, Lydgate addresses the martyr directly, asking his permission to recount a different tale:

> Now, glorios martir [Edmund], which of gret meeknesse
> For Crystes feith suffredist passioun,
> Qwyke my penne, enlumyne my rudenesse,
> To my dulnesse make a dirreccioun,
> That I may undir thy supportacioun
> Compile the story hangyng on this matere
> Off seyn Fremond, thyn owyn cosyn dere! (II. 995–1001)

Lydgate was not the first author to cite a familial link between Edmund and Fremund but the *Lives* is the first occasion where their narratives are contained in the same text. It is therefore necessary to consider the reasons why Lydgate made this interpolation and the extent to which the inclusion of Fremund informs our reading of the poem and inflects the development of Edmund's saintly identity.

According to local tradition, after his death Fremund's body was taken to Offchurch in Warwickshire, where his tomb became a place of pilgrimage. In about AD 931 his remains were taken to Cropredy in Oxfordshire, where the south transept still bears his dedication. The *Dunstable Chronicle* refers to a dedication of an altar to St Fremund in 1207 following the translation of some of his relics from Cropredy, and in 1212 to a proliferation of miracles associated with this new shrine.[45] Despite this, the shrine at Cropredy continued to be venerated until early in the sixteenth century. Testamentary bequests confirm the presence of the shrine in Cropredy church. In 1489 Richard Danvers of nearby Prescote Manor bequeathed money to the chapel of St Fremund:

> To Sir Raunhoh, chaplain of St Frethemund, to pay for my soul, 20s. To the fabric of the prebendal church of Cropredy, 100s. To the repair of the chapel of St Fremund where his shrine is situated, 20s.[46]

Richard Danvers' son John married Ann Stradling, through whom he acquired a property at Dauntsey in Wiltshire. John appears to have maintained his devo-

---

[45] *Annales monastici*, ed. Henry Richard Luard, Rolls Series 36, vol. 3 (London, 1866), pp. 29 and 39.
[46] Will of Richard Danvers, proved 20 February 1489, in *Some Oxfordshire Wills Proved in the Prebendary Court of Canterbury, 1393–1510*, ed. John R.H. Weaver and Alice Beardwood (Banbury, Oxon: Cheney & Sons Ltd., 1958), p. 41.

tion to St Fremund in his new parish. John and Ann are buried in Dauntsey church and antiquarian evidence attests that above their tomb was once a stained glass window depicting St Fremund carrying his head in his hands in reference to the manner of his death. Beneath were John and Ann's four sons and above their heads a scroll entreating 'Sancte Fredismunde ora pro nobis'.[47] In John's will of 1514 he left twenty shillings to Cropredy church and twenty shillings to 'St Frethemund's chapel', while Ann also remembered the chapel in 1539 when she bequeathed 'a cowe' each to the churches of Culworth and Cropredy and 'ten ewes' to the 'Chapel of Saynte Fredysmunde in Cropredy'.[48] The cult of Fremund therefore seems to have enjoyed some local popularity associated with one of his shrine sites. Nationally, however, evidence of his cult is scarce. No parish churches were dedicated in his honour.[49]

The earliest written version of his legend is extant in Dublin, Trinity College, MS B.2.7, a manuscript dating from the early thirteenth century. This prose life was perhaps composed for Dunstable Priory (Bedfordshire) to coincide with the translation of Fremund's relics here in 1207. This prose life was translated into Latin hexameters in the 1220s by Henry of Avranches.[50] The *Vita Sancti Fremundi* is preserved, along with the *Vita Sancti Edmundi*, in Matthew Paris's compilation of Henry's hagiographic works.[51] It tells of the birth of Fremund to a childless couple, foretold by a three-day-old infant. Fremund becomes king but is torn between his commitment to his royal office and his devout piety. Eventually he abdicates and becomes a hermit on a remote island, rejecting the devil's temptation to resume his royal duty. He does, however, respond to his parents' request for assistance against the Viking assailants responsible for Edmund's death. Fremund meets the Danes in battle and, with the assistance of an angel who makes his diminutive force appear one thousand times larger, defeats the numerically superior Danes but is killed by the traitor Oswy, who strikes off Fremund's head. Fremund is recognised as a saint and miracles occur at his tomb, which is discovered by three infirm women and also attested by the prophesied presence of a sow and her piglets. Further miracles occur and news of the burial is taken to Bishop Birin at Dorchester. Although Henry wrote lives of both Edmund and Fremund and alluded to the familial connection between them, there is no evidence that he paired their lives in the manner assumed by Lydgate. Townsend suggests that, like

---

[47] See Rev. Canon Wood, 'A Forgotten Saint?', *The Antiquary* 27 (May, 1893), 202–7; 203.
[48] Cited by Wood, 'A Forgotten Saint?', 203.
[49] Arnold-Foster, *Studies in Church Dedications*, III.
[50] Rigg summarises Henry of Avranches' life in *Anglo-Latin Literature*, pp. 182–3. It has been edited by David Townsend, 'The *Vita Sancti Fremundi* of Henry of Avranches', *Journal of Medieval Latin* 4 (1994), 1–24.
[51] See Townsend and Rigg, 'Medieval Latin Poetic Anthologies', 352–90.

the earlier prose life on which it was based, the *Vita Sancti Fremundi* was probably composed for Dunstable Priory as part of its campaign to promote the cult.[52]

Fremund also features in a mid-fourteenth-century manuscript of the *South English Legendary*, now British Library, MS Stowe 949.[53] It is perhaps significant that Fremund makes his first appearance in the *South English Legendary* in the same manuscript in which St Frideswide is first seen. Both saints were connected with Oxfordshire and this may suggest a local provenance for the manuscript. John of Tynemouth included Fremund in his mid-fourteenth-century compendium of saints' lives, *Sanctilogium Angliae, Walliae, Scotiae et Hiberniae*, now extant in British Library, MS Cotton Tiberius E1 in which 156 saints' lives and festivals are arranged in calendrical order.[54] This was revised in the fifteenth century, with the content rearranged alphabetically. This was possibly undertaken by John Capgrave, under whose name the collection is most commonly known, although scholarly opinion remains divided on the matter of attribution.[55] This in turn was printed in 1516 by Winken de Worde, with some alterations and the addition of fifteen new lives, as *Nova Legenda Anglie*.[56]

In each subsequent version Fremund's legend remains substantially the same as the early thirteenth-century original. It is unclear from whence Lydgate derived his information regarding Fremund. His legend is not included in Bodley 240. He claims that 'off Burchardus folwe I shall the style/ That of seyn Fremund whilom was secretarye/ Which of entent dide his liff compile' (III. 162–4). Burchardus, assumed to be a fictional character, is generally named as one of Fremund's companions on his island wilderness. Lydgate was clearly aware of other versions of Fremund's legend. In contrast to his depiction of Edmund's life, Lydgate retells Fremund's legend with few alterations. The question of why he chose to include Fremund alongside Edmund remains unanswered, but the similarities between the lives of the two saints may offer some explanation.

In addition to the familial connection there are further points of correspondence. Like Edmund, Fremund was of royal stock, according to Lydgate the son of King Offa of Mercia (Edmund's brother-in-law) and Queen Botyld.[57] His virtues

---

[52] Townsend, 'The Vita Sancti Fremundi', 5.

[53] St Fremund is no. 3192 in *The Index of Middle English Verse*, by Carlton Brown and Rossell Hope Robbins (New York: Columbia University Press for the Index Society, 1943). See *The Early South English Legendary*, ed. Carl Horstmann, Early English Text Society, os 87 (London: Early English Text Society, 1887), xiii–xxiv, for tabulation of the contents of the MSS of the *SEL*. See also Horstmann's reflections of the differing content of each MS, ix.

[54] *Nova Legenda Anglie*, ed. Horstmann, ix–xv.

[55] *Nova Legenda Anglie*, ed. Horstmann, xv–xvi.

[56] *Nova Legenda Anglie*, ed. Horstmann, xvi–xxi.

[57] This is not the same Offa whom Edmund succeeds to the throne of East Anglia. Although

were such that when his parents 'gan approachen to the stage/ Off decrepitus' (III. 283–4) they resigned their throne to Fremund, who ruled well and justly in their stead (III. 288–329). However, when the young Fremund 'hadde regned but a yeer' (III. 330) he renounced his birthright to become a hermit on the isle of 'Ilefaye' (III. 338), a place 'lyk a desert' (III. 350) where he lived a life of 'abstynence and contemplaioun' (III. 408) with two companions, 'to god alway doyng reuerence' (III. 377). After seven years his peaceful life was disrupted. Hearing of the death of his kinsman, Edmund, the aged Offa desperately sought his son in order that he might defend his kingdom from the same marauding Vikings and 'ageyn the Danys to make a mortall werre' (III. 427). Fremund reluctantly resumed his royal duties and met the Danes in battle, winning a resounding victory against seemingly unconquerable odds: 'with foure and twenty that day withoute obstacle/ Slouh fourty thowsand, only be myracle' (III. 531–2). Fremund, however, was betrayed: as he knelt to give thanks for his victory the 'ful traitourly' Oswy, a noble of his father's in league with the Danes, 'smet off his hed' (III. 567). Scorched by the holy blood, Oswy cried out for mercy and, in an episode reminiscent of the aftermath of Edmund's martyrdom, Fremund's decapitated head spoke to the traitor and offered him forgiveness (III. 591–602). Fremund then rose, seized his head, and walked. Pausing between 'Whittone and Harborugh' (probably Wigston, near Leicester and Market Harborough, both now in Leicestershire) he touched the ground with his sword, whereupon a spring burst forth in which he washed the blood from his severed head, after which he finally 'gaff up the gost' (III. 617–37). The repentant, and presumably startled, Oswy carried Fremund's body to 'Offecherche' (Offchurch, Warwickshire), where it was enshrined (III. 638–45). Fremund wrought many miracles, including the cure of three crippled virgins, who in gratitude carried his body to the banks of the river 'Charwelle' (Cherwell river, Oxfordshire), where they reburied it in 'a toumbe off gret delit' (III. 646–700). The site became renowned as a place of healing and many miracles occurred there (III. 701–42). Following a vision and a series of miraculous signs, Fremund was translated for the last time, to 'Dunstaple' (Dunstable, Bedfordshire) (III. 743–826). Lydgate's account concludes with the description of more miracles and an invocation for Fremund, 'martir, mayde and kyng' (III. 827) to remember his faithful devotees (III. 827–47). By assigning the same tripartite epithet to Fremund which he uses for Edmund, Lydgate is reinforcing the connection between the two saints. To some extent, however, this connection is one of counterpoint rather than straightforward equivalence. For example, whilst Edmund is a successful and exemplary king, Fremund renounces his royal status. Similarly,

a historically attested king, there is no evidence that Offa of Mercia had a son named Fremund.

Edmund is a great warrior who eventually chooses pacifism, whereas Fremund is recalled from his contemplative life to the active world of warfare.

Winstead suggests that Fremund functions as a 'corrective' to Edmund, a means of reminding King Henry of the secular duties of a king which should not be eschewed in favour of personal preferences, no matter how pious.[58] However, it seems unlikely that Lydgate would criticise, however subtly, the protagonist of his text and patron of his abbey. Instead, Anthony Edwards notes that the trajectory of Fremund's life is in direct contrast to Edmund's own, a technique he believes Lydgate employs in order to emphasise Edmund's saintly excellence.[59] This is far more plausible, particularly if Fremund's life is seen as a sequel to Edmund's. The presence of the same Danish villains means that Fremund's story is a continuation of Edmund's. Lydgate's summary at the end of Book II of the new narrative he is about to introduce indicates that the event of central significance is Fremund's defeat of the Danes:

Thoruh thy [Edmund's] fauor I cast me for tassaye
To declare of humble affeccioun
How seyn Fremond be miracle dide outraye
Hyngwar and Vbba thoruh his hih renoun
And them venquysshid in this regioun (II. 1002–6)

The constraints of the pre-existing legend, the irreducible minimum of which is that Edmund was killed by the Danes, prevent Lydgate's Edmund from defeating the invaders. Lydgate, however, who presents Edmund as exemplary in every other aspect of his being, could not allow the Danes to go unpunished. Fremund's victory therefore completes the narrative by ensuring earthly retribution, just as Edmund's martyrdom ensures his spiritual superiority.

Whether the young king read the poem which Lydgate wrote for him or admired the lavish illustrations is unknown. Yet how the *Lives* was received in actuality does not diminish the significance of its ability to function simultaneously as both a devotional manuscript and a work of secular instruction. As a devotional object the *Lives* seeks to offer Edmund as a model of kingly piety whom Henry VI should seek to emulate, and also reminds Henry of his own devotions to the saint and the vow taken before his shrine. It is likely that Abbot Curteys took advantage of the king's visit to promote the rights and liberties of the abbey and ensure a place for

---

[58] Karen A. Winstead, *John Capgrave's Fifteenth Century* (Philadelphia: University of Pennsylvania Press, 2007), p. 131.

[59] Edwards, 'John Lydgate's *Lives of Ss Edmund and Fremund*: Politics, Hagiography and Literature', in *Changing Images*, ed. Bale, pp. 133–44; p. 140.

it in his benefactions. Lydgate hopes that the king will be 'diffence and protectour' (I. 166) and suggests that in return Saint Edmund 'shal to the kyng be ful proteccioun/ Ageyn alle enemies' (I. 160–1). This concept of mutual assistance and interdependence attests to the special relationship perceived to exist between kings and saints, mediated here through the abbey of Bury St Edmunds. It establishes from the outset of the poem the notion that whilst the king's benefaction may be of value to the abbey and its saintly patron, St Edmund's support would be of equal worth to any upon whom he chose to bestow it. However, by writing the reader into the text Lydgate transforms the *Lives* from simply a devotional object into one which is simultaneously sacred and secular. In order to present the saint as a suitable kingly role model Lydgate was able to capitalize on his position as both a monk of Bury and apologist for the Lancastrian regime to shape and recast the legend in order to fit his own purposes. It seems likely that he played on the young King Henry's religious sensibilities to exhort the virtues of kingly conduct (a model of kingship which might accord with Henry's own proclivities and ideals) in order to demonstrate that it was possible to be both kingly and holy. Pearsall describes the *Lives* as 'surrounded by a mass of rhetorical circumstance'.[60] Ultimately it was this unique combination of events and individuals which resulted in the particular portrayal of Edmund in Lydgate's life. In a poem intended to instruct the young king and influence him in both his temporal and devotional activities, Henry VI as anticipated reader exercises considerable influence over the text and its illustrations. Despite these evident preoccupations, Lydgate's *Lives* is in many ways the most balanced and complete version of Edmund's saintly biography. The miracles described, for example, evince the most even distribution in terms of types of miracles and status of recipients of any version in the hagiographic tradition. Lydgate's Edmund emerges as a saint for all circumstances.

---

[60] Derek Pearsall, *John Lydgate* (London: Routledge and Kegan Paul, 1970) p. 282.

PART II

Relics, shrines and pilgrimage
Encountering St Edmund at Bury

CHAPTER 6

Sacred immanence, the incorrupted body and the shrine of St Edmund

'It is fully proved in his case … that though his spirit be in the enjoyment of heavenly glory, yet it has the power to revisit the body and is not by day or night far separated from the place where the body lies.'[1]

Sacred immanence

IN 1043 King Edward the Confessor visited the abbey of Bury St Edmunds. As the towers of the church became visible in the distance the king dismounted from his horse and walked the last mile on foot, acknowledging that he was crossing the boundary into the spiritual estate under the jurisdiction of St Edmund.[2] In another account recorded by Herman, an old blind man from Northumberland, travelling to Bury with a group of fellow pilgrims, was miraculously restored to sight after kneeling and praying to St Edmund when the bell tower of the abbey church came into sight across the Suffolk fields.[3]

The perceived power of relics as sites of particular miraculous potency was a persistent and influential trope in the medieval cult of saints. The concept of 'holy radiation', whereby the saint's power was most potent in close proximity to his/her relics, provided the ultimate rationale for medieval pilgrimage, along with the understanding that visiting the saint in person evinced a suitable commitment to, and faith in, the saint's powers. The so-called 'holy hole' at Winchester under the *feretory* platform, which Crook suggests allowed pilgrims to crawl beneath the shrine, 'presumably in order to absorb the holy radiation emanating from Swithun's remains', is a particularly striking example of the belief that proximity to relics was of the highest importance.[4]

The monks of Bury, in common with the keepers of many shrines, were keen to remind the faithful of the benefits of visiting the saint in person, undoubtedly

---

[1] Abbo *Passio*, XVIII; Hervey, *Corolla*, p. 55.
[2] Herman, *De Miraculis*, ed. Arnold, *Memorials*, I, p. 48.
[3] Herman, *De Miraculis*, ed. Arnold, *Memorials*, I, p. 371.
[4] John Crook, 'The Romanesque East Arm and Crypt of Winchester Cathedral', *Journal of the British Archaeological Association* 142 (1989), 1–36; 19.

mindful of the financial rewards this brought to their communities in the form of donations and offerings, and the collections of Edmund's miracles include a number of individuals who appeal for help from afar but are fully healed only when they make the journey to Bury. In this pragmatic context, the trope of visibility in the narrative of the aged Northumbrian is symbolically redolent: 'see' St Edmund and you will see again.

Abbo of Fleury reminds his readers of the mystical confederacy between a saint and his or her remains:

> It is fully proved in his [St Edmund's] case (as in that of all the other saints who already reign with Christ) that though his spirit be in the enjoyment of heavenly glory, yet it has the power to revisit the body and is not by day or night far separated from the place where the body lies, in union with which it has earned the joys of blessed immortality, of which even now it has the fruition.[5]

The notion of Edmund occupying a liminal location between this world and the next is depicted in the last of the Morgan miniatures (New York, Pierpont Morgan Library, MS M. 736, fol. 22v). Crowned by angels leaning down from heaven and venerated by monks reaching up from below, Edmund exists in the space between.

The relationship between the saint and his remains is frequently expressed in Edmund's violent defence of his relics and punishment of those who mistreat them. In an incident analogous to the punishment of the eight thieves who attempted to rob the abbey church, Herman recounts the occasion of an unexpected visit to the abbey by Edward the Confessor. The king brought with him both English and Danish retainers and desired that they should enjoy the abbey's hospitality together.[6] Osgod Clapa, a Danish lord of Edward's household, swaggered into the abbey church the morning after their arrival, adorned with garish jewellery and brandishing his war axe. This disrespectful behaviour offended the saint, and the presence of a Dane arrayed for battle perhaps roused unpleasant memories. Osgod Clapa was struck with madness and King Edward arrived in the church to find his steward raving. The monastic community intervened, praying on behalf of the Dane, and Osgod's composure was restored. In addition to attesting once again to St Edmund's dislike of those who violated the sanctity of his shrine, this episode also emphasises the role of the monastic community in the

---

[5] Abbo *Passio*, XVIII; Hervey, *Corolla*, p. 55.
[6] Herman, *De Miraculis*, ed. Arnold, *Memorials*, I, pp. 54–6.

rehabilitation of the afflicted, offering a further incentive for those who sought Edmund's help to visit the saint in person.

Edmund's enforcement of the highest standards of care of his remains was felt beyond the bounds of the Liberty and helped to ensure its continued independence. Jocelin of Brakelond cites the example of attempts to raise the ransom to free Richard I from imprisonment in Germany (1192–94), when the question of whether St Edmund's shrine should be partly stripped to contribute to the cost was argued before the Barons of the Exchequer. The abbot of Bury refused to grant permission, but invited any who dared to come to the abbey and attempt to remove the precious materials. Each judge replied with an oath: "'I shall not go'; "Nor I. St Edmund vents his rage on the distant and the absent: how much greater will his fury be on those near at hand who seek to rob him of his clothing?'"[7] The chronicler concludes that whilst there was 'not one treasure in England that was not given or exchanged for money', the shrine of St Edmund remained intact.[8]

The importance of the preservation of Edmund's remains to his saintly identity is particularly apparent on occasions when it was called into question. The version of *De Miraculis* commonly attributed to Abbot Samson includes an incident which occurred during the abbacy of Leofstan (1044–65), in which a woman from Winchester who was mute visited Bury in the hope of a cure. She was duly healed by the saint and also visited by him in a series of visions, in which Edmund complained about the monks' neglect of his shrine. Having restored her speech, perhaps to enable her to deliver this envoy, Edmund exhorted the woman to chide the monks on his behalf. In response to her rebuke, Abbot Leofstan undertook to inspect Edmund's remains, perhaps concerned that they, as well as the fabric of the shrine, had suffered. The monk Egelwyn, a former keeper of the shrine who removed the saint's body to London to protect it from the Viking raids of the early eleventh century, now a very old man, was summoned and verified that the corpse was indeed Edmund's. Not content that the corpse appeared intact 'and differed little from a living body', Abbot Leofstan resolved upon another test. Ordering one of the monks, Thurstan, to take hold of the feet, the abbot grasped the head, and the two monks pulled in opposite directions. The corpse remained whole, but Edmund, understandably irked by this impudent rough handling, retaliated: Abbot Leofstan was struck with a temporary blindness and dumbness (wryly appropriate, given the healing of the mute woman which initiated the incident), and suffered a permanent withering of both the hands which he had irreverently placed upon the saint.[9]

---

[7] Jocelin, *Chronicle*, p. 86.
[8] Jocelin, *Chronicle*, p. 86.
[9] Samson, *De Miraculis*, ed. Arnold, *Memorials*, I, pp. 131–4.

An interesting contrast may be seen between this account of the inspection of Edmund's body and a similar moment in the life of St Æthelthryth of Ely. A Danish raider, hearing the legend of Æthelthryth's post-mortem incorruption, made an opening in the shrine and forced a stick inside in order to ascertain the presence of the body.[10] The imagery is redolent of sexual transgression, with the saint's female body vulnerable to penetration. Monika Otter suggests that this is an allegory for the potentially problematic presence of an intact female body in the midst of a male community and is meant as a warning to the monks not to be tempted; this is powerfully reinforced by the blinding of the Dane, who is therefore unable to see the saint's body, let alone touch it.[11] It is notable that whilst similar intrusions are made upon the bodies of Edmund and Æthelthryth, it is only in relation to the latter that the language of sexual transgression is deployed. Once again, Edmund's corporeal presence is seen as unproblematic and advantageous for his guardian community, in comparison to that of his female Fenland neighbour.

The incorrupt body

In Edmund's case, the physical prestige of his relics was two-fold: Bury claimed to possess the entire corpse (along with various secondary relics) and attested to the lack of decay and continued preservation of the corpse.[12] The claim that the body was intact was doubly significant: it indicated Edmund's chastity and was also a signifier of his special merit. Æthelthryth similarly evinced her chastity through bodily incorruption and the miraculous post-mortem healing of a wound to the neck. However, her wound was an incision made by a surgeon's knife in an attempt to drain a suppurating growth, presumably a cut made with skill or at least great care, and its healing would not be medically unprecedented. In contrast, Edmund's head was completely severed by the slashing swords of the Danes. It is tempting to read this as another instance of hagiographic 'one-upmanship' in relation to Bury's neighbours at Ely.

---

[10] *Liber Eliensis*, ed. E.O. Blake, Camden Third Series, 92 (London: Royal Historical Society, 1962), pp. 55–6 and 229 (the incident is recounted twice).

[11] Monika Otter, 'The Temptation of St Æthelthryth', *Exemplaria* 9 (1997), 139–63. See also Blanton, *Signs of Devotion*, pp. 137–8.

[12] Norman Scarfe has suggested that Edmund's apparent bodily incorruption, and indeed that of many other medieval saints described as enjoying similar preservation, may in fact have been the result of embalming or some other similar preservative technique. A useful survey of the evidence is Norman Scarfe, 'The Body of St Edmund: An Essay in Necrobiography', *Proceedings of the Suffolk Institute of Archaeology* xxxi (1969), 303–17. Edmund's intact body is depicted in Harley 2278, fol. 117.

The prevalence of miracles concerning the preservation of Edmund's body attests to the value placed upon this element of Edmund's sanctity by the Bury monks. The most vivid and compelling example is Jocelin of Brakelond's account of the fire which devastated the abbey church in June 1198.[13] The extent of the damage was such that it was necessary to construct a new shrine casing, in which the relics were placed on 22 November of the same year. However, unbeknownst (as he thought) to the convent, Abbot Samson took this opportunity to examine Edmund's remains. Three days later, in the dead of night 'while the convent slept', Abbot Samson and fourteen specially selected monks, vested in albs, made their way through the dark of the abbey church to the presbytery. Proceeding to Edmund's shrine, they removed the heavy panels of precious metal and lifted out the coffin, placing it carefully on a nearby table. They prised out the sixteen long nails which secured the lid and opened the casket to reveal a shrouded corpse which Jocelin claims fitted 'so perfectly' within the coffin, both in length and in breadth, 'that a needle could scarcely have been inserted between the wood and either the head or the feet'. Ordering all but the Sacrist and Walter the Physician, the two senior monks in attendance, to stand back, Abbot Samson stepped forward and began carefully to remove the wrappings which covered the corpse:

> The abbot, then, looking closely, first came upon a silk cloth covering the whole body, and after that a linen cloth of wonderful whiteness, and over the head a small linen cloth, and then another fine-spun silk cloth, like the veil of a nun. And after that they found the corpse wrapped in linen, and then at last all the features of the Saint's body were visible.[14]

The tension of the moment is evident in Jocelin's breathless stream of conjunctions: when confronted with the martyred king, Abbot Samson was filled with misgiving, perhaps remembering the fate of his predecessor, Abbot Leofstan (1044–65). Having reassured the saint that his intentions were entirely devout, he cautiously proceeded to examine the body, touching St Edmund's eyes and his 'very large and prominent nose', feeling his breast and his arms, and raising his left hand and placing his fingers between the saint's. He counted the toes upon feet which he found to be 'stiffly upright, as of a man who had died that very day'. The head was securely joined to the body, and a little raised on a small cushion. In order to verify his inspection he called forth six of the monks, whereupon the others also rushed forward to witness the 'marvels' within the coffin. This done, they re-wrapped the body as they had found it and returned it to the shrine, atop

---

[13] Jocelin, *Chronicle*, pp. 94–102.
[14] Jocelin, *Chronicle*, p. 100.

a 'precious new silk cloth' given to the abbey that year by Archbishop Hubert of Canterbury. When the coffin had been transferred to the new shrine three days before, 'a golden angel the length of a man's foot' bearing a golden sword in one hand and a banner in the other had been found attached to the coffin above Edmund's heart, with an inscription above the figure identifying him as St Michael whose image 'guards the sacred corpse'. Next to the golden angel the abbot now placed a silk box containing a 'parchment document written in English' by Egelwyn, a previous guardian of the shrine, to which the abbot added an account of the night's events and the findings of the inspection. Jocelin notes that immediately beneath the image of St Michael was an opening in the coffin lid through which he claims previous wardens of the shrine would touch the body, presumably to ascertain its continuing presence and preservation, all the while prevented from wrong-doing by the protective presence of the archangel. Jocelin also adds the curious observation that at each end of the coffin were two iron rings, which he likens to those found 'on a Norse chest', a particularly interesting detail considering the perpetrators of Edmund's demise and speculation as to the initial promotion of his cult in Danish-ruled East Anglia.[15] Following the placing of the documents, the panels were carefully reattached to the shrine and Edmund was once more left in peace.

Clearly determined to preserve the abbey's investment in the new shrine and its precious contents, Abbot Samson appointed new wardens and devised regulations 'for the better and more diligent care of the sanctuaries'. It was also at this time that the area between the shrine and the high altar, previously covered by the wooden dais which had been ignited by untended candles, was filled with stone and cement to prevent the risk of fire in the future. Although ultimately blaming the fire upon the lax management of the custodians, Jocelin of Brakelond indicates that an alternative explanation for the blaze was disseminated in the aftermath which attributed it to Edmund's dissatisfaction at the care afforded to him by the monks. Jocelin recounts that an unknown 'distinguished person' experienced a vision in which 'the holy martyr Edmund appeared to be lying outside his shrine, groaning, and seemed to say that he had been robbed of his clothes, and that he was emaciated from hunger and thirst, and that his burial-place and the portals of his church were badly cared for'. Abbot Samson concluded that the saint had caused the fire to chastise the monks for their laxity in charitable giving and care of the poor. The brethren, however, favoured an alternative explanation, blaming Samson's reforms for reducing the standard of living within the monastery by

---

[15] H.E. Butler suggests that this may have been a gift from the archbishop of Trondheim, who visited the abbey in 1181/82. *The Chronicle of Jocelin of Brakelond*, ed. and trans. H.E. Butler (London and Edinburgh: Nelson's Medieval Classics, 1949, rpt 1951), p. 15.

removing many of their privileges and placing the chamber, sacristy and cellary under direct abbatial control, with the result that they were 'dying of hunger and thirst'.[16] A delegation sent to the abbot bemoaned their condition, claiming 'we ... are the naked limbs of St Edmund, and the convent is his naked body, because we have been robbed of our ancient customs and liberties'.[17] Although exploited here towards political ends, the extent to which Edmund's saintly identity was constructed and defined in terms of the convent's, and *vice versa*, is striking.

It is unlikely to be coincidental that the incident involving Abbot Leofstan is first recorded in the miracle collection compiled during Samson's abbacy. Leofstan acts as a useful antetype, whose mistreatment of Edmund and subsequent punishment contrasted with Samson's own careful handling and justified his reforms. Locating the first examination in a historically distant period also serves to emphasise the antiquity of the miracle. The fire supposedly caused by Edmund facilitated Samson's refurbishment of the abbey and its timely nature must have been seen as a further indication that Samson was acting in the saint's favour. Both incidents reinforce that paying due respect to Edmund and his physical remains was of the utmost importance. The monks' interpretation of the vision reported to Samson also reveals the symbiotic nature of the relationship between St Edmund and his monastic guardians: just as he expected them to look after him, he also felt their pains when they were mistreated; the monks were the limbs of St Edmund who acted on his behalf in the world, but they were also his protective clothing and nourishment. The anxiety surrounding the condition of Edmund's remains, evinced in the various examinations undertaken, thus reiterates their fundamental importance to the cult at Bury.

Invention and translation: 'Sutton' to Beodricesworth

Bury St Edmunds is the primary site associated with Edmund's cult, but before exploring in detail the nature of the pilgrimage experience at Bury it is important to note that this was not the location of St Edmund's initial burial.[18] Abbo claims that once the Danish army had retreated, Edmund's surviving Christian followers retrieved his severed head from the wolf assiduously guarding it and reunited it with his body, to which it was miraculously rejoined. They buried the now intact corpse in the woods near the site of his demise.[19] According to Abbo, the East

---

[16] For Samson's reforms see Jocelin, *Chronicle*, pp. 96–8 and Gransden, *A History of the Abbey*, pp. 23–31.
[17] Jocelin, *Chronicle*, p. 97.
[18] For a summary of the ongoing debate surrounding the location of the martyrdom see above, Introduction, p. oo.
[19] Abbo *Passio*, XIV; Hervey, *Corolla*, pp. 43–5.

Anglians erected a 'chapel of rude construction' over Edmund's grave, where his body rested undisturbed for 'many years'.[20] However, once the 'conflagration of war and the mighty storms of persecution were over', the people of East Anglia turned their attention to the resting place of their erstwhile king. A bright light could be seen emanating from the chapel, and miracles were reported to have occurred. Although Abbo does not elaborate upon the nature of these miraculous happenings, the version of *De Miraculis* commonly attributed to Abbot Samson cites a particular occurrence as the decisive moment in the establishment of Edmund's miracle-working reputation. A blind man, led by his boy, had taken shelter in the wooden hut containing the tomb. Suddenly, a bright light filled the chapel, whereupon the blind man recovered his sight.[21] Abbo reports that as news of this wondrous occurrence spread, the people of East Anglia built a church at Beodricesworth (the name of the settlement which later became known as Bury St Edmunds, or 'St Edmund's burgh') of 'immense size, with storeys admirably constructed of wood'.[22] Edmund's remains were translated to Beodricesworth with 'great magnificence', and upon the opening of the coffin the body was found to be intact and uncorrupted, despite the passing of many years.[23] Edmund's intercessory ability was thus firmly established. The significance of this event is reflected by its illustration in one of the Pierpont Morgan initials (New York, Pierpont Morgan Library, MS M. 736, fol. 26v), one of the few narrative scenes which accompanies the *miracula*.

The translation of Edmund's body was fundamental to the establishment of his saintly credentials. Prior to the controls over the canonisation process exerted by the papacy from the twelfth century, the act of translation was closely bound up with the proclamation of an individual's sanctity, with the physical act of moving their bodily remains to a new location symbolically representing and attesting to their new spiritual status.[24] Translation frequently involved elevation as well as relocation, the rationale for which may clearly be seen in the indignant complaint of the chronicler reflecting on the delay in the translation of St Erkenwald's remains, who protests that 'someone who shines forth so gloriously in the heavens should surely not be buried in such a foul garment as the earth'.[25] Ben

---

[20] Abbo *Passio*, XIV; Hervey, *Corolla*, p. 45.
[21] Samson, *De Miraculis*, ed. Arnold, *Memorials*, I, 109–10.
[22] Abbo *Passio*, XIV; Hervey, *Corolla*, p. 45.
[23] Abbo *Passio*, XIV–XV; Hervey, *Corolla*, pp. 45–7.
[24] For papal controls over canonisation see Eric W. Kemp, *Canonization and Authority in the Western Church* (London: Oxford University Press, 1948).
[25] *The Saint of London: The Life and Miracles of St Erkenwald*, ed. and trans. E. Gordon Whately (Binghamton, New York: Medieval and Renaissance Texts and Studies, 1989), pp. 119–20.

Nilson notes that although high-status tombs in general became taller and more elaborate during the course of the Middle Ages, to the extent that architecturally and artistically they came to rival shrines, the bodies of the non-saintly usually remained buried beneath the level of the floor, with the elaborate tombs serving as coverings rather than containers.[26] This reflects the desire of the devout to honour the bodies of the sacred dead, removing them from the all-too-temporal muck eloquently described by Erkenwald's chronicler. Physical elevation is indicative of spiritual status, as the saints are both physically and morally closer to God. They occupy a liminal location, with their elevation above the earth symbolising their triumph over worldly concerns, but the resting place of their remains upon a shrine base retaining their connection with the world of their devotees, ensuring the saint's ability to hear the prayers of the faithful and intercede on their behalf.

Edmund's first translation must have taken place in the earlier part of the tenth century, as, in 945, Edmund, king of England (939–46) and namesake of the East Anglian martyr, donated the town of Beodricesworth to the church of St Edmund, making it one of the richest in the country. In 1020 King Cnut, perhaps in an act of expiation for the murder perpetrated by his Viking ancestors, and possibly in fear of the saint's supposed role in the death of his father, Sweyn, sanctioned the replacement of the community of secular priests with Benedictine monks. He also initiated the building of a new church for the monastery, or at least the extension of the existing one, which was consecrated by Archbishop Æthelnoth in 1032.[27]

In common with many saints, Edmund was re-translated on a number of occasions. After the Conquest, Abbot Baldwin began work on a grand new church, whence Edmund's relics were translated on 29 April 1095, presided over by Walkelin, bishop of Winchester (d.1098) and Ranulf Flambard (c.1060–1128).[28] The major part of the Romanesque building was probably completed by 1142, and whilst alterations and additions were made throughout the following centuries, the Romanesque fabric remained the core of the church.[29] Edmund's translation took place in the context of the consecration of many of the great Anglo-Norman churches, accompanied by the translation of relics: St Augustine's, Canterbury

---

[26] Ben Nilson, *Cathedral Shrines of Medieval England* (Woodbridge: The Boydell Press, 1998), p. 18.

[27] This is stated in one of the marginal notes in the Easter Tables, opposite years 1032–35, in the mid-eleventh-century Bury Psalter, now MS Reg. Lat. 12 in the Vatican Library, f. 17v. Cited in Gransden, *A History of the Abbey*, p. 106.

[28] Herman, *De Miraculis*, ed. Arnold, *Memorials*, I, pp. 86–91.

[29] See Eric Fernie, 'The Romanesque Church of Bury St Edmunds Abbey', *BAA: Bury*, pp. 1–15.

received numerous relics in 1091;[30] several years earlier, in 1088, Paulinus was translated into the new cathedral of Rochester;[31] Winchester was consecrated in 1095, although the translation of St Swithin was delayed for several months.[32] The translation of saints as a result of building campaigns was often a matter of architectural necessity, as the new layout and dimensions might not accommodate the saint in his or her previous shrine, and a new site might be desirable in order to facilitate pilgrimage. Such events were also highly symbolic. Nilson suggests that when a disruption in the history of a church occurred, particularly in the wake of the Norman invasion, its shrine became a locus of nostalgic identity:

> The new ecclesiastical hierarchy linked itself to the holiness and prestige of its Anglo-Saxon predecessors by ostentatiously translating the old saints into newly re-built churches. They thereby acquired the saint as patron and linked themselves with the entire history of the see and its possessions, negating the discontinuity of tradition and reaffirming the ancient heritage of the church.[33]

Thus it was not just the location to which the saint was moved that was significant, but the implied authority this bestowed upon those initiating the translation. This is reiterated by the numerous examples of translations which are described as being carried out against the wishes of the saint or in an inappropriate fashion. In one instance in late twelfth-century Worcester a number of people are reported to have experienced visions of St Wulfstan (c.1008–95) demanding that his body be translated. Believing he was enacting the saint's wishes, one night in 1198 Bishop John (1196–98) opened the tomb in the presence of the convent and placed the bones in a newly prepared shrine and the accompanying vestments and ornaments in another. However, John died three weeks later, and the saint appeared in a vision to explain that this was punishment for carrying out the translation without papal approval and without due reverence.[34] Whilst this says as much about increasing papal control over canonisation (the translation took place five

---

[30] The translations were described by Goscelin of Saint-Bertin, 'Historia translationis Sancti Augustini Episcopi', ed. Jacques-Paul Migne, *Patrologia Latina*, clv, cols 33–4.

[31] J. Philip McAleer, *Rochester Cathedral, 604–1540: An Architectural History* (Toronto, Buffalo and London: University of Toronto Press, 1999), pp. 17, 45.

[32] John Crook, 'St Swithun of Winchester', in *Winchester Cathedral: Nine Hundred Years, 1093–1993*, ed. John Crook (Chichester: Phillimore, 1993), pp. 57–68.

[33] Nilson, *Cathedral Shrines*, p. 19. See also Paul A. Hayward, 'Translation-narratives in Post-Conquest Hagiography and English Resistance to the Norman Conquest', *Anglo-Norman Studies* xxi (1999), 67–93.

[34] This incident is cited in Emma Mason, *St Wulfstan of Worcester, c.1008–1095* (Oxford: Basil Blackwell Ltd, 1990), p. 278.

years before Wulfstan's formal recognition as a saint and was therefore not officially sanctioned), it also serves to illustrate the important symbolic function of translation, as, if the saint in question objected, then the consequences were likely to be dire; a similar dialectic is in operation when Edmund intervenes to prevent his forced translation, amounting to kidnap, by the bishop of London.[35]

Although the location of Edmund's initial burial remains uncertain, more is known about the placement of his remains once they were removed to Beodricsworth. His corpse, along with the *'bera'* (bier) upon which it had been transported, was housed in a *rotunda* in the monks' cemetery. A *rotunda* is a circular chapel particularly associated with *mausolea*, places of burial. Inspired by the circular shape of the Church of the Holy Sepulchre in Jerusalem, this architectural form was symbolically redolent. Commonly associated with the church built by Cnut which was accommodated into Baldwin's Romanesque church, it stood in the angle between the north transept and the choir until it was demolished in 1275 to make way for the building of the new Lady Chapel founded by Simon de Luton (1257–79). Edmund's body was by this time in the presbytery and the secondary relics remaining in the *rotunda* were removed to a chapel in the monks' cemetery to the south of the abbey church.[36] A circular, centrally planned church was a relatively common form for a royal mausoleum or *martyrium*, the former based upon the prototype of the imperial chapel at Aachen and the latter derived from the Holy Sepulchre in Jerusalem.[37] As Gransden notes, a circular chapel was therefore particularly appropriate for St Edmund's remains, invoking simultaneously two fundamental elements of his sanctity within its architectural form.[38]

Upon the completion and dedication of Abbot Baldwin's great Romanesque church, Edmund's body was translated into the presbytery, the usual setting for a major shrine. Despite a series of remodellings and replacements, it is apparent that the shrine remained in this location for the remainder of the life of the abbey.[39] In common with the placing of shrines in most Anglo-Norman churches, Edmund was housed behind the high altar.[40] In his account of the fire of 23 June 1198, Jocelin of Brakelond mentions that a great rood beam, which supported reliquaries and from which reliquaries were also suspended, had 'by God's will'

---

[35] Arnold, *Memorials*, I, pp. 45, 123–5.
[36] 'rotunde capelle S. Eadmundi in cimiterio monachorum ex parte aquilonali presbiterii, in quo corpus S. Eadmundi requieuit ante translacionem suam', College of Arms, MS Arundel 30, fol. 8v. See also *Bury Chronicle*, p. 58.
[37] See Richard Gem, 'Towards an Iconography of Anglo-Saxon Architecture', *Journal of the Warburg and Courtauld Institutes* 46 (1983), 1–18; 9–12.
[38] Gransden, *A History of The Abbey*, p. 107.
[39] See *Incendium Ecclesiae*, ed. Arnold, *Memorials*, III, pp. 283–7.
[40] On the positioning of shrines see Nilson, *Cathedral Shrines*, pp. 63–73.

been removed to be renovated with new carvings and replaced with a curtain which was destroyed in the fire.[41] John Crook suggests that the beam is most likely to have been supported on the chord piers of the apse, allowing the shrine to be more precisely located.[42]

The architecture of pilgrimage

Saints' shrines were potent locations reverberating with the hopes and expectations of those who sought divine assistance or came to give thanks for help already received. In addition to the emotional impact of visiting a shrine, the physical experience would have transcended the normal frame of reference for almost all pilgrims. As mentioned above, the abbey church at Bury was the third-longest Romanesque building in northern Europe, surpassed only by the churches of Cluny and Winchester.[43] For the majority of medieval pilgrims this would be the largest building they would ever encounter.

The scale of the church was matched by its architectural and artistic splendour. Pilgrims entering the monastic precinct from the west would pass beneath the imposing 5.86m (19ft 3 in) wide gateway of St James' tower. This grand entrance was undoubtedly designed to impress and mark the significance of the transition from the temporal world beyond the gates to the spiritual realm within: pilgrims passed from darkness beneath the tower into the light of the western courtyard, where they were confronted by the extraordinarily large western front of the abbey church.[44] At around 73m (240ft) it was almost twice the width of Winchester (39m/128ft), the only British church larger overall than Bury.[45] J. Philip McAleer claims that the west front at Bury was 'perhaps the most complex façade structure ever built in Britain or, indeed, on the Continent'.[46] There were three main elements: a west transept with an axial crossing tower, flanking double-storied chapel blocks and flanking octagons. The design is unusual: McAleer notes that a west transept is found at only four other churches in Britain: Ely, Kelso, Kilwinning and Peterborough. The axial west tower is similarly rare and found only at Ely and

---

[41] Jocelin, *Chronicle*, p. 95
[42] John Crook, 'The Architectural Setting of the Cult of St Edmund in the Abbey Church, 1095–1539', in *BAA: Bury*, pp. 34–44; p. 38.
[43] For comparative figures see Eric Fernie, *The Architecture of Norman England* (Oxford: Oxford University Press, 2002) Appendix 1: Dimensions, pp. 304–5.
[44] For the symbolic significance of doorways see M. Cecilia Gaposchkin, 'Portals, Processions, Pilgrimage and Piety: Saints Firmin and Honoré at Amiens', in *Art and Architecture*, 2 vols, ed. Blick and Tekippe, pp. 217–42.
[45] Fernie, *Architecture*, Appendix 1: Dimensions, pp. 304–5.
[46] J. Philip McAleer, 'The West Front of the Abbey Church', *BAA: Bury*, pp. 22–33; p. 22.

Kelso. The rarity of axial towers on major churches before the Gothic period leads McAleer to suggest that Bury was making a particular architectural statement. He notes that single axial towers are more commonly associated with Anglo-Saxon churches and postulates that by adopting this form Bury sought to remind viewers of the community's pre-Conquest heritage.[47] Chapel blocks of this type associated with a west front are not found elsewhere in Britain; the closest comparisons are the comparatively modest two-storey chapels opening directly off the transept arms at Ely. The flanking octagons are even more unusual and seem to be unique to Bury.[48] The architectural form of the abbey church was thus distinctive and designed to impress. This is exemplified by various changes made to the layout of the church after building had begun which resulted in an irregular floor plan, including the departure of the line of the arcade wall northwards from the axis of the church by three degrees and the lengthening of the presbytery and the addition of an aisle to the east of the transepts. Fernie suggests that this is unlikely to be erroneous and instead resulted from a deliberate decision to widen the nave and aisles and lengthen the presbytery in order to ensure that the dimensions of the abbey church surpassed those of long-term rival Norwich, where work on the new cathedral began in 1096.[49]

In addition to the architectural magnificence of the west front, the details of its embellishment were also redolent with symbolism. Particularly striking would have been the pair of great bronze doors which are recorded in the *Gesta Sacristarum* as being made by Master Hugo (fl. c.1130–50) during the abbacy of Anselm (1121–48) when Ralph and Hervey were sacrists:

> Double doors in the front of the church were sculpted by the hands [lit. 'fingers'] of Master Hugo, who in other works surpassed all others, in this magnificent work he surpassed himself.[50]

No other bronze doors are known in England from this period, prompting speculation as to Master Hugo's origins and the model upon which the doors were based.[51] Although it is not known which abbey first installed bronze doors, the

---

[47] McAleer, 'The West Front', p. 29.
[48] For further details see McAleer, 'The West Front', pp. 23–9.
[49] Fernie, 'The Romanesque Church', pp. 1–15; esp. 8–12. See also Stephen Heywood, 'Aspects of the Romanesque Church of Bury St Edmunds in their Regional Context', *BAA: Bury*, pp. 16–21; esp. 19–21.
[50] *Gesta Sacristarum*, Arnold, *Memorials*, II, 289–90.
[51] James notes that bronze doors seem to have been more common in southern Italy and suggests that Anselm may have been seeking to emulate examples he encountered whilst abbot of St Saba's, where he possibly met Master Hugo and subsequently brought

commissioning of a similar pair for Saint-Denis by Abbot Suger (1122–51) attests to their association with high-status royal shrines. Suger's commentary on the 'cast and gilded doors' explains their symbolic significance, which at Saint-Denis was conveyed to pilgrims by inscriptions:

> Whosoever thou art, if thou seekest to extol the glory of these doors,
> Marvel not at the gold and the expense but at the craftsmanship of the work,
> Bright is the noble work; but, being nobly bright, the work
> Should brighten the minds, so that they may travel, through the true lights,
> To the True Light where Christ is the true door.
> In what manner it be inherent in this world the golden door defines:
> The dull mind rises to truth through that which is material
> And, in seeing this light, is resurrected from its former submersion.[52]

It is probable that the doors at Bury were similarly gilded. The gilding is particularly significant as it represents the light of God by which the minds of pilgrims are illuminated and brought to truth. At Bury this would be particularly effective as pilgrims emerged from the darkness beneath St James' gate to be confronted with the blazing brightness of the doors.

The shrine

The sensory spectacle was sustained as pilgrims entered the abbey church, whereupon they encountered a multitude of sights and sounds and smells. Although it is not always possible to ascertain the individual motivations of those who visited the abbey of Bury St Edmunds and made offerings at its altars and shrines, for the majority St Edmund is likely to have been the main attraction. The focus of cultic practice at Bury, as at many other pilgrimage sites, was the shrine of the saintly patron. Simon Coleman and John Eade explain that the presence of a

---

him to Bury (James, *On the Abbey Church*, p. 128). In contrast, Zarnecki suggests that Master Hugo originated from Lower Lorraine. Bronze doors are not known in this region but some have been related to Mosan art (George Zarnecki, *English Romanesque Lead Sculpture: Lead Fonts of the Twelfth Century* (London: Alec Tiranti, 1957), pp. 7–8, 25 n. 11). The debate is summarised by Elizabeth C. Parker, 'Master Hugo as Sculptor: A Source for the Style of the Bury Bible', *Gesta* 20.1 (1981): Essays in Honour of Harry Bober, 99–109; 99–100. For the bronze doors in the context of other metalworking at Bury see Marian Campbell, 'Medieval Metalworking and Bury St Edmunds', *BAA: Bury*, pp. 69–80.

[52] Abbot Suger, *On the Abbey Church of Saint-Denis and its Art Treasures*, ed. and trans. Erwin Panofsky (Princeton, NJ: Princeton University Press, 1948), pp. 47–9.

physical object embodying the cultic figure is an important aspect of the pilgrimage experience:

> The culmination of most acts of pilgrimage is arrival at a sacredly charged space ... The pilgrim knows that the spiritual summit of the journey has been reached because the sacred is not simply focused in a specifically marked area, but more particularly is embodied by a specific object or set of objects.[53]

As the container which protected these potent relics from harm and the public gaze, the shrine was the physical manifestation of the wonders within. Blick and Tekippe suggest that this endowed reliquary shrines with authority in their own right.[54] The often lavish materials from which a shrine was constructed displayed the power of the sainted individual within but were also instrumental in shaping the psychological response of a pilgrim. This was recognised by medieval shrine custodians, and is perhaps most eloquently expressed by Abbot Suger:

> The material – gold and precious stones – clothe the object in light, and reflect or make manifest the transcendent, invisible, and all-powerful nature of visibility ... Thus, when – out of delight in the beauty of the house of God – the loveliness of the many-coloured gems has called me away from external cares, and worthy meditation has induced me to reflect, transferring that which is material to that which is immaterial, on the diversity of the sacred virtues: then it seems to me that I see myself dwelling, as it were, in some strange region of the universe which neither exists entirely in the slime of the earth nor entirely in the purity of Heaven; and that, by the grace of God, I can be transported from this inferior to that higher world in an anagogic manner.[55]

The appearance and physical splendour of the shrine were therefore fundamental aspects of the pilgrimage experience. As Blick and Tekippe affirm, pilgrimage was an overwhelmingly sensory experience:

> The story of pilgrimage and its practice cannot be told without thoughtful consideration of the visual culture developed to enhance and propagate the cults of saints in Europe. These physical objects helped the pilgrim to

---

[53] Simon Coleman and John Elsner, *Pilgrimage; Past and Present: Sacred Travel and Sacred Space in the World Religions* (London: British Museum Press, 1995), p. 48.
[54] Blick and Tekippe, *Art and Architecture*, I, 'Introduction', xxv.
[55] Abbot Suger, *On the Abbey Church of St Denis*, pp. 63–5.

experience the sacred place. Certain aspects of pilgrimage sites signalled nuances of meaning and importance to visitors. The architectural forms, shrines, altars, wall paintings, stained glass, and sculpture coalesced; dignifying and enhancing the sacred spaces, thereby eliciting appropriate responses from devotees.[56]

Ostensibly, reconstructing the appearance of Edmund's shrine should be readily achievable as no fewer than twelve of the miniatures accompanying Lydgate's *Lives* include a visual depiction.[57] Nicholas Rogers suggests that they chart the development of the shrine during the later Middle Ages and are of particular use, due to the lack of documentary evidence for the shrine during this period.[58] However, the majority are representations of the shrine at various stages in its history up to the translation of 1095. Only two miniatures purport to be contemporary representation in the 1430s: fol. 4v depicts the youthful Henry VI praying before the shrine, and fol. 9 depicts Lydgate likewise engaged. The general lack of period-specific depictions must raise the question of the reliability of the artist's information for the appearance of the shrine during the preceding four centuries.

In her discussion of depictions of the shrine of Thomas Becket on medieval pilgrim badges Sarah Blick poses similar questions as to the accuracy of artistic representations:

> Many medieval artists were not interested in the specifics of the shrine [of Thomas Becket at Canterbury]; rather their goal was to render an ideal 'shrine', either because they had not actually seen it or because an accurate depiction was unimportant.[59]

She concludes that the purpose of such an image was not verisimilitude, as only a 'general notion of 'shrine' was required' in order to fulfil the function of a pilgrim souvenir.[60] As we have seen, one of Lydgate's stated aims for his *Lives* was to act as a 'remembraunce' of Henry VI's stay at Bury, thus fulfilling a similar function to a pilgrim badge in textual form. In this context it is likely that a

---

[56] Blick and Tekippe, eds, *Art and Architecture*, 'Introduction', xvi.
[57] These may be found on: fol. 4v, Henry VI kneeling before the shrine; fol. 9, Lydgate praying at the shrine; fols 100v, 106, 108v, 109, 110v, 112v, 113v, 114v, 115, 117.
[58] Nicholas Rogers, 'The Bury Artists of Harley 2278 and the Origins of Topographical Awareness in English Art', in *BAA: Bury*, pp. 219–27.
[59] Sarah Blick, 'Reconstructing the Shrine of St Thomas Becket, Canterbury Cathedral', in *Art and Architecture*, ed. Blick and Tekippe, pp. 405–42; pp. 412–13.
[60] Blick, 'Reconstructing the Shrine', p. 419.

precise representation of the shrine, particularly as it appeared centuries prior to the young king's visit, was not of primary importance. Henry had seen the shrine recently and could reasonably be expected to remember what it looked like; instead it was intended to provoke a more affective response, encouraging Henry to remember his experience of the shrine and its patron and monastic guardians. Maintaining the general visual consistency of the depiction ensured immediate recognition and identification. The miniatures are probably therefore most useful as an indicator of the mid-fifteenth-century convent's perception of the glory and splendour of the shrine and of its attempts to impress this upon an important patron.

The early origin and development of shrines in England related to the structure of tombs and burial practices. Burial within a church was reserved for those of the highest status, with tombs eventually developing into rectilinear stone or wooden chests on the floor of the church, sometimes surmounted by a gabled roof, attested to by Bede in his description of the burial place of St Chad as 'a wooden coffin in the shape of a little house'.[61] Elevation of the bodies of sainted individuals became increasingly common so that shrines, comprising two parts, the *feretory* and the base, became distinct from tomb chests and marked out their inhabitants as especially deserving of veneration.[62]

Jocelin provides an indication of the structure of the base of Edmund's shrine. He recounts an incident from Abbot Samson's younger years when, following a failed mission to Rome on behalf of the abbey, he was so fearful of the abbot's retribution that when he returned to Bury he took refuge 'under St Edmund's shrine'.[63] This suggests that it took the common form of a *foramina* tomb, an architectural design which featured a superstructure pierced with holes or with niches which enabled the faithful to gain closer access to the reliquary above in order to benefit from the 'holy radiation' of the remains, as illustrated in the well-known image from the Anglo-Norman verse *Life of St Edward the Confessor*, written in England in the late 1230s or early 1240s.[64] The tomb of Thomas Becket in the crypt at Canterbury Cathedral was encased in this type of structure, and the remains of a similar example at Salisbury, wherein St Osmund was enshrined, are extant.[65]

---

[61] Bede, *Ecclesiastical History*, ed. McClure and Collins, IV.3, p. 178.
[62] For the development of tomb forms and burial practices see Nilson, *Cathedral Shrines*, pp. 34–5.
[63] Jocelin, *Chronicle*, pp. 43–5; p. 44.
[64] Cambridge University Library, Ms. Ee.3.59, fol. 33r. For *foramina* shrines see Nilson, *Cathedral Shrines*, pp. 44–5.
[65] D. Stroud, 'The Cult and Tombs of St Osmund at Salisbury', *The Wiltshire Archaeological and Natural History Magazine* 78 (1984), 50–2.

The other component of greater shrines was the *feretory* or *feretrum*, a term which could refer to various related objects but most commonly pertained to a house-shaped reliquary chest, with a gabled, often ridged, roof: an embellishment on the idea of a coffin. Descriptions of the artwork of English *feretra* are rare, but the most common decorative scheme seems to have been images of the life of the saint on the sides of the *feretory*, with more universal Christian images occupying each end. Although there is no record of the overall scheme which decorated Edmund's shrine, Jocelin implies that in part at least it conformed to this pattern: an image of Christ in Majesty adorned the front of the shrine and Jocelin reports that whilst the silver panels became loose and most of the stones fell out as a result of the fire, the 'golden Majesty' remained stable and intact, and was 'more beautiful after the fire than before, because it was solid gold'.[66] Rogers suggests that the overall appearance of the shrine may have resembled early Mosan work, a style of ornamentation associated with Netherlandish Romanesque art and architecture of particularly high quality, such as the shrine of St Hadelin at Visé.[67] No pre-Reformation English *feretra* survive, but evidence suggests similarity in shape and detail with Continental examples, and also indicates relative continuity and uniformity in form throughout the Middle Ages. The size of a *feretory* could vary according to the nature of the relics it housed, with an incorrupt body such as Edmund's requiring larger accommodation than a portion of a saint or a collection of disarticulated bones. Nilson suggests that a *feretory* for an intact adult corpse would be at least 160cm long, and probably 40–60cm wide.[68] The basic structure of the *feretory* was usually wooden and was decorated according to the wealth of the shrine and its patrons, with more modest shrines painted and sometimes gilded, and the more elaborate encased in precious metal. The decoration of Edmund's shrine clearly reflected his elevated saintly status, as Jocelin recounts that it was encased in sheets of silver affixed with nails and encrusted with precious stones, many likely to have been gifts from wealthy patrons in thanks for a cure or in hope of securing assistance. Precious stones were believed to possess magical properties, particularly those of healing, and in addition to their obvious aesthetic attraction their perceived innate qualities added to the allure of the *feretory* which they adorned.[69]

Such richly ornamented shrines were tempting targets for thieves, as attested by a number of Edmund's most wrathful miraculous interventions. Although he

---

[66] Jocelin, *Chronicle*, p. 95.
[67] Hanns Swarzenski, *Monuments of Romanesque Art: The Art of Church Treasures in North-West Europe* (London: Faber and Faber, 1954), fig. 226, pp. 349–51; Peter Lasko, *Ars Sacra, 800–1200* (Harmondsworth: Penguin Books, 1972), pp. 181–4, pls 195–7.
[68] Nilson, *Cathedral Shrines*, p. 35.
[69] Nilson, *Cathedral Shrines*, p. 38; cf. *Miracula Erkenwaldi*, p. 220 n. 27

proved himself willing and able to defend his remains, it seems that the monks of Bury sought to assist their saintly patron in deterring intruders. The Harley 2278 miniature of Lydgate praying before the shrine (fol. 9) depicts an iron grille running between circular piers, partitioning the sanctuary from the ambulatory, for which there is archaeological evidence.[70] Defences of this kind, particularly iron grilles or fences, were a commonly employed means of protecting the shrine and its contents.[71] Security was a serious concern and in some places a watching loft was installed which enabled the guardians of the shrine to observe pilgrims and ensure correct behaviour; examples are extant at Peterborough and St Albans. It is unknown whether such an arrangement pertained at Bury, but fols. 9 and 109 of Harley 2278 show two monastic custodians, with the former also depicting a lay figure in a furred blue gown, a book open on his lap as he observes the shrine. He bears a white wand which may suggests that he was employed to point out the salient features of the architecture and iconography, but he may equally have been required to maintain order amongst visiting pilgrims.[72]

It has been suggested that Henry III gave another entirely new shrine in 1269, although this seems to be based upon an erroneous observation made by J.C. Wall,[73] and Rogers maintains that this in fact relates to the shrine of St Edward the Confessor.[74] It is certainly the case, however, that a number of significant modifications were made over the years, affecting, intentionally or otherwise, the experience of a visiting pilgrim. In the late 1190s, for example, Abbot Samson embarked on a campaign of rebuilding and renovation of the precinct and church. In particular, Samson 'concentrated all his efforts on making a most precious canopy above the shrine of the glorious martyr Edmund, so that his work of art would be put in a position from which it could in no circumstances be taken down, and where no man would dare lay a hand on it'.[75] By the later Middle Ages

---

[70] Arthur B. Whittingham, *Bury St Edmunds Abbey, Suffolk* (London: Her Majesty's Stationery Office, 1971), p. 13.

[71] For the grille at St Albans see Martin Biddle, 'Remembering St Alban: The Site of the Shrine and the Discovery of the twelfth-century Purbeck Marble Shrine Table', in *Alban and St Albans: Roman and Medieval Architecture, Art and Archaeology*, ed. Martin Henig and Phillip Lindley, British Archaeological Association Conference Transactions xxiv (Leeds: British Archaeological Association, 2001), pp. 124–61.

[72] An analogous arrangement is attested to by Erasmus during his visit to the shrine of St Thomas at Canterbury: *Opera Omnia Desiderii Erasmi Roterodami*, 1–3 (Amsterdam, 1972), p. 490.

[73] Nichola Coldstream, for example, cites this suggestion in 'English Decorated Shrine Bases', *Journal of the British Archaeological Association* cxxix (1976), 15–34; 25. Cf. James C. Wall, *Shrines of British Saints* (London: Methuen and Co., 1905), p. 221.

[74] Rogers, 'The Bury Artists of Harley 2278', p. 224.

[75] Jocelin, *Chronicle*, p. 86.

most major shrines were protected with wooden covers that mimicked the shape of the *feretory* beneath. They were lifted vertically by means of ropes and pulleys, and in addition to protecting the *feretory* from dust and theft would contribute to the mystery and mystique of the pilgrimage experience by limiting visual access to the holy remains. Its efficacy as a protective covering is attested by the author of the account of the great fire of 1465 which devastated the abbey church, in which he attributes the survival of the shrine to the wooden cover which fell down upon it when the ropes holding it aloft burnt through.[76] J.J.G. Alexander suggests that the miniature in which Henry VI kneels in prayer to St Edmund depicts the shrine with its cover lowered.[77]

The earlier fire of 1198 also caused widespread damage in the abbey church, although, according to Jocelin, it ultimately proved propitious, as it ensured that the area around the shrine 'might be more carefully supervised and the abbot's plan carried out more speedily and without delay: this was to place the shrine, with the body of the holy martyr, more safely and more spectacularly in a higher position'.[78] Abbot Samson's plan to 'have marble blocks made for raising and supporting the shrine' conforms with renovations made to numerous other shrines during the twelfth century.[79] Nilson observes that the development of major shrines during the Middle Ages was 'continually upward'.[80] The reliquary containing St Alban's remains was raised up behind the high altar by Abbot Simon (1166–83) and at Winchester during the 1150s Bishop Henry of Blois (1129–71) elevated St Swithun onto a large platform built into the eastern apse of the Norman cathedral, with pilgrims able to benefit from proximity to the relics by crawling through the 'holy hole' beneath.[81]

In addition to structural modifications, Edmund's shrine was augmented by the gifts of pilgrims. A number of the miniatures in Harley 2278 depict a distinctive purple panel adorning one end (fols. 9, 100v, 109, 117). Scarfe suggests that this was intended to allow inspection of the contents, but Rogers's suggestion, that it was an inset piece of semi-precious stone such as porphyry, seems more likely.[82] It is tempting to connect this detail with the gift of the Bury man Wulmar, revived

---

[76] *Incendium Ecclesiae*, ed. Arnold, *Memorials*, III, p. 286.
[77] J.J.G. Alexander, 'Painting and Manuscript Illumination for Royal Patrons in the Later Middle Ages', in *English Court Culture in the Later Middle Ages*, ed. V.J. Scattergood and J.W. Sherborne (London, 1983), pp. 141–62; pl. 11.
[78] Jocelin, *Chronicle*, p. 96.
[79] Jocelin, *Chronicle*, p. 96. See Crook, 'The Architectural Setting', p. 41
[80] Nilson, *Cathedral Shrines*, p. 62.
[81] Crook, 'The Romanesque East Arm and Crypt of Winchester Cathedral', 19.
[82] Scarfe, 'The Body of St Edmund', caption to pl. xlviii; Rogers, 'The Bury Artists of Harley 2278', p. 224.

from a trance by Edmund on his return from Rome, who offered 'some marble' at the shrine in thanks for his recovery.[83] The custom of giving jewellery towards the adornment of the shrine continued into the fifteenth century. Wills proved in 1457 and 1463, for example, each make provision for such donations.[84] Henry III made several gifts of gold, including 'a fine crown with four flowers on its rim, worth £10 in all', to be attached to the shrine.[85] In 1285 Edward I granted fines for trespass against the assize of weights and measures to the abbey *'reparacioni et decorationi feretri sancti Eadmundi'*.[86] Henry de Lacy, Earl of Lincoln, gave two gold crosses, one worth 66s 8d, which were affixed to the shrine, as was a carbuncle.[87] The miniature depicting Lydgate praying before the resting place of his patron (fol. 9) shows four crosses, one at each corner of the gabled *feretory*, two of them perhaps the gift of Henry de Lacy.

The same miniature, along with fol. 109, depicts three-dimensional figures, possibly votive additions, on the crest of the *feretory*, including a knight on horseback. Edmund's *miracula* indicate his particular intercessory patronage of the knightly classes in the immediate post-Conquest period and it is possible that these figures depict the gift of such an individual in gratitude for Edmund's intervention. However, the pair of figures visible in fol. 109 are ambiguous, as, rather than being securely attached to the shrine, they seem to emanate from either end of the gabled roof. Given the proposition that the Harley miniatures depict 'the idea of a shrine', this suggests that additional symbolic resonance should be attached to these objects. The context of the miniature on fol. 109 is significant, as it illustrates Edmund's violent retribution against a man who attempted to steal a jewel from the shrine by biting it, only for his teeth to become securely attached.[88] The mounted figures resonate with Edmund's role as defender of his abbey and may depict his avenging spirit emanating forth to smite the unlucky thief. The shrine would be a suitable location in which to remind pilgrims of Edmund's defence of his relics and his abbey. Whether or not the Harley miniature depicts the shrine as it actually appeared, or whether it presents an imagined evocation of Edmund's saintly persona, in the context of the *Lives* as a mirror for princes

---

[83] Herman, *De Miraculis*; Arnold, *Memorials*, I, pp. 80–3; and Samson, *De Miraculis*, ed. Arnold, *Memorials*, I, pp. 160–2.

[84] *Wills and Inventories from the Registers of the Commissary of Bury St Edmund's and the Archdeacon of Sudbury*, ed. Samuel Tymms, Camden Society, os xlix (London: Printed for the Camden Society, 1850), pp. 13, 35.

[85] For Henry III and the cult of St Edmund see Gransden, *A History of the Abbey*, pp. 245–8. On Henry's gifts to Bury see Gransden, 'The Abbey of Bury St Edmunds and National Politics in the Reigns of King John and Henry III', *Monastic Studies* 11 (1991), 83–6.

[86] *The Chronicle of the Abbey*, ed. Gransden, p. 83.

[87] James, *On the Abbey*, p. 136.

[88] Bodley 240, ed. Arnold, *Memorials*, I, pp. 373–4; Lydgate, *Lives*, III, 1184.

is seems likely that this was another means by which Lydgate sought to promote Edmund's martial characteristics which he hoped Henry VI would imitate in defence of the abbey and its interests.

Edmund is similarly described in one of the few miracles recounted by Jocelin in which Henry of Essex, an affluent knight, in spite of his wealth refused to donate to Edmund's shrine and 'even used force and illegality to dispossess the church of an annual rent of 5s, which he appropriated for himself'.[89] However, Jocelin recalls that 'the good fortune that had smiled on him in these and similar activities now intervened to bring him unending tribulation, and behind the illusion of a happy beginning worked out a sorrowful end for him'.[90] In March 1163 Robert de Montfort, Henry's 'kinsman and his equal in birth and manhood', accused him of treason and cowardice whilst accompanying Henry II on his Welsh campaign of 1157. Henry of Essex refused to accept the charge and Robert refused to withdraw it, so the king ordered that the matter be settled by trial by combat. The knights met at Reading 'on an island not far from the abbey'.[91] Jocelin recounts that both fought hard but Robert began to gain the advantage. As Henry's strength failed he experienced a vision:

> Henry looked round and was astonished to see, at the water's edge, the figure of the glorious king and martyr, Edmund, dressed in armour and apparently floating in mid-air. He was looking at Henry sternly, shaking his head repeatedly, and gesturing angrily and indignantly in a threatening fashion ... The sight of [Edmund] alarmed and frightened Henry, and he recollected that wickedness in the past leads to shame in the present. So becoming quite desperate, he turned to attack, abandoning defence in favour of aggression. But the more powerfully he struck out, the more powerfully he was himself struck, and the more vigorously he attacked, the more vigorously he was attacked. In short, he was defeated and fell to the ground.[92]

Henry survived and led a reformed life, becoming a monk and cultivating 'the study of virtue'.[93]

Recovering the responses, appropriate or otherwise, of individual pilgrims to St Edmund is in most instances unachievable. However, efforts to do so illuminate additional dimensions of Edmund's cult which would otherwise be unknown.

---

[89] Jocelin, *Chronicle*, pp. 61–2.
[90] Jocelin, *Chronicle*, p. 62.
[91] Jocelin, *Chronicle*, p. 62.
[92] Jocelin, *Chronicle*, p. 63.
[93] Jocelin, *Chronicle*, p. 63.

Even for those few with access to the textual cult in manuscript form, pilgrimage to the shrine would have constituted a distinct cultic experience. At the shrine St Edmund was encountered in public and his saintly identity was primarily mediated through the sensory onslaught orchestrated with knowing skill by his monastic guardians.

CHAPTER 7

The devotional and iconographical context of the shrine

The context of the shrine

WHATEVER its precise appearance, it is apparent that the shrine of St Edmund was significant in a number of ways in terms of projecting a particular version of Edmund's sanctity to pilgrims. It was the focus of cultic devotion and a means of displaying the wealth and prestige of the cult and the involvement of its important patrons. Its function as the container of the saint's remains, and the symbolic resonance of the materials from which it was constructed, also rendered it a potent object in its own right. The shrine, however, did not exist in isolation. Numerous objects commonly found in shrine chapels were present in the vicinity of Edmund's remains. Candelabra or tall candlesticks were usual, and the presence of the latter is attested at St Edmund's shrine by the annotations in College of Arms, MS Arundel 30 which refer to the '*magno candelabro*'.[1] Four of the Harley 2278 miniatures likewise depict the shrine with a large candlestick at each corner (fols 4v, 9, 100v, 106). Hanging basins might provide additional light, but could also be receptacles for holy water or for the receipt of offerings. Books belonging to the shrine could be stored in chests or cupboards nearby, or chained, and at some shrines wooden *tabulae* (decorated panels) provided written or pictorial exposition of the life and miracles of the saint. Nilson concludes that the overall impression offered by a thriving medieval shrine 'must have been one of sumptuous clutter'.[2] However, features such as these, although undoubtedly contributing to the experience of a pilgrim to Bury, are for the most part generic and common to many great shrines and it is rather in the specific orchestration of the east end of the abbey church at Bury that most may be discerned about the convent's attempts to determine the reception of its saint by the medieval faithful.

---

[1] London, College of Arms, MS Arundel 30, fol. 211.
[2] Nilson, *Cathedral Shrines*, p. 53.

The devotional context

A tract on the dedication of the altars, chapels and churches at Bury St Edmunds, along with details in the Bury Customary, both preserved in the *Liber Albus*, indicate that St Edmund's shrine was surrounded by a host of other relics and secondary altars. The presence of secondary cults in addition to the main patron was common at the majority of shrine churches, although the number of secondary cults differed; St Augustine's, Canterbury, for example, was particularly crowded, with a number of significant shrines clustered in the east end of the church, as illustrated in Cambridge, Trinity Hall, MS 1, fol. 77.[3] Useful details about the pre-Conquest cults at Bury may be gleaned from a mid-eleventh century psalter in the Vatican where the litany and calendar indicate the major feasts of the abbey.[4] Many of the secondary cults at Bury were widespread in medieval England; the cult of the Virgin Mary, for example, grew in prominence and popularity throughout the Middle Ages.[5] This was partly evinced in the dedication of the church: the first church at Beodericesworth to which Edmund was translated in the mid-tenth century was dedicated to St Mary, and its replacement, probably the circular *rotunda* chapel, was dedicated in 1032 'in honour of Christ, St Mary and St Edmund'.[6] There was still a church dedicated to St Mary when building began on Abbot Baldwin's (1065–97) great new abbey church, and although this was demolished to accommodate the southern arm of the new building, Abbot Anselm (1121–48) replaced it with another St Mary's to serve as a parish church within the abbey's precinct, where its fifteenth-century successor still stands.[7] The

---

[3] See Richard Gem, 'The Significance of the Eleventh-Century Rebuilding of Christ Church and St Augustine's, Canterbury, in the Development of Romanesque Architecture', in *Medieval Art and Architecture at Canterbury before 1220*, ed. Nicola Coldstream and Peter Draper, British Archaeological Association Conference Transactions, v (1982), pp. 1–19; p. 8.

[4] The litany in Vatican MS Reg. Lat. 12, ff. 159–61, is printed in *Anglo-Saxon Litanies of the Saints*, ed. Michael Lapidge, Henry Bradshaw Society, cvi (London: The Boydell Press for the Henry Bradshaw Society, 1991), pp. 296–9; the calendar is printed in *English Benedictine Kalendars before AD 1100*, ed. Francis Wormald, Henry Bradshaw Society, lxxii (London: The Boydell Press for the Henry Bradshaw Society, 1988).

[5] For the cult of the Virgin Mary at Bury St Edmunds see Antonia Gransden, 'The Cult of St Mary at Beodricesworth and then in Bury St Edmund Abbey to c.1150', *Journal of Ecclesiastical History* lv, pt 4 (2004), pp. 627–53 and Gransden, *A History of the Abbey*, pp. 106–10. For the cult of the Virgin Mary in general see Rubin, *Emotion and Devotion*.

[6] This is stated in one of the marginal notes in the Easter Tables, opposite years 1032–35, in the mid-eleventh century Bury Psalter, now MS Reg. Lat. 12 in the Vatican Library, f. 17v. Cited in Gransden, *A History of the Abbey*, p. 106.

[7] For the demolition of the old St Mary's church see *De dedicationibus, altarum, capellarum, etc., apud Sanctum Edmundum*, in *The Customary of the Benedictine Abbey*

presence of the cult of the Virgin within the abbey church was enhanced by the construction of the Lady Chapel in 1272, with the verses in MS Arundel 30 indicating that a significant quantity of Marian imagery adorned this structure.[8]

In addition to the Nativity of the Virgin Mary, the two pre-Conquest translations of St Edmund (30 and 31 March respectively) and the dedication of the church in 1032, the other feasts entered in the calendar in gold majuscules include those of the popular saints Paul (29 June), Benedict (21 March) and All Saints (1 November). By the time the *De dedicationibus* was composed in the twelfth century a number of other widespread saints were venerated at Bury, including the apostles Andrew and James, John the Evangelist and Sts Denis, Faith, Giles, Margaret, Martin and Michael.[9] Devotion to less widely venerated saints, such as St Saba, is likely to have developed as a result of the personal affiliation of a particular monastic official; the cult of St Saba, for example, to whom the northernmost of the three apsidal chapels was dedicated, is known nowhere else in medieval England, and was introduced by Abbot Anselm (1121–48), who had previously been abbot of St Saba in Rome.[10] Saints with a particular local significance were also common at larger shrine churches, and at Bury the cult of Little St Robert developed in the later twelfth century after the death of a local boy was blamed upon the town's Jewish community, a situation analogous to the cult of St William at Norwich which flourished four decades earlier.[11] The emergence of the cults of Robert and William in the mid to late twelfth century can be located in the context of devotional enthusiasm and institutional competition which existed in the wake of Becket's demise and exponential growth in posthumous popularity. The presence of two other cults at Bury, however, is less readily explicable.

---

of Bury St Edmunds, ed. Antonia Gransden, Henry Bradshaw Society, xcix (London: Henry Bradshaw Society, 1973), pp. 114–21; p. 116, ll 22–3 to p. 117, ll 1–2. The construction of the parish church of St Mary under Abbot Anselm by the sacrists Ralph and Hervey is described in the *Gesta Sacristarum*, ed. Arnold, Memorials, II, p. 289. See also Arthur B. Whittingham, 'St Mary's Church, Bury St Edmunds', *Journal of the British Archaeological Association* xxi (1865), 187–8.

[8] College of Arms, MS Arundel 30, fol. 209v.

[9] Gransden, *A History of the Abbey*, pp. 113–17.

[10] *De dedicationibus*, in *Bury Customary*, ed. Gransden, p. 116, ll 1–10, p. 121, l. 10. For the location of the chapel see James, *On the Abbey Church*, pp. 137, 149, 161, 180. Frequent references to the cult of St Saba in the *Bury Customary* indicate its significance at Bury; see pp. 11–12; p. 55, l. 19; p. 69 n. 1; p. 71, l. 4; p. 73, l. 11; p. 83, l. 30; p. 84, l. 5; p. 85, l. 15. The cult of St Nicasius was similarly idiosyncratic; see Gransden, *A History of the Abbey*, pp. 113–14.

[11] For the development of the cult of Little St Robert see Gransden, *A History of the Abbey*, pp. 117–21 and Anthony Bale, *The Jew in the Medieval Book: English Antisemitisms 1350–1500* (Cambridge: Cambridge University Press, 2006), pp. 105–44.

Local companions

In addition to the saints indicated above, the only other feasts entered in the calendar in gold majuscules are those of Sts Jurmin and Botulph. A marginal annotation in the Bury copy of the chronicle of John of Worcester claims that both saints were translated to Bury during the time of Abbot Leofstan (1044–65).[12] The Bury customary refers to 'the altar of Sts Botulph, Thomas, Jurmin and their reliquaries', indicating that their shrines were served by a shared altar after their translation into Baldwin's abbey church. Due to the pressure of space in the presbytery James suggests that their reliquaries were probably located to the east of St Edmund's shrine. Little is known of Jurmin, other than that he was a seventh-century East Anglian prince. The author of the *Liber Eliensis* claims that he was the son of King Anna (r.640–54) and praises his 'holiness of life and meritoriousness with regard to justice' which 'commended him as blessed' and notes that he was buried alongside his father at Blythburgh (Suffolk).[13] As an East Anglian prince Jurmin was a worthy companion for Edmund and served to emphasise his regional royalty. Furthermore, as son of Anna and thus brother of St Æthelthryth and her sainted sisters, whom the Ely author refers to as 'the holy progeny', Jurmin's royal pedigree is illustrious. Placing his remains alongside Edmund's co-opted some of his familial prestige and established Bury as a rival to Ely as the resting place of the East Anglian holy royal dynasty.

Botulph was also an East Anglian saint and a contemporary of Jurmin. Born in the region, he built a monastery at Icanhoe which the author of the *Anglo-Saxon Chronicle* claims he began in 654: 'This year King Anna was slain, and Botulph began to build that minster at Icanhoe', where he was abbot until his death c.680.[14] Botulph built his monastery on land given by the king of East Anglia (either Ethelhere (c.654–5) or Ethelwold (c.655–64)), echoing the royal favour which Bury sought throughout the Middle Ages. The monastery at Icanho was eventually destroyed in Danish raids, providing a reminder of the origins of St Edmund's own cult.[15]

The importance of the cults of Jurmin and Botulph at Bury is evident in the litany of the Bury psalter, where they, along with St Edmund, St Peter, St Benedict

---

[12] *The Chronicle of John of Worcester*, 3 vols, II, ed. R.R. Darlington and Patrick McGurk, trans. Jennifer Bray and Patrick McGurk (Oxford: Clarendon Press, 1995); III, ed. Patrick McGurk (Oxford: Clarendon Press, 1998); I (forthcoming); III, pp. 316–17.

[13] *Liber Eliensis*, pp. 14 and 22.

[14] *The Anglo-Saxon Chronicle*, ed. Whitelock, p. 28.

[15] See F.S. Stevenson, 'St Botolph (Botwulf) and Iken', *Proceedings of the Suffolk Institute of Archaeology and History* xviii (1924), 30–52 and Stanley E. West, Norman Scarfe and Rosemary Cramp, 'Iken, St Botolph, and the Coming of East Anglian Christianity', *Proceedings of the Suffolk Institute of Archaeology and History* xxxv (1984), 279–301.

and All Saints, are the only saints to share with Christ the honour of a double invocation.[16] Their close association with St Edmund is also apparent in one of the twenty-two prayers appended to the psalter requesting protection of the church of St Mary and St Edmund along with Michael and Gabriel and Botulph and Jurmin.[17] The cult of St Jurmin seems to have been exclusive to Bury St Edmunds and St Botulph was venerated in only a few other locations.[18] Their placing within Baldwin's abbey church and their physical proximity to Edmund's shrine indicates their high status within the hierarchy of cults at Bury, and whilst their presence must partly be accounted for by their local provenance, their cults also provide an interesting counterpoint to St Edmund and may best be understood in this context. They speak to particular elements of Edmund's sanctity: his regional identity and his royal pedigree, and locate him within a long-established tradition of indigenous sanctity.

Edmund's East Anglian identity is similarly celebrated in a number of the liturgical compositions associated with Bury St Edmunds. *In hoc mundo*, a monophonic chant consisting of six pairs of verses, was copied in the thirteenth century but perhaps originated in the twelfth. It is preserved on a single bifolium which contains monophonic items in honour of various saints, including another sequence in honour of St Edmund, *Dulci symphonia*, seemingly copied in liturgical order.[19] Lisa Colton suggests that the two sequences concerning St Edmund may have been performed from this manuscript as part of Mass on St Edmund's Day.[20] According to Colton, the vernacular is rarely used in the liturgy, but she notes that the tenth line of *In hoc mundo* claims that 'Rex "her" dicens in deserto, quod "hic" sonat in aperto lingua sub ytalica' (the king says "here" in the place where he is abandoned, that is uttered aloud as "*hic*" in the Latin tongue).[21] The insertion of the head's vernacular utterance in an otherwise Latin text is reminiscent of Abbo of Fleury's account of this incident in the *Passio*.[22] Its repetition in two divergent sources indicates that it was considered an integral

---

[16] André Wilmart, 'The Prayers of the Bury Psalter', *Downside Review* xlviii (1930), 198–216; 215.

[17] See Wilmart, 'Prayers', 204–5.

[18] Gransden, *A History of the Abbey*, pp. 111–12.

[19] The verses and music are preserved in Oxford, New College, MS 362, Fragment IX, fols 31r–32v. In addition to two sequences in honour of St Edmund, *In hoc mundo* and *Dulci symphonia*, the other saints celebrated are the Virgin Mary, St Michael, St Catherine and an unknown, unnamed saint.

[20] For further discussion of *In hoc mundo* and *Dulci symphonia* and transcriptions of the verses and music, see Lisa Colton, 'Music and Identity in Medieval Bury St Edmunds' in *Changing Images*, ed. Bale, pp. 87–110; pp. 93–5 and figures 1 and 2.

[21] Translation by Colton, 'Music and Identity', p. 95.

[22] Abbo *Passio*, XIII; Hervey, *Corolla*, p. 41.

part of Edmund's life. In particular, its appearance in a chant associated with the Mass of St Edmund signifies that the saint's indigenous identity was an officially authorised legendary element which the abbey at Bury sought to promote.

Similarly, *Ave miles celestis curie*, a mid-fourteenth-century motet, describes St Edmund as '*Rex patrone patrie, matutina lux Saxonie, lucens nobis in meridie, sidus Angligenarum*' ('King of our protectress, of our homeland, morning light of Saxony, shining upon as at midday, star over the children of Anglia').[23] Colton observes that the shining star motif is common in texts associated with translation ceremonies, and might therefore relate this motet to the liturgy of the Translation of St Edmund.[24] As discussed above, Nilson notes that the numerous translations of Anglo-Saxon saints which took place in the wake of the Norman Conquest were carried out as a means of emphasising the continuity of local tradition.[25] Thus the translation of St Edmund into the presbytery of the new Romanesque church in 1095 would be an ideal moment to emphasise his local identity by placing him alongside other regional saints. The significance of this was clearly not lost on the composers of the motet, and whilst this is known from a fourteenth-century source it possibly represents a continuous tradition which is textually embodied at a date some centuries after its initial development.

The close physical association between the shrines of Edmund, Botulph and Jurmin is likely to have invited comparisons from pilgrims, with the undoubtedly more splendid patronal shrine emphasising Edmund's saintly pre-eminence. Attention would also be drawn to the alleged condition of the relics of each saint contained within these shrines. The author of the *Liber Eliensis* notes that Jurmin was translated from his original resting place at Blythburgh to 'Bederichesworthe, which they now called *Sanctus Edmundus*', implying the translation of his entire remains.[26] In contrast, the relics of St Botulph were the subject of competitive acquisitiveness. The author of the *Liber Eliensis* claims that 'the head of the blessed confessor Botulph and his larger bones' were still at Ely in 1093, at least thirty

---

[23] This motet is one of several which was copied in the 1330s or 1340s into the flyleaves of a twelfth-century Bury library book, now Oxford, Bodleian Library, MS e Musaei 7, items 7 and 8, fols Vv–VIr. It is edited and described in detail in Manfred F. Bukofzer, 'Two Fourteenth-Century Motets on St Edmund' in his *Studies in Medieval and Renaissance Music* (New York: Norton, 1950), pp. 17–33. They have since been re-edited in *Motets of English Provenance*, ed. Frank Harrison and Peter Lefferts (Monaco: Éditions de l'Oiseau-Lyre, 1980), from which texts and translations have been drawn unless otherwise stated. For further discussion of the lyrics of the motet see Colton, 'Music and Identity', pp. 98–102.

[24] Colton, 'Music and Identity', p. 102.

[25] Nilson, *Cathedral Shrines*, p. 19. See also Crook, *English Medieval Shrines*, pp. 107–32, esp. 107–19.

[26] *Liber Eliensis*, p. 22.

years after the translation to Bury.[27] It therefore seems that at best Bury gained possession of some of the smaller bones. In addition to his shrine in the presbytery, there was also a chapel dedicated to Botulph elsewhere in the east end of the abbey church, possibly in a position corresponding to the Lady Chapel in the north, or in the south transept. The Bury *Rituale* preserved in MS Harley 2977 refers to St Botulph's arm as a separate relic, and it seems likely that this would be enshrined in his chapel, with the greater portion remaining alongside St Jurmin in the presbytery. Botulph's fragmented remains would have provided a striking contrast with Edmund's bodily wholeness: a symbol of his physical and spiritual purity which also emphasised Bury's exclusive claim on him as patron and therefore as the principal recipient of his saintly intercession. The main feast days of the two saints also provided a balanced counterpoint to that of St Edmund on 20 November: Jurmin was remembered in February and Botulph in June, and it is likely that the monks of Bury hoped that the distribution of these feast days throughout the year would ensure a regular flow of visitors, and therefore income, to the abbey.

Secondary relics of St Edmund

In addition to the body contained within the main *feretrum*, evidence for additional secondary relics associated with St Edmund further illuminate the way in which the abbey sought to promote the cult of its patron. In his account of the fire of 1198 Jocelin describes his relief that the 'great beam which used to be beyond the altar had been taken down to be renovated with new carving' and was therefore spared from the conflagration.[28] This was a cause for celebration not only for the sake of the beam itself, which was evidently elaborate and valued highly enough to be restored rather than replaced, but primarily because the objects normally placed on the beam had also been saved:

> By chance, too, the cross and the 'Mariola' and the 'John' and the casket with the shirt of St Edmund, and the monstrance with the other relics that used to hang from the same beam, and other reliquaries which stood on the beam all had been taken down earlier: otherwise everything would surely have been destroyed by the fire, as was the painted hanging which had been put up in place of the beam.[29]

---

[27] *Liber Eliensis*, p. 266.
[28] Jocelin, *Chronicle*, p. 95.
[29] Jocelin, *Chronicle*, p. 95.

The 'Mariola' and the 'John', attributed by some to Master Hugo, presumably occupied the customary position at the foot of the rood, and although there is some doubt as to their provenance, they were evidently of considerable value. Jocelin claims that they were ornamented 'with a great weight of gold' and recalls an incident in 1175 when the convent considered selling the images in order to pay Pope Alexander III for a privilege granting the abbey exemption from all except papal authority.[30] The accompanying reliquaries atop the beam reflect the relatively common practice of placing relics in this location. A rood beam offered an acceptable position for a minor shrine which did not need to be readily accessible to pilgrims and enabled conservation of precious floor space. The diagrammatic drawing of the east end of St Augustine's, Canterbury indicates relics occupying a similar position atop the reredos.[31]

The 'other relics' to which Jocelin refers in this location are not specified, but other sources refer to relics which would conceivably have been placed near St Edmund due to their biographical or symbolic associations. For example, Abbo refers to Oswen, 'a woman of blessed memory', one of the secular guardians of the shrine before Cnut's introduction of Benedictine monks, who tended St Edmund's remains until 'shortly before these recent times of ours':

> This venerable woman, either from some divine intuition, or from excess of devotion, made it her constant practice to open the sepulchre of the blessed martyr year by year, at the anniversary of the Lord's Supper, and to trim and pare his hair and nails. These relics, one and all, she studiously collected, and stored in a casket; nor did she ever omit, as long as she lived, to cherish them with an affection that was wonderful, having placed them in a casket on the altar of the church to which I have referred. And there they are still preserved with due veneration.[32]

The inference is that Edmund's corpse was not only intact but possessed of such saintly vigour that it continued to evince signs of life. John Lydgate invokes these relics in a fifteenth-century prayer 'To St Edmund':

> Thyn hooly nailles and thy royal heer
> Greuh by miracle, as seith þe cronycleer,
> Kept clos in gold and siluere, as I reede ...

---

[30] Jocelin, *Chronicle*, p. 6. For discussion of the provenance of the images see Gransden, *A History of the Abbey*, p. 109.
[31] For the location of secondary reliquaries see Nilson, *Cathedral Shrines*, pp. 57–8.
[32] Abbo *Passio*, XV; Hervey, *Corolla*, p.47.

Which be conserved yit in thyn hooly place,
With other relyques, for a memoryall,
Frute of this marter growing up by grace.³³

Lydgate implies that the hair and nails were still present in the abbey at the time of the prayer's composition, or at least that the convent thought them significant enough to assert their continuous presence. The intimate nature of these relics affirms the abbey as the careful and privileged guardian of St Edmund and their symbolic resonance as indicators of Edmund's sanctity and continued corporeal preservation makes it likely that they continued to be housed in close proximity to the main shrine.

Similarly, Jocelin maintains that the convent possessed a relic of St Edmund's clothing. This is corroborated by the Bury *Rituale*, which indicates that the garment was carried in procession on important feast days; for example, the procession on Christmas day included the 'shrine with [the relic of] the shirt of St Edmund'.³⁴ Herman refers to similar relics on a number of occasions, including during his account of Abbot Leofstan's (1044–65) inspection of Edmund's remains, where he states that 'the saint is stripped of his holy martyr's vestments, in some places stained red with blood, in others riddled with arrow holes'.³⁵ This seems to be the occasion when the garments are permanently removed from the body and preserved as separate relics as Herman concludes his account of the incident by informing his readers that 'the clothes, stripped from the martyr, are kept in the sacrary coffer with the reliquaries', perhaps the chest atop the beam to which Jocelin refers.³⁶ Herman expounds the efficacy of secondary relics when he claims that the blood-stained garments provide 'the common people' with access to 'the benefits of the shrine's divine power', especially when they are taken from their container and shown to pilgrims, and asserts their power to heal.³⁷ The *camisia* therefore acts as a visible synecdoche of the sacred corpse hidden from human view and reiterates the martyr's transformation of death into holy triumph by enacting miracles of healing whilst simultaneously displaying the wounds which caused his demise. The presence of the shirt relic further explains the anomaly of the depiction of Edmund's martyrdom in the Morgan miniatures, where he is clad

---

33 John Lydgate, 'To Saint Edmund', *Minor Poems of John Lydgate*, Part I, ed. Henry Noble MacCracken, EETS, es 107 (London, New York and Toronto: Oxford University Press, 1911, rpt 1961), pp. 124–7, ll 52–4 and 57–9.
34 *Rituale*, London, British Library, MS Harley, 2977, fol. 8, cited in James, *On the Abbey Church*, pp. 183–6.
35 Herman, *De Miraculis*, ed. Arnold, *Memorials*, I, p. 53.
36 Herman, *De Miraculis*, ed. Arnold, *Memorials*, I, p. 54.
37 Herman, *De Miraculis*, ed. Arnold, *Memorials*, I, pp. 53–4.

only in a loin cloth in some scenes, in imitation of Christ in the St Albans Psalter, but in others is clothed, as, in order both to emphasise the Christological nature of Edmund's martyrdom and to legitimate the shirt relic, Edmund has to appear in both guises.

Jocelin's account of the search for St Edmund's cup in the immediate aftermath of the fire indicates that this was also regarded as a significant relic:

> Then, to our horror, some of our brethren shouted with a loud wailing that St Edmund's cup was burnt. But when some of them were looking here and there among the cinders and ashes for stones and sheets of precious metal, they drew out the cup in perfect condition lying in a heap of cinders that were no longer burning, and they found it wrapped in a linen cloth that was half burnt. The oak box itself, in which the cup had long been stored, was burnt to dust, and only the iron bands and lock were found. When we saw this miracle, we all wept for joy.[38]

If it was normally kept atop the beam then the cup would most likely have been removed along with the other reliquaries during the restoration work, but its discovery by monks who were searching for stones and precious metal, presumably from the shrine, suggests that it stood in close proximity to Edmund's remains. This is corroborated by a miracle account which claims that a Dunwich man who suffered from dropsy was carried to St Edmund's shrine at the insistence of his family and friends, whereupon he drank from the cup and was duly healed.[39] Similar incidents include the healing of a rich woman who is cured of a fever after travelling to Bury and drinking from the cup,[40] and likewise Gervasius, a Cluniac monk of St Saviour's, Southwark, who the author of the miracle collection claims recounted to him directly the story of his cure from an intermittent fever and an additional unspecified 'malady' after his admittance to the infirmary at Bury and the administering of St Edmund's cup.[41] The idea of a life-restoring cup, presumably owned by Edmund whilst alive, has clear Eucharistic connotations and further serves to sacralise Edmund's life as well as death.

The cup of St Edmund also occurs in a less immediately explicable context. The author of the *Bury Chronicle* cites a dispute which occurred in 1300 between the abbey and Edward I concerning jurisdiction over the manor of Warkton in

---

[38] Jocelin, *Chronicle*, pp. 95–6.
[39] Samson, *De Miraculis*, ed. Arnold, *Memorials*, I, pp. 189–91.
[40] Samson, *De Miraculis*, ed. Arnold, *Memorials*, I, p. 187
[41] Samson, *De Miraculis*, ed. Arnold, *Memorials*, I, pp. 202–4

Northamptonshire as a result of the king's reform of the forests.[42] The author of this part of the chronicle uses the conventional format of dating an event by the regnal year, in this case the 'twenty-eighth year of the reign of King Edward', although interestingly he refers to him as the fourth king of that name, thus including the three Anglo-Saxon King Edwards in his enumeration. This sense of pre-Conquest continuity is particularly relevant in the context of a land dispute in which the claimants sought to establish their ancient customary rights. The author claims that 'it is well known that the manor from ancient times was not a part of the king's demesne' and recounts the story of a 'certain lord of this manor' and his wife who lived 'many years ago' who gave the manor to the abbey in gratitude to St Edmund for saving both their lives and their souls.[43] According to the *Chronicle*, the devil, jealous of the couple's devotion, 'sought to deceive them under the guise of religion' and incited them to extremes of religious fervour.[44] He convinced them that they must pursue martyrs' deaths but because there was no-one in the neighbourhood who would kill them 'they both rashly undertook to commit an accursed murder ... by savagely attacking their own bodies'.[45] The author recounts that their custom was 'that every day after lunch, when thanks had been returned to God, a drink called the "*plenum*" or "brimming cup" of St Edmund should be quaffed in honour of the glorious king and martyr Edmund', and that when they partook of their customary drink on the day of their intended suicide, 'a small ray of light flickered in the darkness and deep shadows'.[46] At this point the narrative changes from the past tense into the historical present, accentuating the immediacy and drama of the events:

> When the *plenum* of St Edmund is fetched the devil's evil influence is put to flight; when the sacred cup is tasted with devotion the enemy flies, blinded.[47]

The couple realise that they have been deceived, and hurry to Bury to offer repentance and thanks, giving the manor of Warkton with all its appurtenances to the abbey '*inperpetuum*', spending the rest of their days within the monastic purview 'in the old hall called Bradfield'.[48] Gransden suggests that the purpose of the story 'is to prove that Warkton was not ancient demesne because it had not belonged

---

[42] *The Chronicle of the Abbey of Bury St Edmunds*, ed. Gransden, pp. 158–60. See also her Introduction, xxxv, for the historical context of this dispute.
[43] *Chronicle*, ed. Gransden, pp. 158–9.
[44] *Chronicle*, ed. Gransden, p. 159.
[45] *Chronicle*, ed. Gransden, p. 159.
[46] *Chronicle*, ed. Gransden, p. 160.
[47] *Chronicle*, ed. Gransden, p. 160.
[48] *Chronicle*, ed. Gransden, p. 160.

to the king before the Conquest'.[49] The propagandist element of the narrative is clear, as the author resorts to ancient oral custom, whether a genuine tradition or invented at the time of the dispute, in order to justify his abbey's landholdings. The role of the cup of St Edmund within the narrative is less readily explicable. The author does not suggest that the cup once belonged to St Edmund; rather it is a symbolic toast drunk to the memory of the saint. The imagery of the 'sacred cup' which puts to flight the devil has unmistakable Eucharistic overtones, particularly fitting in the context of the couple's quest for self-sacrifice and the emphasis placed upon Edmund's status as an exemplary martyr. The reference to the brimming cup also has more secular connotations of high-status ceremonial toasting of lords and warriors, a tradition with ancient origins which continued throughout the Middle Ages in north-western Europe.[50] The cup of St Edmund preserved at the abbey seems to have originated in a similarly secular context, rather than as a cup used by Edmund as a Eucharistic chalice, but was transformed by its miracle-working reputation, emphasised by its close physical association with the shrine, into a sacred relic.

Further relics speak to an alternative aspect of Edmund's sanctity. The Bury Rituale indicates that during the Feast of the Translation of St Edmund (29 April) the saint's sword was carried in procession and that his war banner was also preserved in the abbey church.[51] Banners were frequently hung at shrines in the hope they would become imbued with the power and blessing of the saint prior to battle or, as at Bury, the saint's own flag might be displayed.[52] Banners captured from defeated enemies could also be given to a shrine in thanks for a saint's intervention on behalf of the victors, such as the banner of Isaac Comnenus (r.1184–91), the defeated prince of Cyprus, which Richard I sent to the shrine of St Edmund in 1191.[53] The author of *The Rites of Durham* describes a vision experienced by John Fossour, Prior of Durham (1342–74), the night before a battle was to be fought against the Scots:

---

[49] *Chronicle*, ed. Gransden, p. 159, n. 1.
[50] For drinking customs see Marjorie A. Brown, 'The Feast Hall in Anglo-Saxon Society', in *Food and Eating in Medieval Europe*, ed. Martha Carlin and Joel T. Rosenthal (London and Rio Grande: The Hambledon Press, 1998), pp. 1–14; Stephen Pollington, 'The Mead-Hall Community', *Journal of Medieval History* 37.1 (2011), 19–33.
[51] BL, Harley MS 2977, fols 49v–50r. Printed in James, *On the Abbey Church*, p. 90.
[52] See Nilson, *Cathedral Shrines*, pp. 51–2.
[53] *The Chronicle of the Reigns of Henry II and Richard I, AD 1169–92, commonly known under the name of Benedict of Peterborough*, 2 vols, ed. William Stubbs (London: Longmans, Green, Reader and Dyer, 1867), II, p. 164. See also W.T. Mitchell, 'The Shrines of English Saints in Wartime before the Reformation', *Pax: The Quarterly Review of the Benedictines of Prinknash* 30 (1940), 71–80; 79.

> [the vision commanded] him to taike the holie corporax cloth, which was within the corporax, wherewith St Cuthbert did cover the chalice, when he used to say masse, and to put the same holie relique, like unto a banner, upon a speare point, and on the morrowe after to goe and repaire to a place on the west parte of the citie of Durham, called the Readhills, and there to remayne and abyde till the end of the said battell.[54]

The Scots were duly defeated and the monks incorporated the corporax cloth into a lavish banner of silk and velvet, which continued to ensure victory in battle to any who bore it, 'by the especiall grace of God Almightie and the mediacione of holie Saint Cuthbert', until its destruction at the Reformation.[55]

John Lydgate similarly describes Edmund's war banner which he bore 'lyk a wys kyng' in battle against the Danes (Prologue, 9) depicted in the miniature of the Battle of Thetford on fol. 50, which Lydgate avers 'shal kepen and conserue/ this lond from enmyes' (Prologue, 41–2). Edmund's banner had come to be regarded as a powerful relic in its own right when it was borne before the victors at the battle of Fornham (Suffolk) in 1173 when the army of Henry II under his Constable Humphrey de Bohun and the Chief Justice Richard de Luci routed the rebellious forces of Henry the Young King led by Robert de Beaumount, Earl of Leicester.[56]

The presence of Edmund's sword and banner at the shrine clearly alluded to his military prowess. Comparison with the banner made before the battle of Durham emphasises this further: whereas at Durham the banner was created from a devotional item associated with St Cuthbert, its counterpart at Bury was Edmund's own war banner, requiring no modifications. Edmund's complex saintly identity meant he was inherently suited to manifest his power in numerous and varied contexts. As we have seen, Edmund's martial kingship, to which his sword and banner pertain, was an element of his sanctity actively promoted by the abbey. However, in the textual and codicological cult he is more frequently depicted posthumously as an active military figure, whereas the physical presence of the sword and banner owned in life by the king suggests that in the context of his shrine the abbey sought to promote his knightly vigour both pre- and post-mortem.

---

[54] *The Rites of Durham: being a description or brief declaration of all the ancient monuments, rites, and customs belonging or being within the monastical church of Durham before the suppression, written 1593*, ed. Joseph T. Fowler, Surtees Society, cvii (Durham: Published for the Surtees Society by Andrews and Co., 1903), p. 20.

[55] *The Rites of Durham*, ed. Fowler, p. 22–3.

[56] Roger of Hovedon, *Chronica Magestri Rogeri Houedene*, 4 vols, ed. William Stubbs, Rerum Britannicarum Medii Aevi Scriptores, 51 (London: Longman, 1868–71), II, p. 55.

That similar objects can be invested with alternative meanings attests once again to the flexibility of Edmund's saintly identity. This is equally true of the whole assemblage of secondary relics associated with St Edmund at Bury. The shirt, cup, sword and banner were items which had been directly used and handled by the king, contributing to their potency as secondary relics. It is possible that they formed part of the regalia, but none is described as being made of precious materials or as being particularly valuable in its own right. Instead, the temporal and domestic nature of these items contributes a sense of authenticity and real human presence.

Although not strictly relics, additional items located in the vicinity of the shrine likewise attest to Edmund's sanctity in a variety of ways. The account of the great fire of 1465 refers to a wooden chest containing the bones of the sacrist Egelwyn, 'the former servant and charioteer of the martyr', who bore his body to safety in London during the Danish incursions of the early eleventh century, along with the bones of unspecified 'others'.[57] The author notes that the casket was located 'high up, near the king's tomb', possibly indicating a position atop the reliquary beam. Their preservation so close to St Edmund is explicitly characterised as a reward for their loyalty to their royal master, a trait which persisted beyond the grave, as the author records that when the fire had taken hold in the presbytery 'some men had employed great force in trying to move them, inasmuch as the heat had already got to them; but, though the chest could ordinarily be lifted with one hand, they were unable to stir it'. He wonders admiringly, 'was not this truly a faithful servant, who refused to forsake his king?'[58] The high standards of duty and devotion which Edmund expected, and the potential rewards for providing such service, are therefore clear.

The devotional context in which Edmund's shrine existed contributed to his characterisation as a saint of particular potency and comprehensive appeal. Pilgrims were reminded of the efficacy of his relics by references to those who cared for his intact corpse and offered physical evidence of its post-mortem vitality. The fragmented nature of the remains of his companion, Botulph, drew attention to Edmund's own wholeness. The special rewards available to those who served him loyally were also emphasised, no doubt calling to mind the well-known fates of those who had dared defy him. His association with other East Anglian royal saints attested to his regional and regal identity, and his wonder-working banner, along with other military emblems offered in tribute, confirmed his ability to defend his followers, whether within his own lands or as patron of more distant campaigns.

---

[57] *Incendium Ecclesiae*, ed. Arnold, *Memorials*, III, pp. 286–7.
[58] *Incendium Ecclesiae*, ed. Arnold, *Memorials*, III, p. 287.

The iconographical context

An additional means by which the convent could determine Edmund's reception by the medieval faithful in the context of pilgrimage to his shrine was through the way in which he was imagined visually in the artistic schemes adorning the interior of the abbey church. One of the key sources regarding the iconographic context of the cult of St Edmund at Bury is London, College of Arms, MS Arundel 30, in which are recorded a series of inscriptions accompanying works of art in various media in the abbey church. The complex interrelationship of text and image are alluded to by Gilbert Crispin, abbot of Westminster (1085–1117), in an imagined dialogue with a Jew who questions what he perceives to be the Christian practice of worshipping images. Crispin explains that 'just as letters are shapes and symbols of spoken words, pictures exist as representations and symbols of writing'.[59] Embellishing artistic works with textual inscriptions was a relatively common practice and the habit of recording these inscriptions is attested elsewhere.[60] James, for example, transcribed a set of inscriptions from stained-glass windows in Canterbury Cathedral which had been recorded in an early fourteenth-century hand in a roll in the Cathedral and Chapter archives.[61] The inscriptions relate to a series of windows in the cathedral church, now lost, featuring an extensive Old and New Testament typological sequence.[62] James conjectures that these were probably located in a portion of the choir.[63] Although on a different scale and containing different subjects, the Canterbury manuscript nevertheless evinces a similar impulse to record inscriptions as is seen in Arundel 30. The nature of the roll in which the Canterbury inscriptions are recorded led James to speculate as to its original function. He notes that it is 9.5 inches wide and 8 feet 10 inches long, consisting of three skins fastened together with pins which he identifies as post-medieval. The writing is very large and some parts of the text are either rubricated or underlined in red. Based primarily upon the size

---

[59] Gilbert Crispin, *Disputatio Iudeu et Christiani*. Cited in Michael Camille, 'Seeing and Reading: Some Visual Implications of Medieval Literacy and Illiteracy', *Art History* 8.1 (1985), 26–49; 32.

[60] See, for example, Richard Gameson, *The Role of Art in the Anglo-Saxon Church* (Oxford: Clarendon Press, 1995), p. 80; Sabrina Longland, 'A Literary Aspect of the Bury St Edmunds Cross', *Metropolitan Museum Journal* 2 (1969), 45–74.

[61] M.R. James, *The Verses Formerly Inscribed on Twelve Windows in the Choir of Canterbury Cathedral, reprinted from the manuscript with an introduction and notes by Montague Rhodes James*, Cambridge Antiquarian Society publications, Octavo series, 38 (Cambridge: Deighton Bell, 1901). The roll is number C 246 in the Cathedral and Chapter archives.

[62] For a transcription of the sequence see James, *Verses*, pp. 7–37.

[63] James, *Verses*, pp. 37–42.

of the writing, James suggests that the roll was hung up for display to pilgrims to the cathedral in order to facilitate their appreciation and understanding of the windows in a similar way to the display of lists of relics or institutional histories.[64] The significance afforded to the verses is attested by their preservation in the Catalogue of the Library made under Prior Henry of Eastry (d.1331).[65] The monastic community at Canterbury clearly valued the verses and took care to preserve them, an impulse which may be analogous with the intention of the Arundel 30 scribe.

Arundel 30 is the only record of the images implied by the inscriptions, so much remains unknown. It is unclear, for example, whether the inscriptions on the artworks at Bury were likewise highlighted to pilgrims by presenting them in a scroll, but the Canterbury example does emphasise the care taken by the guardians of saints' remains to ensure that pilgrims were appropriately guided and instructed, a desire reflected in other aspects of the orchestration of the pilgrimage experience at Bury discussed above. Based on the iconography suggested by the Arundel 30 inscriptions it is, however, possible to speculate concerning their role in determining Edmund's portrayal.

Arundel 30 contains two sequences of inscriptions relating to St Edmund which are likely to have been in the vicinity of the shrine, on fol. 1 and fol. 208, the nature of which provides a striking indication of the way in which the abbey sought to present its patron. Eleven inscriptions in leonine verse accompanying a sequence of images are recorded on fol. 1. These are designated in Arundel 30 as being '*in quadam cortina*' (on a certain curtain).[66] Jocelin of Brakelond notes that at the time of the fire in 1198 'the great beam which used to be beyond the altar had been taken down to be renovated with new carving'. St Edmund's shrine was located 'beyond', that is, east of, the high altar and this beam therefore seems a likely location from which hangings depicting the life and miracles of St Edmund could be suspended. The inscriptions are counter-chronological, as they begin with two post-mortem miracles before detailing in reverse the events of Edmund's martyrdom and royal rule. Combined with the idiosyncratic Latin of the verses this may suggest a scribe copying with little regard or understanding of meaning. However, I believe it is more likely to indicate something about the way in which the images, and therefore the events of Edmund's life, were encountered visually, with the scribe placing first in the list the images which he saw first, that is, those closest to his eye level, before looking upwards and recording each subsequent image in turn.

---

[64] James, *Verses*, p. 2.

[65] Cotton, MS Galba E.iv. The catalogue is printed in Edward Edwards, *Memoirs of Libraries*, 2 vols (London: Trübner and Co., 1859), I, pp. 122–236; p. 167.

[66] London, College of Arms, MS Arundel 30, fol. 1.

This is significant, as it means that the images closest to pilgrims as they viewed the hanging were depictions of Edmund's arguably most violent posthumous miracles. The first miracle concerns Leofstan, the local sheriff who denounced the right of the accused to claim sanctuary in the abbey church and challenged St Edmund's jurisdiction in legal matters and whom Edmund caused to be afflicted with demons by way of punishment.[67] The second describes the death of King Sweyn. A favourite with manuscript illuminators, an image of Sweyn's demise appears in both the Pierpont Morgan manuscript and in Harley 2278 (see Plate III). Six lines of verses are associated with this incident although they are extremely repetitive and are therefore unlikely to indicate six separate scenes. It is possible that the copyist was improvising upon the theme of the original inscription, or that he was composing inscriptions to describe the images which he saw upon the curtain.

The death of Sweyn appears again in a six-line sequence of inscriptions on fol. 208 of Arundel 30 where the images are designated as being located '*ad reliquias*' (at, or near, the relics). Considering the defining role of this narrative as evinced in the codicological cult discussed above it is likely that the relics they accompanied were Edmund's. The architectural arrangement of the presbytery, along with evidence in Arundel 30 of other art works in this area of the abbey church, leaves little wall space for this sequence of images to occupy. It therefore seems likely that these images were located in stained glass somewhere in the presbytery, perhaps in windows between the eastern-most radiating chapel and the chapels to the north and south.

The repetition of the death of Sweyn underlines its significance in the construction of the cult at Bury. It is also noteworthy that the only two posthumous narratives depicted appear to be those which involve punishment of individuals who attempt to violate the abbey and its patron. These are foolish individuals acting in lone defiance of the saint, in contrast with the *tota plebs* who collectively invoke Edmund's help against Sweyn and the *plebs* of the *cortina* sequence who are overcome by the invading Danes. It is likely that the *plebs* would be depicted in the images, possibly at or near the eye level of the pilgrims, encouraging visitors to the shrine to read themselves into the narrative, with such reflexive representation encouraging devotees to believe that the prayers of people like them would be heeded by St Edmund, whilst also alluding to the dire consequences for those who transgressed.[68] Both the Leofstan and Sweyn narratives offer the opportunity

---

[67] Herman, *De Miraculis*, ed. Arnold, *Memorials*, I, p. 48.

[68] For the presence of the recipients of miracles, both benign and punitive, in images in the vicinity of shrine see Blick and Tekippe, eds, *Art and Architecture*, 'Introduction', xvii. See also Anne F. Harris, 'Pilgrimage, Performance and Stained Glass at Canterbury Cathedral', in the same volume, pp. 243–84.

to remind pilgrims that the power of the saint was most potent in the vicinity of his relics.

Furthermore, the scenes *ad reliquias* and those *in quadam cortina* are the only two sequences of Edmund images which are detailed in Arundel 30 as being located in areas of the church likely to have been visited by pilgrims. A similar message concerning Edmund's power and the proprietorial nature of his sanctity is conveyed by the inscriptions accompanying illustrations in the monks' choir which are recorded in Bodley 240, which depicted the punishment of thieves who attempted to steal horses from the abbey church.[69] This location would have been inaccessible to pilgrims and it is significant that the convent consigned to a private location a narrative in which the thieves successfully violate the abbey, as opposed to the public setting of the miracles of Leofstan and Sweyn, against whom Edmund intervenes before they are able to cause real harm. Perhaps the story of the horse thieves was meant to teach the monks humility and remind them of the need for vigilance, whereas Leofstan and Sweyn offered less ambiguous and more compelling instances of Edmund's intercessory might to present to pilgrims.

It is possible that the Arundel 30 inscriptions existed only in manuscript form. They may have been composed in response to images or may represent plans for an imagined decorative scheme, or perhaps even scribal doodling.[70] This might explain the multiple versions of some inscriptions, if the scribe were experimenting with different textual forms. Even if we assume that the inscriptions in Arundel 30 represent a faithful record of the imagery within the abbey church, this does not mean that these were the only images of St Edmund to have existed, but it does suggest that these were the only ones to have been accompanied by inscriptions at the time when the authors of the manuscript were writing. In an essay on the miracle windows of the Trinity Chapel at Canterbury, Anne F. Harris suggests that inscriptions accompanying imagery played a figurative rather than just a literal role. She argues that the pictures can be understood without the words, which many pilgrims would be unable to read. She suggests that it is not what they say that is most significant, but that they are recognisable as text and therefore connote the authority of text.[71] As such they are intended to imbue the images which they accompany with additional veracity. Whether or not the two

---

[69] Bodley 240, ed. Arnold, *Memorials*, II, p. 362.

[70] Baudri de Bourgueil (Baldricus Burgulianus), Archbishop of Dol (1046–1130), for example, is well known for his experimentation in verse composition, offering several versions of the same visual subject. See Baudri de Bourgueil, *Poèmes*, 2 vols, ed. Jean-Yves Tillette (Paris: Belles Lettres, 2002), II, pp. 151–7.

[71] Harris, 'Pilgrimage, Performance and Stained Glass', in *Art and Architecture*, ed. Blick and Tekippe, pp. 260–1.

sequences at Bury were the only ones to be accompanied by inscriptions, Harris's suggestion seems apt, as these images of Edmund are fundamentally concerned with conveying his spiritual power.

The visual presentation of Edmund's authority in the abbey church would be further reinforced if, as Sandy Heslop has suggested, the Morgan miniatures cycle may actually be designs for, or based upon, a series of images, perhaps a series of hangings in the vicinity of the shrine.[72] This interpretation is primarily based upon the internal dynamics of the manuscript. To some extent the miniatures are ideally suited to be viewed on the page. Figures gesture across the folios at one another and the narrative disruptions caused by turning the page are addressed by the movement of figures through the margins; for example, during the transportation of Edmund's relics to London, Egelwyn departs into the right hand margin of fol. 20r and reappears overleaf on fol. 20v. Heslop concludes that the Morgan cycle is therefore 'better adapted to the successive pages of a book, or more concerned with the continuity of the story than with isolated "iconic" moments'.[73] However, some aspects of the pictorial organisation make the miniatures better suited to an alternative method of viewing. The scenes are grouped in short narrative sequences, usually of three or six scenes, and are organised around the central event: the martyrdom. The moment of Edmund's death and the subsequent hiding of his head are shown in a double scene (fol. 14v), unique in the manuscript, emphasising the centrality of these events both in Edmund's legend and in the miniatures sequence, occupying as they do the sixteenth and seventeenth scenes respectively of the total thirty-three. The miniatures either side of this visual meridian display a certain symmetry: the Danes who arrive on fol. 9v leave on fol. 15. This almost typological method of arrangement has illustrative and textual precedents: Heslop argues that the St Albans Psalter evinces a similar arrangement and cites David Howlett's exposition of similar structural principles in the so-called 'Biblical style'.[74] The numerous visual equivalences of the Morgan cycle would be best appreciated if the images were viewed as a complete set, with each individual sequence intact. The total number of miniatures (thirty-two) does not neatly accord with the tripartite arrangement of the sequences,

---

[72] T.A. Heslop, 'Arranging the Episodes: The Picture Cycles in Two Twelfth-century Manuscripts', Research Seminar, University of York, 24 February 2010. I am grateful to the author for a copy of this paper. A similar transmission of imagery across media may be seen in medieval illustrations of St Cuthbert, see Malcolm Baker, 'Medieval Illustrations of Bede's *Life of St Cuthbert*', *Journal of the Warburg and Courtauld Institutes* xli (1978), 16–49.

[73] Heslop, 'Arranging the Episodes'.

[74] Heslop, 'Arranging the Episodes'. David Howlett, *British Books in Biblical Style* (Dublin: Four Courts, 1997).

unless the subdivided fol. 14v is treated as two. Subdividing the miniatures into their sequences results in eleven sets of three. If these images were originally for public display a likely location would be between the columns of the presbytery, perhaps as tapestry hangings, leading pilgrims through the narrative of Edmund's life and death as they circumambulated the shrine. The nature of the imagery of the Morgan cycle has been discussed above, and would certainly accord with the expression of Edmund's punitive authority seen in the Arundel 30 inscriptions, most notably with the repetition of the death of Sweyn.

The Frenze palimpsest brass

It is possible that the death of Sweyn appeared in at least one other location in the abbey church. In May 1987 the inscription plate from one of the monumental brasses in the disused church at Frenze (Norfolk) was removed from its slab for inclusion in the Monumental Brass Society's centenary exhibition at the Victoria and Albert Museum.[75] The inscription commemorates George Duke, who, according to the monument, died in 1551:

Heare under lyeth George duke Esquyre, who maryed Anne the dawghter of syr thom' Blenerhaysett knight the whyche George dyed the xxv. daye of July In the yeare Of oure lorde god a M'. CCCCC. Li: whose sowle God pardon. Amen.

When the plate was lifted it was discovered that the brass was a palimpsest.[76] On the reverse is an image of a king seated in bed beneath a crown-shaped canopy. The bed rests on a tiled floor raised above the grass in the foreground by a low plinth with three triangular projections. The king is pierced with a spear, from the shaft of which is suspended a drawstring bag. The king's soul, a naked infant with a grotesque face, is seized by a hirsute winged demon. Following the exhibition the brass was returned 'king side down' to its original position in Frenze church, but a rubbing taken at the time of the exhibition indicates the remarkably close similarity between this image and the iconography of the death of Sweyn found in other contexts, most notably the miniatures in the manuscripts

---

[75] John Page-Phillips, *Witness in Brass: The Catalogue of the Monumental Brass Society Centenary Exhibition* (London: Victoria and Albert Museum, 1987), p. 39, no. 205.

[76] Nicholas Rogers discusses the brass in 'The Frenze Palimpsest', in *Contexts of Medieval Art: Images, Objects and Ideas: Tributes to Nigel Morgan*, ed. Julian Luxford and M.A. Michael (London: Harvey Miller, 2010), pp. 223–37. On palimpsests in general, see John Page-Phillips, *Palimpsests: The Backs of Monumental Brasses*, 2 vols (London: Monumental Brass Society, 1980).

of Lydgate's *Lives*, both in Harley 2278 where the impish devil seizes Sweyn's soul (fol. 103v) and in Yates Thompson 47 and the Arundel Castle manuscript where the king grasps the spear as it enters his body, from which is suspended a money bag (fol. 83).

The 1550s re-engraving of the memorial inscription has been assigned to Bury St Edmunds and it seems likely that the original engraving also originated in East Anglia. John Goodall notes that several aspects of the design can be paralleled in East Anglian art: for example, indented bases with roundels may be seen in windows from North Tuddenham (Norfolk), c.1460, East Harling (Norfolk) c.1462–80 and Long Melford (Suffolk), also late fifteenth century. The tufts of grass in the foreground are also similar to those found on brasses made at both Norwich and Bury.[77] This indicates an East-Anglian provenance and suggests a date in the latter part of the fifteenth century.[78] This accords with John Page Phillips' suggestion that the brass may originally have been one of a sequence made to re-cover St Edmund's shrine following the fire which devastated the abbey church in 1465.[79] The convent's predilection for adorning the area surrounding the shrine with images of the death of Sweyn makes this attribution plausible. Brass plates would also be a relatively inexpensive means of re-embellishing the shrine with a fire-proof material which would nevertheless, when polished, provide a suitably splendid covering for St Edmund's relics. Traces of gilding found during the examination of the brass for the 1987 exhibition make its use in a high-status context even more likely.[80]

Whilst this method of embellishing a shrine appears to have been unusual, it is not without precedent. The dark limestone sarcophagus of St Henry of Finland (d.1156) at Nousisainen (Finland) was similarly covered with brass plates.[81] Made c.1420 and probably of Flemish origin, the tomb represents what Anthony Cutler describes as the 'cosmopolitan artistic atmosphere' of Finland in the fifteenth century and its close connections with other major northern European centres of artistic manufacture.[82] On the lid of the tomb was a large bronze plate with a

---

[77] John Goodall, 'Death and the Impenitent Avaricious King: A Unique Brass Discovered at Frenze, Norfolk', *Apollo*, ns 126 (October 1987), 264–6; 265.

[78] For further assertions of the brass's East Anglian provenance see Nicholas Rogers, 'The Frenze Palimpsest', *Monumental Brass Society Bulletin* no. 64 (Oct. 1993), pp. 75–7.

[79] John Page-Phillips, 'Palimspsest Brasses', in *Monumental Brasses as Art and History*, ed. Jerome Bertram (Stroud: Alan Sutton, 1996), pp. 132–45; pp. 134 and 136, figure 104.

[80] Rogers, 'The Frenze Palimpsest', p. 223.

[81] M.R. James, 'The Sepulchral Brass of St Henry of Finland', *Proceedings of the Cambridge Antiquarian Society* x (1901–2), 215–225.

[82] Anthony Cutler, 'The *Mulier Amicta* Sole and Her Attendants. An Episode in Late Medieval Finnish Art', *Journal of the Warburg and Courtauld Institutes* 29 (1966), 117– 134; 130.

figure of the deceased saint, whilst the side plates show scenes from the martyrdom and miracles of the twelfth-century English bishop sent to Finland by Pope Adrian IV (1154–59), who met his death in the aftermath of the Finnish 'crusade' of 1154.[83] Hans Eichler suggests that the now lost tomb of Wicbold von Dobilstein, bishop of Kulm, made in 1398 in the cathedral of Altenberg, near Cologne, was similarly covered at the sides with engraved brasses of narrative compositions, in this instance of the passion of Christ, while on the upper plate was the figure of the deceased. Although it was not the shrine of a saint, Eichler maintains that the same workshop which made this tomb was responsible for Henry of Finland's shrine.[84] This clearly indicates a tradition of adorning tombs in this way and therefore establishes a precedent for the Frenze brass to have originated in a similar context at Bury St Edmunds.

In contrast, Goodall suggests that the scene depicts the death of an unrepentant avaricious king and the fate of his soul, likening the image to that of avarice in the illustrations of the *Ars moriendi* (art of dying) tradition which was extremely popular in north-western Europe by the fifteenth century. However, he concedes that this image does not accord exactly with the known *Ars moriendi* iconography, which is remarkably homogenous in its representation of the temptations of the dying. Instead, he proposes that the Frenze image represents a hitherto unknown tradition. The uneven edges of the brass suggest that it was originally displayed in a frame and Goodall surmises that the image of avarice along with the four other temptations and the five virtues of the dying would originally have made a composition of around 1.5m square, which he suggests once adorned the wall of a church to edify and admonish the congregation. His primary objection to the shrine attribution seems to be the lack of iconographic precedents for the death of Sweyn at Bury which could have provided a model for the engraver.[85] However, I have demonstrated that this was not the case, and that examples were in fact abundant in a variety of media.

Although differing in his interpretation of the sequence, Goodall correctly surmises that the Frenze brass was unlikely to have been an isolated panel. The established iconography of the scene suggests that another plate to the right of the extant panel would depict St Edmund engaged in the act of spearing Sweyn. The plate varies from 3mm to 5mm in thickness and now measures 40 × 20 cm, although it was originally slightly larger, as the top edge lacks the border which

---

[83] See Tancred Borenius, 'St Henry of Finland, an Anglo-Scandinavian Saint', *Archaeological Journal* lxxxvii (1930), 340–56 and Plate I.

[84] Hans Eichler, 'A Flemish Brass of 1398', *The Burlington Magazine for Connoisseurs* 61, no. 353 (August 1932), 84–7; 85.

[85] Goodall, 'Death and the Impenitent Avaricious King', 265–6.

surrounds the other sides of the image. Assuming that each plate would have been of roughly equal dimensions, and assuming that each side of the shrine would have been covered in plates, it is likely that twenty to twenty-four plates would have covered the shrine.[86] If the engravers maintained the tradition of depicting universal Christian images such as the Crucifixion or the Virgin and Child on the ends of the shrine, this would still have allowed at least sixteen plates to be devoted to scenes from the life and miracles of St Edmund. The extreme selectivity evinced by artists depicting Edmund in other contexts negates Goodall's anxiety concerning the large number of scenes that it would be necessary to depict in order to fully illustrate the legend.[87] Similarly, his surprise that no other plates have been found and that this plate was not reused until 1551 overlooks the chaotic nature of the post-Reformation art market. Faced with a deluge of materials, it is plausible that a workshop in Bury or its vicinity would not have reused a plate from the shrine until twelve years after it was dismantled. The question of whether or not other plates are still extant has surely not been definitively answered. The discovery of this plate twenty-three years ago suggests that others may still be in existence, lying face down in the floors, or against the walls, of Norfolk and Suffolk churches.

The exclusive nature of iconography should also not be emphasised. Barbara Abou-El-Haj notes the similarity between the iconography of the death of Sweyn in the Morgan miniature and the slaying of Discord by Faith in a St Albans Prudentius manuscript of about 1125, which she suggests was probably the model for the Morgan artist.[88] Rather than complicating the attribution of the Morgan miniature, this co-mingling of iconographic traditions further nuances Edmund's miraculous smiting because, as Abou-El-Haj notes, it was Edmund's refusal to renounce Christianity which led to his martyrdom, and thus his presentation in the guise of avenging faith is entirely appropriate.[89] Likewise, Sweyn is an avaricious king and Edmund does indeed bring death, so the suggestion that these images embody the *Ars moriendi* tradition is apposite. The similarity between the death of Sweyn scenes and the image of death striking a young man whilst his wife looks on, aghast, that accompanies the Office of the Dead in the Macclesfield Psalter also serves to remind the viewer of the saints as conduits of the universal and enduring power of God, ultimate arbiters in matters of mortality.[90]

---

[86] This is based on the assumption that a *feretory* for an intact adult corpse would be at least 160cm long, and probably 40–60cm wide. For discussion of the relative size of *feretra* see Nilson, *Cathedral Shrines*, p. 35.
[87] Goodall, 'Death and the Impenitent Avaricious King', 266.
[88] Abou-El-Haj, 'Property, Privilege, and Monastic Art Production', 12.
[89] Abou-El-Haj, 'Property, Privilege, and Monastic Art Production', 12.
[90] University of Cambridge, The Fitzwilliam Museum, MS I-2005, *The Macclesfield Psalter*, fol. 235v.

The chronology of these images of the death of Sweyn is uncertain. It is unlikely that they were all present simultaneously, and indeed uncertain that all of them were in fact present, so any conclusions must be provisional. What can be ascertained with some certainty is a continued interest at Bury St Edmunds in this particular incident. Just as the manuscript illuminators chose to emphasise certain elements of Edmund's sanctity, so too the artists and craftspeople who decorated his shrine and its surroundings over a period of at least 150 years highlighted this scene as a central image of Edmund's saintly identity. The nature of the imagery in the context of pilgrimage is striking. As the defining feature of Edmund's post-mortem activities presented in numerous media in the abbey church, presumably of particular interest to pilgrims who sought his intercession, he appears a forbidding saint. However, as demonstrated above, far from being deterred by images of an aggressive saint engaged in acts of violent retribution, pilgrims to the shrine of St Edmund were intended to be impressed by the scope of his powers and reassured of his ability to intervene on their behalf, no matter what problem they brought to his attention.

Once again, this is also reflected in the fragmentary remains of the motet collection from Bury, which reveal an interest in ideal forms of kingship.[91] *Rex visibilium*, for example, is dedicated to Jesus Christ the King and demonstrates a preoccupation in righteous war and a divine struggle against evil in its laudatory lines: '*Rex invinctissime regnorum omnium, princeps milicie celorum civium*' ('Invincible king of all kingdoms, leader of the army of the citizens of heaven'). Beneath this the tenor line emphasises the infinite *status quo*: '*Regnum tuum solidum permanebit in eternum*' ('Your firm kingdom will endure forever').[92] A motet in honour of St Benedict, *Lux refulgent monachorum*, reflects the Benedictine provenance of the collection. The opening line proclaims that '*Lux refulgent monachorum Regis in palacio*' ('The light of the monks shines in the palace of the king').[93] Colton suggests that these motets 'express Bury's perceived identity as a seat of royal sanctity on a par with the court itself, or with Westminster Abbey ...; this may reflect the importance of the Liberty of Bury St Edmunds ... within which the abbot's powers rivalled that of the reigning monarch'.[94] In this context she suggests that the 'palace of the king' could equally well refer to the universal Church of God or to the abbey church which housed the remains of St Edmund.[95]

---

[91] The following motets are preserved in Oxford, Bodleian Library, MS e Musaeo 7 (s. xiv) and discussed by Colton in 'Music and Identity', pp. 101–4
[92] Translation from *Motets of English Provenance*, ed. Harrison and Lefferts, p. 189.
[93] Translation from *Motets of English Provenance*, ed. Harrison and Lefferts, p. 189.
[94] Colton, 'Music and Identity', p. 104.
[95] Colton, 'Music and Identity', p. 104.

The pilgrimage route

Attempting to determine the route by which pilgrims approached the shrine of St Edmund at Bury is important, as pilgrimage is generally characterised as a physical experience; Edith Turner, for example, characterises it as first and foremost a 'kinetic ritual'.[96] This is true of both the pilgrims' journeys to the sacred site and the ritual movements performed on their arrival, such as perambulating around a shrine. Coleman and Elsner suggest that the act of encircling the sacred object ritually defines the space as holy, as it distinguishes it from the journey undertaken to reach the shrine:

> The circumambulation continues the theme of the pilgrim's movement but rather than involving a directional, linear striving to reach the goal now encapsulates the sacred centre in a circular embrace.[97]

Thus at many greater shrine churches the physical movement of pilgrims as well as the visual and auditory experience was carefully orchestrated and formed an important element of the reception of the holy.

Evidence from Bury provides some indications of how pilgrims physically approached St Edmund's shrine. Abbot Curteys' *Register* indicates that Henry VI entered the abbey church via the south transept on his arrival at Bury on Christmas Eve in 1433.[98] This was likely to be partly a result of practical necessity: the west tower of the church partially collapsed in January 1430, when the south side fell; the following year the east side fell; and in April 1432 the north and west sides were taken down. Indulgences for its repair were granted by a papal bull of Eugenius IV (1431–39) and in 1435 a Colchester mason, John Wode, was given a contract for

---

[96] Victor and Edith Turner, *Image and Pilgrimage in Christian Culture* (Oxford: Blackwell, 1978), Introduction, xiii. Conversely, scholarly interest has also been paid to objects or locations which invite devotees to undertake 'mental pilgrimages' without leaving their current locations. See, for example, Jeanne Nuechterlein's discussion of Hans Memling's shrine of St Ursula made before 1489 for St John's Hospital, Bruges, where it is still located. Nuechterlein argues that this shrine encourages the viewer to reflect on the act of pilgrimage as well as being an object of devotion in its own right. Jeanne Nuechterlein, 'Hans Memling's St Ursula Shrine: The Subject as Object of Pilgrimage', *Art and Architecture*, ed. Blick and Tekippe, pp. 51–75.

[97] Simon Coleman and John Elsner, *Pilgrimage, Past and Present: Sacred Travel and Sacred Space in the World Religions* (London: British Museum Press, 1995), pp. 32–3.

[98] Curteys's Register, BL Add. MS 14848, fol. 128r-v; this passage is reprinted in Ord, 'Account of the Entertainment of King Henry the Sixth', *Archaeologia* 15 (1806), 65–71.

five years to rebuild the tower.[99] The west end would therefore have been a less desirable route for the king to enter the church by on this occasion.

Allowing pilgrims access to a shrine by means other than the west door also had more general practical benefits. Accessing a shrine in the presbytery via the west door and thence the nave would require pilgrims to negotiate the numerous grilles and screens surrounding the tombs and chapels in their path and although this would certainly contribute to the anticipation of the occasion, the resulting logistical problems were likely to have been considerable. This arrangement would also require more extensive management to ensure that the movement and direction of pilgrims was maintained in accordance with the wishes of the church administrators. An alternative arrangement which accommodated these considerations seems to have been in place at a number of locations. At Ely and Westminster, for example, pilgrims entered the church via a door in the north transept.[100] The evidence from Winchester is particularly compelling, where the north door of the nave, located in the western-most bay of the north aisle, was known as St Swithun's Door, suggesting that this was the entrance used by pilgrims to the shrine of the saint.[101] Similarly, the so-called 'Judgement Porch' at Lincoln was constructed c.1260 as part of the remodelling of St Hugh's Choir which took place between 1256 and 1280. The Angel Choir was built to extend the presbytery and increase the space behind the altar for the accommodation of pilgrims and the remodelled space was provided with its own door to the east of the south transept to facilitate their ingress and egress.[102] At Bury, as at Lincoln, the cloister was to the north of the monastic church and thus an entrance for pilgrims to the south would have been similarly convenient.

At Bury, the location of the *rotunda* chapel to the north of the Romanesque church may have complicated the route taken by pilgrims, as even after Edmund's

---

[99] The fall of the tower is recorded in Curteys's Register, British Library, MS Add. 14848, fols 105–6. See also James, *On the Abbey Church*, p. 122 and John Gage, 'Historical Notices of the Great Bell Tower of the Abbey Church of St Edmundsbury', *Archaelogia* xxiii (1831), 329–30.

[100] Nilson, *Cathedral Shrines*, pp. 93–4. For further discussion of the route taken by pilgrims to Westminster Abbey see Francis B. Bond, *Westminster Abbey* (London, 1909), p. 67. For Ely see Thomas D. Atkinson, *An Architectural History of the Benedictine Monastery of St Etheldreda at Ely*, 2 vols (Cambridge: Cambridge University Press, 1933), I, p. 28.

[101] St Swithun's Door at Winchester is discussed by C.R. Peers and H. Brakespear, 'Architectural Description of Winchester Cathedral', *Victoria County History: Hampshire and the Isle of Wight*, vol. 5, ed. William Page (London: Constable, 1912), p. 58.

[102] Lynne Broughton, *Interpreting Lincoln Cathedral: The Medieval Imagery* (Lincoln: Lincoln Cathedral Publications, 1996), pp. 59–66.

translation into the presbytery it is likely to have remained a significant feature of the pilgrimage experience until its demolition in 1275 and would most likely have been integrated into the pilgrimage route to enrich the encounter with St Edmund's remains and provide an additional opportunity for the convent to elicit offerings. Avoiding the crossing was a persistent necessity in monastic churches, and pilgrims entering via the south transept therefore presumably proceeded anti-clockwise around the presbytery and then returned the way they had come and exited by the same doorway. Certainly after the demolition of the *rotunda* in 1275 it would be highly desirable for pilgrims to enter the precinct via this route, ensuring that they passed, and made offerings at, the chapel in the cemetery where the secondary relics were rehoused. The bier and other relics would provide a prelude to the main spectacle of the great shrine in the presbytery. The absence of the coffin from the bier on which it once rested would have created a sense of expectation for what was to come, with the funerary connotations of the bier contrasting with the spiritual glory signified by the shrine. These connotations would not have been lost with the destruction of the *rotunda*, as the removal of the relics from the vicinity of Edmund's shrine increased the time, and therefore the anticipation, between encountering the secondary relics and the body of St Edmund himself.

It is unlikely, however, that the south transept was the only entrance for pilgrims. The majority of greater shrines were accessed via the nave, since this was the public part of the church and the most convenient place for pilgrims to gather before visiting the shrine.[103] This would also allow them to pass and make offerings at altars and subsidiary nave shrines, which could be of considerable financial benefit to the religious community.[104] As discussed above, the architecture of the west front of the abbey church at Bury attests to its significance in the ritual life of the building. In addition, particular details of its ornamentation and design affirm its symbolic importance. It appears that a frieze ran across the width of the façade above the three huge portals. The frieze as a form of external decoration was uncommon on medieval churches. Zarnecki notes that the majority of Romanesque examples are found in the Mediterranean region, where he suggests surviving Roman buildings provided the model.[105] This accords with the Roman connotations of the three giant arches on the west front at Bury, and at Lincoln where the frieze survives.[106] Only two fragments of the Bury frieze survive and

---

[103] Nilson, *Cathedral Shrines*, p. 94.
[104] For the financial value of shrines see Nilson, *Cathedral Shrines*, pp. 134–82.
[105] George Zarnecki, *Romanesque Sculpture at Lincoln Cathedral*, Lincoln Minster Pamphlets, 2nd series, no. 2 (Lincoln: Friends of Lincoln Cathedral, 1970), p. 3.
[106] Fernie notes that the giant arches at Lincoln and Bury have been compared to a Roman monument such as the Porte de Mars in Rheims. Fernie, *Anglo-Norman Architecture*,

are preserved in Moyse's Hall Museum in Bury.[107] One sculpture is of an angel, carved at what Zarnecki suggests was probably the angle of a door-jamb.[108] The second relief depicts the torments of the usurer (identifiable by the sack of money he carries), who is being thrust into a Hell-mouth by devils whilst snakes coil around him, indicating that the frieze depicted the Last Judgement, a popular theme above church portals as it reminded the faithful that the church was God's house and that they must be suitably repentant upon entering. In the context of pilgrimage it was particularly relevant for individuals to be spiritually prepared as they approached the shrine to ask the saint to intercede for God's favour on their behalf. The deployment of this iconography in the context of pilgrimage is attested elsewhere by the Judgement Portal at Lincoln.[109]

The octagons flanking the west front of the abbey church at Bury are one of the most unusual elements of the design and seem to have been unique.[110] The significance of circular churches as royal *mausolea* or *martyria* is discussed above and the connotations of Cnut's *rotunda* would also pertain in this context. The original elevation and function of the west front octagons is unclear but their shape would certainly recall Cnut's *rotunda* which was obscured by the building of the Romanesque church. This feature may once again serve to highlight the continuity with the pre-Conquest cult and remind pilgrims of the presence of St Edmund within the church by presenting them with an architectural form with which they may have come to associate Edmund's remains. Equally, the integration of the octagons as one small part of an enormous and elaborate whole contributed to a compelling architectural articulation of the dominance of the abbey.

Both routes into the abbey church therefore had their own practical and symbolic advantages and both may have been used. Entering the abbey church through the vast, elaborate and symbolically resonant west front prepared pilgrims for the glories within and reminded them of the wealth of the abbey and the power of the saint whose remains it housed. Approaching from the south and pausing in the monks' cemetery at the chapel containing his bier and other secondary relics built anticipation, with the empty bier attesting to Edmund's defeat of death, and his spiritual glory proclaimed by the jewel-encrusted shrine which housed his remains. Once they were inside the church, the visual and auditory experience was designed to impress and shape the pilgrims' perception of Edmund's saintly

p. 110. For the Lincoln frieze see Zarnecki, *Romanesque Sculpture at Lincoln Cathedral*, pp. 3–13.

[107] For the fragments of the Bury frieze see George Zarnecki, *Further Studies in Romanesque Sculpture* (London: Pindar Press, 1992), pp. 327–8 and figures 1 and 3.
[108] Zarnecki, *Further Studies*, p. 327 and figure 1.
[109] Broughton, *Interpreting Lincoln Cathedral*, pp. 59–66.
[110] McAleer, 'The West Front', pp. 23–9.

identity. Edmund's bodily wholeness contrasted with the fragmented remains of another East Anglian saint, St Botulph, whose presence along with St Jurmin reminded the faithful of Edmund's regional identity and promoted East Anglia as a region renowned for sanctity. Similarly, the iconographical context in which the shrine was situated reassured pilgrims that Edmund was a saint of national importance, a conqueror of kings, who was able in death to offer to his spiritual subjects the support and protection which in life he had been unable to provide. Ultimately, a pilgrim to the shrine of St Edmund at Bury would have encountered splendour befitting the erstwhile king of East Anglia and a nationally important saint.

PART III

Beyond Bury
Dissemination and appropriation

CHAPTER 8

Writing St Edmund into the East Anglian landscape

The power of his moral excellence which brightly lights up England might be transferred through us to other parts of the world, and thus he may receive a worthy increase on account of his merits.[1]

Dissemination and appropriation: the case of pilgrim badges

THUS far the focus has primarily been upon the development of Edmund's saintly identity at the cult centre: the hagiographic tradition which developed at the abbey, the miracles attributed to Edmund's uncorrupted remains and the devotional and iconographical setting of the shrine in the abbey church. However, in order to examine the true extent of the cult in its regional context it is necessary to move beyond Bury and consider the nature of devotion to St Edmund as manifested in a variety of contexts and locations throughout East Anglia.

Evidence of the cult in outlying areas of the region should not necessarily be taken as an indication of entirely independent devotional traditions, devoid of the abbey's influence. Pilgrim souvenirs are a good example of the way in which the cult could be disseminated throughout Norfolk and Suffolk, and further afield, through physical media. Although found throughout East Anglia and beyond, pilgrim badges were produced at Bury as mnemonic objects intended to perpetuate the pilgrims' imaginative and emotional connections with St Edmund established during their time in his presence.[2] Known by contemporaries as 'signs', they were worn as a marker of the pilgrimage undertaken by that individual.[3] Marike De Kroon demonstrates that in many cases pilgrim badges reflected the actual experience of pilgrims by depicting images and architectural forms encountered by

---

[1] Samson, *De Miraculis*, ed. Arnold, *Memorials*, I, p. 177.
[2] Thomas Head discusses the extent to which devotees formed personal relationships with the saints: *Hagiography and the Cult of Saints*, p. 12.
[3] For a discussion of the terminology associated with pilgrim badges see Jennifer M. Lee, 'Searching for Signs: Pilgrims' Identity and Experience Made Visible in the *Miracula Sancti Thomae Cantuariensis*', in *Art and Architecture*, ed. Blick and Tekippe, I, pp. 473–91.

them at the shrine site, reinforcing their function as commemorative souvenirs.[4] The role of pilgrim souvenirs as private devotional objects is attested by a number of badges either pasted or sewn into Books of Hours or depicted in the margins, attempting to capture the *virtus* of the object in paint.[5] In addition, badges were also thought to possess their own physical efficacy. It was common practice to press souvenirs against the shrine in order that they might absorb some of the power of the remains within, transforming them into contact-relics and allowing pilgrims to carry home with them some of the saint's *virtus*.[6]

Three distinct designs for St Edmund pilgrim badges have been identified. The simplest consists of a garb of arrows held together by a knotted belt, alluding to the manner of Edmund's martyrdom.[7] The significance of the belt is unclear, as there are no references to a relic of this kind, so it is likely to be aesthetic rather than symbolic. In some examples the arrows are held together by a crown. This changes the overall tone of the badge, as it affords equal prominence to Edmund's kingship in addition to the manner of his death. The most common pilgrim badge features a version of Edmund's martyrdom. The earliest iteration of this design depicts Edmund uncrowned, bound to a tree and pierced with many arrows.[8] Based on the details of the underclothes, or braies, that Edmund wears in these badges, Spencer dates the design to c.1250–1350.[9] A slightly later variant includes

---

[4] Marike de Kroon, 'Pilgrim Badges and their Iconographic Aspects', in *Art and Architecture*, ed. Blick and Tekippe, I, pp. 385–403; esp. pp. 387–8, 391–2, 394–5, 401.

[5] For example, impressions of twenty-nine pilgrim badges formerly stitched onto a blank leaf of a Flemish Book of Hours, c.1460–80, reproduced in Brian Spencer, *Pilgrim Souvenirs and Secular Badges*, Medieval Finds from Excavations in London, 7 (Woodbridge: The Boydell Press in association with the Museum of London, 1998, 2nd edn 2010), figure 10, p. 19. A leaf from another Flemish Book of Hours, c.1512, shows the martyrdom of St Sebastian surrounded by a border of pilgrim badges. Sir John Soane's Museum, London, MS 4, fol. 122v.

[6] For contact relics see Brian Spencer, *Salisbury and South Wiltshire Museum Medieval Catalogue. Part 2: Pilgrim Souvenirs and Secular Badges* (Salisbury: Salisbury and South Wiltshire Museum, 1990), Introduction, pp. 16–18. For the amuletic use of relics and other sacred objects see Richard Kieckhefer, *Magic in the Middle Ages* (Cambridge: Cambridge University Press, 2000). Documentary evidence for the practice is unsurprisingly sparse but is referred to in documents relating to the two-centuries-long dispute at Le Puy between the hospital of St Mary and local merchants over the right to manufacture and sell pilgrim badges. A fifteenth-century document states that the hospital would allow only 'legitimate' badges (presumably those produced under its auspices) to be pressed against the statue of St Mary. See Esther Cohen, '*In haec signia*: Pilgrim-Badge Trade in Southern France', *Journal of Medieval History* ii (1976), 193–214; 213 n. 29.

[7] No. 133 in Spencer, *Salisbury and South Wiltshire Museum Medieval Catalogue*, p. 82.

[8] Nos 199–200b in Spencer, *Pilgrim Souvenirs and Secular Badges*, p. 180.

[9] Spencer, *Pilgrim Souvenirs and Secular Badges* (Salisbury: Salisbury and South Wiltshire Museum, 1990), p. 49.

the wolf waiting at Edmund's feet, gazing up expectantly whilst the body of the king, often wearing only a loin-cloth, is pierced with fewer arrows.[10] A more elaborate form featuring archers on either side of Edmund persisted at least until the fifteenth century.[11] A third design appears to have emerged in the early fifteenth century. In these badges the presentation of Edmund differs considerably: robed and crowned, he holds either a single arrow or occasionally a bundle, the symbol of his martyrdom.[12] The contrast with the near-naked, tortured body is striking and offers a markedly different version of Edmund's sanctity, emphasising his spiritual triumph rather than his physical suffering.

As an item intended to disseminate the cult of a saint and stimulate remembrance among devotees it was essential that the badge was distinct and easily recognisable.[13] It is thus reasonable to assume that the depiction of Edmund on pilgrim badges provides an indication of his standard iconographical forms, or at least the way in which the convent sought to promote his image beyond the abbey. There is a marked contrast with the way in which Edmund was depicted in the abbey church, where, as we have seen, the visual emphasis was upon his punitive intercession. The version of Edmund chosen by the abbey for pilgrims to translate into the wider world was, understandably, that of the more munificent intercessor.

This brief introduction to pilgrim badges, one of the most obvious means by which Edmund's saintly identity was dispersed, raises a number of issues concerning the relationship between the cult at Bury and its manifestation further afield. The noticeable difference between the representation of Edmund in the abbey church and on the pilgrim souvenirs invokes the possibility of further variance in the visual codes associated with St Edmund. Chapter 10 therefore investigates the largest surviving body of imagery of St Edmund: his representation in many media in the churches of Norfolk and Suffolk.

The construction of alternative visual Edmunds is reminiscent of the variety of intercessory activities evinced in the miracle collections in Part I. The majority of miracles attributed to Edmund occurred in the vicinity of his shrine but a number are also recorded in locations beyond Bury. Although the *virtus* of the saints was strongest in the vicinity of their relics, its power was believed to extend beyond the confines of their shrines. Edmund's more widely dispersed

---

[10] No. 200c in Spencer, *Pilgrim Souvenirs and Secular Badges*, p. 180; No. 133 in Spencer, *Salisbury and South Wiltshire Museum Medieval Catalogue*, p. 82; *BAA: Bury*, Plate xxv-h.

[11] See James Robinson, 'A Late Medieval Pilgrim Badge from Chaucer House, Tabard Street, SE1', *The London Archaeologist* 6.3 (1989), 60–9.

[12] No. 135 in Spencer, *Salisbury and South Wiltshire Museum Medieval Catalogue*, p. 82.

[13] De Kroon, 'Pilgrim Badges and their Iconographic Aspects', p. 386.

miraculous activities will be therefore be considered in Chapter 9, with emphasis upon the extent to which it is possible to characterise miracles based on geographic location.

Finally, in Chapter 11, the discussion will depart from the region altogether to consider alternative textual representations of St Edmund. The overwhelming majority of regional hagiographic output originated at Bury, but Edmund does appear in sermon manuals and collections of saints' lives written elsewhere in England, thus offering the opportunity to consider Edmund in a non-Bury-based textual context and to examine how this compares with the larger body of material produced on home territory.

Writing St Edmund into East Anglia

Underpinning these discussions is the geographical scope of the cult: the locations beyond Bury in which Edmund was venerated. In addition to church and chapel dedications, one of the ways this may be determined is by mapping the legend of St Edmund onto the East Anglian landscape and noting the extent to which his life relates to the region as a physical entity. Bury was the epicentre of the cult and the ultimate destination for pilgrims to St Edmund, but other sites throughout Norfolk and Suffolk also came to be associated with the saint by the authorial practice of naming locations at which notable events of his legend occurred. As an authorising process and a method of cultic construction this is distinct from, although closely related to, the interest demonstrated in particular by Abbo and Geoffrey of Wells in the general physical characteristics of East Anglia. It is certainly the case that the naming of locations associated with St Edmund similarly adds authenticity to the legend and embeds the cult within the local landscape, identifying Edmund as a saint with a distinct regional identity. However, the topographical specificity evinced by some authors seems to function in a distinct way, and when considered in the context of pilgrimage activity and the physical presence of the cult these features acquire additional significance.

The map at the front of this volume shows the geographical distribution of the locations which came to be associated with St Edmund. Their dispersal throughout the region is striking, extending as they do from Hunstanton on the north-west coast of Norfolk to Bures on the boundary between Suffolk and Essex in the south. Edmund is located at seats of royal governance (Bures and Thetford) and by Lydgate at 'Castre', possibly Caistor St Edmund, an important strategic Roman fort (perhaps also the '*castro*' referred to by the Bodley 240 compiler).[14]

---

[14] See John A. Davis, *Venta Icenorum: Caistor St Edmund Roman Town* (East Dereham: Norfolk Archaeological Trust, 2001).

The legend locates Edmund at places across the length and breadth of the ancient kingdom of East Anglia (Table 1).

Stephen Reimer suggests that it seems 'almost as if someone deliberately set out to make sure that every region of the kingdom was represented in the story'.[15] This is particularly notable in the narrative first recorded by Geoffrey of Wells concerning Edmund's arrival in East Anglia and the events leading up to his coronation in which the young prince arrives at the furthest north-west corner of his new kingdom, around Hunstanton, journeys to its centre where he resides for a year at Attleborough, before travelling to its southern extremity to be crowned at Bures. There is no readily discernible reason why Edmund should have landed in north-west Norfolk. Even given Geoffrey's misinterpretation of Abbo's claim that Edmund descended from the Old Saxons to mean that he was born in Saxony, it would more feasible for him to land somewhere on the east coast, perhaps at the Saxon port of Ipswich.[16] The most plausible motivation for Edmund to land near Hunstanton is that it enables him, as Reimer suggests, to traverse the entire kingdom in the first actions of his reign.

Coleman discusses the relationship between texts and places of religious significance, noting the important function of texts as 'authoritative charters' which define the sanctity of a space or object.[17] In turn, sites associated with holy figures act as embodiments of myth-history and can serve as witnesses of the truth of a text or revelatory event: as the pilgrim encounters a holy place, he or she experiences physically what had previously perhaps been known only through sacred narrative or its visual illustrations.[18] Coleman concludes that in many cases texts and places are inextricably linked and mutually dependent, as 'they both physically exist and gain mythological significance from their location in words as well as in a landscape.'[19] It is likely that the relationship between text and place was not always so neatly reciprocal. Coleman acknowledges that there are instances of shrine guardians 'generating' sacred texts in order to justify the charisma attributed to a particular location.[20]

---

[15] Stephen R. Reimer, 'Unbinding Lydgate's *Lives of Saints Edmund and Fremund*', in *The Book Unbound: Editing and Reading Medieval Manuscripts and Texts*, ed. Sîan Echard and Stephen Partridge (Toronto: University of Toronto Press, 2004), pp. 176–89; p. 181.

[16] Keith Wade, '*Gipeswic* – East Anglia's First Economic Capital, 600–1066', in *Ipswich From The First To The Third Millennium*, ed. N. Salmon and R. Malster, (Ipswich: The Ipswich Society, 2001), pp. 1–6.

[17] Coleman and Elsner, *Pilgrimage; Past and Present*, p. 202.

[18] Coleman and Elsner, *Pilgrimage; Past and Present*, p. 203.

[19] Coleman and Elsner, *Pilgrimage; Past and Present*, pp. 202–3.

[20] Coleman and Elsner, *Pilgrimage; Past and Present*, p. 203.

Table 1 Topographical references

Narrative context	Abbo	De Miraculis	Geoffrey of Wells	Bodley 240	Lydgate
Landing in East Anglia; miraculous springs appear			Maydenebure (prob. St Edmund's Point nr. Hunstanton)	Maydenboure (prob. St Edmund's Point nr. Hunstanton)	Maydenburuh (prob. St Edmund's Point nr. Hunstanton
Builds a royal town			Hunstanton	Honystanestoun	Hunstanton
Pre-coronation			Attleborough	Athlesburgh/ Civitas Athle	Attleborough
Coronation			Bures (St Mary)	Villa de Bure	Bures
Holding court when Danes invade	Hægelisdun[1]		*	'In quodam castro'/'in castello'	Castre (Caistor St Edmund)
Battle			*	Theofordiam	Thetford
Martyrdom			*		Hoxne
Hidden head	Haglesdun		*	Heylesdun	Heylesdone
Initial burial		Sutton	*	Hoxne	
Resting place of relics	Bedrices-gueord/ Bedrici-curtis	Bedericsworth	*	Bedricesworthe	Bury St Edmunds

Note: [1] Hægelisdun/Haglesdun/Heylesdone has traditionally been read as 'Hellesdon', a village now incorporated into the north-western suburbs of Norwich. However, the debate concerning the location of Edmund's martyrdom continued to incite scholarly debate (and local pride). See Introduction for further details.

A likely site of this kind associated with Edmund is St Edmund's wells in Old Hunstanton (Norfolk), which today are still identified as a series of ponds in the vicinity of the church. Geoffrey of Wells is the first author to mention the wells (there is no evidence to connect him with this location, although the toponymic equivalence is intriguing).[21] In his account of Edmund's arrival in East Anglia he relates that the young prince knelt and gave thanks for a successful sea crossing from 'Saxony':

---

[21] A second spring associated with St Edmund lies close to Hoxne, to the north of Abbey Farm on the site of a Benedictine priory founded in 950 and dedicated to St Athelbright or Ethelbert. A deep moat or square pond encloses a small island on which was a freshwater spring, said to have emerged on the spot where Edmund's head was found guarded by the wolf. However, this spring does not feature in the medieval legend and appears to have acquired a folkloric association with the cult in the post-medieval period.

At that place also, as he rose from his knees, and mounted his horse, there broke from the ground twelve springs of extraordinary clearness, which continue to flow, even in these days, to the admiration of all who behold them as they glide perpetually to the sea with a pleasant and cheerful murmur.[22]

A notable instance of the elision of topography and sanctity is found in Harley 2278. The miniature on fol. 34 (see Plate IV) shows Edmund enthroned as symbolic personifications of the body politic circle round him: knights battle near his head; a church lingers near his heart; a sailing boat and a plough team toil near his feet. He is its ruler who ensures its harmonious functioning and this is represented by his synergy with the landscape itself, with the lush, green, undulating hills echoing the shape of his throne and the blue of the cloth evoking the watery fertility first celebrated by Abbo; just as East Anglia is girded by waters, so too is its king encircled. Edmund is the embodied signifier of his kingdom and its people.

The presence in saints' lives of topographical features such as holy wells is usually taken as an indication of the influence of popular devotion on the development of a cult.[23] 'Popular religion' is a complicated term which defies precise definition, but which is sometimes understood to mark a distinction between learned and elite religion and the religion of the less-learned masses. As Simon Yarrow notes, the notion of 'elite and popular religion' has continued to 'exercise' historians.[24] Yarrow cites a volume of Studies in Church History published in 2006 which, although aiming to unpick the elite–popular binary, he in fact believes 'confirmed the enduring afterlife of two-tier tradition'.[25] Some of the difficulties arising from this definition are readily apparent. In his important study of religious culture in England between 1050 and 1250, Carl Watkins sets out to challenge many of the assumptions about religious belief, such as the extent to which it is possible to divide people into discrete types, the possibility of defining 'learned' and 'unlearned' and distinguishing who belonged in each category, noting the reductive binaries often produced by assuming a correlation between patterns of belief and the social groupings of believers. He cites, for example, the

---

[22] Geoffrey of Wells, *De Infantia*, ed. Arnold, *Memorials*, I. 99–100.

[23] Graham Jones discusses the numerous examples of medieval churches associated with wells which appear to have been places of much older, and in many cases pre-Christian, religious practice. Graham Jones, *Saints in the Landscape: Heaven and Earth in Religious Dedications* (Stroud: Tempus, 2007), pp. 125–7. For a detailed study of holy wells see James Rattue, *The Living Stream: Holy Wells in Historical Context* (Woodbridge: Boydell, 1995).

[24] Simon Yarrow, 'Miracles, Belief and Christian Materiality: Relic'ing in Twelfth-Century Miracle Narratives', in *Contextualising Miracles*, ed. Mesley and Wilson (2014).

[25] *Elite and Popular Religion*, ed. Kate Cooper and Jeremy Gregory, Studies in Church History, 42 (Woodbridge, 2006).

case of monks and the aristocracy, noting that aristocratic families 'supplied the cloisters with recruits, were bound to them by the frequent exchange of gifts for prayers, and celebrated association with the life of renunciation because it seemed so valuable to the sinner in the world', concluding that 'monk and warrior were not marooned on either side of a cultural divide'.[26]

In the context of saints' cults the presence of natural markers is normally taken to suggest the spontaneous development of popular devotion independently of the authorised cult. Topographical references in a legend are a particularly clear indication of this, as they suggest cultic activity in locations other than the cult centre. Catherine Cubitt notes the particular prevalence of topographical features in the legends of martyred and murdered Anglo-Saxon royal saints, which she identifies as an indication of the popular origins of these cults.[27] She cites Bede's description of the early cult of St Oswald in which it appears that devotion to the martyred Northumbrian king developed in distinct ways in contrasting locations. At the battlefields of Heavenfield near Hexham (Northumbria), where Oswald defeated Caedwalla and the British, and *Maserfelth*, where he met his death, pilgrims appear to have been primarily non-elite. Miracles at these sites included the healing of animals as well as humans, brought about through the mediation of natural features such as the soil of *Maserfelth*, which was deemed so potent that it was excavated by devotees to the depth of a grown man. In contrast, devotion to Oswald at the ecclesiastical sites of St Peter's, Bamburgh (Northumberland), the monastery at Bardney in Lindsey (Lincolnshire) and a church built by the monks of Hexham (Northumberland) near Heavenfield focussed upon the corporeal relics of St Oswald where high-status participants benefitted from human healings and exorcisms, with no mention of animal cures.[28]

There is no evidence for such extreme polarisation at the inception of the cult of St Edmund. An ancient oak tree at Hoxne (Suffolk) was identified as St Edmund's Oak until the time it fell in September 1848 (a monument now marks the spot). This association was facilitated by the supposed discovery within the remnants of the tree of 'a piece of curved iron, possibly an arrowhead', although subsequent investigation has identified this as a rusty nail or piece of bent wire.[29]

---

[26] Carl Watkins, *History and the Supernatural in Medieval England* (Cambridge: [publisher], 2007), 5–6.
[27] Cubitt, 'Universal and Local Saints in Anglo-Saxon England', pp. 424–32; 'Sites and Sanctity', 53–83.
[28] Alan Thacker, '*Membra Disjecta*: The Division of the Body and the Diffusion of the Cult', in *Oswald: Northumbrian King to European Saint*, ed. Clare Stancliffe and Eric Cambridge (Paul Watkins: Stamford, 1995), pp. 97–127.
[29] Abstract of Proceedings, *Proceedings of the Suffolk Institute of Archaeology* 7 (1888–89), p. xli.

Trees are often seen as points of intersection between popular and learned religion, due to their connotations of both the Crucifixion and the sacred trees of pre-Christian Germanic traditions.[30] It is possible that the doubt which persists today concerning the location of the martyrdom also existed when Edmund's legend was first recorded, perhaps as a result of the upheaval of the Viking incursions. Edmund's body seems to have been translated to Bury within around seventy years of his death and it is possible that the then-secular community and later the Benedictines sought to promote the site of Edmund's final resting place over the site of his martyrdom as a means of consolidating the cult in one location.

As discussed in Part I, Abbo's *Passio* contains indications that devotion to St Edmund developed at least in part from popular impetus. The additional details of the perception of St Edmund provided by Geoffrey of Wells indicate either that the popular cult had continued to develop in the century and a half since Abbo was writing and that as a monk of Bury and possibly a local man Geoffrey was more aware of local legends; or, conversely, that he invented the stories. If legends associating Edmund with additional sites in East Anglia had emerged in the interim between Abbo and Geoffrey, there was a clear political utility in writing the sites which had come to be associated with St Edmund into the Bury-based legendary, as it appropriated them for the official cult and enabled their meaning to be determined and managed by Edmund's monastic guardians. This was also a means by which the abbey could promote their interests and influence within the region. The Liberty of St Edmund, comprising the eight and a half hundreds in west Suffolk, was a physical and delimited territory, but establishing the presence of St Edmund throughout the region implies that there was also a sense in which the Liberty was a flexible concept, a spiritual rather than temporal entity, that the abbey's sphere of influence could and should be no more circumscribed than the life and footsteps of St Edmund himself. Thus the multiplication of sites associated with St Edmund should not be seen as competing with the cult centre at Bury, but rather as extending the cult across the East Anglian landscape.

The local and regional cult: the Snettisham procession

The distribution of satellite sites was thus integral to the dissemination of the cult throughout the region. The question remains, however, of how these sites functioned in the more practical sense of how devotion to St Edmund was manifested in these places and how this related to the cult centre at Bury. In most cases evidence suggesting physical cult activity at these locations is lacking, for example,

---

[30] James H. Wilks, *Trees of the British Isles in History and Legend* (London: Frederick Muller Ltd, 1972), p. 134.

at Attleborough, named as the location where Edmund spent a year learning the psalter before his coronation. This does not necessarily indicate a disjuncture between the textual cult and its physical realisation but speaks instead to the inevitable loss of records and material evidence over time.

In contrast, there is evidence to suggest long-term devotional activity associated with the place of Edmund's arrival in East Anglia at Hunstanton. The evidence comes not from Hunstanton itself, but from the nearby village of Snettisham, approximately five miles west of Hunstanton and slightly inland, and around fifty miles north-west of Bury St Edmunds. The churchwardens' accounts from Snettisham survive in a single volume dating from 1467/68 to 1581/82 and provide a remarkably detailed and invaluable insight into the calendar customs of the village over a century.[31] They include references to various dances, games, Mayes, processions and the intriguingly entitled Snettisham 'Rockfeste'.[32] Numerous references are also made to festive activities relating to St Edmund. A number of these are simply for costs 'at seynt Edmundys' but others specify that the event is a procession. The entry for 1514/15 refers to the 'Capella[m] S[an]c[t]I Ed[mund] i'.[33] The chapel is specified as the destination on only one occasion; presumably the procession was so ingrained in the local consciousness that no further elucidation was deemed necessary. Other entries in the churchwardens' accounts indicate that Snettisham participated in the processions of other communities, most notably Ingoldisthorpe, a nearby parish.[34] The nature of the payments for the St Edmund procession, however, indicates that this was Snettisham's own celebration. The involvement of the community is indicated by the nature of some of the payments which specify that the churchwardens contributed funds 'besyd ye gaderyng of Snettisham' or 'besyd the gaderyng of the town'.[35] The procession therefore seems to have been one in which the whole community participated.

It is unclear when the procession took place but the context of some of the entries suggests that they should be read in relation to costs for other activities;

---

[31] Norwish Record Office, PD 24/1. The fullest treatment of the Snettisham Church Wardens' Accounts is by James Cummings, 'Contextual Studies of the Dramatic Records in the Area Around the Wash c.1350–1550' (Leeds: unpublished Ph.D. thesis, University of Leeds, 2001), pp. 193–231.

[32] The nature of the Rockfeste is unclear but it probably took place on 'Rock Monday', the first Monday after the twelve days of Christmas, when women typically resumed spinning (using a distaff, or 'rock') after the seasonal festivities. For rituals and rites associated with the Christmas season see Ronald Hutton, *The Stations of the Sun: A History of the Ritual Year in Britain* (Oxford: Oxford University Press, 1996), pp. 9–24.

[33] Norfolk Record Office, PD 24/1, fol. 36v.

[34] For the Ingoldisthorpe procession see Cummings, 'Contextual Studies', pp. 197–200.

[35] Norfolk Record Office, PD 24/1, 1500/1–2/3, fol. 80v and PD 24/1, 1503/4, fol. 83.

for example, the cost of 4d for 'y[e] schaft[es] of holy Thursday' is immediately followed by 6d 'for Ingaldysthorp p[ro]cession' and 10d for 'washyng ageyn Sent Edm[u]nd'.³⁶ It therefore seems likely that these three processions occurred each year as part of a season of spring festivities.³⁷ The entry for xd for 'washyng ageyn sent Edm[u]nd[es]' in 1491/92 is immediately followed by a payment also of xd 'to ye vykyr of honstant[u]n ffor a lombe'.³⁸ This suggests that the destination of the St Edmund procession was the cliff-top chapel at Hunstanton, presumably the 'sent Edm[u]nd[es]' which was 'washed' and cleaned in preparation for the festivities. It is possible that the festivities were timed to commemorate the Feast of the Translation of St Edmund on 25 April. The concurrence of place and time is, however, more generally appropriate, with the connotations of springtime renewal and regeneration befitting the location in which Edmund, the youthful king, arrived in East Anglia and where the kingdom itself erupted forth in miraculous springs in recognition of his sanctity. The participation of the clergy at Hunstanton and the nature of other preparations, such as washing surplices and the bearing of shafts (presumably displaying banners), suggests that this was a formally recognised ceremonial occasion.

The participation of the villagers of Snettisham in the festivities of other communities raises the possibility that surrounding villages likewise contributed to the St Edmund procession. In particular, if the procession did take place on the Feast of the Translation, it is tempting to imagine the communities of north-west Norfolk joining together to celebrate their regional patron and his legendary presence in their area. Rita Tekippe notes the commonalities between pilgrimage and processions and the way in which the latter could function as a means of sacralising the local landscape.³⁹ Duffy likewise asserts the importance of the local in medieval pilgrimage:

> For many medieval Christians, going on pilgrimage was ... not so much like launching on a journey to the ends of the earth, as of going to a local market town to sell or buy geese or chickens: shrines were features by which they mapped the familiar, as much as signposts to other worlds and other social realities; a local, not a liminal, phenomenon.⁴⁰

---

[36] Norfolk Record Office, PD 24/1, fol. 69.
[37] For rogationtide rituals see Hutton, *Stations of the Sun*, pp. 277–87.
[38] Norfolk Record Office, PD 24/1, fol. 31v.
[39] Rita Tekippe, 'Pilgrimage and Procession: Correlations of Meaning, Practice and Effects', in *Art and Architecture*, ed. Blick and Tekippe, pp. 693–751; esp. 693–7 and 701.
[40] Eamon Duffy, 'The Dynamics of Pilgrimage in Late Medieval England', in *Pilgrimage: The English Experience from Becket to Bunyan*, ed. Colin Morris and Peter Roberts (Cambridge: Cambridge University Press, 2002), pp. 164–77; pp. 165–6.

Thus secondary sites associated with St Edmund served an important function not only in mapping the cult onto the landscape for the benefit of the monastic community at Bury, but also for devotees removed from the cult centre. Writing the region into the legend both served to symbolically appropriate the region into the cult and also integrated the saint into numerous localities, potentially facilitating the identification of the local inhabitants with their regional patron and strengthening the sense in which Edmund continued to preside over the whole of his East Anglian kingdom.

CHAPTER 9

Miracles beyond Bury

An additional means of determining the variety of responses to the cult is by considering the miracles with which Edmund is credited. As discussed above, the majority of miracles are associated with Edmund's corporeal relics, both before and after their enshrinement in the abbey church. This is to be expected, given the *virtus* associated with a saint's remains. However, the narrative of Egelwyn's flight to London in the first decade of the eleventh century, bearing Edmund's remains to safety away from renewed Viking incursions, demonstrates the potency of the relics regardless of their geographical location. Herman relates Edmund's punishment of the arrogant Dane, 'filled with fierce intent', who disrespectfully approached the *feretory* and attempted to remove the pallium as the relics lay in their temporary home in St Gregory's church, London. The man was struck blind, but quickly repented, whereupon his sight was restored.[1] According to Herman, Aelfhun, bishop of London (c.1002–c.1015), was so impressed by the miracles wrought by Edmund during his London sojourn that he attempted to translate the body from St Gregory's to the episcopal seat of St Paul's. However, despite Egelwyn's ability to move the *feretory* with ease, the bishop and his helpers were unable to lift it, as 'although his devotion was good, such an intention was at odds with the will of the saint'.[2] Yarrow suggests that this miracle should be read in the context of *furta sacra*, or relic thefts, in which the ability to translate the saint to a new location was taken as an indication of his or her silent assent.[3] In contrast, this miracle indicates Edmund's unwillingness to be relocated to St Paul's and speaks instead of his desire to return home to his own kingdom. Yet ultimately this display of saintly homesickness demonstrates that Edmund's miracle-working ability was not constrained by the location of his relics, whilst simultaneously underlining the particular *virtus* associated with his remains.

Secondary relics associated with Edmund were also credited with manifesting miraculous abilities, such as his banner, borne before the victors at the battle of Fornham in 1173, or an arrow reputedly used at the martyrdom which thwarted attempts to remove it from its enshrined position in St Edmund's church in

---

[1] Herman, *De Miraculis*, ed. Arnold, *Memorials*, I, p. 44.
[2] Herman, *De Miraculis*, ed. Arnold, *Memorials*, I, pp. 44–5.
[3] Yarrow, *Saints and their Communities*, pp. 35–6.

London.[4] This indicates that the extent to which Edmund's miracles differed according to their location is less significant than the occurrence of miracles in relation to relics. Thus the primary distinction here will be between miracles which occurred in the presence of relics and those which did not. A number of miracles in each collection suggest that wonders occurred in the absence of relics, whether primary or secondary. These miracles will be considered here, in particular the difference between the types of miracles which occurred through the direct mediation of relics and those which did not, and the resulting extent to which Edmund's saintly identity was perceived to differ according to proximity to his shrine.

In this instance relics also include Edmund's living body, in order to account for miracles associated with him before his martyrdom, such as the bursting forth of the springs at Hunstanton. 'Presence' is a loose term, but for my current purposes I have defined a miracle as occurring in the presence of relics if: it occurred in or near the abbey church; if a relic of St Edmund is specified in the narrative, regardless of the location of the miracle; if a relic is not mentioned in the narrative but one is known to have existed in that location at a concomitant date. Due to the inextricable links between the abbey and the *banleuca* of Bury St Edmunds I have also included miracles occurring within the abbey's immediate vicinity in this category. In some cases it can be difficult to determine the exact location at which a miracle took place. In many cases the monastic authors were understandably keen to emphasise the occurrence of miracles at the shrine as a means of promoting pilgrimage to the abbey, frequently describing journeys to Bury undertaken by supplicants which are duly rewarded with intercessory benevolence. For this reason I have assumed that any ambiguity indicates that a miracle occurred elsewhere. This is frequently supported by the narrative context in which miracles occur. For example, a miracle in Bodley 240 (the location of which is unspecified), describing a man who promises his son to St Edmund in return for the boy's restoration to health, is flanked by two miracles which the scribe states occurred in the diocese of Chichester. Although not conclusive, this suggests a short sequence of narratives acquired from Chichester, whether orally or passed on in manuscript form, to be copied at Bury, and therefore suggests that the second, unattributed miracle may also share this locational provenance. This ambiguity, however, makes it unfeasible in most instances to perform a detailed analysis of the type of miracles which occurred in the absence of relics in relation to their distance from the cult centre at Bury.

---

[4] For the battle of Fornham see Roger of Hovedon, *Chronica Magestri Rogeri Houedene*, ed. Stubbs, II, p. 55. For further discussion see above, Chapter 2, pp. 149–51. For the arrow see Bodley 240, ed. Arnold, *Memorials*, I, pp. 375–6.

It is, however, interesting that at the inception of the textual cult, in Abbo's *Passio*, all the miracles occur in the context of Edmund's relics, probably representing the limited dissemination of the cult at this date and the desire to promote Bury as the location in which Edmund's *virtus* could be experienced. As the cult developed over time increasing numbers of miracles occur in locations other than those connected with Edmund's relics but the total proportion of miracles without relics remains relatively stable at between 17 and 33 per cent. This most likely reflects the continued efforts of the convent to retain control of the cult and promote the benefits of visiting the shrine, whilst simultaneously indicating that Edmund's miracle-working abilities were sufficiently great that they extended beyond the confines of the abbey church. As texts originating at Bury, each collection represents available knowledge of miracles attributed to St Edmund, which was certain to have been greater concerning events in the church or its immediate surroundings.

A telling distinction can be seen in the types of miracles which occurred within or without the presence of relics. Revelations concerning Edmund's incorruption were, unsurprisingly, all associated with his relics, as in each instance his bodily wholeness is attested by the examination of his corpse. Similarly, the majority of natural wonders are either performed by Edmund during his lifetime or concern the guarding of his head by the wolf. A small number of weather miracles are also attributed to the presence of relics, such as the ending of a drought leading to an abundant harvest which Herman claims took place after the bishop ordered that Edmund's body be borne outside the church at the time of his translation in 1095.[5] The number of punishment miracles taking place in the absence of the relics may initially seem surprising, considering the pattern noted above for Edmund's punitive interventions to be associated with violations of his shrine or the abbey church. However, Edmund also intervenes to protect the broader territory of the Liberty and the abbey's landholdings elsewhere, and the death of Sweyn accounts for a considerable proportion of these miracles. Edmund's ability to intervene to prevent encroachments upon the abbey's lands and privileges and, in the case of Sweyn, those of the kingdom as a whole therefore forms a significant aspect of his saintly identity and it is natural that this should be emphasised in the miracle collections.

Healing and helping

The least consistent statistics relate to miracles of healing as well as rescue and assistance. The relative size of the samples in some collections (Abbo's *Passio*, the Pierpont Morgan illustrations and Geoffrey's *De Infantia*) and the extent to

---

[5] Herman, *De Miraculis*, ed. Arnold, *Memorials*, I, pp. 90–1.

which this distorts the impression given by the statistics has been discussed above in relation to the nature of Edmund's miracles and how these evolved over time. However, focussing upon the collections where the number of miracles in these categories provides a meaningful sample (Herman's *De Miraculis*, Samson's *De Miraculis*, Bodley 240 and Lydgate's *Lives*) still reveals notable disparities. In both versions of *De Miraculis* and the *Lives* the proportion of healing miracles which occurred in the presence of relics ranges between 80 and 100 per cent and miracles of rescue and assistance between 40 and 100 per cent. In contrast, the figures for the same categories in Bodley 240 are starkly different: 9 and 7 per cent respectively. This reflects the overall trend of the Bodley miracles, in which, on average, only 14 per cent are associated with relics of St Edmund, meaning that the vast majority (86 per cent) occurred elsewhere. The reasons why the convent should wish to emphasise Edmund's particularly potent ability to heal and help his devotees in the vicinity of his shrine are self-evident, so the extent of the anomaly in Bodley 240 is particularly striking: why should the compiler of this collection alone place so much emphasis upon miracles which occurred in locations other than Bury?

This discrepancy may be accounted for by the provenance of the miracles in this collection. Fifty-four are miscellaneous narratives which seem to have been collected at the abbey by the scribe from various sources including extant documents and oral testimony of recent events. In contrast, the remaining accounts consist of two discrete sets associated with locations other than Bury St Edmunds: seventeen miracles are recorded at the chapel of St Edmund in Wainfleet (Lincolnshire) and seven from the chapel of St Edmund at Lyng (Norfolk). In neither case are relics of St Edmund mentioned and this necessarily has a considerable effect upon the overall proportions of Bodley 240. These miracles were likely compiled in their respective locations and disseminated to Bury where they were copied by the Bodley scribe. In addition to elucidating the processes of textual augmentation, Wainfleet and Lyng are also eloquent examples of the complex networks of patronage and cultural exchange which influenced the dissemination of the cult.

Miracles from Wainfleet (Lincolnshire)

The abbey held land and property in Wainfleet in the region of the Wash in Lincolnshire, including a chapel dedicated to St Edmund, in an area which Gransden suggests was of particular importance to the abbey, as the salterns clustered around the Wash were the principal source of the abbey's salt.[6] The strategic importance of the area is attested by the presence in the immediate vicinity of Wainfleet of three further churches or chapels belonging to other monastic

---

[6] Gransden, *A History of the Abbey*, p. 224.

houses: All Saints' church was a possession of Bardney Abbey (near Lincoln); St Thomas's church in Northolme, now part of Wainfleet, belonged to Kyme Priory (near Sleaford, Lincolnshire); and St Mary's to the Priory of Stixwould (near Lincoln).[7] St Edmund's chapel was therefore an important outpost of the abbey, a marker of its regional presence. Similarly, in the face of fierce monastic rivalry for control of valuable resources it would have suited the abbey to promote St Edmund's personal interest in the area, manifested in his numerous miraculous interventions on behalf of local devotees.

Further connections existed between Bury and this area of the Wash. Henry de Lacy, earl of Lincoln (1272–1311) was a generous benefactor of the abbey. The Douai register records Henry's donation of a gold cross worth 66s 8d which stood atop Edmund's shrine and another gold cross with jewels with a great carbuncle at the foot (possibly the jewel referred to by the Bodley scribe) which was suspended from one side.[8] Henry is likewise recorded by the Bodley scribe as presenting a further 'great jewel' to St Edmund's shrine at Bury, as well as making valuable bequests and generous land transactions in gratitude for his deliverance from peril in Aquitaine in 1308, which he credited to his invocation of the saint.[9] From the early thirteenth century, the properties of the earls of Lincoln and those of the abbey in the area around the Wash were in close proximity and although this resulted in conflict which was not resolved until the end of the century, the opportunities for interaction were also considerable. Gransden, for example, discusses the exchange of books between the abbey and the earls of Lincoln in the thirteenth and fourteenth centuries.[10] The Bodley miracles from Wainfleet are dated 1373–74 and therefore are not a direct result of the particularly close relationship which the abbey enjoyed with Henry de Lacy. They also date from a period when the title of the Lincolnshire earldom fell extinct for over a hundred years following the death of Henry of Grosmont in 1361.[11] However, the monastic guardians would be aware of miracles occurring in a chapel under their jurisdiction.

Miracles from Lyng (Norfolk)

The fragmentary ruins of St Edmund's chapel at Lyng (Norfolk) are three-quarters of a mile south-east of the present parish church of St Margaret. The chapel was

---

[7] Nikolaus Pevsner and John Harris, *The Buildings of England: Lincolnshire* (London: Penguin Books, 1973, rpt 1978, rev. 1989 by Nicholas Antrim), p. 776.
[8] Douai Register, see James, *On the Abbey Church*, p. 136.
[9] Bodley 240, ed. Arnold, *Memorials*, II, pp. 366–7.
[10] Gransden, *A History of the Abbey*, pp. 224–5.
[11] For the history of the earldom see *Debrett's Peerage and Baronetage*, ed. Patrick Montague-Smith (London: Macmillan for Debrett's Peerage Ltd., 1995). CS420 DEB

originally part of a nunnery dedicated to St Edmund, reputedly founded to commemorate the site of a battle with the Danes during their ninth-century campaign which culminated with the death of Edmund in 869.[12] In 1176 the nuns moved to Thetford and occupied the Priory of St George, similarly founded to commemorate a battle between Edmund and the Norsemen, but which by the later twelfth century had diminished to two canons, Folchard and Andrew, following the deaths of the rest of their colleagues, facilitating the nuns' relocation.[13] The history of Lyng hereafter is obscure but it seems to have persisted as a chapel dedicated to St Edmund under the control of the prioress of St George's, as in 1286/87 the prioress was given permission to hold an annual fair at Lyng on the Feast of St Edmund and in 1437/38 was granted a licence to sell the Lyng property to the rector of Lyng with the chapel, nine acres of land and property in Feltwell, Foulden and Hockwold in return for an annual pension of 4 marks which was paid up until the Dissolution.[14] By the fifteenth century there was also a guild dedicated to the saint.[15] Preceding its transfer to the Lyng nuns, St George's at Thetford had been a priory of St Edmund's Abbey and it is likely that the new proprietors would have maintained close links with the motherhouse, thus enabling the dissemination of miracles attributed to Edmund at the chapel at Lyng.

The extent to which saints could be accessed at locations other than their primary shrine or cult centre is evident in these local miracles. The role of visual imagery in attesting to the presence of the saint is also apparent, as two of the Wainfleet miracles refer to an '*ymago sancti Edmundi, situate in capella monachorum sancti Edmundi*'.[16] In one example from Wainfleet, sailors who are wrecked off the coast near Skegness (Lincolnshire) make a vow '*ad sanctum Edmundum et ejus capellam de Wainflet*'.[17] The phraseology is telling, as it indicates that for these sailors, presumably local men, the primary *locus* for their devotion to St Edmund is their local chapel, not the cult centre at Bury. This reiterates Duffy's assertion that for many medieval men and women the cult of saints functioned primarily at a local level.[18]

---

[12] Blomefield, *Norfolk*, VIII, p. 250. See also a guide to the church by M.J. Sayer, *Lyng* (East Dereham: C&J Murray, 1970).

[13] The transfer is described in a charter of Abbot Hugh (1157–80), *Monasticon Anglicanum: A History of the Abbies and other Monasteries, Hospitals, Friaries and Cathedral and Collegiate Churches*, ed. William Dugdale, rpt ed. John Caley, Henry Ellis and Bulkeley Bandinel, 6 vols (London: Longman, Hurst, Rees, Orme and Brown, 1817–30), IV, pp. 477–7.

[14] Blomefield, *Norfolk*, VIII, p. 250.

[15] Ken Farnhill, *Guilds and the Parish Community in Late Medieval East Anglia: c.1470–1550* (York: York Medieval Press, 2001), pp. 172–211.

[16] Bodley 240, ed. Arnold, *Memorials*, III, pp. 327–8.

[17] Bodley 240, ed. Arnold, *Memorials*, III, p. 331.

[18] Duffy, 'The Dynamics of Pilgrimage', pp. 165–6.

This is reflected in the origins of the recipients of miracles at both Wainfleet and Lyng: in each collection the majority of devotees originate from within a fifteen-mile radius of the chapel. The majority of miracles similarly occurred either at the chapel in question or in or near the home of the recipient and are therefore equally local in their distribution. Two of the Wainfleet miracles occur at sea, reflecting its coastal location and speaking to the maritime preoccupations of its inhabitants.

However, in each collection St Edmund is also credited with intervening at a greater distance or assisting devotees of non-local origins. In the Wainfleet miracles, Matildis of Westchester (perhaps near Camberley in Surrey) has the use of her hand and arm restored after praying in the chapel, and a child from York who appears drowned is restored after his parents make a vow to St Edmund.[19] At Lyng, a woman from Kent who is both blind and deaf recovers her sight and hearing after she is advised to travel to St Edmund's chapel.[20] Although the location at which the miracle of the child from York occurred is unspecified, it is notable that in each of the other cases the supplicants travel to the respective chapels, where they are cured. In the final case a chaplain, along with men from North Lincolnshire and South Yorkshire, are released from captivity in Spain after being captured and imprisoned on their return from pilgrimage to Compostella.[21] The origins of the men suggest they may have landed on the Lincolnshire coast on their return home and chose to give thanks at Wainfleet as this was the nearest chapel dedicated to St Edmund.

All the miracles from Wainfleet and Lyng are benign acts of healing or rescue and assistance, reinforcing the notion that Edmund's punitive identity was a phenomenon of the early cult and a preoccupation of the convent at Bury St Edmunds. At Wainfleet and Lyng, people were more concerned with the tribulations of everyday life and St Edmund demonstrates his ability to intervene on behalf of members of the local communities regardless of the location in which they find themselves in need, and to extend this munificence to devotees from further afield, especially if they are willing to show their devotion by visiting one of his chapels in person.

Soldiers and sailors

Although miracles of healing or rescue and assistance which may be designated as taking place in the absence of relics occur in different proportions in the collections originating at the abbey as opposed to those compiled at Wainfleet and

---

[19] Bodley 240, ed. Arnold, *Memorials*, III, pp. 328–9 and 332–3.
[20] Bodley 240, ed. Arnold, *Memorials*, III, pp. 338–9.
[21] Bodley 240, ed. Arnold, *Memorials*, III, pp.

Lyng, the nature of the wonders enacted by St Edmund nevertheless follows similar patterns. The majority involve travellers in peril, often at sea, who invoke St Edmund and are duly saved, such as a clerk from Lichfield whom Edmund dragged from the sea by his hair after the man fell overboard *en route* to Jerusalem.[22] The compilers of these miracles understandably emphasise the vows made by pilgrims in which devotees promise to visit the shrine or make an offering in exchange for intercession.[23] In one example, a group of pilgrims returning from Rome found themselves in peril when their boat sprung a leak and began to sink. Two men of St Edmund's jurisdiction, Robert and a priest named Wulfward, convinced the passengers of the boat to place their trust in St Edmund and make a pledge of money for their safe deliverance. A collection was made and the boat continued its journey to port in safety. The money was taken to Bury, where it was offered to the saint.[24] It is notable that in both of these examples, as in numerous others, the recipients of the miracles were on pilgrimage. This display of devotion marks them as worthy recipients of Edmund's patronage. The locations to which they journey (Jerusalem, Rome, Compostella) are also significant. Bury could not expect to compete with these international destinations and their importance for medieval Christians made it appropriate for St Edmund to assist devotees on their journeys. In contrast, Edmund is not credited with assisting pilgrims to other English shrines which might represent realistic competition.

St Edmund and St Nicholas

Edmund's particular patronage of those at sea also entailed the possibility of disseminating his cult even farther afield. Thus in addition to helping English devotees travelling abroad he is credited with assisting foreign travellers who encounter difficulties whilst journeying to England. Samson's *De Miraculis* includes the story of the influential Abbot Lambert of Angers, whose boat was prevented from sailing for England from Barfleur due to unfavourable winds.[25] An aged monk, Nicholas, advised the abbot to pray to St Edmund, reassuring him that St Nicholas, the customary patron of sea-goers, would not be offended, as St Edmund's power was particularly potent in English waters. The abbot followed the monk's advice and the crossing was made in ten hours. Lambert's successful crossing and its commemoration in the record served to enhance the prestige of St

---

[22] Samson, *De Miraculis*, ed. Arnold, *Memorials*, I, pp. 95–6.
[23] Finucane discusses the importance of vows to saints in *Miracles and Pilgrims*, pp. 35–6.
[24] Samson, *De Miraculis*, ed. Arnold, *Memorials*, I, pp. 95–6.
[25] Samson, *De Miraculis*, ed. Arnold, *Memorials*, I, pp. 176–8.

Edmund by placing him in the company of internationally recognised saints. The curiously coincidental name of the mysterious aged monk who advised the abbot implies that St Nicholas himself acknowledged Edmund's power and jurisdiction. Abbot Lambert's status and position made him an ideal conduit through which Edmund's miracle-working reputation could be transmitted overseas. As the aged monk predicts, on account of this miracle 'the power of his [Edmund's] moral excellence which brightly lights up England might be transferred through us to other parts of the world, and thus he may receive a worthy increase on account of his merits'.[26]

The association between Sts Edmund and Nicholas is likewise found in further miracle narratives. The clerk from Lichfield, whom Edmund hoisted by the hair, avers that as St Nicholas was famous for helping sailors, so too was St Edmund the patron of those shipwrecked at sea.[27] Similarly, in 1190, a young man from Shimpling (Suffolk) was captured in a battle overseas, tortured and imprisoned, but was released when he invoked Sts Edmund and Nicholas.[28] When Richard I set sail for the Holy Land in 1190 his crusading fleet sailed under the joint protection of St Thomas, St Nicholas and St Edmund.[29]

Similarly, James Robinson suggests that Edmund's patronage of sailors and those travelling at sea may be reflected in an aspect of his visual iconography, proposing that the shape of the most iconographically complex pilgrim badge, in which Edmund is flanked by archers, may be likened to an anchor.[30] He notes that the anchor was a form associated with Edmund by a number of pilgrims. In 1173 fishermen from Dunwich, caught in a storm, invoked St Edmund and were saved. In gratitude they travelled to Bury, where they offered an *ex voto* wax anchor at the shrine.[31] Robinson maintains that it is highly likely that large quantities of similar images decorated the shrine at Bury, and suggests that the badge itself could have been worn as a charm for protection at sea.[32]

Whilst Robinson offers no explanation for the development of this particular aspect of Edmund's saintly identity, it can most likely be traced to Edmund's arrival in East Anglia, which involved a successful sea voyage. Geoffrey of Wells makes it clear that, due to Edmund's presence on board the ship, the East Anglian

---

[26] Samson, *De Miraculis*, ed. Arnold, *Memorials*, I, p. 177.
[27] Samson, *De Miraculis*, ed. Arnold, *Memorials*, I, pp. 95–6.
[28] Bodley 240, ed. Arnold, *Memorials*, I, p. 374.
[29] *The Chronicle of the Reigns of Henry II and Richard I*, ed. Stubbs, II, p. 116. This is illustrated in a fifteenth-century copy of the St Alban's Chronicle, now London, Lambeth Palace Library, MS 6, fol. 142.
[30] Robinson, 'A Late Medieval Pilgrim Badge from Chaucer House', 60–9.
[31] Bodley 240, ed. Arnold, *Memorials*, I, p. 367.
[32] Robinson, 'A Late Medieval Pilgrim Badge from Chaucer House', 69.

delegation are 'preceded and followed by the grace of God'.[33] Although this event is often overshadowed by Edmund's more dramatic posthumous activities, it nevertheless associates him from the outset with voyages by sea, and may go some way to explaining the emphasis placed on this aspect of his identity. Robinson's suggestion is not entirely convincing, as, if this element of Edmund's sanctity was as pre-eminent as he suggests, it might be expected that this would be referred to explicitly in his iconography, for example in a pilgrim badge depicting a ship. Nevertheless, it is certainly the case that Edmund's patronage of sea-going travellers formed a significant part of his saintly identity in relation to miracles occurring in the absence of relics and that this was also manifested visually in offerings made at the shrine, two features which were likely to be mutually reinforcing, indicating once again the interactions between textual and visual manifestations of the cult, as well as the way in which incidents happening beyond Bury were ultimately integrated into the official narrative.

The association between Edmund and Nicholas is also evident on lead tokens discovered in St Mary's church at Bury. They were apparently struck in imitation of silver groats and pennies, and Bury is named on a number of them and the town's arms also appear, suggesting that they originated locally. Golding identifies twenty-one distinct types, of which nineteen refer to St Nicholas, mostly by way of invocation (*pie Nicholae ora pro nob.*), and some depict a mitre or mitred figure.[34] In addition, seven of the tokens are inscribed on the reverse with the opening words from the *Ave Rex* antiphon to St Edmund which Lydgate recounts was inscribed before Edmund's shrine.[35] Golding suggests that the tokens were struck during the reign of Henry VII, but otherwise little is known about them.[36] Lead trade tokens of a similar size and material were produced to provide currency of a sufficiently small denomination for the purposes of everyday commerce, in the same way that pennies were clipped to create halves or quarters.[37] The ecclesiastical overtones of the Nicholas and Edmund coins, however, suggest that they were not used in lieu of currency. Golding notes that many are pierced with two or three holes, suggesting that they were suspended from a cord or sewn onto clothing, much like pilgrim badges. Their discovery in St Mary's church in Bury, where there was a guild of St Nicholas, makes Golding's suggestion that they

---

[33] Geoffrey of Wells, *De Infantia*, ed. Arnold, *Memorials*, I, p. 99.
[34] Charles Golding, *The Coinage of Suffolk. Consisting of the Regal Coins Leaden Pieces and Tokens of the Seventeenth and Nineteenth Centuries* (London: Printed privately by the author, 1868), pp. 14–19.
[35] Lydgate, *Lives*, Prologue, ll. 73–80.
[36] Golding, *The Coinage of Suffolk*, p. 14.
[37] Golding, *The Coinage of Suffolk*, pp. 21–3.

were commemorative tokens issued by the guild to mark major festivals highly plausible.[38]

One of three leper hospitals in the town was also dedicated to St Nicholas.[39] Abbey accounts indicate that in 1249 9d was paid to the kitchener for 'wafres' for the monks on the feasts of St Edmund (20 November) and St Nicholas (6 December), with the provision of similar treats on these days suggesting the high regard in which St Nicholas was held by the abbey.[40] In addition, the verses in Arundel 30 indicate that there was a chapel to St Nicholas in the south transept, decorated with scenes from his legend showing the saint marked with divine favour by a voice from heaven, his consecration as bishop and his deliverance of condemned criminals.[41] No mention is made of St Nicholas' patronage of sailors, perhaps because the convent wanted to emphasise that this role was fulfilled by St Edmund.

Thus consideration of Edmund's miracles which occurred at a remove from his shrine and potentially in the absence of his relics demonstrates that the dissemination of the cult did to some extent affect the development of Edmund's saintly identity, particularly as devotees' perceptions of Edmund originating in outlying communities filtered into the official miracle registers. Finucane reiterates the importance of considering the development of a saint's reputation in context:

> Unqualified statements about the 'growth of the cult' of a saint may be misleading, suggesting that such 'growth' was an abstract, even automatic, process unrelated to the society in which it occurred. The awareness of curative cults was not silently and mysteriously communicated to peasants in their huts or to knights in their halls, but was physically carried to them by living individuals.[42]

It is therefore particularly important when examining trends in miracles over time not to lose sight of the separate collections in which they originate. At the inception of the cult, in Abbo's *Passio*, all the miracles were associated with Edmund's relics

---

[38] Golding, *The Coinage of Suffolk*, p. 15–16, illustrated in Plate 2.
[39] For the medieval hospitals of Bury see *Charters of the Medieval Hospitals of Bury St Edmunds*, ed. Christopher Harper-Bill, Suffolk Charters 14 (Woodbridge: The Boydell Press for the Suffolk Records Society, 1994) and Joy Rowe, 'The Medieval Hospitals of Bury St Edmunds', *Medical History* ii (1958), 253–63. For the treatment of leprosy in general see Carole Rawcliffe, *Leprosy in Medieval England* (Woodbridge: The Boydell Press, 2006).
[40] London, British Library, MS Harley 645 (the 'Kempe' register of the abbey), fol. 193v, cited in Gransden, *A History of the Abbey*, p. 257.
[41] MS Arundel 30, fol. 208.
[42] Finucane, *Miracles and Pilgrims*, p. 156.

as his proponents attempted to bolster the burgeoning cult and promote Bury as the official cult centre. A similar situation pertains a century later when Herman composed *De Miraculis*. Perhaps in response to post-Conquest uncertainties the convent once again sought to reinforce the link between the saint and his resting place. By the time *De Miraculis* was revised at the turn of the thirteenth century, perhaps by Abbot Samson himself, the cult was more securely established. Miracles were occurring further afield and it is possible that the convent promoted Edmund's national and international reputation in response to Becket's growing popularity. When the miracles in Bodley 240 were compiled the cult had spread still further, to the extent that the majority of miracles occurred beyond Bury, and other communities were recording miracles associated with their own chapels and cult images. Lydgate's *Lives* offers a more balanced view of the range of Edmund's activities. As a text so entirely invested in promoting the abbey and its saintly patron it is unsurprising that the focus is upon Edmund's activities on home territory. Even in one of Lydgate's few miracles to take place in the absence of Edmund's relics (the narrative of a boy healed by Edmund after a fall from London Bridge) Anthony Bale sees Bury attempting to forge connections between the abbey and the Lancastrian regime. He suggests that the anachronistic presence of Lord Fanhope (d.1443) in the miracle may be explained by his role as a counsellor to Henry VI:

> Far from attempting to wrest the miracle from Bury, [this miracle] may attempt to knit, imitatively and flatteringly, Henrician and Lancastrian models of piety and polity, lordship and counsel, with the city of London, through the image of Fanhope. London, the capital, becomes connected, through [this miracle], with Edmund's ancient capital, Bury. Through the potent image of the endangered child, recalling Henry VI himself, the miracle imagines a kind of sacramental, civic and distinctly urban authority, seamlessly uniting secular, clerical and royal jurisdictions.[43]

As expected of a convent which sought so consistently to promote its patron and its abbey, each miracle served its purpose in furthering a version of Edmund's saintly identity which suited the abbey. As Geoffrey of Wells acknowledged in his description of the process by which the convent determined the 'official' version of Edmund's life, even miracles which originated beyond Bury were ultimately filtered through the abbey's authors and scribes and it should therefore be unsurprising that the miracle collections tend to reinforce aspects of Edmund's sanctity seen elsewhere at the cult centre. Moving beyond the cult centre to consider miracles which occurred in other locations has, perhaps inevitably, led back to Bury.

---

[43] Bale, 'St Edmund in Fifteenth-Century London', pp. 145–61; p. 155.

CHAPTER 10

Images of St Edmund

TRANSACTIONS between Bury and the cult in outlying areas are especially visible in the dozens of images of Edmund which adorned East Anglian churches. Visual culture was fundamental to the dissemination of saintly identities at the parochial level as well as at the cult centre. Richard Gameson maintains that some communities 'immortalis[ed] their particular holy man or woman in paint, stone, wood and precious metals as much as, if not more so, than in verse and prayer'.[1] Hagiographic art could fulfil many functions and its didactic potential was recognised by contemporaries. The familiar, homogenised code of church art provided a highly visible, pervasive reminder of the events described in sermons and commemorated in services. Contemporary authors frequently invoked Gregory I in support of art as a means of instructing the illiterate.[2] In *Dives and Pauper*, for example, an early fifteenth-century prose commentary on the Ten Commandments, Dives, a layman, asks his adviser, Pauper, to teach him about images, the 'book of lewyd peple'.[3] However, the notion of medieval church art as simply picture books for the illiterate fails to acknowledge the complex range of potential responses. Gameson, for instance, suggests that 'by the means of depictions, one could appropriate and possess any saint or particular figure'.[4] 'Appropriation' implies a degree of ownership which the elevated status of saints within medieval religion renders surprising; saints were, after all, the conduits through which flowed the power of God. Rather than a one-way transaction, with the saint obediently at the behest of the community, the decision to depict a particular saint represented the creation of a mutually beneficent relationship, the 'debt of interchanging neighbourhood' referred to by Caxton in his translation of

---

[1] Richard Gameson, 'The Early Imagery of Thomas Becket', in *Pilgrimage: The English Experience from Becket to Bunyan* ed. C. Morris and P. Roberts (Cambridge, 2002), pp. 46–89; p. 46.
[2] For discussions of the Gregorian topos see Lawrence G. Duggan, 'Was Art Really the Book of the Illiterate?', *Word and Image* 5 (1989), 227–51 and Celia Chazelle, 'Pictures, Books and the Illiterate: Pope Gregory I's Letters to Serenius of Marseilles', *Word and Image* 6 (1990), 138–53. Richard Marks also discusses these issues in *Image and Devotion in Late Medieval England* (Stroud: Sutton, 2004), pp. 26–7.
[3] *Dives and Pauper*, ed. Priscilla Heath Barnum, 3 vols, Early English Text Society, os 275, 280 and 323 (London: Oxford University Press for the Early English Text Society, 1976, 1980 and 2004), I, p. 91.
[4] Gameson, 'Early Imagery', p. 45.

the *Golden Legend*.[5] An individual or parochial community would have hoped to attract the intercessory favour of the one depicted in return for identifying that particular saint as especially worthy of devotion. It was above all the reputation of the holy man or woman to act effectively on their behalf, whether based upon evidence from their life or, frequently, their posthumous activities, which encouraged those who sought their favour and intercession.

Images played a key role in this process, able to represent the identity of a saint as understood by those involved in the creation of the image, whether at the level of commissioning, design or production. It is therefore important to consider the context in which an image may be found, both its physical location within a church and the social and cultural context in which it originated, as this helps to determine the ways in which individuals and communities perceived saints such as Edmund. For ease of reference Table 2 shows a statistical breakdown of images by type, which are also categorised based on iconography in Table 3.

Although it is not universally the case, some images survive within their original contexts, facilitating speculation concerning their relationship to the 'holy geography' of a church as a whole. Images from parish churches are particularly useful as they survive in relatively large numbers, enabling direct comparisons to be made. Indeed, Duffy notes that Edmund is the most frequently depicted native saint.[6] Interestingly, he makes this observation whilst discussing representations of female saints, including St Æthelthryth. Given her widespread popularity it is perhaps surprising that Æthelthryth does not appear more frequently in church imagery. Blanton suggests that this may be accounted for by the early construction of the cult as a textual entity as a means of eliding the problematic presence of the female body at Ely, which in turn may have affected her popularity with the laity.[7] She is also most commonly depicted in her role as abbess and monastic foundress, an aspect of her cult perhaps more appealing to the clergy. In contrast, the promotion from the outset of Edmund as a saint of the East Anglian people is reflected in his broader demotic appeal, and is manifest in the visual vocabulary through which he was represented.

Table 2 indicates that at least ninety images of Edmund are known to have existed in churches in Norfolk and Suffolk, and of these nearly sixty are

---

[5] Caxton, trans., *The Golden Legend*, ed. Ellis, VI, p. 97.

[6] Eamon Duffy, '"Holy Maydens, Holy Wyfes": The Cult of Women Saints in Fifteenth- and Sixteenth-Century England', in *Women in the Church: Papers Read at the 1989 Summer Meeting and the 1990 Winter Meeting of the Ecclesiastical History Society*, ed. W.J. Shiels and Diana Wood, Studies in Church History 27 (Oxford: Bail Blackwell, 1990), pp. 175–96; pp. 178–9.

[7] Blanton, *Signs of Devotion*, p. 267.

Table 2 Images of Edmund by medium

Type	Number documented	Number extant	Date ranges (approximate)
Painted glass	27	13	1250–1558
Chancel screen panels	15	14	15th C
Unspecified 'image'	8	0	Unknown
Wall paintings	8	6	12th–14th C
Bench ends	6	6	15th C
Roof bosses	4	4	1327–1480
Font images	3	3	1400–1475
Sculpted stone figures (miscellaneous)	4	3	Late 12th–15th C
Sculpted stone figure (on porch)	1	1	15^4
Sculpted stone figure (on tower)	1	1	c.1472
Sculpted stone figure (spandrel)	1	1	15^3
Carved wooden wall post	1	1	15th C
Embroidered cope	1	0	1501
Engraved brass plate	1	1	1450–1500
Inscribed brass bell	1	0	Unknown
Misericord	1	1	15th C
Painted cloth frontal	1	0	14^3
Pulpit image	1	1	
Retable	1	1	1300–1350
Stone inscription	1	1	c.1450–80
Painted indulgence	1	0	15th C
Totals	**88**	**58**	**1100s–1558**

Table 3 Images of Edmund by iconography

Iconographic type	Frequency
Individual	51
Martyrdom	10
Wolf and head	10
Narrative	2
Text	2
Unknown	13

extant, although this number would undoubtedly have been higher before the Reformation.[8] Edmund is depicted in numerous formats, most frequently in

---

[8] For Reformation in general, see Duffy, *Stripping of the Altars*, esp. pp. 377–593. For documents pertaining to the destruction of the shrine at Bury see *Three Chapters of Letters*, ed. Wright.

painted glass and on chancel-screen panels, and most often appears as an individual standing figure bearing his attribute, the arrow. The range and frequency of depiction in each media as well as the iconographic types broadly accord with the manner in which most saints were depicted in English medieval churches.[9] The relative numbers of some types of images may be accounted for partly by fashion; for example, the taste for painted murals declined in the later Middle Ages at the same time that other formats, particularly the painted chancel screen, came into favour.[10] Issues of destruction and survival are also influential. Painted glass and wall paintings were undoubtedly easier for reformers and iconoclasts to remove by breaking or whitewashing than a stone sculpture high on the roof of a porch or the side of a tower. The particular vulnerability of certain types of images is reflected in the disparity between the numbers we know to have existed and those which survive, a trend which is likely to have continued after the periods of reforming zeal. More problematic are the unspecified 'images' frequently referred to in antiquarian sources.[11] Nevertheless, images of St Edmund survive in sufficient quantities to enable them to illuminate a particular aspect of cultic devotion.

The chronological range within which images of Edmund occur is similarly broad, ranging from twelfth-century sculptures and wall paintings in the chancels of St Edmund's, Emneth (Norfolk) and St Edmund's, Fritton (Norfolk) respectively, to glass installed in the north window of St Peter Parmentergate, Norwich in 1558. However, the distribution of images within this range is by no means even. The twelfth-century sculpture at Emneth is uniquely early, and although a few images survive from the thirteenth and fourteenth centuries, it is in the fifteenth century that we see an exponential growth in numbers, with around two-thirds of known images dating from after 1400. This apparent growth in Edmund's popularity in the later Middle Ages may be to some extent misleading, and it should not be assumed that a lack of earlier images represents a lack of devotion. Such a summation would depend upon the remaining images representing the full extent of the visual cult and this is evidently not the case. Churches were remodelled and rebuilt throughout the Middle Ages, and it was during the later fifteenth century,

---

[9] For Norfolk, for example, see Ann Eljenholm Nichols, *The Early Art of Norfolk: A Subject List of Extant and Lost Art Including Items Relevant to Early Drama* (Kalamazoo: Medieval Institute Publications/Western Michigan University, 2002).

[10] See Simon Cotton, 'Medieval Rood Screens in Norfolk – Their Construction and Painting Dates', *Norfolk Archaeology* 35 (1984), 44–54.

[11] See Nichols, *Early Art*, p. 10. It should be noted that Nichols assumed a fifteenth-century date for all unspecified images unless otherwise stated. This assumption has not been reproduced in my statistics.

at the time of greatest prosperity, that the majority of rebuilding took place in Norfolk and Suffolk.

To some extent the geographical distribution of images accords with a variety of geological, demographic and social determinants: settlement tends to be denser in areas with good soil, and in turn settlement density affects the distribution of wealth and the presence of industry, particularly the worsted textile industry.[12] Once again, however, although the overall distribution of his cult may be attributed to general determinants such as these, the most fundamental factor governing Edmund's presence was the whim or preference of certain groups or individuals.

Patronage and popularity

Key to understanding how Edmund is depicted is knowing who created an image and for what purpose. As Richard Marks notes, 'images did not function in a vacuum, but were framed by current ideologies and local power structures ... by their environment and by the particular historical moment they occupied'.[13] Although the function and reception of images may have altered over time, appreciating the context in which they originated invariably adds further nuance. Certain factors would have contributed to the likelihood of Edmund being depicted; the dedication of the church and the presence of a guild are two of the most readily discernible.[14]

Dedication images

WALL PAINTINGS, ST EDMUND'S CHURCH, FRITTON (NORFOLK)

There are some notable examples of what may be termed 'dedication images'. The wall paintings in St Edmund's, Fritton (Norfolk) are of various dates, but the images of Edmund in the remarkable tunnel-vaulted Saxon apse of the church date from the twelfth century. Discovered in 1967 surrounding a small Saxon window, the paintings consist of seven scenes. The martyrdom itself is in the spandrel above the window and flanking it are two very faint figures representing

---

[12] These patterns are illustrated in *An Historical Atlas of Norfolk*, ed. P. Wade-Martins, 2nd edn (Norwich: Norfolk Museums Service, 1994) pp. 18–19, 42–4, 76–7, 78–9, 94–5 and *An Historical Atlas of Suffolk*, ed. David Dymond and Edward Martin, 2nd edn (Ipswich: Suffolk County Council, 1989), pp. 20–1, 76–8, 80–2, 140–2.

[13] Marks, *Image and Devotion* p. 25.

[14] For discussion of patronal images see Marks, *Image and Devotion* pp. 64–85 and for guild images see Farnhill, *Guilds and the Parish Community*, pp. 34–40.

the True Church on the left, and Unbelief or Paganism on the right. Below these are four archers, two on either side, bows bent as they shoot at the bound king. Below these again are, on the right, a saint usually identified as St Peter by the key which appears next to him, and on the left, an unknown figure without a halo. The figure of Edmund is extremely fragmentary but he is readily identifiable by his crown, which has a square, castellated top, and by the many arrows that protrude from his body.

The manner in which the Danish archers at Fritton are depicted is unusual. Images in similar media and contexts, such as the fourteenth-century wall painting of the martyrdom at Troston (Suffolk), include the standard image of grotesque, animalistic figures in short tunics. At Fritton, however, the figures are more respectably attired and elegantly postured. Although an unprovable assertion, it is possible that the alleged founding of the church by Cnut may have perpetuated a more nuanced attitude to the Danes than evinced elsewhere.[15]

Another iconographically unusual feature is the second figure that appears in the martyrdom frame, who seems to pull one of the arrows from Edmund's body. This is not part of the standard iconography of the martyrdom, in which Edmund usually stands alone except for the Danish archers. It is possible that this figure represents one of Edmund's followers who searched for the king's body after the departure of the Danes. This is also alluded to by the presence of the wolf, which stands on its hind legs, front paws braced, presumably against another tree, head turned to look at Edmund, ready to stand guard after the king is beheaded. Thus the artist has conflated narrative time in these images in order to convey the most significant elements of Edmund's identity: his kingship (evident in his crown), his martyrdom and his East Anglian origins (represented by the loyal follower and the presence of the wolf). The presence of the flanking figures of the True Church and Unbelief reflects the understanding that Edmund died a martyr's death in defence of his faith. Likewise, the presence of St Peter alludes to Edmund's role in promoting and preserving East Anglian Christianity, just as Peter ensured Christianity's spread during the earliest days of the Church. Thus these early paintings offer an important indication of the nature of Edmund's saintly patronage.

Taverham antiphon window, St Edmund's church, Taverham (Norfolk)

Although similarly dedicated to St Edmund, the stained glass at Taverham (Norfolk) offers a different perspective on the dissemination of Edmund's saintly identity. The only medieval glass now in the church is the north-west nave

---

[15] J.P. Wilkinson, 'Fritton Parish Church, Norfolk', church pamphlet (1930).

window (N5). The main lights contain a simple Crucifixion scene which is largely restored and not originally in this location.[16] The medieval glass in four of the six tracery lights, however, appears to be *in situ*. Each contains a demi-figure of an angel wearing a diadem and an ermine tippet and holding an inscribed scroll.[17] The texts are incomplete but David King identifies them as follows: *Miles Regis* (A2); *P[ro] sal[ute]* (A4); *Ave rex ge[n]tis an[glorum]*.[18] This is clearly part of the antiphon sung at Vespers on the eve of the Feast of St Edmund.[19] Blomefield records the antiphon similarly written on the now-lost roodscreen in Fundenhall church (Norfolk).[20] The most widespread dissemination of the antiphon would have been through its adoption by the Sarum rite, but the direct influence of the abbey at Bury is also apparent. Lydgate exhorts readers of his *Lives* to recite 'with hool herte and dew reuerence' an 'Antephone and Orison' in order to gain an indulgence of two hundred days 'write and registred afforn his hooly shryne'.[21] The presence of the text of the antiphon on or near the shrine would be an effective means of disseminating it to pilgrims, and its use as a textual mnemonic is evinced in the lead pseudo-coins discussed above.

Although now lost, the antiphon window once contained the arms of the Braunche family along with donor figures, leading King to suggest that the glass was probably installed around 1478, when Robert Braunche of Stody and Hunworth presented it to the church.[22] As a local man it is possible that Braunche went on pilgrimage to Bury. The presence of the antiphon at Taverham may therefore be as a result of general knowledge of it from the Sarum rites, via its dissemination through pilgrim souvenirs or from direct experience in the abbey church at Bury. This exemplifies that whilst images of St Edmund may derive from the dedication of the church, a far more complex network of influences and individuals are likely to be involved.

Despite these notable examples, the relationship between dedication and depiction is further complicated by the overall evidence from Norfolk and Suffolk, where, of the twenty-three churches dedicated to Edmund, only eleven are known to have contained an image of the saint, and of the nine guilds dedicated to Edmund

---

[16] David King, 'An Antiphon to St Edmund in Taverham Church', *Norfolk Archaeology* 35 (1977), 387–91.
[17] For other example of angels holding inscribed scrolls see Christopher Woodforde, *The Norwich School of Glass-Painting in the Fifteenth Century* (London: Oxford University Press, 1950), pp. 137–42.
[18] King, 'An Antiphon', 388.
[19] See Colton, 'Music and Identity', 89–95.
[20] Blomefield, *Norfolk*, V, p. 174.
[21] Lydgate, *Lives*, Prologue, 73–80 and Antiphon and Orison (unnumbered in Horstmann's edition).
[22] King, 'An Antiphon', 389.

in Norfolk only four of these accord with the parochial dedication.[23] Whilst it is likely that these apparent anomalies may be accounted for by depredation, either of an image or of records relating to guilds, it is noteworthy that guild records do survive for two churches dedicated to Edmund and refer to guilds with alternative patrons.[24] Duffy avers that there is 'little sign in the later Middle Ages of strong individual devotion to the parish patron', and notes that few surviving screens portray such individuals, who also occur infrequently as recipients of bequests.[25] In determining the presence of an image within a church the affiliation of the parish may therefore be more significant than its dedication. In the case of St Edmund, affiliation of a church or chapel with the abbey at Bury, either directly or via the connections with patrons of the abbey, would be likely to influence his inclusion.

Personal patronage

In addition to the patronage of an institution, the proclivity of the individual is also likely to be a significant factor in determining the presence of a saint. Although the medium and circumstances of patronage may differ considerably, the underlying principles of selection detailed in hagiographic narratives may illuminate the choices of saints within a material context. In his fifteenth-century *Legendys of Hooly Wummen*, Osbern Bokenham (1393–1447), Augustinian friar at Clare (Suffolk), describes the circumstances of the composition of each life, informing us, for example, that the legend of St Anne was composed for John and Katherine Denston, who had a daughter named Anne, and that the lives of Sts Elizabeth and Katherine are dedicated to Elizabeth de Vere and to Katherine Denston and Katherine Howard, respectively.[26] St Anne is also invoked in her capacity as patroness of conception and fertility, representing a common appeal to saints associated with specific occupations or circumstances. Although documentary references are sparse, bequests to rood screens exhibit similar patterns of patronage; for example, at North Burlingham (Norfolk) the names of the donors of the rood screen correlate with the saints and frequently occur on the panel with their 'name' saint.[27]

---

[23] For dedications see Frances Arnold-Foster, *Studies in Church Dedications*, III, p. 359 and for guilds see Farnhill, *Guilds and the Parish Community*, pp. 172–211.

[24] Farnhill, *Guilds and the Parish Community*, pp. 172–211.

[25] Duffy, *Stripping of the Altars*, p. 162.

[26] Osbern Bokenham, *Legendys of Hooly Wummen*, ed. Mary S. Serjeantson, Early English Text Society, os 206 (London: Humphrey Milford, 1938), ll. 2092, 5054 and 6365–6 respectively.

[27] The donors at Burlingham include Edward Lacy, John and Cecilia Blake, Thomas and Margaret Benet and John Benet; amongst the saints are Edward the Confessor, John the

Thornham Parva retable

A comparable contiguity between patron and saint is evident on the mid-fourteenth-century retable now in St Mary's, Thornham Parva (Suffolk). Along with the frontal now in the Musée de Cluny (Paris), the inclusion of Sts Dominic and Peter Martyr is suggestive of Dominican patronage, with the most convincing attribution being to Thetford Dominican Priory.[28] Founded in 1335, it correlates with the date of the painting of the retable.[29] Connections can also be made to account for the retable's relocation from the Priory at the Dissolution and its rediscovery in a stable loft on the nearby Thornham Hall estate in 1926.[30] The choice of saints is also illuminating: flanked by the two Dominicans, the pairs proceeding inwards towards the central Crucifixion panel are Catherine of Alexandria and Margaret of Antioch, John the Baptist and Edmund, and Peter and Paul. The two apostles are standard across contexts, due to their role in the establishment of the Church, and the two female saints were both famed for their learning and preaching and thus accord with Dominican ideology. Edmund and John the Baptist are less readily explicable in this otherwise explicitly Dominican context. A convincing connection based on nomenclature, however, can be made between the saints and the founders of Thetford Priory: John de Warenne, earl of Surrey (d.1347) and Edmund de Gonville (d.1351), a wealthy local priest and founder of Gonville Hall in Cambridge.[31] The otherwise unusual pairing can therefore be explained by reference to the retable's patrons.

Baptist, Thomas Becket, Benedict and Cecilia. Cited in Cotton, 'Medieval Roodscreens in Norfolk', 44–5.

[28] Christopher Norton, David Park and Paul Binski, *Dominican Painting in East Anglia: the Thornham Parva retable and the Musée de Cluny frontal* (Woodbridge: Boydell, 1987). For the provenance of the retable see Norton, 'History and Provenance', in *Dominican Painting*, pp. 82–101; esp. pp. 82–91.

[29] Binski, 'Style and Date', in *Dominican Painting*, pp. 57–81. See also Mary Kempski, 'A Technical Comparison of the Thornham Parva Retable with Contemporary Paintings, with Particular Reference to East Anglia' and Marie Louise Sauerberg, Helen Howard and Aloce Tavares da Silva, 'The Wall Paintings of c.1300 in the Ante-Reliquary Chapel, Norwich Cathedral and the Thornham Parva Retable: A Technical Comparison', both in *The Thornham Parva Retable: Technique, Conservation and Context of an English Medieval Painting*, ed. Ann Massing, Hamilton Kerr Institute Painting and Practice Series 1 (London: Harvey Miller Publishers for the Hamilton Kerr Institute and the University of Cambridge, 2003), pp. 143–4 and 174–88 respectively.

[30] For how the retable came to be at Thornham Hall see Norton, 'History and Provenance', in *Dominican Painting*, pp. 95–101.

[31] For the foundation of Thetford Priory in relation to the retable and frontal see Norton, 'History and Provenance', in *Dominican Painting*, pp. 87–8 and n. 22.

The iconography of St Edmund

THE NORWICH CATHEDRAL CLOISTER BOSSES

As part of the monastic precinct, the images of St Edmund in the cloisters of Norwich Cathedral Priory exist in a different physical context and are therefore not directly comparable to the majority of East Anglian parish church imagery. It is possible that their context, in particular their intended monastic audience, may have resulted in representations of Edmund different from those on display to the general populace, although the tendency of the cathedral to act as a prototype for work replicated elsewhere is also well known.[32] However, this is one of the few examples where multiple images of St Edmund survive in one location as part of a larger iconographic scheme and as such contributes a unique perspective to a discussion of Edmund's visual cult.

Although completed as part of the original cathedral building, the cloisters, along with much of the structure, probably sustained considerable damage during rioting in Norwich in 1272 and were rebuilt between 1300 and 1450 as part of an extensive programme of repair. This included the sculpture and painting of the approximately four hundred keystone bosses which hold in place the ribs of the vaulting.[33] The north walk was the last to be restored, and the bosses here depict scenes from the lives of the saints. Most are shown during their martyrdom, what Rose describes as 'their most characteristic moment'.[34] Thus St Martin is shown dividing his cloak with the peasant (CNJ3) and St Laurence appears roasting on the gridiron (CNI5).[35] Most saints are afforded only one boss, but Edmund appears twice, bound to the tree and pierced with arrows in the seventh bay (CNI7) and with his followers discovering the wolf guarding his severed head in the ninth (CNH7). This suggests that the creators of the bosses considered Edmund to be of suitable significance to be included twice: only Thomas Becket occupies a greater number, with his martyrdom depicted in a sequence of five images (CNH3/5/6/8, CNI1).

---

[32] The cathedral as an architectural prototype is discussed by Malcolm Thurlby, 'The Influence of the Cathedral on Romanesque Architecture' and Richard Fawcett, 'The Influence of the Gothic Parts of the Cathedral on Church Building in Norfolk', in *Norwich Cathedral: Church, City and Diocese, 1096–1996*, ed. Ian Atherton, Eric Fernie, Christopher Harper-Bill and Hassel Smith (London: Hambledon 1996), pp. 136–57 and pp. 210–227 respectively.

[33] See Martial Rose, *Stories in Stone: The Medieval Roof Carvings of Norwich Cathedral* (London: Herbert, 1997), pp. 23–50.

[34] Rose, *Stories in Stone*, p. 42.

[35] References to boss and bay numberings are given throughout in accordance with those in Rose, *Stories in Stone*; see especially the plan of the cloisters on p. 47.

Edmund also appears in the east walk, the first to be rebuilt, begun under Bishop John Salmon (1299–1325) and Prior Henry Lakenham (1289–1310). The eastern bosses were completed in two phases: the first group, which spans eight bays running south from the entrance of the Chapter House to the Dark Entry, was completed between 1316–19. The imagery here is mostly foliate, with some figural images such as the Green Man, and numerous hybrids and mythical creatures.[36] The second phase, rebuilt between 1327 and 1329, runs northwards across six bays from the Chapter House to the Prior's Door, through which the monks passed on their way through the cloisters to services in the cathedral. The subject of this later sequence, the first sequence of narrative bosses carved in England, was the passion of Christ.[37]

It is in the context of the passion narrative that Edmund can be found. His martyrdom appears in the second bay and forms one of the 'orbital' bosses around the central scene of the Resurrection (CEB3). Edmund is also depicted above the Prior's Door, where, along with Moses and Sts Peter and John the Baptist, he flanks an image of Christ enthroned. The inclusion of Edmund, the only non-biblical saint, in this illustrious group again attests to the exceptionally high regard in which he was held. The image here is of Edmund crowned and made whole, and provides a sharp contrast with the bound and helpless individual depicted during his martyrdom in the second bay and the two north walk images. Edmund's presence in the Resurrection bay prefigures his appearance above the Prior's Door, and alludes to his spiritual glorification in the company of heaven. It also reiterates the sacrificial nature of Edmund's own martyrdom. Despite there being only two images of Edmund, their association with the passion sequence invests them with a similar narrative progression of their own: just as Christ's passion culminates in His heavenly enthronement, so Edmund's suffering and death ensure his place amidst the celestial company. For the creators of the bosses the martyrdom was the most characteristic scene from Edmund's life and defined him in relation to other saints. His presence in the Resurrection bay, however, reiterates that whilst death marks the end of a saint's earthly life it is also the beginning of their heavenly existence.

THORNHAM PARVA WALL PAINTINGS

The only other extant sequence of Edmund images in East Anglia is the early fourteenth-century wall painting cycle at Thornham Parva (Suffolk). Painted on the north wall of the nave, opposite the ornate Norman south door which formed

---

[36] The imagery of the bosses in this walk is discussed by Sarah Mittuch in 'Medieval Art of Death and Resurrection', *Archaeology Today* 209 (May/June 2007), 34–40.

[37] Rose, *Stories in Stone*, p. 11.

the main entrance to the church, five visible scenes run from east to west. Along with a mid-thirteenth-century cycle in the north transept of St Helen's church, Cliffe-at-Hoo (Kent), it is one of only two surviving cycles of Edmund wall paintings in England. On the opposite wall scenes from the Infancy of Christ run west to east, suggesting that the paintings were designed for a viewer entering the church at the west end and proceeding around the interior in an anti-clockwise direction. The paintings on both walls extend east as far as the chancel screen and at their western limit are obscured by an eighteenth-century bow-fronted gallery. The Virgin Mary, dedicatee of the church, features prominently in the Infancy cycle and the theme of the incarnation of the saviour relates to the notion of Edmund as saviour of his kingdom, dying on behalf of his people. Thus Edmund is portrayed as a type of Christ, embodying universal Christian truths of salvation and redemption.

Simultaneously, certain details of the Edmund cycle attest to aspects of his saintly identity of particularly local relevance. The first scene depicts Edmund on horseback riding away from a battlemented tower. This is iconographically extremely unusual and illustrates the narrative, first recorded by Geffrei Gaimar in his *Estoire des Engleis* around 1135–40, of Edmund's attempt to flee from the Danes following the East Anglians' defeat in battle:

> The [Danes] fought with great ferocity and emerged victorious on the battlefield. God! What a calamity it was for their lord and king Edmund, who was driven back into a stronghold where his principle place of residence was. The heathens pursued him there, and Edmund came out to meet them. The first people who met him took him prisoner, asking him 'Where is Edmund? Tell us where he is.' 'That I will, and willingly so, you can be sure: for as long as I have taken refuge here, Edmund has been here, and I have been with him. When I left, he left as well. I have no idea whether he will get out of your clutches.'[38]

Edmund is held by the Danes until he is recognised by one of Ingwar and Ubba's retinue, and is subsequently put to death.

Estoire was probably composed for Constance, wife of Ralph Fitz Gilbert, a minor Lincolnshire magnate.[39] Up until the accession of Edgar in 959 it is primarily based upon the Northern Recension of the *Anglo-Saxon Chronicle* and follows

---

[38] The most recent edition and translation is by Ian Short, *Geffrei Gaimar. Estoire des Engleis* (Oxford: Oxford University Press, 2009), ll. 2871–90, pp. 156–9.

[39] For the Fitz Gilberts see Short. *Geffrei Gaimar*, ix–xi and notes to the text, ll. 5899, 6258, 6350–1.

its annalistic format, although its narratives are heavily influenced by Romance traditions.[40] At this date the Edmund textual tradition was still largely bifurcated along chronicle and hagiographic lines and Edmund's depiction in *Estoire* is thus primarily drawn from chronicle sources in which he engages the Danes in battle. As we have seen, the traditions would not be united textually until the compilation of Bodley 240 in the third quarter of the fourteenth century, around half a century later than the date usually ascribed to the paintings. The rest of the scenes are part of the standard hagiographic tradition and this raises a number of possibilities concerning the source upon which the cycle as a whole was based. The paintings might be later, which would enable them to be based upon Bodley 240, which contains all the narrative elements depicted visually in the paintings. However, based on stylistic analysis this seems unlikely. The other possibility is that elements of the chronicle tradition had already been incorporated into Edmund's life by the early fourteenth century and the Thornham cycle is based either on oral traditions which were not yet formally recorded or upon an otherwise unknown text or visual source. This is also implied by evidence from the Cliffe-at-Hoo cycle, which likewise contains Edmund's flight from the Danes. Dating from the mid-thirteenth century and geographically further removed from the cult centre, they suggest that this version of Edmund's legend was being disseminated at an earlier date than previously assumed. In terms of the development of Edmund's saintly identity this scene is a curious addition, as his attempts to flee to some extent undermine the notion of the willing heroic martyr. Short suggests that Geffrei includes local traditions and romance elements throughout *Estoire* in order to enliven his text for his secular baronial audience.[41] This incident is therefore part of the same trend that Geoffrey of Wells alludes to at a similar date, where increasing interest in St Edmund led people to elaborate upon the legend. In much the same way as the details Geoffrey contributes concerning Edmund's youth and upbringing, his flight from the Danes serves to humanise an example of otherwise saintly perfection, rendering him more accessible to his devotees. The wall paintings are therefore indicative of the growth of local traditions and Edmund's increasing popularity.

The remaining scenes are part of a more standardised iconographic tradition. The next scene has been destroyed by the insertion of a later window but almost certainly showed the martyrdom, as in the Cliffe-at-Hoo cycle, probably in the

---

[40] For the literary context see Legge, *Anglo-Norman Literature*, pp. 27–36; 276–8, also Rosalind Field, 'Romance as History, History as Romance', in *Romance in Medieval England*, ed. Maldwyn Mills, Jennifer Fellows and Carol M. Meade (Cambridge: D.S. Brewer, 1991), pp. 164–73.

[41] Short, *Geffrei Gaimar*, xxxix.

conventional format of the tree-bound and sagittated king, in accordance with his depiction in other wall paintings, including East Anglian examples at Boxford, Fritton and Troston. In what originally comprised the third scene, two tonsured monks support Edmund's wound-ridden corpse whilst his head is miraculously reattached, the join clearly visible on his neck. Next, Edmund's body, accompanied by the wolf, is carried on a bier in a house-shaped casket topped with three small crosses. These scenes are derived from Abbo's *Passio* and are likewise depicted in the Pierpont Morgan miniatures, although in the manuscript version the visual narrative adheres more closely to the textual source in depicting as laypeople the followers who find and reattach Edmund's head and bury his body.[42] It is possible that the context of the wall paintings made it more desirable to depict Edmund's followers as monks. The presence of the Morgan manuscript in the abbey church and its presumably limited readership meant that less ambiguity was likely to arise concerning the role of the convent as Edmund's guardian, whereas in an alternative location, at a remove from the shrine, it was apt to remind viewers of the resting place of Edmund's remains.

The final visible scene illustrates the miraculous crossing of the narrow bridge during Egelwyn's transportation of the relics to London to escape the renewed Danish raids. The figures of Egelwyn and the donkey, presumably to the left of the scene, are obscured by the gallery, but the cart, painted on an enormous scale, is clearly visible. The artist has used the arch of the north door to represent the bridge and in addition to being a neat visual trick, this also sets up an evocative relationship between the paintings and the physical experience of the viewer.

Thornham Parva is approximately eighteen miles east-north-east of Bury and therefore could not claim to be on Egelwyn's route south-west to London. However, Thornham Parva is situated a few miles east of what is now the A143, the main road between Bury and Great Yarmouth and a major arterial route in the region. It is also just west of the A140, the Cromer to Ipswich road, likewise a long-established cross-country route. At a day or two's walk from Bury it is likely that pilgrims travelling from the north or the east, either from elsewhere in Norfolk or Suffolk or from further afield via one of the ports, would have passed through Thornham Parva. In this context the cart evokes Edmund's own pilgrimage of sorts, establishing a relationship between the pilgrims' journey and that undertaken by Edmund's relics. It is tempting to assume that the final image in the cycle, now obscured by the gallery, would have been of Bury, located at the west end of the church in the direction of the pilgrim's journey towards the shrine. The wall paintings recount both a historical narrative and the ongoing, lived experience of the viewer.

---

[42] See Pierpont Morgan MS M. 736, fols 15v–18r.

The cathedral bosses and the Thornham Parva paintings attest to the variety of depictional possibilities. Edmund could appear either as a glorified individual in the company of heaven, during his martyrdom or in reference to a post-mortem incident, particularly in the company of his lupine guardian. In the majority of instances Edmund is depicted in one of these three ways.

EDMUND THE MARTYR

Edmund's association with the martyrs of the early Church is made explicit in the spandrels above the west door of St Laurence's church in Norwich, dating from the third quarter of the fifteenth century. In the triangular spandrel to the left of the door, stretched across his gridiron, is the patronal saint. To the right is Edmund, bound to a tree and being shot from close quarters by several archers, many arrows already protruding from his body (Figure 1). The allusion to decapitation is further emphasised by the wolf lurking in foliage at the bottom of the spandrel, waiting to take possession of the saint's head which will soon be struck from his body. Edmund's martyrdom likewise appears in two mid-thirteenth-century roundels now in the east chancel window of St Mary's, Saxlingham Nethergate (Norfolk), where he is afforded two bosses, with Sts James and John in another and St Peter in a fourth. This implies not only that is Edmund continuing a long tradition of defending the faith but that he is being represented as on a spiritual par with the earliest founders of Christian sainthood. His martyrdom therefore integrates him into the continuous narrative of Christian history, establishing a link with individuals from all periods which transcends conventions of era or nationality.

Images of the martyrdom span a broad chronological period: from the mid-thirteenth-century roundels at Saxlingham Nethergate to the glass installed in St Peter Parmentergate, Norwich in 1558, indicating the longevity of this mode of representation. They also appear in a range of media. In addition to glass and the carved spandrels mentioned above, Edmund's martyrdom was depicted in the Norwich Cathedral roof bosses, a fifteenth-century misericord in the church at Norton (Suffolk) (Figure 2), wall paintings at Fritton (Norfolk), Troston (Suffolk) and Stow Bardolph (Norfolk), although the latter image is no longer extant. Considering its longevity and appearance in a variety of forms, it is surprising that relatively few representations of the martyrdom are known in East Anglian churches, accounting for just over a ninth of the total. However, this may be accounted for by the evident range of iconographical choices, reflecting the interpretive flexibility afforded to Edmund in other cultic contexts.

Figure 1 Carved stone spandrel of the martyrdom from St Lawrence (Norwich)

EDMUND IN GLORY

By far the most widespread mode of representation is of Edmund as a single figure, clutching his attribute, the arrow. Accounting for nearly 60 per cent of known images, the majority depict Edmund crowned, robed and glorified, and whilst he holds the arrow, the symbol of his martyrdom, he bears no wounds from his ordeal (Figure 3). The emphasis is upon Edmund's status as a martyr and the spiritual consequences of this event rather than the physical act of martyrdom itself. As in the final miniature in the Pierpont Morgan manuscript (fol. 22v), Edmund is glorified. The medium of these images and their relative positioning within the holy geography of the church is also significant. The majority are either painted glass or painted rood-screen panels, and the connotations of each reinforce the spiritual nature of Edmund's sanctity.

Although stained glass undoubtedly fulfilled a highly decorative function, it also had theological connotations. Sarah Crewe describes the perceived mystical association of light with the spirit of God, for which it was a common metaphor.[43]

---

[43] Sarah Crewe, *Stained Glass in England, c.1180–1540* (London: Her Majesty's Stationery Office, 1987), pp. 7–8. For detailed discussion of medieval glass see also Richard Marks, *Stained Glass in England during the Middle Ages* (London: Routledge, 1993).

Figure 2 Carved wooden misericord from Norton (Suffolk)

Figure 3 Stained glass roundel from Saxlingham Nethergate (Norfolk)

Thus when light shone through a painted-glass window, bringing to life the colours and shapes therein, this could be seen as analogous to the spirit of God radiating through the individuals depicted. In a general sense this may represent the omnipresence of the Holy Spirit, penetrating all aspects of creation just as light illuminates the multitude of scenes depicted in glass. However, it is particularly relevant to images of saints, as it reiterates the role of the sainted individual as a conduit between humankind and God: their likenesses in glass refract light just as they were believed to refract the power of God. The saint is quite literally glorified, and although scenes of all types could be depicted in glass, it is a particularly appropriate medium in which to show saints as they were believed to exist in heaven.

Edmund is represented on screen panels in much the same way as in painted glass, royally attired and with the same attribute. Similarly, the physical context and associations of the screens also invests them with additional meaning. More than two hundred chancel screens in various stages of preservation survive in Norfolk and Suffolk, the majority of which date from the fifteenth century, and of these around one hundred retain painted panels.[44] Fifteen panels depicting Edmund survive, twelve in their original screen framework, with three disarticulated or re-framed. The original focus was usually the rood suspended from the rood beam, from which the structures derive the name by which they are commonly known. At the foot of the crucifix were Mary and John, and often on the tympanum above or behind them was a scene of the Last Judgement. The positions of the saints beneath the rood therefore represented the heavenly hierarchy. Duffy maintains that the presence of the saints on these screens and their relationship to the other figures 'spoke of their dependence on and mediation of the benefits of Christ's passion, and their role as intercessors for their clients not merely here and now but at the last day'.[45] This is reiterated by the position of the screens within the internal dynamic of the church, marking as they did the move from lay to clerical areas of authority: just as the screens were the portals to the holiest part of the church, so the saints were spiritual portals

---

[44] East Anglian screens are surprisingly poorly documented but the main studies include: W.G. Constable, 'Some East Anglian Roodscreen Paintings', *Connoisseur* lxxxiv (1929), 141–7; W.W. Lillie, 'Screenwork in the County of Suffolk, III: Panels Painted with Saints', *Proceedings of the Suffolk Institute of Archaeology* xxi (1933), 179–202; W.W. Williamson, 'Saints on Norfolk Roodscreens and Pulpits', *Norfolk Archaeology* xxi (1957), 299–346; Simon Cotton, 'Medieval Roodscreens in Norfolk', 44–54; Julian Eve, *Saints and the Painted Roodscreens of North East Norfolk* (Norwich: J.R. Eve, 1997); Helen E. Lunnon, 'Observations on the Changing Form of Chancel Screens in Late Medieval Norfolk', *Journal of the British Archaeological Association* 163.1 (2010), 110–31.

[45] Duffy, *Stripping of the Altars*, p. 158.

between humankind and God. Edmund is thus once again represented in his capacity as spiritual intermediary, with emphasis upon his heavenly rather than earthly lineage. Representations of St Edmund as an individual figure therefore appear to correspond with the iconographic scheme suggested in the cathedral cloisters, emphasising the saint as intercessor. The emphasis is upon Edmund post mortem, but he is restored and glorified. He grasps the implement of his martyrdom, symbolising that his death was not a defeat, but a victory: his martyrdom is literally within his own grasp.

EDMUND THE KING

Examining the iconographic context in which Edmund is found in these same media (stained glass and chancel-screen panels) reveals a further aspect of his saintly identity. Where an image of Edmund occurs as one of a series of saints, he is frequently found alongside other sainted monarchs. The preservation of the surviving screens varies considerably and it is not possible in all cases to identify each figure. Whilst Edmund may be distinguished with considerable certainty on each screen due to his characteristic attribute, the identity of many of his companions is at best ambiguous and in some cases entirely unknown. At Catfield (Norfolk), however, and on the south screen at Barton Turf (Norfolk) it is clear that each individual is drawn from amongst the ranks of sainted English monarchs. Although the screen at Catfield is damaged, two of the figures can be identified by their attributes as Sts Edmund and Olaf, with others believed to be Ethelbert of East Anglia, Margaret of Scotland, Oswin of Deira and Edward the Confessor. The variety of ways in which even this relatively small sample achieved the status of saint and the subsequent influence this has upon their perceived identity differs considerably; it is difficult, for example, to draw many comparisons between the peaceable diplomat Edward the Confessor and the warrior-king Olaf (killed in battle and most often seen brandishing his war axe) other than that both were kings. The feature of their sanctity which unifies these figures is therefore their royalty. This is reiterated by Edmund's appearance: on all but the screen at Stalham he is crowned and richly robed; at Barton Turf, for example, his elaborately patterned mantel is trimmed with ermine. In addition, on around half the screens he is shown not only with an arrow, the means by which he achieved his heavenly status, but also a sceptre, a symbol of his earthly authority. Nichols similarly notes that in the king sequences on Norfolk screens none of the monarchs is nimbed, an omission which she feels places further emphasis upon their temporal status.[46] Edmund similarly appears in the company of other sainted kings in the glazing schemes of a number of churches including St Peter Mancroft

---

[46] Nichols, *Early Art of Norfolk*, p. 317.

Figure 4 St Edmund and Henry VI on the chancel screen at Ludham (Norfolk)

(Norwich), Outwell, Marsham, Salle and Stody (all Norfolk). Anglo-Saxon kings such as Sts Kenelm, Edward Martyr, Edward the Confessor and Ethelbert feature frequently. Where individuals are identified by means of a label, such as at St Peter Mancroft, the use of '*rex*' similarly emphasises their temporal status.

POLITICS AND PROPAGANDA: EDMUND AND HENRY VI

Devotion to the saints could also have a political dimension. As an erstwhile king of the region, Edmund's cult was particularly strong in East Anglia, but in addition to being worshipped locally, he was for several centuries a particular favourite of the English monarchy. In addition to the influence of individual preference in determining the presence of his iconography in the Norfolk parish church, the visual cult must also therefore be located in its political context, both locally and nationally. A particular instance of this occurs when Edmund appears alongside Henry VI (Figure 4).

The majority of these images of Edmund as king, both in windows and on screens, were installed during the mid-fifteenth century, the period that saw the deposition and reinstatement of Henry VI. Sequences of English kings were frequently used to present Henry VI's royal ancestry as a way of justifying the Lancastrian hold on the throne, and this appears to be the case, for example, in the original glazing at Salle (Norfolk).[47] Nothing remains of the main-light glazing of the side-chancel windows, but antiquarian evidence indicates that Edmund was once depicted here amongst other sainted kings, popes and archbishops in the main lights of the three triple-light windows on either side of the church.[48] An element of political propaganda in the Salle glazing is indicated by the presence in the sequence of the only non-English king, Louis IX of France, whom David King suggests was probably chosen by the designer of the scheme in reference to and in support of Henry VI's claim to the dual monarchy of England and France through his descent from Louis IX.[49] This is supported by the patronage implied by the inscriptions and heraldry which indicate links with Cardinal Beaufort and William de la Pole, both key supporters of Henry VI.[50] In addition to emphasising Edmund's own royalty, images such as these demonstrate that he was a useful *exampla* of an indigenous, saintly, pre-Conquest king who would therefore be an appropriate inclusion in a royal genealogy, and whose image could be deployed in support of another monarch, in this case Henry VI.

Following Henry VI's eventual demise in 1471, within a few years the late king was himself revered as a saint.[51] His cult flourished in East Anglia and images of Edmund paired with Henry VI appear on the chancel screens at Barton Turf and

---

[47] Richard Marks discusses other series of English kings to appear in ecclesiastical glazing schemes, including All Souls College, Oxford, which contains similar elements of genealogical propaganda, in Marks, *Stained Glass in England*, pp. 88–9. For uses of royal genealogies as Lancastrian propaganda in other media see McKenna, 'Henry VI of England and the Dual Monarchy', 145–62.

[48] North side, left to right: St Lucius, Pope Eleutherius, St Fagan, St Ethelbert, Pope Gregory I, St Augustine, unknown, Pope Boniface, St Laurence of Canterbury. South side, right to left: St Alphege, Pope Urban I, St Edmund King & Martyr, St Thomas Becket, Pope Silvester, St Edward King and Martyr, St Edmund Rich, Pope John I, St Louis IX of France. Sequence reconstructed by David King, in 'Salle Church – The Glazing', *Archaeological Journal* cxxxvii, 1980, 333–5; p. 335.

[49] King, 'Salle Church', p. 335. Again, see McKenna, 'Henry VI of England and the Dual Monarchy', pp. 145–62.

[50] King, 'Salle Church', p. 335.

[51] The cult of Henry VI is exhaustively documented by Paul Grosjean in *Henrici VI Angliae Regis Miracula Postuma* (Bruxelles: Société des Bollandistes, 1935); see also Francis Aidan Gasquet, *The Religious Life of King Henry VI* (London: G. Bell, 1923); Wolffe, *Henry VI*, especially pp. 3–24 and pp. 351–60; J.W. McKenna, 'Piety and Propaganda: The Cult of Henry VI', in *Chaucer and Middle English Studies in Honour of R.H. Robbins*, ed. Beryl Rowland (London: Allen and Unwin, 1974), pp. 72–88; Katherine Lewis, '"Imitate, too, this king in virtue, who could have done ill, and did it not": Lay Sanctity and the Rewriting of Henry VI's Manliness', in *Religious Men and Masculine Identity in the Middle Ages*, ed. P.H. Cullum and K. Lewis (Woodbridge: Boydell, 2013), pp. 126–142.

Ludham (Figure 4).⁵² Although Edward IV was understandably concerned about Henry's apparent apotheosis and attempted to suppress the fledgling cult of the king he had deposed, Richard III, in a gesture of expiation and reconciliation, had Henry's body exhumed and translated to Windsor in 1484. Henry VII likewise sought to promote the cult of his predecessor, petitioning the papacy for his canonisation in an attempt to legitimate the Tudor dynasty by associating it with his saintly relative.⁵³ In this post-mortem context, the long-established and successful cult of Edmund would provide the fifteenth- and sixteenth-century cult of Henry VI with a historical context and precedent and reinforce it by association.⁵⁴ Edmund the royal saint was therefore not only part of an established tradition of holy monarchs, but a useful and relevant tool in the world of later medieval political propaganda. This facet of Edmund's saintly identity may be appreciated by considering the national political context in which it was re-imagined. Evidence of patronage survives in very few cases, but where it does exist it can additionally illuminate the means by which the cult of St Edmund was manipulated to serve political ends at a local and personal level.

THE TOPPES WINDOW, ST PETER MANCROFT, NORWICH

The east window in the north chancel chapel of St Peter Mancroft, Norwich, was the gift of Robert Toppes, the richest merchant in Norwich and an active participant in the stormy political life of the city, including the troubles of the 1430s and 1440s.⁵⁵ The window displays Toppes's arms, his merchant's mark and the arms of his wife's landed family, and may have been glazed by the time of the consecration in 1455.⁵⁶ Although the panels of the Toppes window are no longer *in situ*, King has reconstructed the original glazing scheme based upon surviving panels and fragments and the observations of a number of antiquarians.⁵⁷ The thirty main-light panels contained scenes from the Infancy of Christ and the Death, Funeral

---

52 Richard Marks discuss the visual cult of Henry VI at a national level in 'Images of Henry VI', in *The Lancastrian Court*, ed. Jenny Stratford Harlaxton Medieval Studies XIII, (Donnington: Shaun Tyas, 2003), pp. 111–24.
53 Wolffe, *Henry VI*, pp. 3–21.
54 This element of the cult is also clear from the additional miracles added to Lydgate's *Lives* which Bale argues were also connected with William de la Pole. See Bale, 'St Edmund in Fifteenth Century London', in *Changing Images*, ed. Bale, pp. 145–61.
55 For the background to this disturbance and details of the political unrest in the city in this period see Norman Tanner, 'The Cathedral and the City', in *Norwich Cathedral: Church, City and Diocese*, ed. Atherton et al., pp. 255–80; pp. 255–69.
56 David King, *The Medieval Stained Glass of St Peter Mancroft, Norwich, Corpus Vitrearum Medii Aevi* Great Britain, vol. 5 (Oxford and New York: Published for the British Academy by Oxford University Press, 2006) lxxviii.
57 King, *The Medieval Stained Glass of St Peter Mancroft, Norwich*, clxix–clxxxi.

and Assumption of the Virgin Mary. The tracery lights contained three series: Old Testament figures; sainted English bishops and archbishops; and (mainly) sainted English kings, amongst whom Edmund is to be found. The extant kings are all nimbed and hold either swords or sceptres or, in Edmund's case, the usual arrow. It seems likely that the kings were arranged in chronological order of date of death, and King has based his reconstruction of the missing figures upon this premise.[58]

Edmund's presence in the Toppes window is literally marginal, appearing as he does in one of the tracery lights, and his connection with the main subjects is not readily apparent. The national political significance of sequences of English kings created during this period has been discussed above. In this context, however, some aspects of the series assume significance in a local context. St Alban, for example, was not a royal saint but his presence may have arisen from local political considerations, being a possible reference to the devotion of Humphrey, duke of Gloucester, to the English proto-martyr.[59] Gloucester was popular in Norwich, in contrast to William de la Pole, duke of Suffolk, who King suggests is portrayed as the Jew interrupting the Funeral of the Virgin in the main lights below.[60] The exact significance of this reference is ambiguous; on the one hand de la Pole is depicted as committing a heinous act, whereas in adjacent panels we see the Jew converted, and subsequently being handed the palm given to St John by the Virgin. This ambiguity is likely to have arisen as a result of de la Pole's participation in the factional unrest in the city and his support of the cathedral priory's claims over those of the citizens, as, whilst de la Pole was now dead and the troubles had largely subsided, the memory of his involvement would have lingered.

Similar themes are implied by the presence of Athelstan in the sequence of holy kings. Athelstan was a monarch renowned for his piety and for the number and importance of his charters, and is a possible reference to the recent signing of a new royal charter for the city in 1452. The charter marked the official reconciliation of the city with the king, following the years of political unrest which

---

[58] King, *The Medieval Stained Glass of St Peter Mancroft, Norwich*, clxxxix–cxcii. The reconstructed sequence is: St Alban, St Oswald, St Oswin, St Ethelbert, St Alcmund, St Kenelm, St Edmund, King Athelstan, King Edgar, St Edward the Confessor. It will be noted that not all the figures are kings, and that likewise not all were sainted, points I will return to below.

[59] Gloucester's relationship with the Abbey of St Albans and its patron is discussed by K.H. Vickers in *Humphrey, Duke of Gloucester: A Biography* (London: Archibald Constable, 1907) pp. 329–32. See also Jane Kelsall, *Humphrey Duke of Gloucester, 1391–1447* (St Albans: Fraternity of the Friends of Saint Albans Abbey, 2000).

[60] The figure of the Jew is wearing a surcoat over full plate armour in pale blue glass on which are painted three leopards' faces in silver stain, a reference to William de la Pole, whose arms were *Azure a fess between three leopards' faces two and one or*. King, *The Medieval Stained Glass of St Peter Mancroft, Norwich*, clxxxvi.

erupted in Gladman's Insurrection in 1443. Henry VI visited Norwich in February 1453, followed by Margaret of Anjou in April of that year, and these royal visits, symbolic of the city's reconciliation with the monarchy, may have suggested the themes of political hostility and reconciliation found in the Toppes window. The sainted English kings, including Edmund, may therefore have also been part of the city leaders' attempts to confirm the restitution of good relations between themselves and the king by asserting Henry's legitimacy and royal pedigree.

ST MARY'S CHURCH, LAKENHEATH (SUFFOLK)

In addition to secular politics, Edmund's image could also be deployed in ecclesiastical disputes. An example of appropriation of this kind can be seen in the wall paintings in the parish church of St Mary the Virgin, Lakenheath (Suffolk), near the Cambridgeshire border. Evidence of the original twelfth-century church survives in the fine chancel arch, but otherwise the extant fabric belongs to later building phases, including the extension of the nave westwards in the mid-thirteenth century, the alteration of the north aisle windows in the fourteenth century and the heightening of the nave and the addition of the angel hammer-beam roof in the fifteenth. These successive building phases are significant, as they are reflected in the five successive series of wall paintings which seem to have accompanied each remodelling.

The paintings were largely uncovered during restoration works to the roof in the 1860s but subsequently deteriorated significantly.[61] Conservation work in 2009 revealed additional paintings and clarified the complex sequences apparent in the various layers.[62] These were summarised by the conservators:[63]

Scheme 1 (c.1220) A series of angels and associated decoration on the soffits and piers (N0–N3).
Scheme 2 (c.1250) Decorative scroll work and fictive tapestry on the spandrels of N3–N5 and associated decoration on soffits (N0–N3/4).
Scheme 3 (c.1330) Passion cycle and Virgin and Child with St Edmund (N3). Large figures of saints (N1 and N2 spandrels) and associated decora-

---

[61] The pre-restoration condition of the paintings is described by Tobit Curteis in his 2003 Condition Survey: 'St Mary's Church, Lakenheath, Suffolk: Technical and Condition Survey of the Wall Paintings' (Tobit Curteis Associates, April 2003).

[62] I am grateful to the conservators for allowing me to visit during the restoration work and examine the wall paintings in detail. I am particularly indebted to the Project Manager, Matthew Champion, for supplying me with a copy of the Conservation Record and associated images and for our numerous conversations on the subject.

[63] Mark Perry, 'Church of St Mary the Virgin, Lakenheath, Suffolk: Wall Painting Conservation Record' (The Perry Lithgow Partnership, September 2009), p. 4.

tion on the arcade mouldings (N0–N3). Painted fragments at the east end of the north aisle.

Scheme 4 (c.1500?) Unidentified traces on N3. The Risen Christ, nave lower east wall.

Scheme 5 (17th C.) Traces of cartouche frames at clerestory level (N1–N3). Painted text on the upper south arcade.

Thus St Edmund appears in the third scheme, probably painted during the first third of the fourteenth century. Evidence of this scheme has been found only in bays N1–N3 but it appears to have been more substantial.[64] Extremely partial remains of life-size figures are apparent in the upper-arcade spandrels of N2 and N1. The figure in N2 is tentatively identified by the conservators as Paul but the other has no identifying attributes. Substantial remains of the third scheme may also be seen in the decoration within the arch mouldings. N3 occupies the position directly opposite the south door and these images are therefore the first to be seen upon entering the church. There are two sequences: the passion in the spandrel area and a large, seated Virgin and Child below. The passion cycle originally comprised six scenes. In the top register from left to right is an iconographically unusual Harrowing of Hell, in which a crowned figure assists Christ in leading the righteous from the gaping Hell Mouth, the Resurrection and *Noli Me Tangere*. On the tier below are the Flagellation and the Carrying of the Cross and below this an extremely fragmentary Crucifixion.

The Virgin and Child is barely visible and was first tentatively identified by David Park in 1998, although the conservation works clarified the head of Christ and details of the Virgin's hair and drapery.[65] Cleaning also revealed that the beautifully painted figure of St Edmund, readily identifiable by his crown and arrow, is positioned to the right of the Virgin and Child as part of the same image. The juxtaposition of a single saint with the holy family is unique in English wall painting and raises the intriguing possibility of why Edmund appears in this context. Given the affiliation of the church to Ely it is also surprising that no images of St Æthethryth have been found. As patron of the ecclesiastical establishment in charge of Lakenheath she would be a more obvious choice to occupy the privileged position at the foot of the Virgin and Child. Matthew Champion suggests that the unique iconography may be explained by the history of the conflict between Bury St Edmunds and Ely for control of the parish, now in the diocese of St Edmundsbury and Ipswich, but in the Middle Ages under the jurisdiction of Ely but located

---

[64] Perry, 'Wall Painting Conservation Record', p. 6.
[65] David Park, Courtauld Institute of Art, unpublished survey (1998), cited in Perry, 'Wall Painting Conservation Record', p. 7.

within the Hundred of Lackford within the Liberty of St Edmund, the eight and a half hundreds in west Suffolk granted to the abbey by Edward the Confessor in 1044.[66] The resulting tension is exemplified in an incident described by Jocelin concerning market rights.[67] The abbot's jurisdiction within the Liberty was deemed to be absolute, but in 1201 King John infringed the abbey's rights by granting the prior of Ely the right to hold a market in his parish of Lakenheath.[68] Abbot Samson (1182–1211) paid 50 marks for an inquisition which found that his market at Bury, fourteen miles hence, suffered as a result. Following Samson's pledge of forty further marks and the gift of two palfreys, the king issued a new charter stating that no market could be established within the Liberty without the abbot's consent. King John sent a mandate to the justiciar, Geoffrey Fitz Peter (justiciar 1198–1213, earl of Essex 1199–1213), ordering him to demolish the market. Gilbert passed this duty to the sheriff of Suffolk but because he knew that he 'could not enter the Liberty of St Edmund or exercise any power there' he ordered the abbot by writ to implement the king's command. The bailiff of the hundred was sent to Lakenheath but was insulted and forcibly removed. Enraged at this blatant violation of his authority, Samson sent six hundred well-armed men who destroyed the stalls and seized livestock.[69] Although the third scheme of wall paintings is dated to around a century after the dispute concerning the market the message they convey may reflect ongoing tensions surrounding jurisdiction over the parish. Champion suggests that the presence of St Edmund in such a prominent position in the lay-controlled area of the church suggests that the parishioners felt their allegiance lay with Bury rather than Ely.[70] Edmund raises his left hand as if in blessing, presumably indented to reflect the mutual bond between the saint and his devotees.

Furthermore, the iconographically unusual additional figure in the Harrowing of Hell scene bears some similarities to the image of St Edmund below: both are crowned and share certain facial similarities. Champion suggests that Edmund may therefore be assisting Christ as he guides souls out of Hell.[71] If this is the case it would be iconographically unique but to some extent is supported by the visual language of the scene. In addition to the similarities to the Edmund figure below,

[66] For the Liberty see Gransden, *A History of the Abbey*, pp. 236–44.
[67] Jocelin, *Chronicle*, pp. 117–19.
[68] A copy of the charter, dated 25 March 1201, was entered in the king's charter rolls. See *Rotuli chartarum in Turri Londinensi asseravti*, ed. Thomas D. Hardy, vol. 1, 1199–1216 (London: Record Commissioners, 1837), p. 91.
[69] Jocelin, *Chronicle*, pp. 118.
[70] Matthew Champion, 'Devotion, Pestilence and Conflict: The Medieval Wall Paintings of St Mary the Virgin, Lakenheath', in *Art, Faith and Place in East Anglia*, ed. T.A. Heslop et al. (Woodbridge: Boydell, 2012), pp. 88–104. I am grateful to him for discussing his theories with me in person.
[71] Champion, 'Devotion, Pestilence and Conflict', pp. 99–100.

the crowned figure stands in place of the columns used to demarcate the other scenes in the top register. Visually, this enables the Harrowing of Hell to occupy a larger area whilst maintaining the register's compositional symmetry. In addition, a column connotes solidity and strength, an apposite attribute reminiscent of the protective blessing gesture of the larger Edmund below. The depiction of the Hell Mouth is also distinctive, appearing more boar-like than the usual feline, draconic or leviathan representations.[72] The boar was the emblem of the De Veres, who controlled large landholdings in Suffolk and Cambridgeshire.[73] They also held five and a half fees in the Liberty of St Edmund and therefore owed forty days of military service a year to the abbot, their feudal over-lord.[74] Relations between the abbey and its military tenants, including the De Veres, were not always harmonious. Shortly after Samson's succession in 1182 he summoned the knights to pay homage to him and requested of them an aid, an occasional tax a landlord was permitted to claim from his tenants. Officially the abbot of Bury St Edmunds owed the service of forty knights but, like other tenants-in-chief, had enfeoffed knights in excess of his quota. On this basis the fifty-two knights of St Edmund refused to pay for the additional twelve, instead stating that the cost for forty knights would be borne between them all. An infuriated Samson vowed to pay back the knights 'injury for injury'.[75] The opportunity arose some years later when, in 1196, Samson took the matter to the king's court, where the justiciar, Hubert Walter, decreed that each knight must answer individually for himself and his holdings. Samson compelled the knights to recognise their service to St Edmund and travelled with them and their wives to London to make their recognitions in the king's court. The last of the knights to comply was Aubrey de Vere (second earl of Oxford, 1194–1214), who succumbed when Samson impounded and sold his cattle.[76]

If the wall paintings were created in response to conflicts between Bury and Ely, then reference to other areas in which the abbey's jurisdiction was questioned seem pertinent. St Edmund, champion of the Liberty, leads the vulnerable figures away

[72] Gary D. Schmidt, *The Iconography of the Mouth of Hell: Eighth-Century Britain to the Fifteenth Century* (Sellinsgrove: Susquehanna University Press, 1995), pp. 35–60.

[73] Michael Powell Siddons, *Heraldic Badges in England and Wales*, 4 vols (Woodbridge: The Boydell Press for the Society of Antiquaries of London, 2009). For De Vere badges see II, pt. II: *Non-Royal Badges*, pp. 299–303. For boars in general see III: *Ordinaries*, pp. 16–17. The De Vere boar is depicted in a stained glass roundel of c.1340–60, now in the Ely Stained Glass Museum.

[74] Jocelin incorporates a list of the knights of St Edmund and their fees into his chronicle. See Jocelin, *Chronicle*, pp. 106–8. See also Helena M. Chew, *The English Ecclesiastical Tenants-in-Chief and Knight Service* (London: Oxford University Press, 1932), pp. 18–23.

[75] This incident is described by Jocelin, *Chronicle*, pp. 26–7.

[76] For more details see Gransden, *A History of the Abbey*, pp. 56–9.

from the boar-like Hell Mouth of secular landlords towards Christ and the Church. The decision to place Edmund in this context makes it plausible to read this image as a deliberate statement concerning the proclivities of the parish. Edmund's surprising and iconographically unique presence in the Lakenheath wall paintings seems once again to attest to his role as protector of the abbey's rights and privileges.

EDMUND OF EAST ANGLIA: WOLVES AND WUFFINGS

The final examples to be considered are a group of images whose provenance cannot so easily be determined. These are carved wooden bench ends found at Gimingham, Neatishead, Walpole St Peter (Figure 5) and Wiggenhall St Mary in Norfolk and Hadleigh (Figure 6) and Hoxne in Suffolk. They depict Edmund's head, which, according to his hagiographers, had been cast into the woods by the Danes following his decapitation, being guarded by the wolf. These images are problematic primarily due to their lack of provenance. They are difficult to date precisely but can be loosely assigned to 1400–1500. The benches are no longer in their original locations within their respective churches and are rare survivors of more extensive sets which are now lost. In addition, the bench ends at Walpole St Peter appear to have been reset. It is thus particularly difficult to assess how Edmund was being depicted in these contexts. However, these images may still contribute to our knowledge of the cult, and rather than dismissing them it is instead necessary to approach them via alternative sources and methodologies.

The wolf was an important motif of the official cult, attested to by its presence on several surviving seals of the abbots of Bury St Edmund's and on pilgrim souvenirs.[77] The story of the wolf and the head is first recounted by Abbo and the incident is thereafter repeated throughout the medieval tradition. It forms part of the martyrdom narrative: chronologically it is the next scene to be described and takes place soon after Edmund's death. It is Edmund's first posthumous miracle, representing the saint's ability to overcome the wolf's usually savage nature.[78] It

---

[77] For examples of the seals of the Abbots of Bury St Edmunds see Roger H. Ellis, *Catalogue of Seals in the Public Record Office: Monastic Seals* (London: Her Majesty's Stationery Office, 1986), p. 15, no. M140 and p. 16, nos M142–4; for pilgrim badges including the wolf see Spencer, *Pilgrim Souvenirs and Secular Badges*, p. 182. The association of the image of the wolf with the abbey at Bury was so strong that to this day local folklore claims that the abbots kept wolves as pets in the abbey grounds. This is apocryphal and seems to derive from canine skulls recovered during excavations in the abbey grounds, now on display in Moyse's Hall Museum, Bury.

[78] Aleksander Pluskowski cites numerous examples of saints enjoying amicable relations with wolves. The Early Desert Fathers, for example, frequently shared their living space with wolves and other fierce animals and the wolf also appears frequently in Celtic hagiography. See Aleksander Pluskowski, *Wolves and the Wilderness in the Middle Ages* (Woodbridge: Boydell, 2006) pp. 167–9.

Figure 5 Wolf and head bench end from Walpole St Peter (Norfolk)

Figure 6 Wolf and head bench end from Hadleigh (Suffolk)

also alludes to the later rejoining of Edmund's head and body by virtue of the saint's physical purity as a result of his virginity. It is thus a key moment of transition, encapsulating Edmund's transformation from earthly king to heavenly saint. As such, it appears that we are once again being offered an image of the glorified saint displaying his *virtus*. However, as explored above in relation to images in painted glass and on chancel screens, an additional aspect of Edmund's sanctity is revealed when the images are contextualised, in this case in relation to evidence from archaeology and ethnography.

Edmund was probably the last of the pre-Danish kings of East Anglia, the last of the royal dynasty of the Wuffings who had ruled Norfolk and Suffolk for at least three hundred years.[79] Etymologically, the name Wuffa appears to be a diminutive form of Wulf, and should be translated as 'little wolf', with the patronymic form 'Wuffingas' being a variant of 'Wulfingas', literally 'the kin of the wolf'.[80] The wolf may also have been of significance to the Wuffing rulers above and beyond the genealogical origins of their clan, as an emblematic personification of their founder.[81]

The importance of the wolf to the kings of East Anglia is reflected artistically. The Sutton Hoo ship burial, for example, believed to be the burial-place of the Wuffings during the late sixth to early seventh centuries, yielded several artefacts featuring an image of a wolf, most notably the purse lid retrieved from Mound One bearing the 'man between beasts' motif (Figure 7). The lower limbs of the animals are entwined with the legs of the man, whose arms appear to reach towards their front paws. The proximity of the wolves' open mouths to the man's ears is suggestive of them whispering or speaking directly to him, possibly representing the communication of ancestral knowledge from the dynasty's totemic guardian beast. The relationship between the three figures is reiterated by the repeated patterning and colouration, for example the blue millefiore gems on the wolves' forelegs and the man's abdomen. Sam Newton suggests that the 'peculiar flanking position of the beasts could be regarded as a representation of

---

[79] Little is known of the history of the Wuffings. A late eighth-century regnal list now in London British Library, Cotton MS Vespasian B vi traces the dynastic genealogy of the Wuffings back through fourteen generations and twenty rulers to the Norse god Woden/Óðinn. Cited in Peter Warner, *The Origins of Suffolk* (Manchester: Manchester University Press, 1996), p. 70. Bede similarly describes a king named Wuffa 'from whom the kings of East Anglia are called Wuffings'. Bede, *Ecclesiastical History*, ed. McClure and Collins, II.15, p. 99.

[80] Sam Newton, *The Origins of Beowulf and the Pre-Viking Kingdom of East Anglia* (Cambridge: Brewer, 1993), p. 106.

[81] For the significance of the wolf to the Wuffing dynasty see Newton, *Origins of Beowulf*, p. 106; for a broader discussion of the emblematic wolf in the Middle Ages see Pluskowski, *Wolves and the Wilderness*, pp. 134–53.

the protective presence of the putative ancestral guardian-spirit of the Wuffings'.[82] The possible underlying meaning of this image is thus remarkably similar to the manner in which the wolf is described as guarding the head of St Edmund and how this was subsequently represented artistically.[83] The notion of the wolf as a protective presence is also seen in the fifteenth-century sculpture of the wolf and head atop the porch of the church at Pulham St Mary (Norfolk); along with a wodewose, a woodman and a greyhound, it guards the vulnerable liminal space of the entrance to the church.[84]

Whether notions of ancestral totemism persisted in the intervening centuries between the Sutton Hoo ship burial, the conversion of East Anglia to Christianity and the establishment of Edmund's cult is uncertain and the paucity of the material record from East Anglia in this period obscures attempts to establish the prevalence of wolf imagery. Wolves are, however, present on a seal found at Eye (Suffolk) in the nineteenth century (Figure 8).[85] It is the earliest physical evidence for an English seal and is believed to have belonged to Æthelwold, bishop of Dummoc, who made his confession to the archbishop of Canterbury between 845 and 870.[86] The seal is bronze, appropriately mitre shaped, of two rows of arches supported in the interstices by nine wolves' heads with garnet eyes, the use of garnet being reminiscent of the material of the man-between-beasts images on the Sutton Hoo purse lid. Æthelwold is likely the bishop referred to in some accounts as advising Edmund during his negotiations with the Danes.[87] The date of the seal is important in determining the significance of the wolf-and-head motif. Although a precise date is not known, it is believed that Æthelwold held office until around 870. If it was created following Edmund's martyrdom it is possible that the use of the wolf was a gesture of religious and political defiance, referring simultaneously to the political autonomy and religious sensibility of the region

---

[82] Newton, 'The Royal Money Belt', *Wuffings Website*, http://www.wuffings.co.uk/MySHPages/SHTreasure/SHMoneyBelt.htm (last accessed 27 July 2014).

[83] The wolf's possible status as a sacred animal in Wuffing East Anglia may also account for the popularity of images of the she-wolf and Romulus and Remus from the Roman foundation myth, for example on an eighth-century coin series of King Aethelberht of East Anglia. For further discussion and examples of this motif see Newton, *Origins of Beowulf*, p. 108 and Pluskowski, *Wolves and the Wilderness*, pp. 144–9.

[84] For the architecture and symbolism of church porches see Helen E. Lunnon, 'Making an Entrance: Studies of Medieval Church Porches in Norfolk', 2 vols, Ph.D. thesis, University of East Anglia, School of World Art Studies and Museology, 2012.

[85] Norman Scarfe, *Suffolk in the Middle Ages* (Woodbridge: Boydell, 2004), p. 130 and plate 7 for the discovery of the seal.

[86] T.A. Heslop, 'English Seals from the Mid-Ninth Century to 1100', *Journal of the British Archaeological Association* cxxxiii (1980), 1–16; 2–3.

[87] Ridyard, *Royal Saints*, p. 221.

Figure 7 Sutton Hoo purse lid

in the wake of the Danish conquest. However, the likelihood of such an object's being produced in the immediate aftermath of the Danish incursion is slight, suggesting that it dates from during, or before, Edmund's reign. If the seal was made before Edmund's martyrdom it would reinforce the link between Sutton Hoo and the wolf and head, and suggest that this element of Edmund's life is in part a back formation by hagiographers to explain an earlier visual tradition and represents continuity in the popular use of the emblematic wolf in East Anglia.

It is of course impossible to determine the extent to which those who adorned their churches with the image of Edmund and the wolf were aware of such connotations. It is possible that the wolf came to be understood in a more generic heraldic sense, representing the royal dynasty without its previous totemic associations. The use of a symbol rather than a narrative scene distances the image from the sequence of events it represents, enabling the symbol to be invested with meaning above and beyond its immediate context. Edmund himself becomes a symbol, once again of kingship but in this instance specifically regional East Anglian kingship, in a similar way to which the wolf and head is a symbol of Edmund as a saint. Thus the bench ends bearing this striking image, far from being rendered redundant by their lack of iconographic and social context, may still contribute to the debate surrounding Edmund's saintly identity if approached through alternative methods and sources.

Figure 8 Æthelwold seal

'MARTYR, MAYDE AND KYNGE'

This tripartite epithet, repeatedly afforded to St Edmund by Lydgate throughout the *Lives*, speaks as much to his visual as to his textual identity.[88] The consideration of Edmund's iconographical presence within East Anglian parish churches has revealed that he could be depicted in one of three distinct ways: either during his martyrdom; as an individual figure with his characteristic feature, the arrow; or by means of a severed head guarded by a wolf. Whilst distinct in their own right, these three categories are afforded further nuance according to their material, physical, iconographic or social context, and where it is not possible to determine their provenance, by reading them through alternative sources and methodologies. Closer interpretation reveals multiple layers of meaning within these types. These variously emphasise Edmund's spiritual glorification, his intercessory ability, and his royalty. They are not restricted to one type of image and are not mutually exclusive; the co-existence of multiple meanings within one image attests to a subtle and complex visual code.

[88] Lydgate, *Lives*, Prologue, 1 and used frequently thereafter.

The martyrdom is arguably the most characteristic, irreducible feature of Edmund's sanctity, ensuring his place in the ranks of the exalted. Images of Edmund bearing his attribute, the arrow, are not narrative scenes like the martyrdom, but rather the culmination of all narratives, the universal image that simultaneously depicts Edmund's royalty, his martyrdom, physical regeneration as a result of his chastity and his spiritual triumph and subsequent potency as intercessor and miracle worker. These elements are all implicit in each image, and through the manipulation of the context in which they were placed could be made to emphasise one whilst encapsulating all. The incident of the wolf and head is miraculous; it is Edmund's first posthumous miracle, and confirms the sanctity which his life and the manner of death had suggested. In this sense it forms part of the narrative of his death, linking his martyrdom with the later miracles attributed to him. As an image of his kingship, however, it relies upon very different conditions to generate meaning. It is to a large extent detached from Edmund's saintly history, emphasising as it does his temporal ancestral lineage; Edmund is in the company of his forebears rather than the company of heaven. Above all, these various visual identities once again demonstrate the complexity of Edmund's saintly identity.

CHAPTER 11

Texts beyond Bury: legendary collections

In addition to the many chronicles and the various hagiographic accounts already discussed, there is one final category of texts in which lives of Edmund appear: he is present in a number of sermon manuals and collections of saints' lives dating from the late thirteenth century to 1516. Whilst there is evidence that some of these collections were widely distributed, none is of East Anglian origin, so whilst this does not necessarily further an understanding of regional devotion, it does offer the opportunity to consider the textual cult as it existed at a remove from the cultural milieu of Bury St Edmunds. In terms of the development of the textual tradition, the legendary texts contribute little additional information. Although unequivocally part of the hagiographic tradition, the length of each life bears more similarity to the chronicle accounts: each version is brief, presenting only the basic details of Edmund's life and death. The interest of these texts is therefore primarily contextual, particularly in terms of the other saints alongside whom Edmund appears. The brevity of the accounts can also be illuminating in its own right as, much like the images of Edmund discussed above, it indicates what was considered to be the core of the narrative and therefore integral to Edmund's saintly identity.

The South English Legendary

The South English Legendary (*SEL*) was initially composed in the 1280s, although only one early manuscript (Bodleian 1486 Laud Misc. 108) survives.[1] The remainder (an impressive fifty-one examples, not including those containing single items) date from the early fourteenth to the late fifteenth centuries. The text underwent numerous revisions, with new material added at various times and this is reflected in the presentation of the legends, which do not follow the ecclesiastical calendar.[2]

---

[1] *The South English Legendary*, ed. Horstmann. All references will be in accordance with this edition and will be given parenthetically in the text.
[2] See Manfred Görlach, *The Textual Tradition of the South English Legendary* (Leeds: University of Leeds, 1974) for a discussion of the history and dissemination of the *SEL* and a survey of extant manuscripts. See also Charlotte D'Evelyn, 'Collections of Saints' Legends', in *A Manual of Writings in Middle English, 1050–1500*, gen. ed. J. Burke Severs (Hamden: Connecticut Academy of Arts & Sciences, 1970), II, pp. 413–18; *The South English Legendary: A Critical Assessment*, ed. Klaus P. Jankofsky (Tübingen: Francke, 1992).

The authorship and origins of the *SEL* are the subject of ongoing critical debate. The dialect of the earliest manuscript suggests a southern or south-west Midlands provenance, probably either at Gloucester or Worcester.[3] The *SEL*'s favouring of St Dominic over St Francis is frequently cited as evidence of Dominican authorship.[4] The intended audience of the *SEL* is more controversial, although it is generally agreed to have been composed as a sermon manual for the use of parish clergy in the instruction of lay parishioners. Bella Millet, for instance, claims that the assumed cultural level is low, the tone is uncourtly and sometimes anti-clerical and 'the addresses to the audience are undeferential to the point of being patronising, and seem to assume public delivery to a sizeable audience, not chamber performance or solitary reading'.[5] The presentation of the legendary material certainly accords with this view. Klaus Jankofsky suggests that the principles of composition applied to the *SEL* seem to be 'a simplification of complicated theological-dogmatic problems and hagiographic traditions', 'an explanatory, interpretative expansion of subject matter' and 'a process of concretization', which he suggests make it suitable for instructing a lay audience.[6] He also suggests that the texts are characterised by the tendency to 'humanise' the saints, and by a 'new tone and mood of compassion and emotional involvement', rendering the saints more approachable and attainable, in keeping with their function as exemplary role models for a lay audience.[7]

This is apparent in the depiction of Edmund in the *SEL*. Edmund is referred to throughout as 'þe holie kyng', but the emphasis is upon his representative piety, rather than his actual historical role as ruler:

---

[3] Görlach, *The Textual Tradition of the South English Legendary*, summarises this discussion.

[4] Dominican origins are often claimed for the collection; see, for example, William A. Hinnebusch, *The Early English Friars Preachers*, Institutum Historicum Ff. Praedicatorum Romae ad S. Sabine, Dissertationes Historicae 14 (Rome: Ad S. Sabine Institutum Historicum Ff. Praedicatorum, 1951) and Warren F. Manning, 'The Middle English Verse *Life of St Dominic*: Date and Source', *Speculum* 31 (1956), 82–91. In contrast, Annie Samson claims the text was intended for the secular gentry. Annie Samson, 'The South English Legendary: Constructing a Context', in *Thirteenth Century England I*, ed. P.R. Coss and S.D. Lloyd. Proceedings of the Newcastle-upon-Tyne Conference, 1985 (Woodbridge: Boydell, 1985), pp. 185–95; pp. 192–4.

[5] Bella Millet, 'The Audience of the Saints' Lives of the Katherine Group', in *Reading Medieval Studies 16: Saints and Saints' Lives: Essays in Honour of D.H. Farmer* (1990), 127–56; 144.

[6] Klaus P. Jankofsky, 'Entertainment, Edification and Popular Education in the *South English Legendary*', *Journal of Popular Culture* 11 (1977), 706–17; 709.

[7] Klaus P. Jankofsky, 'Personalized Didacticism: The Interplay of Narrator and Subject Matter in the *South English Legendary*', *Texas A&I University Studies* 10 (1977), 69–77; 72.

Swyþe fair kny3t and strong he was and hardi and quoynte,
Meoke and milde and ful of milce and large in eche poynte. (p. 297, ll. 5–6)

Apart from this brief generic description we learn little about Edmund's character or activities as a king. The Danes' assault on East Anglia is similarly presented in general terms. We are told only that Hynguar and Hubba were 'in luþere þou3te ... to bringue enguelond to nouþte' (p. 297, ll. 7–8), with no motivation offered for their attack, other perhaps than Hynguar's jealousy of Edmund of whose 'guodnesse' 'he heorde muche telle' (p. 297, l. 17). The *SEL* omits the exchange between Hynguar and Edmund concerning the fate of the East Anglian kingdom and its people, and Edmund arrives at his martyr's fate without the political wrangling and diplomatic negotiations present in other versions of the legend. This de-politicises and de-historicises the events which follow, in which the Christ-like Edmund is located within the timeless context of ongoing Christian history in the company of 'ore louerd' (p. 297, l. 38) and 'seint sebastian' (p. 298, l. 53). He is stoic throughout the tortures inflicted upon him so that 'euere he stod ase him no rou3te' (p. 298, l. 56), calling to God 'wel bliue' (p. 298, l. 56). Edmund's behaviour is exemplary as he submits patiently to the will of God.

The collection as a whole, however, does evince more overtly political concerns, in particular in its presentation of English saints; for example, nearly a quarter of the saints are Anglo-Saxon. Jankofsky maintains that the collection was deliberately designed to appeal to an English audience.[8] He claims this was achieved by a process of acculturation, or 'Englishing', whereby essentially Latin sources were adapted and imbued with a distinctive flavour and mood.[9] A key element of this is the inclusion of historical-factual information about the English saints which is almost entirely absent from the lives of their non-English counterparts:

> Place names and topographical details are mentioned; inheritance laws, death duties, the situation of the poor, the rights of the Church versus state with specific instances of conflict, and historical-geographical accounts of the old English kingdoms and bishoprics are given, and even weather conditions are described when appropriate.[10]

---

[8] Jankofsky, 'Entertainment, Edification, and Popular Education in the *South English Legendary*', 707.
[9] Klaus P. Jankosfky, 'National Characteristics in the Portrayal of English Saints in the *South English Legendary*', in *Images of Sainthood in Medieval Europe*, ed. Renate Blumenfeld-Kosinski and Timea Szell (Ithaca: Cornell University Press, 1991), pp. 81–93, p. 83.
[10] Jankofsky, 'National Characteristics', p. 84.

This is particularly apparent in the description of the Anglo-Saxon kingdoms of England which begins the legend of St Kenelm and which continues for sixty-five lines:

> Fyf kingues þare weren þulke tyme In engelonde i-do,
> For Enguelond was guod and long and sum-del brod al-so.
> A-bouten ei3te hondret mile Engelond long is
> Fram þe South into þe North and to houndret brod i-wis
> Fram þe Est into þe West ... (p. 235, ll. 9–13)

Renee Hamelinck suggests that details such as these are 'meant to remind the audience of the history of the country – a history they could be proud of'.[11] She characterises the collection as a history of the English Church from the coming of St Augustine up to the time of the *SEL*'s composition, and proposes that it demonstrates the Church's decline from Anglo-Saxon prosperity to a weakened position under the Norman kings.[12] In contrast to the nostalgia for the past implicit in Hamelinck's reading, Jankofsky suggests that the *SEL* works to locate its audience firmly in the present, citing the frequent use of adverbial phrases such as 'still' or 'yet' which indicate a continuity of tradition and elision of historical chronology.[13] This is visible in the life of Edmund, where the author concludes by informing his audience that Edmund's miraculously preserved body is 'al hol and sound' and enshrined 'as ri3t was to do' in the town now called 'saint Edmundesbury' in his honour, and that 'a swyþe fair pilegrimage it is, þudere forto fare,/ for-to honour þat holie bodi, þat þare hath i-leie so 3are' (p. 290, ll.). Jill Frederick cites numerous other techniques which contribute to the national tone of the collection and concludes that in relation to its depiction of English saints the *SEL* is 'purely politically centred'.[14] The precise nuances of the *SEL*'s political concerns are undoubtedly various, and it is beyond the scope of this study to investigate them all. However, analysis of the broader textual circumstances of the *SEL* indi-

---

[11] Renee Hamelinck, 'St Kenelm and the Legends of the English Saints in the *South English Legendary*', in *Companion to Early Middle English Literature*, ed. N.H.G.E. Veldhoen and H. Aertsen (Amsterdam: Free University Press, 1988), pp. 21–30, p.27.
[12] Hamelinck, 'St Kenelm and the Legends of the English Saints', p. 21.
[13] Jankofsky, 'National Characteristics', p. 86.
[14] Jill Frederick, 'The *South English Legendary*: Anglo-Saxon Saints and National Identity', in *Literary Appropriations of the Anglo-Saxons from the Thirteenth to the Twentieth Century*, ed. Donald Scragg and Carole Weinberg (Cambridge: Cambridge University Press, 2000), pp. 57–73, p. 67. See also Diane Speed, 'The Construction of the Nation in Medieval English Romance', in *Readings in Medieval English Romance*, ed. Carol M. Meale (Cambridge: D.S. Brewer, 1994), pp. 135–57.

cates that in this context Edmund should be understood in his role as an English, specifically Anglo-Saxon, saint.

Speculum Sacerdotale

The *Speculum Sacerdotale* (*SS*) is a fifteenth-century collection of *Sanctorale* and *Temporale* sermons, of the same type as the *Festial* of John Mirk.[15] It survives in a unique early fifteenth-century manuscript (BL Additional MS 36791).[16] The identity of the author is unknown, but the dialect of the manuscript is Standard English of the early fourteenth century, with some West Midland characteristics.[17] It is likely that the author was a priest, as he claims to be writing 'for serteyne prestes which ben dere and famyliare vn-to me before alle other' who have asked him to provide them with a vernacular collection to read out to their parishoners.[18] Several scholars have suggested that, like John Mirk, they were friars or canons who had responsibility for the pastoral care and instruction of the laity and thus needed comprehensive vernacular collections upon which to draw.[19] The narratives in the *SS* are arranged chronologically and are of four general types: legends of the Blessed Virgin Mary, lives and legends of other saints, *exempla*, and biblical stories. Most of its chapters include narratives and expositions of church ritual and observance. Peter Heath maintains that the *SS* is less naïve and sensational than Mirk's *Festial* and presents doctrine and practice in a more balanced way, suggesting that it is a good indication of the quality and nature of the average parish homily in late medieval England.[20] The sources for the *SS* are in almost all instances either of the *Legenda Aurea* of Jacobo de Voragine or of Johannes Belethus' *Rationale Divinorum Officiorum*.[21] Weatherly erroneously identifies the source of Edmund's life as the *Legenda Aurea*, in which it does not in fact appear; the author most likely relied upon a version of Edmund's life based upon Abbo.

---

[15] John Mirk, *Festial: A Collection of Homilies*, ed. Theodor Erbe, Early English Text Society, es 96 (London: Kegan Paul, 1905).

[16] *Speculum Sacerdotale*, ed. Edward H. Weatherly, Early English Text Society, os 200 (London: Published for the Early English Text Society by Oxford University Press, 1936, rpt 1971). All references will be in accordance with this edition and will be given parenthetically in the text.

[17] See *Speculum Sacerdotale*, ed. Weatherly, xvii–xxi for a detailed exposition of the various linguistic forms of the manuscript.

[18] *Speculum Sacerdotale*, ed. Weatherly, pp. 2–3.

[19] For example, Görlach, *Textual Tradition*, pp. 45–50.

[20] Peter Heath, *The English Parish Clergy on the Eve of the Reformation* (London: Routledge, 1969), p. 101.

[21] Weatherly details the sources by chapter in a table, *Speculum Sacerdotale*, pp. xxvii–xxix.

Given the similarities in form, and arguably the function, it is unsurprising that the version of Edmund's legend found in the *SS* is very similar to the *SEL*. Edmund's generic kingly virtues are once again praised: he is 'symple as the dowue, wyse as the serpent, and benigne to his subiects, discrete with the forward, meteable to the nedy, liberall to wydowes and children' (p. 239, ll. 25–7). The *SS*, however, provides a fuller indication of the reasoning behind the Danes' invasion, suggesting that they were 'purposyng to gete vnder here 30kke this kingdom and to destroye Chistiante' (p. 239, ll. 32–3). This is reiterated by Edmund's response to the Danes' attempts to agree terms for the surrender of East Anglia, where the use of direct speech adds to the power and emotive force of the sentiment:

> 'Let hym take and destroye oure tresoures and riches and sle þe seruauntes and after the kynge, and let the kynge of kyngis se it and rewarde it in his kingdom. But he shal wel knowe that I, Edmund, the Cristen man, shal neuer submitte me to hym þat is a pagane vnto the tyme that he be i-made Cristen.' (p. 240, ll. 2–7)

Unlike the *SEL*, the *SS* explicitly terms Edmund a 'marter' (p. 239, l. 24). This is significant beyond the level of nomenclature and reflects his status in the collection as a whole. In contrast to the *SEL*, the *SS* contains the lives of only two English saints: Edmund and Thomas Becket. This does not necessarily mean that Edmund is not to be understood in his role as a national saint, as the compiler of the *SS* may have considered Edmund and Becket as the two most noteworthy examples of indigenous sanctity. It does, however, clearly highlight his elevated position within the saintly hierarchy of late medieval England. This is similarly the case in the Norwich Cathedral cloister bosses discussed above in which the deaths of Becket and Edmund in the east walk are depicted in multiple bosses, in comparison with the single-scene depictions of other saints. Like the deviser of the cloister bosses, the compiler of the *SEL* is constructing a collection which reflects a broader Christian history than that of one nation. Much like the *SEL*'s comparison of him with St Sebastian, in the *SS* Edmund's death in defence of his faith is emphasised, as it locates him within the long line of Christian martyrs and as a participant in universal Christian history.

Gilte Legende

The *Gilte Legende* (*GiL*) is a translation of Jean de Vignay's *Légende Dorée* of c.1333–40, which is in turn a translation of the *Legenda Aurea*.[22] The author of the

---

[22] *Supplementary Lives in Some Manuscripts of the Gilte Legende*, ed. Richard Hamer and Vida Russell, Early English Text Society, os 315 (Oxford: Published for the Early English

GiL refers to himself as a 'synfulle wrecche' but cannot be securely identified.[23] The language of most of the manuscripts is fairly typical of a London dialect of the mid-fifteenth century. The GiL is referred to as such in the colophon to Bodleian MS Douce 372, which also affirms that it was 'drawen out of Frensshe into Englisshe' in 1438. It survives in varying degrees of completeness in eight manuscripts, three of which (BL MS Add. 11565, BL MS Add. 35298 and Lambeth Palace Library MS 72) contain additional saints' lives, and it is amongst these that Edmund is to be found.[24] Most of the additional lives are of English saints and are de-versified versions of the lives in the SEL. It is therefore unsurprising that the additions to the GiL evince a similar interest in placing the legends within a detailed physical and historical context. It likewise emphasises that Edmund was king 'of a partye of Ynglond that is callid Northfolke and Suffolke' (p. 149, ll. 1–2) and concludes by describing the many miracles which 'nowe' 'shewith daylye' at the shrine of St Edmund at Bury (p.150, ll. 47–8). Why a later compiler should choose to append a selection of English saints to the GiL is unclear, but it is again indicative of the importance placed upon Edmund's indigenous sanctity.

Caxton's Golden Legend

Caxton's Golden Legend (GoL) was based on three versions of the Legenda Aurea: the original Latin, de Vignay's French and the English GiL.[25] He combined and adapted these, and made additions from other sources:

> Against me here might some persons say that this legend hath been translated tofore, and truth it is; but forasmuch as I had by me a legend in French, another in Latin, and the third in English, which varied in many and divers places; and also many histories were comprised in the two other books which

---

Text Society by the Oxford University Press, 2000). All references will be in accordance with this edition and will be given parenthetically in the text.

[23] See *Supplementary Lives*, ed. Hamer and Russell, xx–xxi for discussion of the possible authorship.

[24] See *Supplementary Lives*, ed. Hamer and Russell, xxi–xxvi for discussion of the additional *lives* manuscripts. For the *Gilte Legende* see *Gilte Legende*, 3 vols, ed. Richard Hamer and Vida Russell, Early English Text Society, os 237 (Oxford : Published for the Early English Text Society by the Oxford University Press, 2006).

[25] William Caxton, trans., *The Golden Legend or Lives of the Saints*, ed. Frank S. Ellis (London: Temple Classics, 1900). All references will be in accordance with this edition and will be given parenthetically in the text.

were not in the English book; therefore I have written one out of the said three books.[26]

In reworking the text, Caxton omitted some of the saints found in Voragine's original, but also added legends, many of English and Irish saints. Although printed, the book was hand-finished, with initial letters being supplied in manuscript throughout the text, a common practice in early printed books. The colophon at the end of the work states that the book was finished on 20 November 1483, the first year of the reign of King Richard III. Although Caxton makes no direct reference to this being the feast day of St Edmund, it is tempting to read this as a nationalistic gesture towards one of the pre-eminent English saints by a printer invested in the presentation of texts in the English language.

The legends are arranged according to the liturgical year and each is illustrated with a woodcut which, as well as making the book visually appealing, also had the practical benefit of helping readers navigate through a large and unwieldy text; this is clearly a book intended for private reading rather than simply auditory consumption. In the Preface Caxton claims that he was encouraged to pursue the project by William FitzAlan, the ninth Earl of Arundel, who promised to take a reasonable quantity of copies when completed, and to pay him an annuity of a buck in summer and a doe in winter as recompense for the effort.[27] Whilst this does not amount to a commission, it does indicate that the *GoL* appealed, presumably by design, to a lay audience who would utilise it in a private context. Thus whilst the version of Edmund's life found in Caxton's *GoL* is based entirely upon pre-existing sources and therefore contributes very little to our understanding of how the saint was perceived in terms of the details of his life and death, once again, the context in which his legend was read is informative and indicates his wide appeal. Edmund's saintly identity was sufficiently broad, and sufficiently well established, that it transcended the changes in reading practices and the increasing trend towards private devotion, ensuring his continued popularity in an evolving cultural context.

Kalendre of the Newe Legende of Englande

The trend towards private, lay readership is similarly seen in the *Kalendre of the Newe Legende of Englande*, although the appeal of this text seems even broader; Görlach suggests that 'it is tempting to connect the factual style of this 'encyclopaedia' with a bourgeois readership eager for information but incapable of getting

---

[26] Caxton, *Golden Legende*, Prologue, p. 2
[27] Caxton, *Golden Legende*, Prologue, p. 3

it from Latin texts'.[28] The *Kalendre* was printed by Richard Pynson in 1516 and is the work of an anonymous compiler and translator. It is a précis of the legends of 168 British saints and is the most comprehensive collection of its kind in English. Predating the Reformation by only two decades, it was also the last of the great legendary collections of this kind. At least eleven copies are extant, and although it is unknown how many copies were originally printed, the possibility that there was a second edition suggests its popularity.

The *Kalendre* does not contain original material: it is based on the *Nova Legenda Anglie* printed by Winken de Worde in the same year, which in turn was a revision of John of Tynemouth's late fourteenth-century national legendary, *Sanctilogium Angliae, Walliae, Scotiae et Hiberniae*, which underwent an intermediary revision in the fifteenth century, possibly by John Capgrave.[29] In addition, it also appears that the compiler of the *Kalendre* used some additional materials, possibly the *GiL* and Caxton's *GoL*. Görlach notes that this intertextual indebtedness is particularly apparent in the *Kalendre* version of St Edmund's life.[30] In contrast to the other legendary collections, which include a basic *passio* account of Edmund's demise, the *Kalendre* version considers the whole life of the saint, not just the martyrdom. It begins by informing the reader that Edmund was 'borne in Saxony and was sone to the Kynge Alcmunde, whiche was kynne to Offa, Kynge of Eest Englonde' (p. 83, ll. 1–2), and goes on to relate the circumstances in which Edmund became king of the East Angles and the benign nature of his rule (p. 83, ll. 2–13). Although this aspect of Edmund's legend had been developed by Geoffrey of Wells in the thirteenth century, and the details were therefore not new, it is the first time that they are included in a legendary collection of this kind.[31] Nearly a third of the narrative is devoted to Edmund's early life. Norman Blake believes that this is a deliberate literary strategy which may be accounted for by the context in which the work was produced, suggesting that 'as the possibilities for martyrdom diminished, so the model lives of these saints increased in importance'.[32] This is more akin to the images of Edmund in glory found on chancel screens and in stained glass than the majority of the textual precursors.

---

[28] *The Kalendre of the Newe Legende of Englande*, ed. Manfred Görlach, Middle English Texts 27 (Heidelberg: Universitätsverlag C. Winter, 1994). All references will be in accordance with this edition and will be given parenthetically in the text. For the audience of the text see *Kalendre*, ed. Görlach, p. 7.
[29] For a detailed discussion of the history of the collection see *Kalendre*, ed. Görlach, pp. 7–12.
[30] *Kalendre*, ed. Görlach, p. 15.
[31] For Geoffrey of Wells see above, Chapter Four, pp. 75–9.
[32] Norman F. Blake, *Middle English Religious Prose* (London: Arnold, 1972), p. 14.

A further distinctive feature of Edmund's depiction in the *Kalendre* concerns the saintly company he keeps: in contrast with the universalising trends of the other legendaries in which Edmund features, the tone of the *Kalendre* is unabashedly nationalistic. The influence of John of Tynemouth may be seen in the preponderance of saints connected with Tyneside and the north-east of England, but on the whole, as its title suggests, the *Kalendre* is concerned with celebrating the saints of all England.[33] Once again, a certain nostalgia and attempt to construct an indigenous Englishness is evident in the preference for saints of Saxon origin. The contrast with the wide chronological and geographical sweep of other legendaries is particularly evident in the infrequent references to biblical or universal saints of international provenance. Görlach proposes that the *Kalendre* was intended to complement the international *Legenda Aurea* and that the texts should effectively be treated as two volumes of the same work.[34] However, the care the compiler takes to itemise the shrines and burial places of the saints, effectively forming a sacred atlas of English sanctity akin to the Anglo-Saxon lists of resting places, suggests a more concerted and profound effort to promote national identity.[35]

Whilst ostensibly similar, the particularities of these collections shed illuminating light on the supra-regional textual cult of St Edmund. In their arrangement all follow the basic structure of the *Legenda Aurea*. Part of the popularity of this structure, apart from ease of reference, lies in its adaptability, as authors or scribes could add or omit narratives according to personal or local preferences, or to suit the specific devotional interests or pastoral needs of a projected audience. This was not primarily achieved in the details of the individual narratives, as the nature of the collections meant that these were by necessity relatively brief, although certain features of a saint's character could be afforded prominence. The authors and compilers were, however, able to achieve particular emphases by the selection and organisation of their material.

Both the *SEL* and the *SS* appear to have originated as sermon manuals for use by clerics in the public instruction of lay parishoners. The Fourth Lateran Council of 1215 had decreed that priests were to preach in the vernacular once a week in order to improve the knowledge of the laity, and the author of the *SS* maintains that his aim is to provide an alternative to sermons in 'Latyne or Romayne tonge' indistinguishable to most.[36] Legendary collections were a practical solution to

---

[33] *Kalendre*, ed. Görlach, p. 29, summarises the contents of the text in a table.
[34] *Kalendre*, ed. Görlach, p. 31.
[35] See David Rollason, 'Lists of Saints' Resting-places in Anglo-Saxon England', *Anglo-Saxon England* 7 (1978), 61–93.
[36] *Speculum Sacerdotale*, ed. Weatherly, p. 3. See Leonard E. Boyle, 'The Fourth Lateran Council and Manuals of Popular Theology', in *The Popular Literature of Medieval*

meeting this requirement and by the later Middle Ages priests could choose from a variety of texts. In addition to the *SEL* and the *SS*, the *Northern Homily Cycle* and John Mirk's *Festial* also enjoyed wide circulation. Sermons were most commonly preached on Sundays during the course of the morning Mass (the other two services for the laity on Sundays were Matins and Vespers or Evensong). H. Leith Spencer notes that sermons on the saints were a frequent alternative to preaching the Sunday lesson.[37] The prologue to the *SS* offers guidance as to when a saint's life should be delivered to the congregation:

> Among all other holy customs of holy churche the whiche oweth to be worshipid with a souerayn deuocion, this semeth right commendable and to be kepid with a good diligence and desire. That is to say that in alle the chirches of the worlde, the prested of hyem which are sette to the gouernaunce of the parishenus aftur the redyng of the gospel and of the offeratorie at masse yurne hem vnto the peple and schewe openliche vnto hem alle the solempnitees and festes whiche shall falle and be hadde in the weke folowynge.[38]

Whilst it is probable that a saint's life would be read on his or her feast day, it is also possible that they could be heard at other times, including the preceding Sunday when forthcoming feasts were announced.

Of greater significance in terms of how a saint such as Edmund would be presented in one of these collections is the explanation provided by the author of the *SS* as to why it was necessary to hear the sermons on the saints. He stresses that the saints should 'be scewid vn-to youre peple that God may be glorified in youre chirches' but also identifies their role as models of exemplary conduct:

> The olde fadres a-fore tymes made fro bigynnyng the festyuites of holy apostles and martires whiche were before hem to be louyd and halowed as i-seen, and specially in entent that we, the herers of here blessid commemoracions whiche ben in tymes of here festes redde and songen, myȝte þrouȝ here prayers and medes be in here euerlastynge fellaschip and holpen here in erþe.[39]

Thus in this context Edmund is primarily valued for the *exemplar* of holy living (and dying) which he offered to a congregation, hence the tendency to focus upon

---

England, ed. Thomas J. Heffernan (Knoxville: University of Tennessee Press, 1985), pp. 30–43.

[37] H. Leith Spencer, *English Preaching in the Late Middle Ages* (Oxford: Clarendon Press, 1993), p. 31.
[38] *Speculum Sacerdotale*, ed. Weatherly, pp. 2–3.
[39] *Speculum Sacerdotale*, ed. Weatherly, p. 1.

these generic aspects of his sanctity in favour of his royalty or his historical presence. This was similarly appropriate in the context of private devotion, for which the *GiL*, the *GoL* and the *Kalendre* are likely to have been produced.

In addition to their expository role, the inclusion of large numbers of insular saints in the *SEL*, the additional lives of the *GiL* and the *Kalendre* attest to a desire on the part of their authors or compilers to emphasise the saintly heritage of Britain. Diane Speed suggests that the *SEL* is an important sign of an emerging institution of an English national literature, equating it with the production of verse romances in English which began around the same time.[40] In this context it is clear that Edmund's status as a national saint is particularly significant. To some extent this is emphasised by the *SS*, which includes only two English saints, Thomas Becket and Edmund, as the compiler may have considered Edmund and Becket as the two most noteworthy examples of indigenous sanctity. It also serves to highlight Edmund's exceptionally high status within the hierarchy of English saints.

The legendary collections span a period of over 230 years, during which time the hagiographic tradition underwent significant developments and expansions. In contrast, Edmund's narrative in the legendary collections remains largely static. The authors of these collections were satisfied by the exemplary model offered by the basic details of Edmund's legend, whereas the hagiographic authors continually sought to contribute new information. This is undoubtedly due in part to their close associations with the Abbey of Bury St Edmunds, where successive abbots sought to capitalise on Edmund's reputation as a wonder-working saint of great power in order to attract pilgrims and protect the interests of their monastic community. In this context, updating the legend was a means of demonstrating Edmund's ongoing relevance. The hagiographers' proximity to the source and subject of these stories is also likely to have contributed a degree of authenticity which would be lacking in a work produced elsewhere.

In comparison with the Bury-based hagiographic tradition, Edmund's depiction in the legendary collections neither contributes new material nor contradicts the longer lives. It does, however, indicate that a number of features of the hagiographic tradition are distinct, in particular its emphasis upon Edmund's kingship and his regional identity, two aspects which, as discussed above, are closely linked. This suggests that the regional cult in its textual manifestation is subtly, but significantly, different to how Edmund was imagined on a national scale.

---

[40] Speed, 'The Construction of the Nation in Medieval English Romance', pp. 135–57.

Conclusion
'Martir, mayde and kynge', and more

'Blyssyd Edmund, kyng, martir and vyrgyne,
Hadde in thre vertues by grace a souereyn prys,
Be which he venquysshed al venymes serpentine.'[1]

THIS book has demonstrated that the tripartite epithet repeated by Lydgate throughout the *Lives* does an injustice to the nature and complexity of the medieval cult of St Edmund. He was indeed a royal virgin martyr, but implicit in these terms are a multitude of subtle nuances and inflections that indicate the vitality of Edmund's cult over nearly six and a half centuries.

My stated intention was to explore how, why and when the cult developed. What has become strikingly apparent is that it is not possible to separate these three lines of enquiry. As a constructed saint (to borrow Delooz's term), everything we know about 'saint' Edmund is mediated through the individuals and communities who wrote about him, painted him, sculpted images of him, processed in his name and prayed at his tomb. In studying the cult of a medieval saint we are in fact studying the societies in which the holy man or woman was venerated. The plural is important, as in addition to acknowledging the social setting of cultic development we must also pay attention to the various origins and agendas of those involved. Considering the cult from a variety of perspectives has thus facilitated a greater understanding of the ways in which Edmund's saintly identity developed in response to particular circumstances.

Audience and reception

Part I attests to the value of a longitudinal approach to saints' cults. Reading these lives in relation to hagiographic patterns identified in other cults indicates that whilst Edmund's life developed in line with some devotional trends, in many ways his cult was distinctive. The influence of the monastic community at Bury is overwhelmingly apparent, as most iterations of the legend were

---

[1] Lydgate, *Lives*, Prologue, 1–3.

composed at or for the abbey. Rare and precious manuscripts were largely the preserve of ecclesiastics and the secular elite, who were therefore the most likely to encounter Edmund in this context. High-status lay interaction is evident, whether through the commissioning and design of manuscripts of Lydgate's *Lives*, listening to a vernacular version adapted for their benefit by Henry of Avranches or being allowed to view the sumptuous illustrations of Pierpont Morgan 736. Nevertheless, the textual and manuscript tradition should not be characterised as entirely exclusive or Bury based. The widespread dissemination of the cult in other contexts indicates that Edmund's life and legend were known beyond the cloister. The abridged versions of Abbo's *Passio* which were distributed as far afield as Saint-Denis and Lucca ensured that the details of Edmund's life were circulated within ecclesiastical circles. Similarly, the numerous accounts in sermon manuals and hagiographic compendia facilitated lay access across both a broader social spectrum and geographical area. The absorption rather than dissemination of information is fleetingly visible, tantalisingly alluded to by Geoffrey of Wells' references to the integration of popular traditions into the official cult, suggesting that the tendency to embellish the legend may not always have originated within the abbey.

Edmund's shrine in the abbey church offered a cultic experience available to all who were willing or able to make the journey to Bury. The audience of the cult in this context and the manner in which Edmund was encountered were thus markedly different from the majority of the textual and manuscript tradition, and the presentation of Edmund's saintly identity differed accordingly. Distinguishing between aspects of the Bury-based cult in terms of audience is particularly enlightening, as it highlights that whilst the monastic community was responsible both for the version of Edmund in the textual cult and in orchestrating the experience of pilgrims to the shrine, his saintly identity differed in each case as a result of the audience for which it was intended.

Part III conceived of audience primarily in terms of proximity to the cult centre by consideration of the extent to which manifestations of the cult differed at a remove from the monastic community. The analysis of miracles occurring in the absence of relics revealed hitherto unremarked contrasts with the nature of Edmund's intercessions in the vicinity of his shrine. Once again, this may be accounted for by the varying requirements of his devotees. Thus at Bury Edmund is the powerful and punitive saintly landlord, protecting the rights and interests of his shrine, the abbey and its monastic community. Elsewhere, however, his intercessions reflect the more mundane needs of the communities in which they took place and Edmund becomes the munificent guardian of injured children, the sick and sailors in peril.

People, places and moments

Certain individuals had a fundamental influence on the development of the cult, although the manner of their involvement and their motivations differed greatly. Arguably the most significant was Abbo of Fleury. One wonders how, and indeed if, the legend would have developed without his initial intervention. As a respected hagiographer his version of the legend garnered approval and credibility which might not have been afforded to the work of a less prestigious author. His *Passio* inaugurated the hagiographic tradition and set the tone for subsequent versions. His influence is evident in the repeated deferrals of later authors to his established authority. The time in which Abbo wrote affected his telling of the tale. As a proponent of monastic reform he emphasised Edmund's virginity, in keeping with increasing strictures on clerical celibacy. This aspect of Edmund's sanctity which had such a profound and long-lasting influence on how he was perceived thus originated in response to a particular historical moment. Similarly, whilst the motivations behind Abbo's composition remain the subject of debate, whether commissioned by the monastic community at Bury or by a local secular magnate, the genesis of the St Edmund legend speaks to the desire of East Anglians, most readily evident in Abbo's lengthy praise of the local landscape, to promote the merits of their region and its saintly heritage.

Arguably the greatest flourishing of cultic activity took place in the late eleventh and early twelfth centuries. In the latter part of the eleventh century the monastic community and its saintly patron faced turbulent times, first from attempted encroachment by the bishop of East Anglia and then as a result of the confusion and uncertainty arising from the Norman Conquest. In these contexts Edmund became the defender and protector of his abbey and its privileges, blinding the ambitious bishop and fending off incursions from acquisitive Normans greedy for Bury lands. This remained one of Edmund's defining characteristics, reflected in the Pierpont Morgan miniaturist's emphasis on Edmund's punitive activities. Images of Edmund's wrathful intercessions were also offered to pilgrims to the abbey church, but in the context of his enshrined glory were intended to impress and reassure, rather than intimidate, those who showed correct devotion, once again demonstrating the importance of context.

Herman the Archdeacon played a key role in this stage of Edmund's development. His connections with both the episcopal and abbatial factions facilitated a unique insight and enabled him to effectively involve St Edmund in the dispute. The political connections of Abbot Baldwin should also be emphasised, as these helped to ensure the survival of the abbey and the perpetuation of Edmund's cult, including its dissemination on the Continent. His influence on its physical setting was also profound, as the abbey church he rebuilt survived for much of the

Middle Ages and thus formed the backdrop to the visits of thousands of expectant pilgrims. Abbot Samson was similarly influential and equally determined in his promotion of St Edmund. He also undertook extensive refurbishment of the abbey church, most notably restoring the shrine after the disastrous fire in 1198. He oversaw the reinvigoration of the textual and manuscript cult, rewriting Herman's *De Miraculis* in order to emphasise Edmund's ability to assist as well as punish. Given that Edmund's more benign attributes most commonly feature in miracles occurring at a remove from Bury, this seems to be an attempt to appeal to pilgrims and promote St Edmund to the masses.

At the latter end of the Middle Ages a unique combination of people and historical circumstances led to a remarkable cultic flourishing. During the troubled reign of Henry VI, the shrewd Abbot William Curteys sought to shape the turbulent political circumstances for the benefit of his abbey. His affecting agent was John Lydgate, whose links with both the abbey and the court made him the ideal conduit through which to curry royal favour. Lydgate's *Lives* is a testament both to the complex interrelationships between patron, author, text and audience and to the nature of Edmund's saintly identity, which was flexible enough to be reshaped to offer an *exemplum* of secular kingship.

In addition to notable individuals and historical moments, the influence of less readily definable groups and communities is apparent. The churchwardens' accounts at Snettisham, for example, indicate that this parish community undertook a procession to St Edmund's chapel at Hunstanton every year for over a century, but due to the nature of the records the exact composition of this group, their motivations and what they thought about St Edmund can only be surmised. One of the most noteworthy findings of Part III is the difficulty of determining the involvement of Bury in cultic activity which took place at a remove from the shrine. As a major landholder in the region, the abbey's influence extended beyond the *banleuca* and the Liberty to its many estates and manors elsewhere in Norfolk and Suffolk which in many cases most likely accounted for the presence of St Edmund in, for example, imagery within the parish church. Connections between the abbey and other wealthy patrons could have a similar effect, such as at Wainfleet in Lincolnshire, where the flourishing micro-cult was most likely promoted by the abbey's presence through its landholdings in the area, but also perhaps through the personal devotion of Henry Lacey, earl of Lincoln, a local magnate and generous benefactor of the abbey church.

Methodological insights

Adopting a longer-term view of the cult allows the development of Edmund's saintly identity to be fully appreciated. Similarly, focussing enquiry on medieval

Norfolk and Suffolk allows devotion to St Edmund in his spiritual heartland to be considered in hitherto unattempted depth. Edmund's status as royal favourite has inevitably led to the focus of scholarly attention upon his presence on high-status artefacts such as the Wilton Diptych or in the personal devotions of kings such as Henry III. However, relocating the cult within the region in which it originated reveals elements of Edmund's saintly identity which are barely evinced elsewhere. This is particularly the case regarding Edmund's role as regional patron. In a broader context his kingship is used as a means to integrate him into national history. In the legendary collections, for example, Edmund appears as one of many indigenous English kings who speak to a growing sense of national identity at the time the texts were composed. However, in the regional cult Edmund also manifests features which allude to his East Anglian origins. The prevalence of imagery of the wolf and head is a good example of this, as the longevity of the motif indicates its ongoing significance in the mythic narrative of East Anglia and aligns Edmund with alternative traditions. This distinctive and significant feature of the cult may be fully appreciated only in a regional context.

In large part this study has been a methodological exercise to test the proposition that approaching saints' cults from an interdisciplinary perspective is more rewarding than adhering to traditional disciplinary constraints. The benefits of this approach are apparent throughout. In Part I, literary, art-historical and statistical analysis were brought to bear on texts and images too often considered in isolation from each other, so as to reveal in detail the way in which the legend of St Edmund evolved over five centuries in response to particular circumstances. The methodological challenges of reconstructing the experience of a pilgrim at the shrine of St Edmund at Bury are considerable, as, in contrast to the wealth of printed legends, the material relating to the architectural and art-historical cult centre is disparate and sparse. Above all, therefore, this demonstrates the necessity of approaching saints' cults from an interdisciplinary perspective. The prevalence of imagery relating to the death of Sweyn is a prime example. Discussed by previous scholars in its textual and manuscript setting as a noteworthy example of the manifestation of Edmund's saintly abilities, the extent of its significance has hitherto gone unnoticed, but is duly revealed by juxtaposing an array of sources relating to the abbey church. Similarly, combining seemingly disparate sources around a unifying interpretive approach elucidates the processes by which the cult was disseminated by the monastic community at Bury and appropriated by other individuals and communities to suit their varying purposes. Comparing Edmund with other native saints such as St Æthelthryth reveals the ways in which his cult accorded with devotional trends, as well as highlighting aspects of devotion particular to him. Although beyond the scope of this project, additional comparisons with other saints would further refine this understanding.

'Martir, mayde and kynge', and more

Above all, this study has revealed the complex nature of Edmund's saintly identity. His martyrdom guaranteed his inclusion in the ranks of the holy and his integration into the long history of Christian sanctity. His virginity alluded to his purity and elevated spiritual status and, by association, the inviolability of the community in which it endured. Edmund appealed to ecclesiastical reformers as an image of the clerical ideal and in the context of his kingship allowed him to be presented as a model of royal chastity which other monarchs could emulate. The alleged preservation and intactness of Edmund's corpse as a result of his virginity also allowed the monastic community to lay exclusive claim to his primary relics, securing its monopoly over the cult.

Edmund embodied the institution of the monarchy and appealed to history and indigenous Englishness, providing a sense of continuity and a legitimising link between both the Anglo-Saxon and post-Conquest kingdoms and later royal dynasties. He offered a precedent in light of which contemporary events could be interpreted. As an erstwhile king of Norfolk and Suffolk, Edmund continued to be cast in the role of defender of his people, especially the monastic community which guarded his remains. Other saints offered similar benefits, but Edmund's regional identity made him particularly appealing in an East Anglian context. He was a symbol of the region, its past autonomy and origins, and as its former ruler was ideally placed to offer the protection which in life he had been unable to provide. Above all, multifarious personae allowed Edmund to appeal to numerous sensibilities and to transcend time and context.

In addition to developing an alternative methodology, this study challenges some of the assumptions concerning the medieval cult of saints, such as Ridyard's assertion that the cult of St Edmund was entirely political, or Cubitt's contrasting claims which overstate the influence of popular culture.[2] Rather, both of these are integral, but in differing proportions in different periods. Nor, as Guerevich claims, should it be assumed that 'low' culture always existed in antagonistic relation to 'high' culture.[3] John Arnold offers a far more convincing conceptualisation of medieval religion. He rejects a simplistic idea of 'popular piety' and the 'religion of the laity' as divergent from, and in opposition to, a stable orthodoxy represented by the established Church. Instead he suggests a model of authority inspired by Michel Foucault in which he sees power 'not as a straight line, one

---

[2] Ridyard, *Royal Saints*, p. 216; Cubitt, *Sites and Sanctity*, 53–83.
[3] Aron Gurevich, *Medieval Popular Culture: Problems of Belief and Perception*, trans. János M. Bak and Paul A. Hollingsworth (Cambridge: Cambridge University Press, 1990), esp. pp. 41–3.

thing pushing at another, but as a field of relationships: a web of interactions and tensions that *pull* as much as push us into particular social, cultural and political hierarchies'.[4] The idea of interaction is particularly relevant in relation to the construction of Edmund's identity, which developed over time as a result of ongoing renegotiations between individuals and communities from across the social spectrum. Far from being problematic, I believe that Edmund's historical indeterminacy, which has so troubled historians, was in fact his greatest asset, enabling successive generations of devotees to redefine Edmund to suit their own proclivities and requirements and ensuring his enduring appeal. The aspects of his saintly identity could mean many things to many people. He was indeed 'martir, mayde and kynge', and much more besides.

---

[4] John H. Arnold, *Belief and Unbelief in Medieval Europe* (London: Hodder Arnold, 2005), pp. 7–14; p. 14.

APPENDIX 1

Synoptic account of the legend of St Edmund

EDMUND was born of 'the stock of the Old Saxons', the son of King Alkmund and Queen Siware. He was a prudent and holy child, fulfilling the potential miraculously foretold to his father by a wise woman in Rome before the young prince's birth.

On his way to the Holy Land on pilgrimage, Edmund's uncle Offa, king of East Anglia, visited his relatives. He was so struck by Edmund's virtues that he named him his heir. On his return from Jerusalem, Offa fell ill and died. His attendants travelled to the court of King Alkmund and presented Offa's ring to the young prince as a sign of his inheritance. Reluctantly, Edmund's parents agreed that he must leave, and with many tears they bade him farewell.

On his arrival in East Anglia, at 'Maydensburgh', Edmund knelt and gave thanks for a successful sea crossing. Five miraculous wells sprang forth and thereafter watered the land, bringing great fertility to the area. Edmund founded the town of Hunstanton, which was built nearby.

The new king travelled south across his kingdom to Attleborough, where he spent a year learning his Psalter. At the end of the year he was proclaimed king by public acclamation, and was crowned at the royal seat at Bures. He ruled wisely, administering justice, defending the Church, and offering charity to widows and orphans. He was also a valiant knight, hunting and hawking with his men.

Meanwhile, tales of the East Anglian king reached the Danish court. King Lothbroc taunted his sons, Hinguar and Hubba, claiming that they measured badly against the merits of the foreign ruler. Whilst he was out alone, fishing, Lothbroc's boat was swept away from the Danish shore and carried across the North Sea. Beaching on the East Anglian coast, he was hospitably received by King Edmund, and the two spent many hours together, hunting and talking. However, one of Edmund's huntsman, Bern, was jealous, and lured Lothbroc to the forest, where he killed him. Lothbroc's faithful greyhound returned to court and led Edmund to the body. Bern was cast adrift in a boat without oars and washed ashore on the Danish coast. Unable to admit his own part in their father's murder, Bern told Hinguar and Hubba that Edmund had ordered his death. Enraged, and still rankling from their father's taunts, the Danes set sail for East Anglia.

The Viking army swept across the East Anglian countryside. Killing all in their path, they pillaged and burnt. Edmund rallied his troops and met the Danes in battle near Thetford. The East Anglians gained the victory, but appalled by the bloodshed and loss of life, Edmund vowed not to fight again, resolving instead to offer himself as a sacrifice to the Danes.

A messenger arrived from the Viking leaders, demanding that Edmund pay tribute and worship their pagan gods. The king refused, and was seized by the Danes. Stripped of his royal robes and cruelly beaten, he was tied to a tree and shot full of arrows. Edmund refused to cry out in pain, but continuously prayed for forbearance. Eventually the Danes tired of their sport and beheaded the king, abandoning his body to be devoured by wild animals, but casting his head deep into a thorny thicket to prevent Edmund's followers from giving him a Christian burial.

Once the semblance of peace returned to East Anglia the survivors sought for the body of their fallen king. Discovering the corpse, they were unable to locate the head. They heard a voice calling 'here, here, here', and following the sound came upon a monstrous wolf guarding Edmund's head between his paws. Recognising the sanctity of their martyred king, the East Anglians reunited the head and the body, to which it was miraculously rejoined, with only a thin red line indicating his decapitation. They buried Edmund's remains with great reverence in a small wooden chapel. Miracles began to occur at the chapel, and eventually Edmund was translated to the royal seat of Beodricesworth, where he was enshrined.

APPENDIX 2

Chronology of significant events and texts associated with the cult of St Edmund

c. 840?	Edmund born 'of Old Saxon stock'
c. 855?	Edmund crowned King of East Anglia at Bures (Suffolk)
865	The Great Heathen army invades. Edmund barters horses with the Vikings and they march north to Yorkshire
869	The Vikings return to East Anglia. Edmund is captured and killed
878	Alfred defeats the Vikings at the Battle of Ethandun
c.890	The first account of Edmund's death recorded in the *Anglo-Saxon Chronicle* (Parker manuscript)
893	Asser includes Edmund's death in his *Vita Ælfredi Regis Angul Saxonum*
c.895–910	St Edmund memorial coinage issued
c.905?	Edmund's remains translated to Beodricesworth (later Bury) from their original burial place at 'Sutton'
945	King Edmund grants the secular community control over the *banleuca*
c.985–7	Abbo of Fleury, *Passio Sancti Edmundi*
1010	A Danish army under the leadership of Thurkill the Tall lands at Ipswich. Egelwyn travels with Edmund's relics to London
1013	Edmund's relics returned to Bury St Edmunds
1013	King Sweyn Forkbeard claims control of England. King Æthelred 'the unready' flees England
1014	King Sweyn dies suddenly, allegedly speared by St Edmund
1020	King Cnut replaces the community of secular clerics with Benedictine monks
1021	King Cnut grants the abbey a charter of privileges
1032	Rebuilt or extended abbey church consecrated by Archbishop Æthelnoth
1043	King Edward the Confessor visits Bury and grants the abbey jurisdiction over the eight and a half hundreds of West Suffolk
1044–65	Abbot Leofstan inspects Edmund's remains and finds them intact and uncorrupted

APPENDIX 2   249

Mid. 11th C	Earliest known version of Abbo's *Passio* preserved in Lambeth Palace Library, London, MS 361
c.1150–56	Geoffrey of Wells, *De Infantia Sancti Edmundi*
1153	Abbey estates pillaged by Eustace, son of King Stephen, when the abbey refused his demands for money
1065–97/98	Baldwin abbot of Bury St Edmunds
1066	The Norman Conquest of England
1070–84	Herfast bishop of East Anglia
c.1070–81	Ongoing dispute between the abbey at Bury and the episcopate concerning the location of the episcopal see
1071	Abbot Baldwin travels to Rome, via Lucca, to secure the privilege of exemption from Pope Alexander I
1081	King William I forced to intervene and settle the dispute
1095	St Edmund's relics translated into the new abbey church
Late 11th C	Archdeacon Herman, *De Miraculis Sancti Edmundi*
c.1098–1118	*De Miraculis* revised
c.1100	London, British Library, Cotton Tiberius B. ii, including *De Miraculis* and Abbo's *Passio*
Early 12th C	Promotional tracts circulate with abridged versions of *De Miraculis* (Oxford, Bodleian Library, MS Digby 39 and Paris, Bibliothèque Nationale, MS latin 2621)
1121–48	Anselm abbot of Bury St Edmunds
c.1125–35	New York, Pierpont Morgan Library, MS M. 736 produced at Bury
c.1125–34	*De Miraculis* revised again, probably by Osbert de Clare, prior of Westminster
c.1135–40	Geffrei Gaimar, *Estoire des Engleis*
By 1142	Majority of the Romanesque abbey church completed
1173	Edmund's war banner borne by the victors at the Battle of Fornham
c.1180–1200	Denis Piramus, *La Vie seint Edmund le Rei*
1182–1211	Samson of Tottington abbot of Bury St Edmunds
1198	23 June, fire destroys much of the east end of the abbey church
1198	November, Edmund's relics translated to a new shrine in the abbey church. Abbot Samson inspects the body and finds it uncorrupted
c.1200	Abbot Samson revises Osbert de Clare's version of *De Miraculis* (preserved in London, British Library, Cotton Titus Aviii)
c.1200	*La Passiun de seint Edmund* (anon.)
Mid 13th C	Henry of Avranches, *Vita Sancti Eadmundi*

1275	The *rotunda* of St Edmund demolished to make room for a new Lady Chapel. St Edmund's relics moved to a chapel in the monks' cemetery
1280s	*South English Legendary*
Mid 14th C	Inscriptions pertaining to images in the abbey church recorded (preserved in London, College of Arms, MS Arundel 30)
c.1360–80	Compilation of Oxford, Bodleian Library, MS Bodley 240
c.1370–1449	John Lydgate
Early 15th C	*Speculum Sacerdotale*
1429–46	William Curteys abbot of Bury St Edmunds. Author of *Vita et Passio S. Edmundi Abbreviata*
1430s	Abbey church tower partially collapses
1433–34	Christmas Eve, King Henry VI arrives at the abbey and stays until Easter 1434, during which time he is admitted to the Confraternity of the abbey
c.1435	John Lydgate, *Lives of Sts Edmund and Fremund*
After 1441	Additional miracles appended to Lydgate's *Lives*
Mid 15th C	*Gilte Legende*
1461–83	Descendent manuscripts of Lydgate's *Lives* (London, British Library, MS Yates Thompson 47 and the Arundel Castle manuscript, *sine numero*) copied and illustrated at Bury
1465	Fire devastates much of the abbey church
1467/68	First account of the St Edmund procession at Snettisham (Norfolk)
1483	William Caxton's *Golden Legend*
1516	*Kalendre of the Newe Legende of Englande* printed by Richard Pynson
1535	Thomas Cromwell's Commissioners visit the abbey. They deface the shrine and remove other treasures and relics
1539	The abbey is dissolved
1550s	Inscribed brass plate, possibly from the shrine of St Edmund, re-inscribed in memory of George Duke and laid, image-side down, in St Andrew's church, Frenze (Norfolk)
1581/82	Last record of the St Edmund procession at Snettisham (Norfolk)

Bibliography

Unpublished primary sources
London, College of Arms, MS Arundel 30
Norwich, Norfolk Record Office, PD 24/1

Printed primary sources
Abbo of Fleury. *Passio Sancti Edmundi*, in *Three Lives of English Saints*, ed. Michael Winterbottom, Toronto Medieval Latin Texts, 1 (Toronto: Centre for Medieval Studies, 1972).
Ælfric of Eynsham. *The Lives of Saints*, ed. and trans. W.W. Skeat, 2 vols, Early English Text Society, os 76 and 82 (London: Oxford University Press for the Early English Text Society, 1966).
Aimo. *Vita et Martyrium S. Abbonis*, ed. Jacques-Paul Migne, *Patrologia Latina*, cxxxix, cols 390–2; col. 392.
Anglo-Saxon Chronicle, ed. Dorothy Whitelock with David C. Douglas and Susie Tucker (London: Eyre and Spottiswoode, 1961).
Anglo-Saxon Litanies of the Saints, ed. Michael Lapidge, Henry Bradshaw Society, cvi (London: The Boydell Press for the Henry Bradshaw Society, 1991).
Annales monastici, ed. Henry Richard Luard, Rolls Series 36, vol. 3 (London, 1866).
Asser's Life of King Alfred, ed. W.H. Stevenson (Oxford: Clarendon Press, 1904).
Baudri de Bourgueil. *Poèmes*, 2 vols, ed. Jean-Yves Tillette (Paris: Belles Lettres, 2002).
Bede. *The Ecclesiastical History of the English People*, ed. and trans. Judith McClure and Roger Collins (Oxford: Oxford University Press, 1969, rpt 1999).
Bokenham, Osbern. *Legendys of Hooly Wummen*, ed. Mary S. Serjeantson, Early English Text Society, os 206 (London: Humphrey Milford, 1938).
Caxton, William, trans. *The Golden Legend or Lives of the Saints*, ed. Frank S. Ellis (London: Temple Classics, 1900).
Charters of the Medieval Hospitals of Bury St Edmunds, ed. Christopher Harper-Bill, Suffolk Charters, 14 (Woodbridge: The Boydell Press for the Suffolk Records Society, 1994).
The Chronicle of the Abbey of Bury St Edmunds, 1212–1301, ed. Antonia Gransden (London: Nelson, 1964).
The Chronicle of the Reigns of Henry II and Richard I, AD 1169–92, commonly known under the name of Benedict of Peterborough, 2 vols, ed. William Stubbs (London: Longmans, Green, Reader and Dyer, 1867).

Corolla Sancti Edmundi: The Garland of St Edmund, King and Martyr, ed. Francis Hervey (London: John Murray, 1907).
Cronica de electione Hugonis abbatis postea episcope Eliensis, ed. and trans. Rodney Thomson, *The Chronicle of the Election of Hugh, Abbot of Bury St Edmunds and Later Bishop of Ely* (Oxford: Clarendon Press, 1974).
Curteys, William. 'Account of the Entertainment of King Henry the Sixth at the Abbey of Bury St Edmunds', ed. Craven Ord, *Archaeologia*, 15 (1806), 65–71.
The Customary of the Benedictine Abbey of Bury St Edmunds, ed. Antonia Gransden, Henry Bradshaw Society, xcix (London: Henry Bradshaw Society, 1973).
Da Varazze, Iacopo. *Legenda Aurea*, 2 vols, edizione critica a cura di Giovanni Paolo Maggioni. Seconda edizione rivista dall' autore. Millennio Medievale, 6 (Firenze, 1998–99).
De dedicationibus, altarum, capellarum, etc., apud Sanctum Edmundum, in *The Customary of the Benedictine Abbey of Bury St Edmunds*, ed. Antonia Gransden, Henry Bradshaw Society, xcix (London: Henry Bradshaw Society, 1973), pp. 114–21.
De Voragine, Jacques. *La Légende Dorée : Edition critique dans la révision de 1476 par Jean Batallier, d'après la traduction de Jean de Vignay (1333-1348) de la Legenda Aurea (c.1261-1266)*, ed. Brenda Dunn-Lardeau (Paris : Champion, 1997).
Dives and Pauper, 3 vols, ed. Priscilla Heath Barnum, Early English Text Society, os 275, 280 and 323 (London: Oxford University Press for the Early English Text Society, 1976, 1980 and 2004).
English Benedictine Kalendars before AD 1100, ed. Francis Wormald, Henry Bradshaw Society, lxxii (London: The Boydell Press for the Henry Bradshaw Society, 1988).
Feudal Documents from the Abbey of Bury St Edmunds, ed. David C. Douglas (London: Oxford University Press, 1932).
Gaimar, Geffrei. *Estoire des Engleis*, ed. and trans. Ian Short (Oxford: Oxford University Press, 2009).
Geoffrey of Wells. *De Infancia sancti Edmundi*, in *Memorials of St Edmund's Abbey*, 3 vols, ed. Thomas Arnold, *Rerum Britannicarum Medii Aevi Scriptores* (Rolls Series), 96 (London: Printed for Her Majesty's Stationery Office by Eyre and Spottiswoode, 1890-6), I, pp. 93–103.
De Infancia sancti Edmundi, ed. Rodney Thomson, *Analecta Bollandia*, 95 (1977), 34–42.
Gesta Sacristarum, in *Memorials of St Edmund's Abbey*, 3 vols, ed. Thomas Arnold, *Rerum Britannicarum Medii Aevi Scriptores* (Rolls Series), 96 (London: Printed for Her Majesty's Stationery Office by Eyre and Spottiswoode, 1890-6), II, pp. 289–96.
Gilte Legende, 3 vols, ed. Richard Hamer and Vida Russell, Early English Text Society, os 237 (Oxford: Published for the Early English Text Society by the Oxford University Press, 2006).
The Golden Legend or Lives of the Saints as Englished by William Caxton, 7 vols, ed. F.S. Ellis (London: Temple Classics, 1900).

Goscelin of Saint-Bertin, 'Historia translationis Sancti Augustini Episcopi', ed. Jacques-Paul Migne, *Patrologia Latina*, clv, cols 33–4.
Goscelin of Saint-Bertin. *Liber confortatorius*, ed. C.H. Talbot, *Analecta monastica, troisième série: Studia Anselmiana*, xxxvii (Rome, 1955).
Henry of Avranches. 'The *Vita Sancti Fremundi*', ed. David Townsend, *Journal of Medieval Latin*, 4 (1994), 1–24.
'The *Vita Sancti Eadmundi*', ed. David Townsend, *Journal of Medieval Latin*, 5 (1995), 95–118.
Hermann archdiaconi liber de miraculis sancti Eadmundi, in *Memorials of St Edmund's Abbey*, 3 vols, ed. Thomas Arnold, *Rerum Britannicarum Medii Aevi Scriptores* (Rolls Series), 96 (London: Printed for Her Majesty's Stationery Office by Eyre and Spottiswoode, 1890–96), I, pp. 26–92.
Hermann archdiaconi liber de miraculis sancti Eadmundi, ed. Felix Liebermann, *Ungedruckte Anglo-Normannische Geschichtsquellen* (Strassburg: K.J. Trübner, 1879), 231–81.
Higden, Ranulf. *Polychronicon Ranulphi Higden monachi Cestrensis, together with the English translations of John Trevisa and of an unknown writer of the fifteenth century*, 9 vols, ed. Joseph Rawson Lumby, *Rerum Britannicarum Medii Aevi Scriptores*, 41 (London: Longman, Green, Longman, Roberts and Green, 1865–86).
An Historical Atlas of Norfolk, ed. Peter Wade-Martins (Norwich: Norfolk Musuem Service, 1994).
Incendium Ecclesiae, in *Memorials of St Edmund's Abbey*, 3 vols, ed. Thomas Arnold, *Rerum Britannicarum Medii Aevi Scriptores* (Rolls Series), 96 (London: Printed for Her Majesty's Stationery Office by Eyre and Spottiswoode, 1890–96), III, pp. 283–7.
Inventory of Church Goods during the Reign of Edward III in the Archdeaconry of Norwich, 2 vols, ed. Aelred Watkin, Norfolk Record Society, 19 (Norwich: Norfolk Record Society, 1947–48).
Jocelin of Brakelond. *The Chronicle of Jocelin of Brakelond*, ed. and trans. H.E. Butler (London & Edinburgh: Nelson's Medieval Classics, 1949, rpt 1951).
Jocelin of Brakelond. *Chronicle of the Abbey of Bury St Edmunds*, trans. Diana Greenway and Jane Sayers (Oxford: Oxford University Press, 1989).
John of Worcester. *The Chronicle of John of Worcester*, 3 vols, II, ed. R.R. Darlington and Patrick McGurk, trans. Jennifer Bray and Patrick McGurk (Oxford: Clarendon Press, 1995); III, ed. Patrick McGurk (Oxford: Clarendon Press, 1998); I (forthcoming).
The Kalendre of the Newe Legende of Englande, ed. Manfred Görlach, Middle English Texts, 27 (Heidelberg: Universitätsverlag C. Winter, 1994).
Lantfred. *Translatio et miracula Sancti Swithuni*, ed. E.P Sauvage, *Analecta Bollandiana*, iv (1885), 367–410.
The Letters of Osbert de Clare, prior of Westminster, ed. Edward W. Williamson (London: Oxford University Press, 1929).
Liber Eliensis, ed. E.O. Blake, Camden Third Series, 92 (London: Royal Historical Society, 1962).

Lydgate, John. *Lives of Saints Edmund and Fremund, Altenglische Legenden. Neue Folge*, ed. Carl Horstmann (Heilbronn: Henniger, 1881), pp. 376–445.

Lydgate, John. *Lives of Saints Edmund and Fremund*, in *John Lydgate's Lives of Saints Edmund and Fremund and the Extra Miracles of St Edmund: Edited from British Library MS Harley 2278 and Bodleian Library M*, ed. Anthony Bale and A.S.G. Edwards (Heidelberg: Universitätsverlag, 2009).

Lydgate, John. *Life of Our Lady: A Critical Edition of John Lydgate's Life of Our Lady*, ed. Joseph A. Lauritis, Ralph A. Klinefekter and Vernon F. Gallagher (Pittsburgh: Duquesne University Press, 1961).

Lydgate, John. *The Life of St Alban and Saint Amphibal*, ed. J.E. van der Westhuizen (Leiden: Brill, 1974).

Lydgate, John. *The Minor Poems of John Lydgate*, Part 1, ed. Henry Noble McCracken, Early English Texts Society, es 107 (London: Oxford University Press, 1911).

Lydgate, John. *The Life of St Edmund, King and Martyr: A Facsimile of British Library MS Harley 2278*, with an introduction by A.S.G. Edwards (London: British Library, 2004).

Memorials of St Edmund's Abbey, 3 vols, ed. Thomas Arnold, *Rerum Britannicum Medii Aevi Scriptores*, 96 (London: Her Majesty's Stationery Office, 1890–93).

Mirk, John. *Festial: A Collection of Homilies*, ed. Theodor Erbe, Early English Text Society, es 96 (London: Kegan Paul, 1905).

Nova Legenda Anglie, 2 vols, ed. Carl Horstmann (Oxford: Clarendon Press, 1901).

Osbert de Clare. *Vita beati ac gloriosi regis Anglorum Eadwardi*, ed. Marc Bloch, *Analecta Bollandiana*, 41 (1923), 5–131.

La Passiun de seint Edmund, ed. Judith Grant (London: Anglo-Norman Text Society, 1978).

Piramus, Denis. *La Vie seint Edmund le Rei*, in *Memorials of St Edmund's Abbey*, 3 vols, ed. Thomas Arnold, *Rerum Britannicarum Medii Aevi Scriptores* (Rolls Series) 96 (London: Printed for Her Majesty's Stationery Office by Eyre and Spottiswoode, 1890–6), II, pp. 137–250.

Piramus, Denis. *La Vie seint Edmund le Rei*, ed. Hilding Kjellman (Göteborg, 1935).

Proceedings and ordinances of the Privy Council of England, 7 vols, ed. Harris Nicolas (London: Commissioners on the Public Records of the United Kingdom, 1834–37).

The Rites of Durham: being a description or brief declaration of all the ancient monuments, rites, and customs belonging or being within the monastical church of Durham before the suppression, written 1593, ed. Joseph T. Fowler, Surtees Society, cvii (Durham: Published for the Surtees Society by Andrews and Co., 1903).

Rituale, London, British Library, MS Harley 2977, ed. James, *On the Abbey Church of S. Edmund at Bury*, Cambridge Antiquarian Society publications, Octavo series 28 (Cambridge: Deighton Bell, 1895), pp. 183–6.

Roger of Hovedon. *Chronica Magestri Rogeri Houedene*, 4 vols, ed. William Stubbs, *Rerum Britannicarum Medii Aevi Scriptores*, 51 (London: Longman, 1868–71).
Roger of Wendover. *Chronica sive Flores Historiarum*, ed. Henry O. Coxe (London: The English Historical Society: London, 1841).
Rotuli chartarum in Turri Londinensi asseravti, ed. Thomas D. Hardy, vol. 1: 1199–1216 (London: Record Commissioners, 1837).
The Saint of London: The Life and Miracles of St Erkenwald, ed. and trans. E. Gordon Whately (Binghamton, New York: Medieval and Renaissance Texts and Studies, 1989).
Samson. *De Miraculis Sancti Edmundi*, ed. Thomas Arnold, *Memorials of St Edmund's Abbey*, 3 vols, *Rerum Britannicum Medii Aevi Scriptores*, 96 (London: Her Majesty's Stationery Office, 1890–93, I, pp. 107–208.
Some Oxfordshire Wills Proved in the Prebendary Court of Canterbury, 1393–1510, ed. John R.H. Weaver and Alice Beardwood (Banbury, Oxon: Cheney & Sons Ltd., 1958).
The South English Legendary or Lives of the Saints, ed. Carl Horstmann, Early English Text Society, os 87 (London: Early English Text Society, 1887).
Speculum Sacerdotale, ed. Edward H. Weatherly, Early English Text Society, os 200 (London: Published for the Early English Text Society by Oxford University Press, 1936, rpt. 1971).
Suger, Abbot. *On the Abbey Church of Saint-Denis and its Art Treasures*, ed. and trans. Erwin Panofsky (Princeton, NJ: Princeton University Press, 1948).
Supplementary Lives in Some Manuscripts of the Gilte Legende, ed. Richard Hamer and Vida Russell, Early English Text Society, os 315 (Oxford: Published for the Early English Text Society by the Oxford University Press, 2000).
Symeon of Durham. *Libellus de exordio atque procursu istius, hoc est Dunhelmensis, ecclesie*, ed. and trans. David Rollason (Oxford : Clarendon Press, 2000).
Three Chapters of Letters Relating to the Suppression of the Monasteries, ed. Thomas Wright, Camden Society, London, vol. 26 (London: Printed for the Camden Society by John Bowyer Nichols and Son, 1843).
Virgil. *Aeneid*, trans. Sarah Ruden (New Haven: Yale University Press, 2008).
Wills and Inventories from the Registers of the Commissary of Bury St Edmund's and the Archdeacon of Sudbury, ed. Samuel Tymms, Camden Society, os xlix (London: Printed for the Camden Society, 1850).

Printed secondary sources

A Catalogue of the Harleian Manuscripts in the British Museum, 4 vols (London: British Museum Department of Manuscripts. Printed by command of H.M. King George III, 1808–12).
Abou-El-Haj, Barbara. 'Bury St Edmunds Abbey between 1070 and 1124: A History of Property, Privilege, and Monastic Art Production', *Art History* 6 (1983), 1–29.

Alexander, J.J.G. 'Painting and Manuscript Illumination for Royal Patrons in the Later Middle Ages', in *English Court Culture in the Later Middle Ages*, ed. V.J. Scattergood and J.W. Sherborne (London: [publisher], 1983), pp. 141–62.

Arnold, John H. *Belief and Unbelief in Medieval Europe* (London: Hodder Arnold, 2005).

Arnold-Foster, Frances. *Studies in Church Dedications or England's Patron Saints*, 3 vols (London: Skeffington and Son, 1899), III, pp. 354 and 359.

Ashley, Kathleen and Pamela Sheingorn, eds, *Interpreting Cultural Symbols: Saint Anne in Late Medieval Society* (Athens and London: The University of Georgia Press, 1990).

_____. *Writing Faith: Text, Sign, and History in the Miracles of Sainte Foy* (Chicago: University of Chicago Press, 1999).

Atkinson, Thomas D. *An Architectural History of the Benedictine Monastery of St Etheldreda at Ely*, 2 vols (Cambridge: Cambridge University Press, 1933).

Baker, Malcolm. 'Medieval Illustrations of Bede's *Life of St Cuthbert*', *Journal of the Warburg and Courtauld Institutes* xli (1978), 16–49.

Bale, Anthony. *The Jew in the Medieval Book: English Antisemitisms 1350–1500* (Cambridge: Cambridge University Press, 2006).

_____, ed. *St Edmund, King and Martyr. Changing Images of a Medieval Saint* (York: York Medieval Press, 2009).

_____. 'St Edmund in Fifteenth-Century London: The Lydgatian *Miracles of St Edmund*', in *St Edmund, King and Martyr. Changing Images of a Medieval Saint*, ed. Anthony Bale (York: York Medieval Press, 2009), pp. 145–61.

Bateman, Katherine R. 'Pembroke 120 and Morgan 736: A Re-examination of the St Albans–Bury St Edmunds Manuscript Dilemma', *Gesta* xvii, no. 1 (1978), 19–26.

Beaven, M.R.L. 'The Beginnings of the Year in the Alfreidan Chronicle, 866–87', *English Historical Review* 33 (1918), 328–42.

Beckwith, Sarah. *Christ's Body: Identity, Culture and Society in Late Medieval Writings* (New York: Routledge, 2003).

Beer, Jeannette M.A. *Narrative Conventions of Truth in the Middle Ages* (Genève: Libraire Droz S.A., 1981).

Bertram, Jerome, ed. *Monumental Brasses as Art and History* (Stroud: Alan Sutton, 1996).

Biddle, Martin. 'Remembering St Alban: The Site of the Shrine and the DISCOVERY of the twelfth-century Purbeck Marble Shrine Table', in *Alban and St Albans: Roman and Medieval Archiecture, Art and Archaeology*, ed. Martin Henig and Phillip Lindley, British Archaeological Association Conference Transactions xxiv (Leeds: British Archaeological Association, 2001), pp. 124–61.

Black, W.H. *Catalogue of Arundel Manuscripts in the Library of the College of Arms* (London: printed by S. and R. Bentley, 1829).

Blake, Norman F. *Middle English Religious Prose* (London: Arnold, 1972).

Blanton, Virginia. 'Building a Presbytery for St Ætheltryth: Hugh de Northwold and the Politics of Cult Production in Thirteenth-century England', in *Art and Architecture of Late Medieval Pilgrimage in Northern*

Europe and the British Isles, 2 vols, ed. Sarah Blick and Rita Tekippe, Studies in Medieval and Reformation Traditions, 104 (Leiden and Boston: Brill, 2005), pp. 539–65.

―――. *Signs of Devotion: The Cult of St Æthelthryth in Medieval England, 695–1615* (University Park, PA: The Pennsylvania State University Press, 2007).

Blick, Sarah. 'Reconstructing the Shrine of St Thomas Becket, Canterbury Cathedral', in *Art and Architecture of Late Medieval Pilgrimage in Northern Europe and the British Isles*, 2 vols, ed. Sarah Blick and Rita Tekippe, Studies in Medieval and Reformation Traditions, 104 (Leiden and Boston: Brill, 2005), pp. 405–42.

Blick, Sarah and Rita Tekippe, eds, *Art and Architecture of Late Medieval Pilgrimage in Northern Europe and the British Isles*, 2 vols, Studies in Medieval and Reformation Traditions, 104 (Leiden and Boston: Brill, 2005).

Bloch, Marc. *The Royal Touch*, trans. J.E. Anderson (New York: Dorset Press, 1961).

Blomefield, Francis. *An Essay Towards a Topographical History of the County of Norfolk*, 11 vols, 2nd edn (London: Miller, 1805–10).

Blum, Pamela Z. 'The Saint Edmund Cycle in the Crypt at Saint-Denis', in *Bury St Edmunds: Art, Architecture, Archaeology and Economy*, ed. Antonia Gransden, British Archaeological Association Conference Transactions, xx (Leeds: British Archaeological Association, 1998), pp. 57–68.

Blunt, C.E. 'The St Edmund Memorial Coinage', *Proceedings of the Suffolk Institute of Archaeology* xxxi (1969), 234–53.

Boffey, Julia and A.S.G. Edwards. *A New Index of Middle English Verse* (London: British Library, 2005).

Bond, Francis B. *Westminster Abbey* (London, 1909).

Borenius, Tancred. 'St Henry of Finland, an Anglo-Scandinavian Saint', *Archaeological Journal* lxxxvii (1930), 340–56.

Boureau, Alain. 'Franciscan Piety and Voracity: Uses and Strategies in the Hagiographic Pamphlet', in *The Culture of Print: Power and the Uses of Print in Early Modern Europe*, ed. Roger Chartier, trans. Lydia G. Cochrane (Princeton: Princeton University Press, 1989), pp. 15–58.

Boyle, Leonard E. 'The Fourth Lateran Council and manuals of popular theology', in *The Popular Literature of Medieval England*, ed. Thomas J. Heffernan (Knoxville: University of Tennessee Press, 1985), pp. 30–43.

Brod, Harry, ed. *The Making of Masculinities: The New Men's Studies* (Boston: Allen and Unwin, 1987).

Broughton, Lynne. *Interpreting Lincoln Cathedral: The Medieval Imagery* (Lincoln: Lincoln Cathedral Publications, 1996).

Brown, Carlton and Rossell Hope Robbins. *The Index of Middle English Verse* (New York: Columbia University Press for the Index Society, 1943).

Brown, Marjorie A. 'The Feast Hall in Anglo-Saxon Society', in *Food and Eating in Medieval Europe*, ed. Martha Carlin and Joel T. Rosenthal (London and Rio Grande: The Hambledon Press, 1998), pp. 1–14.

Brown, Peter. *The Cult of Saints: Its Rise and Function in Latin Christianity* (Chicago: University of Chicago Press, 1981).

Bukofzer, Manfred F. *Studies in Medieval and Renaissance Music* (New York: Norton, 1950).
Burrow, John A. *The Ages of Man. A Study of Medieval Writing and Thought* (Oxford: Clarendon Press, 1986).
Camille, Michael. 'Seeing and Reading: Some Visual Implications of Medieval Literacy and Illiteracy', *Art History* 8.1 (1985), 26–49.
Campbell, James. 'Some Twelfth-Century Views of the Anglo-Saxon Past', *Peritia* 3 (1984), 135–50.
Campbell, Marian. 'Medieval Metalworking and Bury St Edmunds', in *Bury St Edmunds: Art, Architecture, Archaeology and Economy*, ed. Antonia Gransden, British Archaeological Association Conference Transactions, xx (Leeds: British Archaeological Association, 1998), pp. 69–80.
Champion, Matthew. 'Devotion, Pestilence and Conflict: The Medieval Wall Paintings of St Mary the Virgin, Lakenheath', in *Art, Faith and Place in East Anglia*, ed. T.A. Heslop et al. (Woodbridge: Boydell, 2012), pp. 88–104.
Chaney, William A. *The Cult of Kingship in Anglo-Saxon England: The Transition from Paganism to Christianity* (Manchester: Manchester University Press, 1970).
Chapman, Anna. 'King Alfred and the Cult of St Edmund', *History Today* 53.7 (July 2003), 37–43.
Chazelle, Celia. 'Pictures, Books and the Illiterate: Pope Gregory I's Letters to Serenius of Marseilles', *Word and Image* 6 (1990), 138–53.
Chew, Helena M. *The English Ecclesiastical Tenants-in-Chief and Knight Service* (London: Oxford University Press, 1932).
Cochelin, Isabella and Karen Smyth, eds. *Medieval Life Cycles: Continuities and Change* (Turnhout: Brepols, 2011).
Cohen, Esther. '*In haec signia*: Pilgrim-Badge Trade in Southern France', *Journal of Medieval History* ii (1976), 193–214.
Cohen, Jeffrey Jerome and Bonnie Wheeler, eds. *Becoming Male in the Middle Ages* (New York: Garland, 1997).
Coldstream, Nicola. 'English Decorated Shrine Bases', *Journal of the British Archaeological Association* 129 (1976), 15–34.
Coleman, Simon and John Elsner. *Pilgrimage; Past and Present: Sacred Travel and Sacred Space in the World Religions* (London: British Museum Press, 1995).
Coletti, Theresa. '*Pauperatus et donum Dei*: Hagiography, Lay Religion, and the Economics of Salvation in the Digby Mary Magdalen', *Speculum* 76 (2001), 337–78.
Colton, Lisa. 'Music and Identity in Medieval Bury St Edmunds', in *St Edmund King and Martyr: Changing Images of a Medieval Saint*, ed. Antony Bale (York: York Medieval Press, 2009), pp. 87–110.
Constable, W.G. 'Some East Anglian Roodscreen Paintings', *Connoisseur* lxxxiv (1929), 141–7.
Cornwall, Andrea and Nancy Lindisfarne. 'Dislocating Masculinity: Gender, Power and Anthropology', in *Dislocating Masculinity: Comparative Ethnographies*, ed. Cornwall and Lindisfarne (London: Routledge, 1994), pp. 11–46.

Cotton, Simon. 'Medieval Rood Screens in Norfolk – Their Construction and Painting Dates', *Norfolk Archaeology* 35 (1984), 44–54.
Crewe, Sarah. *Stained Glass in England, c.1180–1540* (London: Her Majesty's Stationery Office, 1987).
Crook, John. 'The Romanesque East Arm and Crypt of Winchester Cathedral', *Journal of the British Archaeological Association* 142 (1989), 1–36.
———. 'St Swithun of Winchester', in *Winchester Cathedral: Nine Hundred Years, 1093–1993*, ed. John Crook (Chichester: Phillimore, 1993).
———. 'The Architectural Setting of the Cult of St Edmund in the Abbey Church, 1095–1539', in *Bury St Edmunds: Art, Architecture, Archaeology and Economy*, ed. Antonia Gransden, British Archaeological Association Conference Transactions, xx (Leeds: British Archaeological Association, 1998), pp. 34–44.
Cubitt, Catherine. 'Sites and Sanctity: Revisiting the Cult of Murdered and Martyred Anglo-Saxon Royal Saints', *Early Medieval Europe* 9 (2001), 53–83.
———. 'Universal and Local Saints in Anglo-Saxon England', in *Local Saints and Local Churches in the Early Medieval West*, ed. Alan Thacker and Richard Sharpe (Oxford: Oxford University Press, 2002), pp. 423–54.
Cullum, P.H. and Katherine J. Lewis, eds. *Holiness and Masculinity in the Middle Ages* (Cardiff: University of Wales Press, 2004).
Curteis, Tobit. 'St Mary's Church, Lakenheath, Suffolk: Technical and Condition Survey of the Wall Paintings' (Tobit Curteis Associates, April 2003).
Cutler, Anthony. 'The *Mulier Amicta Sole* and Her Attendants. An Episode in Late Medieval Finnish Art', *Journal of the Warburg and Courtauld Institutes* 29 (1966), 117–34.
Davies, Natalie Zemon. 'From 'Popular Religion' to Religious Cultures', in *Reformation Europe: A Guide to Research*, ed. Stephen Ozment (St Louis: Centre for Reformation Research, 1982), pp. 321–41.
Davis, John A. *Venta Icenorum: Caistor St Edmund Roman Town* (East Dereham: Norfolk Archaeological Trust, 2001).
D'Evelyn, Charlotte. 'Collections of Saints' Legends', in *A Manual of Writings in Middle English, 1050–1500*, gen. ed. J. Burke Severs (Hamden: Connecticut Academy of Arts & Sciences, 1970), II, pp. 413–18.
De Kroon, Marike. 'Pilgrim Badges and Their Iconographic Aspects', in *Art and Architecture of Late Medieval Pilgrimage in Northern Europe and the British Isles*, 2 vols, ed. Sarah Blick and Rita Tekippe, Studies in Medieval and Reformation Traditions, 104 (Leiden and Boston: Brill, 2005), I, pp. 385–403.
Delooz, Pierre. 'Towards a Sociological Study of Canonized Sainthood in the Catholic Church', trans. Jane Hodgkin, in *Saints and their Cults: Studies in Religious Sociology, Folklore and History*, ed. Stephen Wilson (Cambridge: Cambridge University Press, 1983), pp. 189–216.
Duffy, Eamon. '"Holy Maydens, Holy Wyfes": The Cult of Women Saints in Fifteenth- and Sixteenth-Century England', in *Women in the Church: Papers Read at the 1989 Summer Meeting and the 1990 Winter Meeting of the Ecclesiastical History Society*, ed. W.J. Shiels and Diana Wood (Oxford: Ecclesiastical History Society, 1990), pp. 175–96.

_____. *The Stripping of the Altars: Traditional Religion in England, 1400–1580* (New Haven and London: Yale University Press, 1992).

_____. 'The Dynamics of Pilgrimage in Late Medieval England', in *Pilgrimage: The English Experience from Becket to Bunyan*, ed. Colin Morris and Peter Roberts (Cambridge: Cambridge University Press, 2002), pp. 164–77.

Dugdale, William, ed. *Monasticon Anglicanum: A History of the Abbies and other Monasteries, Hospitals, Friaries and Cathedral and Collegiate Churches*, rpt., ed. John Caley, Henry Ellis and Bulkeley Bandinel, 6 vols (London: Longman, Hurst, Rees, Orme and Brown, 1817–30).

Duggan, Lawrence G. 'Was Art Really the Book of the Illiterate?', *Word and Image* 5 (1989), 227–51.

Dumville, David N. *English Caroline Script and Monastic History. Studies in Benedictinism, AD 950–1030* (Woodbridge: The Boydell Press, 1993).

Dymond, David and Edward Martin, eds. *An Historical Atlas of Suffolk*, 2nd edn (Ipswich: Suffolk County Council, 1989).

Eaglen, Robin J. *The Abbey and Mint of Bury St Edmunds to 1279* (London: Spink, 2006).

Edwards, A.S.G. and J.I. Miller. 'John Stow and Lydgate's *St Edmund*', *Notes and Queries* 228 (1973), 365–9.

_____. 'John Lydgate's *Lives of Sts Edmund and Fremund*. Politics, Hagiography and Literature', in *St Edmund, King and Martyr. Changing Images of a Medieval Saint*, ed. Anthony Bale (York: York Medieval Press, 2009), pp. 133–45.

Edwards, Edward. *Memoirs of Libraries*, 2 vols (London: Trübner and Co., 1859).

Eichler, Hans. 'A Flemish Brass of 1398', *The Burlington Magazine for Connoisseurs* 61, no. 353 (August 1932), 84–7.

Ellis, Roger H. *Catalogue of Seals in the Public Record Office: Monastic Seals* (London: Her Majesty's Stationery Office, 1986).

Eve, Julian. *Saints and the Painted Roodscreens of North East Norfolk* (Norwich: J.R. Eve, 1997).

Farnhill, Ken. *Guilds and the Parish Community in Late Medieval East Anglia, c. 1470–1550* (York: York Medieval Press, 2001).

Fawcett, Richard. 'The Influence of the Gothic Parts of the Cathedral on Church Building in Norfolk', in *Norwich Cathedral: Church, City and Diocese, 1096–1996*, ed. Ian Atherton, Eric Fernie, Christopher Harper-Bill and Hassel Smith (London: Hambledon 1996), pp. 210–27.

Fernie, Eric. 'The Romanesque Church of Bury St Edmunds Abbey', in *Bury St Edmunds: Art, Architecture, Archaeology and Economy*, ed. Antonia Gransden, British Archaeological Association Conference Transactions, xx (Leeds: British Archaeological Association, 1998), pp. 1–15.

_____. *The Architecture of Norman England* (Oxford: Oxford University Press, 2002).

Field, Rosalind. 'Romance as History, History as Romance', in *Romance in Medieval England*, ed. Maldwyn Mills, Jennifer Fellows and Carol M. Meale (Cambridge: D.S. Brewer, 1991), pp. 164–73.

Finlay, Alison. 'Chronology, Genealogy and Conversion: The Afterlife of St Edmund in the North', in *St Edmund, King and Martyr: Changing Images of a Medieval Saint*, ed. Anthony Bale (York: York Medieval Press, 2009), pp. 27–44.
Finucane, Ronald. *Miracles and Pilgrims. Popular Beliefs in Medieval England* (London, Melbourne and Toronto: J.M. Dent and Sons Ltd., 1977).
Foucault, Michel. 'The Battle for Chastity', in *Western Sexuality: Practice and Precept in Past and Present Times*, ed. Philippe Ariès and André Béjin, trans. Anthony Forster (Oxford: Basil Blackwell, 1985), pp. 14–25.
Frazer, Sir James George. *The Golden Bough: A Study in Magic and Religion*, 12 vols (London: Macmillan, 1906–15).
Frederick, Jill. 'The *South English Legendary*: Anglo-Saxon Saints and National Identity', in *Literary Appropriations of the Anglo-Saxons from the Thirteenth to the Twentieth Century*, ed. Donald Scragg and Carole Weinberg (Cambridge: Cambridge University Press, 2000), pp. 57–73.
Gage, John. 'Historical Notices of the Great Bell Tower of the Abbey Church of St Edmundsbury', *Archaelogia* xxiii (1831), 329–30.
Galbraith, V.H. 'The East Anglian See and the Abbey of Bury St Edmunds', *English Historical Review* xl (1925), 222–8.
Gameson, Richard. *The Role of Art in the Anglo-Saxon Church* (Oxford: Clarendon Press, 1995).
_____. 'The Early Imagery of Thomas Becket', in *Pilgrimage: The English Experience from Becket to Bunyan*, ed. Colin Morris and Peter Roberts (Cambridge: Cambridge University Press, 2002), pp. 46–89.
Gaposchkin, M. Cecilia. 'Portals, Processions, Pilgrimage and Piety: Saints Firmin and Honoré at Amiens', in *Art and Architecture of Late Medieval Pilgrimage in Northern Europe and the British Isles*, 2 vols, ed. Sarah Blick and Rita Tekippe, Studies in Medieval and Reformation Traditions, 104 (Leiden and Boston: Brill, 2005), I, pp. 217–42.
Garnett, George. *Conquered England: Kingship, Succession and Tenure, 1066–1166* (Oxford, New York: Oxford University Press, 2007).
Gasquet, Francis Aidan. *The Religious Life of King Henry VI* (London: G. Bell, 1923).
Gem, Richard. 'The Significance of the Eleventh-Century Rebuilding of Christ Church and St Augustine's, Canterbury, in the Development of Romanesque Architecture', in *Medieval Art and Architecture at Canterbury before 1220*, ed. Nicola Coldstream and Peter Draper, British Archaeological Association Conference Transactions, v (1982), pp. 1–19.
_____. 'Towards an Iconography of Anglo-Saxon Architecture', *Journal of the Warburg and Courtauld Institutes* 46 (1983), 1–18.
_____. 'A Scientific Examination of the Relics of St Edmund at Arundel Castle', in *Bury St Edmunds: Art, Architecture, Archaeology and Economy*, ed. Antonia Gransden, British Archaeological Association Conference Transactions, xx (Leeds: British Archaeological Association, 1998), pp. 45–56.
Gillespie, Alexandra. 'The Later Lives of St Edmund: John Lydgate to John Stow', in *St Edmund, King and Martyr. Changing Images of a Medieval Saint*, ed. Anthony Bale (York: York Medieval Press, 2009), pp. 163–86.

Gillingwater, Edmund. *Historical and Descriptive Account of St Edmund's Bury* (Saint Edmund's Bury: Printed by and for J. Rackham, Angel Hill, 1804).

Girard, René. *Violence and the Sacred*, trans. Patrick Gregory (Baltimore and London: The Johns Hopkins Press, 1977).

Golding, Charles. *The Coinage of Suffolk. Consisting of the Regal Coins Leaden Pieces and Tokens of the Seventeenth and Nineteenth Centuries* (London: Printed privately by the author, 1868).

Good, Jonathan. *The Cult of St George in Medieval England* (Woodbridge: The Boydell Press, 2009).

Goodall, John. 'Death and the Impenitent Avaricious King: A Unique Brass Discovered at Frenze, Norfolk', *Apollo* ns 126 (October 1987), 264–6.

Görlach, Manfred. *The Textual Tradition of the South English Legendary* (Leeds: University of Leeds, 1974).

Gransden, Antonia. 'The Legends and Traditions concerning the Origins of the Abbey of Bury St Edmunds', *English Historical Review* 100, no. 394 (January 1985), 1–24.

———. 'The Abbey of Bury St Edmunds and National Politics in the Reigns of King John and Henry III', in *Monastic Studies: The Continuity of Tradition*, 2 vols, ed. Judith Loades (Bangor: Headstart History, 1991), II, pp. 67–86.

———. 'Abbo of Fleury's *Passio Sancti Eadmundi*', *Revue Bénédictine* 105 (1995), 20–78.

———. 'The Composition and Authorship of the *De Miraculis Sancti Eadmundi* Attributed to "Herman the Archdeacon"', *Journal of Medieval Latin* v (1995), 1–52.

———. *Historical Writing in England*, 2 vols (London: The Hambledon Press, 1997).

———, ed. *Bury St Edmunds: Art, Architecture, Archaeology and Economy*, British Archaeological Association Conference Transactions, xx (Leeds: British Archaeological Association, 1998).

———. 'The Cult of St Mary at Beodricesworth and then in Bury St Edmund Abbey to c. 1150', *Journal of Ecclesiastical History* lv, pt 4 (2004), 627–53.

———. *A History of the Abbey of Bury St Edmunds, 1182–1256* (Woodbridge: The Boydell Press, 2007).

Gravdal, Kathryn. *Ravishing Maidens: Writing Rape in Medieval Literature and Law* (Philadelphia: University of Pennsylvania Press, 1991).

Griffiths, Ralph A. *The Reign of King Henry VI* (Stroud: Sutton Publishing, 1998).

Grosjean, Paul. *Henrici VI Angliae Regis Miracula Postuma* (Bruxelles: Société des Bollandistes, 1935).

Gurevich, Aron. *Medieval Popular Culture: Problems of Belief and Perception*, trans. János M. Bak and Paul A. Hollingsworth (Cambridge: Cambridge University Press, 1990).

Hackwood, Frederick P. *Inns, Ales and Drinking Customs of Old England* (London: T. Fisher Unwin, 1909).

Hahn, Cynthia. '*Peregrinatio et Natio*: The Illustrated Life of Edmund, King and Martyr', *Gesta* xxx, no. 2 (1991), 119–39.

_____. *Portrayed on the Heart: Narrative Effect in Pictorial Lives of the Saints from the Tenth through the Thirteenth Century* (Berkley and London: University of California Press, 2001).

Hamelinck, Renee. 'St Kenelm and the Legends of the English Saints in the *South English Legendary*', in *Companion to Early Middle English Literature*, ed. N.H.G.E. Veldhoen and H. Aertsen (Amsterdam: Free University Press, 1988), pp. 21–30.

Harris, Anne F. 'Pilgrimage, Performance and Stained Glass at Canterbury Cathedral', in *Art and Architecture of Late Medieval Pilgrimage in Northern Europe and the British Isles*, 2 vols, ed. Sarah Blick and Rita Tekippe, Studies in Medieval and Reformation Traditions, 104 (Leiden and Boston: Brill, 2005), I, pp. 243–84.

Harrison, Frank and Peter Lefferts, eds. *Motets of English Provenance* (Monaco: Éditions de l'Oiseau-Lyre, 1980).

Hayward, Paul Anthony. 'Translation-Narratives in Post-Conquest Hagiography and English Resistance to the Norman Conquest', *Anglo-Norman Studies* xxi (1999), 67–93.

_____. 'Geoffrey of Wells' *Liber de infantia sancti Edmundi* and the "Anarchy" of King Stephen's Reign', in *St Edmund, King and Martyr: Changing Images of a Medieval Saint*, ed. Anthony Bale (York: York Medieval Press, 2009), pp. 63–86.

Heath, Peter. *The English Parish Clergy on the Eve of the Reformation* (London: Routledge, 1969).

Heslop, T.A. 'English Seals from the Mid-ninth Century to 1100', *Journal of the British Archaeological Association* cxxxiii (1980), 1–16.

_____ with Elizabeth Mellings and Margit Thøfner, eds, *Art, Faith and Place in East Anglia* (Woodbridge: Boydell, 2012).

Heywood, Stephen. 'Aspects of the Romanesque Church of Bury St Edmunds in their Regional Context', in *Bury St Edmunds: Art, Architecture, Archaeology and Economy*, ed. Antonia Gransden, British Archaeological Association Conference Transactions, xx (Leeds: British Archaeological Association, 1998), pp. 16–21.

Hinnebusch, William A. *The Early English Friars Preachers*, Institutum Historicum Ff. Praedictatorum Romae ad S. Sabine, Dissertationes Historicae, 14 (Rome: Ad S. Sabine Institutum Historicum Ff. Praedictatorum, 1951).

Howell, M.J. 'The Children of Henry III and Eleanor of Provence', in *Thirteenth Century England 4*, ed. P.R. Coss and S.G. Lloyd (Woodbridge, 1992), pp. 57–72.

Hutton, Ronald. *The Stations of the Sun: A History of the Ritual Year in Britain* (Oxford: Oxford University Press, 1996).

James, M.R. *On the Abbey of S. Edmund at Bury*, Cambridge Antiquarian Society publications, Octavo series, 28 (Cambridge: Deighton Bell, 1895).

_____. *The Verses Formerly Inscribed on Twelve Windows in the Choir of Canterbury Cathedral, reprinted from the manuscript with an introduction and notes by Montague Rhodes James*, Cambridge Antiquarian Society publications, Octavo series, 38 (Cambridge: Deighton Bell, 1901).

_____. 'The Sepulchral Brass of St Henry of Finland', *Proceedings of the Cambridge Antiquarian Society*, x (1901–2), 215–25.

Jankofsky, Klaus P. 'Entertainment, Edification and Popular Education in the *South English Legendary*', *Journal of Popular Culture* 11 (1977), 706–17.

_____. 'Personalized Didacticism: The Interplay of Narrator and Subject Matter in the *South English Legendary*', *Texas A&I University Studies* 10 (1977), 69–77.

_____. 'National Characteristics in the Portrayal of English Saints in the *South English Legendary*', in *Images of Sainthood in Medieval Europe*, ed. Renate Blumenfeld-Kosinski and Timea Szell (Ithaca: Cornell University Press, 1991), pp. 81–93.

_____. *The South English Legendary: A Critical Assessment* (Tübingen: Francke, 1992).

Jenkins, Jacqueline and Katherine J. Lewis, eds. *St Katherine of Alexandria: Texts and Contexts in Western Medieval Europe* (Turnhout: Brepols, 2003).

Jones, Graham. *Saints in the Landscape: Heaven and Earth in Religious Dedications* (Stroud: Tempus, 2007).

Kelsall, Jane. *Humphrey Duke of Gloucester, 1391–1447* (St Albans: Fraternity of the Friends of Saint Albans Abbey, 2000).

Kemp, Eric W. *Canonization and Authority in the Western Church* (London: Oxford University Press, 1948).

Kempski, Mary. 'A Technical Comparison of the Thornham Parva Retable with Contemporary Paintings, with Particular Reference to East Anglia', in *The Thornham Parva Retable. Technique, Conservation and Context of an English Medieval Painting*, ed. Ann Massing, Hamilton Kerr Institute Painting and Practice Series 1 (London: Harvey Miller Publishers for the Hamilton Kerr Institute and the University of Cambridge, 2003), pp. 143–4.

Kern, Fritz. *Kingship and the Law in the Middle Ages*, trans. S.B. Chrimes (New York: Harper and Row, 1970).

Kieckhefer, Richard. *Magic in the Middle Ages* (Cambridge: Cambridge University Press, 2000).

King, David. 'An Antiphon to St Edmund in Taverham Church', *Norfolk Archaeology* 35 (1977), 387–91.

_____. 'Salle Church – The Glazing', *Archaeological Journal* cxxxvii, 1980, 333–5.

_____. *The Medieval Stained Glass of St Peter Mancroft, Norwich*, Corpus Vitrearum Medii Aevi Great Britain, 5 (Oxford and New York, Published for the British Academy by Oxford University Press, 2006).

Klaniczay, Gábor. *The Uses of Supernatural Power. The Transformations of Popular Religion in Medieval and Early Modern Europe* (Cambridge: The Polity Press, 1990).

_____. *Holy Rulers and Blessed Princesses: Dynastic Cults in Medieval and Central Europe*, trans. Éva Pálmai (Cambridge: Cambridge University Press, 2002).

Knowles, David, Christopher N.L. Brooke and Vera C.M. London, *The Heads of Religious Houses, England and Wales, Volume 1, 940–1216*, 2nd ed. (Cambridge: Cambridge University Press, 2001).

Lapidge, Michael. 'Byrhtferth of Ramsey and the Early Sections of the *Historia Regum* attributed to Symeon of Durham', *Anglo-Saxon England* 10 (1982 for 1981), 97–122.

———. 'A Tenth-Century Metrical Calendar from Ramsey', *Revue Bénédictine* 94 (1984), 326–69.

———. *The Anglo-Saxon Library* (Oxford: Oxford University Press, 2006).

Lasko, Peter. *Ars Sacra, 800–1200* (Harmondsworth: Penguin Books, 1972).

Lee, Jennifer M. 'Searching for Signs: Pilgrims' Identity and Experience Made Visible in the *Miracula Sancti Thomae Cantuariensis*', in *Art and Architecture of Late Medieval Pilgrimage in Northern Europe and the British Isles*, 2 vols, ed. Sarah Blick and Rita Tekippe, Studies in Medieval and Reformation Traditions, 104 (Leiden and Boston: Brill, 2005) I, pp. 473–91.

Lees, Clare A., ed. *Medieval Masculinities: Regarding Men in the Middle Ages* (Minneapolis: University of Minnesota Press, 1994).

Legge, Dominica. *Anglo-Norman in the Cloisters: The Influence of the Orders on Anglo-Norman Literature* (Edinburgh: Edinburgh University Press, 1950).

———. *Anglo-Norman Literature and Its Background* (Oxford: Clarendon Press, 1963).

Lewis, Katherine J. *The Cult of St Katherine of Alexandria in Late Medieval England* (Woodbridge: The Boydell Press, 2000).

———. '"Lete me suffer": Reading the Torture of St Margaret of Antioch in Later Medieval England', *Medieval Women: Texts and Contexts in Late Medieval Britain: Essays for Felicity Riddy*, ed. Jocelyn Wogan-Browne et al. (Turnhout: Brepols, 2000), pp. 69–82.

———. 'Becoming a Virgin King: Richard II and Edward the Confessor', in *Gender and Holiness: Men, Women and Saints in Late Medieval Europe*, ed. Sarah Salih and Samantha Riches (London: Routledge, 2002), pp. 86–100.

———. 'Edmund of East Anglia, Henry VI and Ideals of Kingly Masculinity', in *Holiness and Masculinity in the Middle Ages*, ed. P.H. Cullum and Katherine J. Lewis (Cardiff: University of Wales Press, 2004), pp. 158–73.

———. 'Anglo-Saxon Saints' Lives, History and National Identity', in *History, Nationhood and the Question of Britain*, ed. Helen Brocklehurst and Robert Phillips (Basingstoke: Palgrave Macmillan, 2004), pp. 160–70.

———. '"Imitate, too, this king in virtue, who could have done ill, and did it not": Lay Sanctity and the Rewriting of Henry VI's Manliness', in *Religious Men and Masculine Identity in the Middle Ages*, ed. P.H. Cullum and Katherine J. Lewis (Woodbridge: Boydell, 2013), pp. 126–42.

Licence, Tom. 'History and Hagiography in the Late Eleventh Century: The Life and Work of Herman the Archdeacon, Monk of Bury St Edmunds', *English Historical Review* cxxiv (June 2009), 516–44.

———, ed. and trans. *Herman the Archdeacon and Goscelin of Saint-Bertin: The Miracles of St Edmund*, Oxford Medieval Texts (Oxford: Clarendon Press, 2014).

Lillie, W.W. 'Screenwork in the County of Suffolk, III: Panels Painted with Saints', *Proceedings of the Suffolk Institute of Archaeology* xxi (1933), 179–202.

Long, Mary Beth. 'Corpora and Manuscripts, Authors and Audiences', in *A Companion to Middle English Hagiography*, ed. Sarah Salih (Cambridge: D.S. Brewer, 2006), pp. 47–69.

Longland, Sabrina. 'A Literary Aspect of the Bury St Edmunds Cross', *Metropolitan Museum Journal* 2 (1969), 45–74.

Loomis, Grant. 'The Growth of the Saint Edmund Legend', *Harvard Studies and Notes in Philology and Literature*, xiv (1932), 83–113.

_____. 'St Edmund and the Lodbrok Legend', *Harvard Studies and Notes in Philology and Literature* xv (1933), 1–23.

Lunnon, Helen E. 'Observations on the Changing Form of Chancel Screens in Late Medieval Norfolk', *Journal of the British Archaeological Association* 163.1 (2010), 110–31.

_____. 'Making an Entrance: Studies of Medieval Church Porches in Norfolk', 2 vols, Ph.D. Thesis, University of East Anglia, School of World Art Studies and Museology, 2012.

Maltby, H.J.M. 'Excavation of the Abbey ruins, Bury St Edmunds', *Proceedings of the Suffolk Institute of Archaeology* xxiv (1949), 256–7.

Manning, Warren, F. 'The Middle English Verse *Life of St Dominic*: Date and Source', *Speculum* 31 (1956), 82–91.

Mansfield, H.O. *Norfolk Churches: Their Foundations, Architecture and Furnishings* (Lavenham: T. Dalton, 1976).

Marks, Richard. *Stained Glass in England During the Middle Ages* (London: Routledge, 1993).

_____. 'Images of Henry VI', in *The Lancastrian Court*, ed. Jenny Stratford, Harlaxton Medieval Studies, xiii, (Donnington: Shaun Tyas, 2003), pp. 111–24.

_____. *Image and Devotion in Late Medieval England* (Stroud: Sutton, 2004).

Martin, A. Lynn. *Alcohol, Sex and Gender in Late Medieval and Early Modern Europe* (Basingstoke: Palgrave, 2001).

Mason, Emma. *St Wulfstan of Worcester, c. 1008–1095* (Oxford: Basil Blackwell Ltd., 1990).

McAleer, J. Philip. 'The West Front of the Abbey Church', in *Bury St Edmunds: Art, Architecture, Archaeology and Economy*, ed. Antonia Gransden, British Archaeological Association Conference Transactions, xx (Leeds: British Archaeological Association, 1998), pp. 22–33.

_____. *Rochester Cathedral, 604–1540: An Architectural History* (Toronto, Buffalo, and London: University of Toronto Press, 1999).

McKenna, J.W. 'Henry VI of England and the Dual Monarchy: Aspects of Royal Political Propaganda, 1422–1432', *Journal of the Warburg and Courtauld Institutes* 28 (1965), 145–62.

_____. 'Piety and Propaganda: The Cult of Henry VI', in *Chaucer and Middle English Studies in Honour of R.H. Robbins*, ed. Beryl Rowland (London: Allen and Unwin, 1974), pp. 72–88.

Mesley, Matthew and Louise Wilson, eds. *Contextualising Miracles: New Historical Approaches*. Medium Ævum Monograph, XXXII (Oxford: The Society for the Study of Medieval Languages and Literature, 2014).

Millet, Bella. 'The Audience of the Saints' *Lives* of the Katherine Group', in *Saints and Saints' Lives: Essays in Honour of D.H. Farmer*, Reading Medieval Studies, 16 (1990), 127–56.
Mills, Robert. *Suspended Animation: Pain, Pleasure and Punishment in Medieval Culture* (London: Reaktion Books Ltd., 2005).
Minnis, Alistair J. and A.B. Scott. *Medieval Literary Theory and Criticism, c.1100–c.1375: The Commentary Tradition* (Oxford: Clarendon Press, 1988).
Mitchell, Shelagh. 'Kingship and the Cult of Saints', in *The Regal Image of Richard II and the Wilton Diptych*, ed. Dillian Gordon, Lisa Monnas and Caroline Elam (London: Harvey Miller, 1997), pp. 115–24.
Mitchell, W.T. 'The Shrines of English Saints in Wartime before the Reformation', *Pax: The Quarterly Review of the Benedictines of Prinknash* 30 (1940), 71–80.
Mittuch, Sarah. 'Medieval Art of Death and Resurrection', *Archaeology Today* 209 (May/June 2007), 34–40.
Montague-Smith, Patrick, ed. *Debrett's Peerage and Baronetage* (London: Macmillan for Debrett's Peerage Ltd., 1995).
Mortimer, Richard, ed. *St Edward the Confessor: The Man and the Legend* (Woodbridge: The Boydell Press, 2009).
Mostert, Marco. *The Political Theology of Abbo of Fleury. A Study of the Ideas about Society and Law of the Tenth-Century Monastic Reform Movement* (Hilversum: Verloren, 1987).
Murray, Jacqueline, ed. *Conflicted Identities and Multiple Masculinities: Men in the Medieval West* (New York and London: Garland Publishing Inc., 1999).
Nelson, Janet. 'Royal Saints and Early Medieval Kingship', Studies in Church History, 20 (1983), 15–30.
Newton, Sam. *The Origins of Beowulf and the Pre-Viking Kingdom of East Anglia* (Cambridge: D.S. Brewer, 1993).
Nichols, Ann Eljenholm. *The Early Art of Norfolk: A Subject List of Extant and Lost Art Including Items Relevant to Early Drama* (Kalamazoo: Medieval Institute Publications, 2002).
Nilson, Ben. *Cathedral Shrines of Medieval England* (Woodbridge: The Boydell Press, 1998).
Norton, Christopher, David Park and Paul Binski. *Dominican Painting in East Anglia: The Thornham Parva retable and the Musée de Cluny frontal* (Woodbridge: Boydell, 1987).
Nuechterlein, Jeanne. 'Hans Memling's St Ursula Shrine: The Subject as Object of Pilgrimage', in *Art and Architecture of Late Medieval Pilgrimage in Northern Europe and the British Isles*, 2 vols, ed. Sarah Blick and Rita Tekippe, Studies in Medieval and Reformation Traditions, 104 (Leiden and Boston: Brill, 2005), I, pp. 51–75.
Orme, Nicholas. *From Childhood to Chivalry. The Education of English Kings and Aristocracy 1066–1530* (London and New York: Methuen, 1984).
Otter, Monika. 'The Temptation of St Æthelthryth', *Exemplaria* 9 (1997), 139–63.
Pächt, Otto, Charles R. Dodwell and Francis Wormald. *The St Albans Psalter (The Albani Psalter)* (London: The Warburg Institute, 1960).

Page-Phillips, John. P*alimpsests: The Backs of Monumental Brasses*, 2 vols (London: Monumental Brass Society, 1980).
_____. *Witness in Brass: The Catalogue of the Monumental Brass Society Centenary Exhibition* (London: Victoria and Albert Museum, 1987).
Parker, Elizabeth C. 'Master Hugo as Sculptor: A Source for the Style of the Bury Bible', *Gesta* 20.1 (1981): Essays in Honour of Harry Bober, 99–109.
_____. *The Scriptorium of Bury St Edmunds in the Twelfth Century* (New York and London: Garland Publishing Inc., 1986).
Pearsall, Derek. *John Lydgate* (London: Routledge and Kegan Paul, 1970).
_____. *John Lydgate (1371-1449): A Bio-bibliography* (Victoria, B.C.: English Literary Studies, University of Victoria, 1997).
Peers, C.R. and H. Brakespear. 'Architectural Description of Winchester Cathedral', in *Victoria County History: Hampshire and the Isle of Wight*, vol. 5, ed. William Page (London: Constable, 1912).
Perry, Mark. 'Church of St Mary the Virgin, Lakenheath, Suffolk: Wall Painting Conservation Record' (The Perry Lithgow Partnership, September 2009).
Pevsner, Nikolaus and John Harris, *The Buildings of England: Lincolnshire* (London: Penguin Books, 1973, rpt 1978, rev. 1989 by Nicholas Antrim).
Pinner, Rebecca. 'Medieval Images of St Edmund in Norfolk Churches', in *St Edmund, King and Martyr: Changing Images of a Medieval Saint*, ed. Anthony Bale (York: York Medieval Press, 2009), 111–32.
_____. 'St Edmund, "Martir, Mayde and Kynge", and Midwife? New Approaches to Medieval and Early Modern Miracles', in *Contextualising Miracles: New Historical Approaches*, ed. Matthew Mesley and Louise Wilson, *Medium Ævum* Monograph, XXXII (Oxford: The Society for the Study of Medieval Languages and Literature, forthcoming)
Pluskowski, Aleksander. *Wolves and the Wilderness in the Middle Ages* (Woodbridge: Boydell, 2006).
Rattue, James. *The Living Stream: Holy Wells in Historical Context* (Woodbridge: Boydell, 1995).
Rawcliffe, Carole. *Leprosy in Medieval England* (Woodbridge: The Boydell Press, 2006).
Reimer, Stephen R. 'Unbinding Lydgate's *Lives of Saints Edmund and Fremund*', in *The Book Unbound: Editing and Reading Medieval Manuscripts and Texts*, ed. Sian Echard and Stephen Partridge (Toronto: University of Toronto Press, 2004), pp. 176–89.
Riches, Samantha. *St George: Hero, Martyr and Myth*, rev. edn (Stroud: The History Press Ltd., 2005).
Ridyard, Susan. *The Royal Saints of Anglo-Saxon England. A Study of West Saxon and East Anglian Cults* (Cambridge: Cambridge University Press, 1988).
Rigg, A.G. *A History of Anglo-Latin Literature 1066-1422* (Cambridge: Cambridge University Press, 1992).
Roberts, Marion. 'The Effigy of Bishop Hugh de Northwold in Ely Cathedral', *Burlington Magazine* 130 (1988), 77–84.
Robinson, James. 'A Late Medieval Pilgrim Badge from Chaucer House, Tabard Street, SE1', *The London Archaeologist* 6.3 (1989), 60–9.

Robinson, Pamela R. '"The Booklet". A self-contained unit in composite manuscripts', *Codicologica* III (1980), 46–69.

Rogers, Nicholas. 'The Frenze Palimpsest', *Monumental Brass Society Bulletin* 64 (October 1993), 75–7.

———. 'The Bury Artists of Harley 2278 and the Origins of Topographical Awareness in English Art', in *Bury St Edmunds: Art, Architecture, Archaeology and Economy*, ed. Antonia Gransden, British Archaeological Association Conference Transactions, xx (Leeds: British Archaeological Association, 1998), pp. 219–27.

Rollason, David. 'Lists of Saints' Resting-places in Anglo-Saxon England', *Anglo-Saxon England* 7 (1978), 61–93.

———. 'The Cults of Murdered Royal Saints in Anglo-Saxon England', *Anglo-Saxon England* 11 (1983), 1–22.

Rose, Martial. *Stories in Stone: The Medieval Roof Carvings of Norwich Cathedral* (London: Herbert, 1997).

Rosewell, Roger. *Medieval Wall Paintings in English and Welsh Churches* (Woodbridge: Boydell, 2008).

Rothwell, Harry. 'The *Life* and Miracles of St Edmund: A Recently Discovered Manuscript', *Bulletin of the John Rylands University Library* lx (1977–78), 135–80.

Rouse, Richard H. '*Bostonus Buriensis* and the Author of the *Catalogus Scriptorum Ecclesiae*', *Speculum* 41 (1966), 471–99.

Rowe, Joy. 'The Medieval Hospitals of Bury St Edmunds', *Medical History* ii (1958), 253–63.

Rubin, Miri. *Emotion and Devotion: The Meaning of Mary in Medieval Religious Cultures*, Natalie Zemon Davies Annual Lecture Series (Budapest and New York: Central European University Press, 2009).

Russell, Josiah Cox and John Paul Heironymous. *The Shorter Latin Poems of Henry of Avranches relating to England* (Cambridge, Mass: The Medieval Academy of America, 1935).

Salih, Sarah, ed. *A Companion to Middle English Hagiography* (Cambridge: D.S. Brewer, 2006).

———. 'Lydgate's Landscape History', in *Locating the Middle Ages: The Spaces and Places of Medieval Culture*, ed. Julian Weiss and Sarah Salih, King's College London Medieval Studies (London: King's College, 2012), pp. 83–92.

Samson, Annie. 'The South English Legendary: Constructing a Context', in *Thirteenth Century England I*, ed. P.R. Coss and S.D. Lloyd. Proceedings of the Newcastle-upon-Tyne Conference, 1985 (Woodbridge: Boydell, 1986), pp. 185–95.

Sauerberg, Marie Louise, Helen Howard and Aloce Tavares da Silva. 'The Wall Paintings of c. 1300 in the Ante-Reliquary Chapel, Norwich Cathedral and the Thornham Parva Retable: A Technical Comparison', in *The Thornham Parva Retable. Technique, Conservation and Context of an English Medieval Painting*, ed. Ann Massing, Hamilton Kerr Institute Painting and Practice Series, 1 (London: Harvey Miller Publishers for the Hamilton Kerr Institute and the University of Cambridge, 2003), pp. 174–88.

Scarfe, Norman. 'The Body of St Edmund; An Essay in Necrobiography', *Proceedings of the Suffolk Institute of Archaeology* xxxi (1969), 303–17.

_____. *Suffolk in the Middle Ages* (Woodbridge: Boydell, 2004).

Schirmer, Walter F. *John Lydgate: A Study in the Culture of the Fifteenth Century*, trans. Ann Keep (London: Methuen, 1961).

Schmidt, Gary D. *The Inconography of the Mouth of Hell: Eighth-Century Britain to the Fifteenth Century* (Sellinsgrove: Susquehanna University Press, 1995).

Scott, Kathleen. 'Lydgate's Lives of Saints Edmund and Fremund: A Newly Located Manuscript in Arundel Castle', *Viator* 13 (1982), 335–66.

_____. *Later Gothic Manuscripts, 1390–1490*, 2 vols (London: Harvey Miller, 1996).

Scribner, Bob. 'Is a History of Popular Religion Possible?', *History of European Ideas* 10 (1989), 175–91.

Sharpe, Richard. 'The Setting of St Augustine's Translation, 1091', in *Canterbury and the Norman Conquest: Churches, Saints and Scholars 1066–1199*, ed. Richard Eales and Richard Sharpe (London: Hambledon, 1995), pp. 1–13.

Siddons, Michael Powell. *Heraldic Badges in England and Wales*, 4 vols (Woodbridge: The Boydell Press for the Society of Antiquaries of London, 2009).

Somerset, Fiona. '"Hard is with seyntis for to make affray": Lydgate the "Poet-Propagandist" as Hagiographer', in *John Lydgate. Poetry, Culture and Lancastrian England*, ed. Larry Scanlon and James Simpson (Notre Dame, Indiana: University of Notre Dame Press, 2006), pp. 258–78.

Speed, Diane. 'The Construction of the Nation in Medieval English Romance', in *Readings in Medieval English Romance*, ed. Carol M. Meade (Cambridge: D.S. Brewer, 1994), pp. 135–57.

Spencer, Brian. *Salisbury and South Wiltshire Museum Medieval Catalogue. Part 2: Pilgrim Souvenirs and Secular Badges* (Salisbury: Salisbury and South Wiltshire Museum, 1990).

_____. *Pilgrim Souvenirs and Secular Badges*, Medieval Finds from Excavations in London, 7 (Woodbridge: The Boydell Press in association with the Museum of London, 1998, 2nd edn 2010).

Spencer, H. Leith. *English Preaching in the Late Middle Ages* (Oxford: Clarendon Press, 1993).

Stevenson, F.S. 'St Botolph (Botwulf) and Iken', *Proceedings of the Suffolk Institute of Archaeology* xviii (1924).

Stroud, D. 'The Cult and Tombs of St Oswald at Salisbury', *The Wiltshire Archaeological and Natural History Magazine* 78 (1984), 50–2.

Swarzenski, Hanns. *Monuments of Romanesque Art: The Art of Church Treasures in North-West Europe* (London: Faber and Faber, 1954).

Tanner, Norman. 'The Cathedral and the City', in *Norwich Cathedral: Church, City and Diocese, 1096–1996*, ed. Ian Atherton, Eric Fernie, Christopher Harper-Bill and Hassel Smith (London: Hambledon, 1996), pp. 255–80.

Tekippe, Rita. 'Pilgrimage and Procession: Correlations of Meaning, Practice and Effects', in *Art and Architecture of Late Medieval Pilgrimage in Northern Europe and the British Isles*, 2 vols, ed. Sarah Blick and Rita Tekippe, Studies in

Medieval and Reformation Traditions, 104 (Leiden and Boston: Brill, 2005), I, pp. 693–751.

Thacker, Alan. 'Kings, Saints and Monasteries in Pre-Viking Mercia', *Midland History* 10 (1985), 1–25.

Thomas, Hugh M. *The English and the Normans: Ethnic Hostility, Assimilation and Identity 1066–c.1200* (Oxford: Oxford University Press, 2003).

Thomson, Rodney M. 'Two Versions of a Saint's Life from St Edmund's Abbey: Changing Currents in Twelfth-Century Monastic Style', *Revue Bénédictine* 84 (1974), 383–408.

_____. *The Archives of the Abbey of Bury St Edmunds* (Woodbridge: The Boydell Press for the Suffolk Records Society, 1980).

Thurlby, Malcolm. 'The Influence of the Cathedral on Romanesque Architecture', in *Norwich Cathedral: Church, City and Diocese, 1096–1996*, ed. Ian Atherton, Eric Fernie, Christopher Harper-Bill and Hassel Smith (London: Hambledon 1996), pp. 136–57.

Townsend, David and A.G. Rigg, 'Medieval Latin Poetic Anthologies (V): Matthew Paris' Anthology of Henry of Avranches (Cambridge, University Library, MS Dd. 11.78)', *Medieval Studies* 49 (1987), 352–90.

Turner, Victor and Edith. *Image and Pilgrimage in Christian Culture* (Oxford: Blackwell, 1978).

Tymms, Samuel. *A Historie of the Church of St Marie Bury St Edmunds* (Bury St Edmunds and London: Jackson and Frost, 1845).

Van Houts, Elizabeth. *Memory and Gender in Medieval Europe, 900–1200* (Basingstoke: Macmillan, 2009).

Vauchez, André. *Sainthood in the Later Middle Ages*, trans. Jean Birrell (Cambridge: Cambridge University Press, 1997).

Vaughan, Richard. *Matthew Paris* (Cambridge: Cambridge University Press, 1958).

Vickers, K.H. *Humphrey, Duke of Gloucester: A Biography* (London: Archibald Constable, 1907).

Wade, Keith. '*Gipeswic* – East Anglia's first economic capital, 600–1066', in *Ipswich From The First To The Third Millennium*, ed. N. Salmon and R. Malster, (Ipswich: The Ipswich Society, 2001), pp. 1–6.

Wall, James C. *Shrines of British Saints* (London: Methuen and Co., 1905).

Ward, Benedicta. *Miracles and the Medieval Mind. Theory, Record and Event, 1000–1215* (Aldershot: Wildwood House, 1987).

Warner, Peter. *The Origins of Suffolk* (Manchester: Manchester University Press, 1996).

Watts, John. *Henry VI and the Politics of Kingship* (Cambridge: Cambridge University Press, 1996).

Weinstein, Donald and Rudolph M. Bell. *Saints and Society. The Two Worlds of Western Christendom, 1000–1700* (Chicago and London: University of Chicago Press, 1982).

West, Stanley E., Norman Scarfe and Rosemary Cramp. 'Iken, St Botolph, and the Coming of East Anglian Christianity', *Proceedings of the Suffolk Institute of Archaeology* xxxv (1984), 279–301.

Whitelock, Dorothy. 'Fact and Fiction in the Legend of St Edmund', *Proceedings of the Suffolk Institute of Archaeology* 31 (1969), 217–33.
Whittingham, Arthur B. 'St Mary's church, Bury St Edmunds', *Journal of the British Archaeological Association* xxi (1865), 187–8.
_____. *Bury St Edmunds Abbey, Suffolk* (London: Her Majesty's Stationery Office, rpt 1971).
Wilks, James H. *Trees of the British Isles in History and Legend* (London: Frederick Muller Ltd, 1972).
Williamson, Tom. *The Origins of Norfolk* (Manchester: Manchester University Press, 1993).
Williamson, W.W. 'Saints on Norfolk Roodscreens and Pulpits', *Norfolk Archaeology* xxi (1957), 299–346.
Wilmart, André. 'The Prayers of the Bury Psalter', *Downside Review* xlviii (1930), 198–216.
Wilson, Stephen, ed. *Saints and their Cults: Studies in Religious Sociology, Folklore and History* (Cambridge: Cambridge University Press, 1983).
Winstead, Karen A. *Virgin Martyrs: Legends of Sainthood in Late Medieval England* (Ithaca and London: Cornell University Press, 1997).
_____. *John Capgrave's Fifteenth Century* (Philadelphia: University of Pennsylvania Press, 2007).
Wogan-Browne, Jocelyn. *Saints' Lives and Women's Literary Culture, c. 1150–1300: Virginity and its Authorizations* (Oxford: Oxford University Press, 2001).
Wogan-Browne, Jocelyn, Nicholas Watson, Andrew Taylor and Ruth Evans, eds. *The Idea of the Vernacular. An Anthology of Middle English Literary Theory, 1280–1520* (Exeter: The University of Exeter Press, 1999).
Wolffe, Bertram. *Henry VI* (London: Eyre Methuen, 1981).
Wood, Rev. Canon. 'A Forgotten Saint?', *The Antiquary* 27 (May 1893), 202–7.
Woodforde, Christopher. *The Norwich School of Glass-Painting in the Fifteenth Century* (London: Oxford University Press, 1950).
Yarrow, Simon. *Saints and their Communities: Miracles Stories in Twelfth Century England*, Oxford Historical Monographs (Oxford: Clarendon Press, 2006).
_____. 'Miracles, Belief and Christian Materiality: Relic'ing in Twelfth-Century Miracle Narratives', in *Contextualising Miracles: New Historical Approaches*, ed. Matthew Mesley and Louise Wilson, *Medium Ævum* Monograph, XXXII (Oxford: The Society for the Study of Medieval Languages and Literature, forthcoming).
Zarnecki, George. *English Romanesque Lead Sculpture: Lead Fonts of the Twelfth Century* (London: Alec Tiranti, 1957).
_____. *Romanesque Sculpture at Lincoln Cathedral*, Lincoln Minster Pamphlets, 2nd series, no. 2 (Lincoln: Friends of Lincoln Cathedral, 1970).
_____. *Further Studies in Romanesque Sculpture* (London: Pindar Press, 1992).

Unpublished secondary sources

Cummings, James. 'Contextual Studies of the Dramatic Records in the Area around the Wash c. 1350–1550' (Leeds: Ph.D. thesis, University of Leeds, 2001).

Heale, N.J. 'Religious and Intellectual Interests at St Edmunds Abbey at Bury and the Nature of English Benedictinism, c. 1350–1450: MS Bodley 240 in Context' (D.Phil. thesis, University of Oxford, 1994).

Heslop, T.A. 'Arranging the Episodes: The Picture Cycles in Two Twelfth-century Manuscripts', Research Seminar, University of York, 24 February 2010.

Marten, Lucy. *The Southfolk and the Northmen: Suffolk 840–1086* (forthcoming).

_____. 'Lordship and Land: Suffolk in the Tenth and Eleventh Centuries' (Norwich: Ph.D. thesis, University of East Anglia, 2005).

Index

Abbo of Fleury, *Passio Sancti Eadmundi* 2 n.5, 7, 33, 34–47, 48–52, 57–9, 63–8, 69, 70, 74, 76, 77, 81, 83, 84, 86, 87, 93, 94, 101, 115 n.1, 116, 121–2, 142, 145, 172, 173, 174, 175, 177, 183, 191, 206, 22, 231, 240, 241, 248, 249
Ælfric of Eynsham 34–5
Æthelwold, Bishop of East Anglia 223–4
Alfred 'the Great' 4–5, 6, 248
Anglo-Saxon Chronicle 4, 5, 7, 16, 22–3, 33, 37, 50, 55, 87, 141, 204, 248
Arundel Castle MS (*sine numero*) 102–5
Asser, *Vita Ælfredi Regis Angul Saxonum* 4–5, 37, 248
Attleborough 76, 79, 104, 173, 174, 178, 246

Baldwin, Abbot of Bury (1065–97) 26, 46, 49, 50, 53–4, 61, 62, 63, 70, 92, 123, 125, 139, 141, 142, 241, 249
Beodricesworth 2, 37, 38, 44, 48, 121–3, 125, 139 n.4, 247
Bures 76, 172, 173, 174, 246, 248
Bury St Edmunds, Abbey of
  Abbots *See individual entries*
  Abbey church
    Architecture
      Bronze doors (*see also* Master Hugo) 127–8
      Choir 125, 152, 155
      Lady Chapel 27, 125, 140, 144, 250
      Monks' cemetery 125, 164–5, 250
      Nave 70, 127, 163, 164
      Octagons 126–7, 165
      Presbytery 119, 125, 127, 141, 143–4, 151, 154, 157, 163, 164
      Rotunda 125–6, 139, 164, 165, 250
      St James' tower 126, 128
      Transepts 125, 126–7, 144, 162–4, 191
      West front 126, 164–5
      Western axial tower 70, 126–7, 162–3, 250
      Western chapel blocks 126–7
    Fire of 1198 26, 119, 124–5, 134, 144, 153, 242, 249
    Fire of 1465 1 n.1, 26–7, 134, 151, 158, 250

Iconography *See individual saints and other figures*
Shrines *See individual saints*
Banleuca 2, 70, 182, 242, 248
Liberty 2–3, 52–3, 117, 161, 177, 183, 218–19, 242

Caistor-St-Edmund 95
Caxton, William, *The Golden Legend* 9, 51, 193, 233–4, 235, 250
Cnut 2, 38, 55, 73, 123, 125, 145, 165, 198, 248
Curteys, William, Abbot of Bury (1429–46) 22, 90, 91, 93 n.16, 97, 110, 162, 163 n.100, 242, 250

de la Pole, William, 1st Duke of Suffolk (1396–1450) 213–15
de Lacy, Henry, Earl of Lincoln (1272–1311) 135, 185
de Northwold, Hugh, Abbot of Bury St Edmunds (1213–29), Bishop of Ely (1229–54) 85

Edmund, King and Martyr
  Accession to the throne of East Anglia 4, 76, 78, 92, 93, 101, 179
  Apotheosis and heavenly glory 45, 65, 72, 115, 116, 189, 203, 207, 208–11, 211, 225, 229, 235
  Birth 7, 86, 101, 256
  Burial 43, 52, 67, 73, 121–5, 174, 247, 248
  Coins minted during reign 4
  Coronation 68, 69, 72, 103, 173, 174, 178
  Kingship and rule 4, 5, 14–15, 42, 45, 53, 54, 57, 66, 68–9, 72, 78, 95–101, 103, 153, 172, 175, 211–12, 222, 228, 235, 244, 246
  Martyrdom 5, 8, 15–17, 18–19, 33, 35, 36, 40, 41, 43, 44, 45, 51, 57, 65, 67–9, 74, 76, 81, 85, 86, 92, 93, 94, 95, 97, 98, 104, 105, 109, 110, 121 n.18, 146, 147, 153, 156, 159, 160, 170–1, 174, 177, 181, 182, 195, 197–8, 202–3, 205, 206, 207–8, 209, 211, 220, 223, 224, 225–6, 235, 244
  Memorial coinage 5–6

INDEX 275

Offa, King of East Anglia, uncle of Edmund 75, 76, 78–9, 101, 235, 246
Parents (Alkmund and Siwara, or Siware) 86, 100, 246
Pilgrim souvenirs and tokens 130, 169–72, 189–90, 190–1, 199, 220
Secondary relics
 Arrow 176, 181–2
 Shirt and garments 28, 59, 144, 146–7, 151
 Sword 149, 150–1
 Banner 100, 149–51, 181, 249
 Cup 147–9, 151
 Hair and nails 145–6
 Bier 67, 125, 164, 165–6, 206
Shrine 24–6, 48, 54, 56, 59, 62, 69, 70, 74, 82, 91, 92, 93, 110, 115–137, 138, 141–4, 144–51, 152–62, 162–3, 171–2, 179, 183, 184, 185, 188, 189–91, 199, 206, 230, 233, 240, 241, 242, 243, 247
Translation 44, 48, 49, 61, 70, 121–25, 130, 140, 141, 143, 149, 164, 179, 183
Virginity and bodily incorruption 10, 13, 15, 17–21, 34, 44–6, 57, 61, 100, 109, 118, 222, 225 226, 239, 241, 244–5
Wolf 15, 43, 52, 74, 121, 171, 174 n.21, 183, 195, 198, 202, 206, 207, 220–5, 226, 243, 247
Wuffings 220–5
Youth and upbringing 7, 76, 77, 81, 86, 92, 93, 99, 101, 205
Edward 'the Confessor' 3, 20, 57, 60, 80 n.29, 98, 115, 116, 131, 133, 148, 200 n.27, 211, 212, 215, 218, 248
Edward I 135, 147
Edward III 28, 103
Edward IV 103, 214
Egelwyn 56, 71, 117, 120, 151, 156, 181, 206, 248
Eleanor of Provence 3, 80 n.29
Ely Abbey, Cathedral from 1109 10, 13, 46, 53, 85, 118, 126, 127, 141, 143, 163, 194, 217–20
Eye 223

Geoffrey of Wells, *De Infantia Sancti Eadmundi* 7, 33 n.1, 75–9, 81, 83, 84, 86, 93, 101, 172, 173, 174–5, 177, 183, 189–90, 192, 205, 235, 240, 249
Gilte Legende 332–3

Haegelisdun 174
Hellesdon 8 n.26, 174
Henry of Avranches, *Vita Sancti Eadmundi* 83–5, 107, 240, 249

Henry III 3, 84, 133, 135, 243
Henry VI 20 n. 77, 22, 89–92, 97–105, 110, 111, 130, 134, 136, 162, 190, 192, 212–14, 216, 242, 250
Herfast, Bishop of East Anglia (1070–85) 49–50, 53–4, 249
Herman, *De Miraculis Sancti Eadmundi* 49–59, 61–2, 63–4, 69, 70, 71 .34–6, 77, 94, 115, 116, 123 n.28, 135 n.83, 146, 154 n.67, 181, 183, 184, 192, 241, 242, 249
Hoxne 8 n.26, 174, 174 n.21, 176, 220
Hugo, Master 127, 128, 145
Hunstanton 28, 76, 172, 173, 174, 178–9, 182, 242, 246

Jocelin of Brakelond, *Chronicle of the Abbey of Bury St Edmunds* 25–6, 60, 83, 117, 119–20, 121 n.16–17, 125–6, 131, 132–4, 136, 144–7, 153, 218–9

Kalendre of the Newe Legende of Englande 234–8

Lakenheath 216–20
Liber Eliensis 53, 118 n.10, 141, 143, 144 n.27
Lincoln Cathedral 27, 163–5
Leofstan, Abbot of Bury (1044–65) 73, 117, 119, 121, 141, 146, 248
Leofstan, Sheriff 54, 154–5
London, British Library, MS Harley 2278 ('the presentation manuscript') 89, 92 n.11, 102–5, 118 n.12, 130 n.58, 133–4, 138, 154, 158, 175
London, British Library, MS Yates Thompson 47 92 n.10, 92 n.11, 102–5, 158, 250
London, College of Arms, MS Arundel 30 26–7, 125 n.26, 138, 140, 152–7, 191, 250
Lucca 2, 46, 240, 249
Lydgate, John
 Prayer to St Edmund 145–6
 The Lives of Sts Edmund and Fremund 13, 17, 22, 34, 79, 82, 88, 89–111, 130, 133, 135–6, 145–6, 150, 158, 172–3, 174, 182, 184–8, 189 n.28, 189 n.31, 192, 205, 250
Lyng 184, 185–7

New York, Pierpont Morgan MS M 736 59, 60, 63–74, 101, 116, 122, 146, 154, 156–7, 160, 183, 206, 208, 241, 249
Norwich (city) 214–16
Norwich Cathedral Priory and diocese 53, 127, 202–3, 207

276 INDEX

Offa, father of St Fremund 108, 109
Osbert de Clare, *De Miraculis Sancti Eadmundi* 59–62, 117, 121, 122, 135 n.83, 147 n. 39–41, 169 n.1, 184, 188, 189 n. 26–7, 192
Oswen 145
Oxford, Bodleian Library, MS Bodley 240 49–50, 60, 79 n.26, 86–8, 90, 91 n.9, 95, 96, 108, 135 n.88, 155, 172, 174, 182, 184–88, 189 n.28, 189 n.31, 192, 205, 250

Peterborough Abbey 27, 34, 55, 126, 133
Piramus, Denis (sometimes Pyramus), *La Vie seint Edmund le Rei* 80–2, 83, 249

Ramsey Abbey 34, 35, 37–9

Saints
    Æthelthryth 10, 13, 21, 45–6, 53, 118, 141, 194, 243
    Anne 11–12
    Becket, Thomas 16, 36, 80 n.29, 84, 130, 131, 140, 192, 193 n.1, 201 n.27, 202, 213 n.48, 232, 238
    Botolph 141–4, 151, 166
    Cuthbert 35, 37, 39, 150, 156 n.73
    Denis 140
    Edmund *See separate entry*
    Edward 'the Confessor' *See main entry*
    Fremund 22, 84 n.49, 92, 98, 105–10, 250
    Jurmin 141–4, 166
    Nicholas 188–91
    Robert of Bury ('Little St Robert') 140
    Saba 127 n.51, 140
    Sebastian 16, 35, 170 n.5, 229, 232
    Virgin Mary 3, 13, 139–40, 142 n.19, 160, 204, 215, 216–17, 231
    William of Norwich ('Little St William') 140
Saint-Denis, Abbey of 2, 46–7, 128, 240, 249
Samson, Abbot. *De Miraculis Sancti Eadmundi* 59–62, 117, 121, 122, 135 n. 83, 147 n. 39–41, 169 n. 1, 184, 188, 189 n.26–7, 192
Samson, Abbot of Bury (1182–1211) 83, 85, 119–21, 131, 133–4, 218–19, 242, 249
Snettisham 177–80, 242, 250
South English Legendary 108, 227–31
Speculum Sacerdotale 231–32
St Albans Cathedral 65, 81 n.36, 133, 215 n.59
St Albans Psalter 64, 65 n.8, 66 n.13, 67, 68, 147, 156, 160
St Peter Mancroft, Norwich 214–16
Suger, Abbot of Saint-Denis 47, 128–9
'Sutton' (as putative place of Edmund's initial burial) 121–2, 174
Sutton Hoo 222–4
Sweyn Forkbeard 55–8, 71, 73, 81, 123, 154–62, 183, 243, 248

Taverham 198–200
Thetford 4, 75–6, 172
Thetford, Battle of 75, 95–6, 105, 150, 174, 257
Thetford, Priory of Our Lady 28, 75, 201
Thetford, Priory of St George 186
Thornham Parva
    Retable 201
    Wall paintings 203–7

Vikings (*including Danes*) *See also martyrdom*
    Great Viking Army (also Great Heathen Army) 1, 4, 87, 95, 121, 247
    Hinguar and Hubba (or Ubba) 41, 66, 76, 83, 94, 95–6, 246
    Lothbroc (also Lodbrok) 7 n.24, 76, 86, 103, 104–5, 246, 248
    Bern 76, 246

Wainfleet 184–7
Westminster Abbey 27, 59, 60, 152, 161, 163, 249
William I ('the Conqueror') 53, 54, 73, 249
Winchester Cathedral 45, 55, 115, 117, 123, 124, 126, 134, 163

www.ingramcontent.com/pod-product-compliance
Lightning Source LLC
Chambersburg PA
CBHW051604230426
43668CB00013B/1973